THE RADICAL NOVEL

IN

THE

UNITED

STATES

1900–1954

Some Interrelations

of Literature and Society

WALTER B. RIDEOUT

 American Century Series
HILL AND WANG · NEW YORK

Library of Congress Catalog Card Number 56–10162

Printed in the United States of America

1234567890

To JEAN

PREFACE

DOUBTLESS some readers will find this book unsatisfactory. The general reader may be put off by the subject matter, for nowadays in the United States the mention of anything having to do with radical politics is likely to be met by suspicion or anger. This book assumes, however, that such a subject as proposed by the title may be discussed and that it is best to discuss it in a reasonable manner. In the following pages I have attempted to conduct neither an attack nor a defense, but rather an examination, as objective an examination as possible, of a body of fiction which once was exaltedly praised in some quarters and now in most quarters is categorically condemned. Even the present title was selected instead of a more colorful one to emphasize my purpose: to put facts into the public domain. If the general reader has picked up this volume in hopes of finding the sort of thing which should be entitled *The Novel on the Barricades* or, conversely, *I Read Red Fiction*, he had better put it down at once.

Certain more specialized readers may find the book unsatisfactory because it — purposely — does not confine itself to one literary technique. The strict literary historian may object to finding some literary analysis and evaluation here, while the formalist critic will surely be unhappy over the very large amount of what he would call "extrinsic" material. Likewise, if the literary critic may object that the book contains too much talk of politics, the political scientist may feel that it contains too little. I can only say that the book, as its subtitle suggests, seemed to me to require an approach which combined techniques and even disciplines. We still know very little about the obscure and enormously complicated relation between a society and its literature. This study is offered as an attempt to increase at least slightly our knowledge of that relation.

I am glad to thank publicly a number of individuals who, either in direct interview or by letter, generously answered out of their personal knowledge the questions that I asked them and who, in some instances, made material available to me: Nelson Algren, Elliot Cohen, Mandel and Winifred Cohen, Malcolm Cowley, Floyd Dell, Margaret DeSilver, John Dos Passos, James T. Farrell, Howard Fast, Waldo Frank, Joseph Freeman, Granville Hicks, Thomas Barry Hunt, Agnes Inglis, Philip Rahv, Isidor Schneider, Fred Thompson, and Edmund Wilson. Except where specifically noted, these individuals are not responsible for any opinions expressed in this book.

To many friends and colleagues I am indebted for various kinds of assistance. William H. Bond and Richard M. Ludwig made available to me certain materials on, respectively, Dos Passos and Steinbeck. Muriel Murray kindly lent me a paper and check list on proletarian fiction which she had formerly prepared. Deming Brown helped me at many points with his knowledge of Soviet-American literary relationships, Wallace Douglas and Harrison Hayford gave me sound information and equally sound advice, while Richard Ellmann was so kind as to read four chapters and to make detailed comments. Again, none of these persons is responsible for any opinions expressed in this book. I wish also to thank the Northwestern University Graduate School Committee on Research for several generous grants which enabled me to carry out my research.

My special thanks are reserved for three people. To Howard Mumford Jones, under whose direction the first version of this book was written as a doctoral dissertation, and to Bessie Jones I have for a long time and in many ways owed much for their help and their friendship. As usual, my greatest debt is to my wife, whose assistance over the years to the author and his book has been surpassed only by her patience with both. I have dedicated this book to her.

Northwestern University   WALTER B. RIDEOUT
January, 1956

CONTENTS

THE RADICAL NOVEL

IN

THE

UNITED

STATES

1900–1954

1.

THE TWO NATIONS

O NE of the effects of modern war is to alienate us from the recent past. The events of the prewar years are accomplished, of course, and do not themselves change, but our attitude toward them changes vastly. In our consciousness war drops like a trauma between "after" and "before," until it is sometimes hard to believe that "before" was a part of us at all. Thus Americans in the nineteen-twenties felt sharply cut away from the Years of Confidence on the other side of World War I, and we in the middle nineteen-fifties, just beyond the halfway point of a troubled century, feel as widely separated from the Years of the Great Depression on the other side of World War II. We can see the people of the thirties, we can hear their voices, as though we watched a newsreel — that peculiarly apt symbol of the time — yet we can reëxperience only by an effort the actual emotional weather through which those people (we ourselves) walked. We see in the newsreel the spurting ticker tape as the stock market crashes, the silent men at closed factory gates, the apple sellers on street corners, the bread lines, the picket lines, the families defiant on the porches of mortgaged farmhouses, and the black dust storms in the sky; then the speakers on city sidewalks, in parks, in hired halls, in auditoriums, the speakers fronted by faces or microphones; then the dams and the bridges and the post-office murals and the crowded union halls, the newspaper headlines, the rattletrap cars along Route 66, and more headlines, the factory gates opening in slow montage, and the sudden explosion of war which fills the screen. We can see these pictures through the mind's newsreel, but only with difficulty can we recreate in and around them the nervous tension, the epidemics of faith or despair, the ever-present sense of the closeness of violence, and even, in the first years of the decade at least, the occasional abrupt conviction that perhaps tomorrow, for good or bad, barricades might rise on all the Main Streets across the land.

It was into such stormy skies that there flared one of the phenomena of the thirties — "proletarian literature" and its major component, the "proletarian novel." Essentially a literary reflection of the current interest in revolutionary Marxism, this fiery phenomenon seemed to a number of admiring observers to be a whole new planet swimming into their ken. One of them, in fact, wrote a history of American literature after the Civil War arguing that its "Great Tradition" had been the tradition of social protest, that proletarian writing, particularly the novel, would be its culminating glory, and that here was an omen of the future when capitalist America, now caught in the dark turmoil of the Depression, would emerge clean and shining as part of classless mankind. Unfortunately for his prophecy the proletarian novel, and all the rest of proletarian literature, hardly survived the second edition of his book. Neither a planet nor a fixed star, perhaps it was a comet, for it flashed briefly and then apparently burned out. Much reformed since that time, the literary historian has insisted that he was using the wrong telescope.

Because literary taste has changed somewhat and because the crises of the fifties are not the crises of the thirties, we now find it conveniently easy to laugh at the efforts of the literary Marxists of the Depression, at least in the intervals when we are not denouncing their politics. The proletarian novel in particular is dismissed as bizarre and improbable. Without offering much proof critics declare in unison that the phenomenon was not even a comet or, in fact, a heavenly body at all; rather, they say, it was only a skyrocket, one of inferior make, which burst with an empty bang, spit out some very dull sparks, and came down like a stick. The difference in estimated magnitude is so immense, however, that we well might wonder why the stargazers of the thirties miscalculated so fantastically — or could it be that those of our own time have, for one reason or another, made some slight error? Clearly here is a question that can not be answered until, like good astronomers, we view the evidence. That is what the present volume proposes to do.

Although this book will from time to time include both critical analyses and value judgments, it must concern itself primarily, because of the nature of its subject, with literary history. In its second and climactic half it will examine at length the politically radical novel of the thirties in order to describe its relation to the society of its time, analyze its characteristics as a body of literature, and determine the nature of its defects and possible virtues. But it must be said at once that neither 1930 nor 1940 is a terminal date. In actuality the proletarian novelists have their descendants, diminished though the race may be, down into the present time; and in their own day they had their ancestors, even though these they usually scorned, ignored, or did not know. The full story of the radical novel in the United States must show that, although it has been confined to the twentieth century, it has come in two waves rather than one. If the writers who in the thirties created the second wave deliberately cut themselves off from those who had created the first, still both waves have this in common: each was an attempt to express through the literary form of the novel a predominantly Marxist point of view toward society. Before we can talk about the radical novel of the thirties, which was produced primarily by writers influenced by Communism, we must, therefore, go back to the earlier years of the century, to the sizeable body of fiction, now largely forgotten, which was brought forth by writers responding affirmatively to Socialism. The first chapters of this book will deal with these writers, precursors in an attempt to unite a certain ideology with art. Here also the intention will be to show the social roots of a body of writing, to describe its character, to designate its relative literary worth. Taken together, the two halves of the book should define the place of radical fiction within our literature. They may also help us to repossess a part of the past.

II

If Karl Marx had lived into the twentieth century, he might have argued, with perverse pleasure, that his prophecies about capitalism's growth were being confirmed by the experience of the

United States. Within the second half of the previous century, he might have said, American capitalism had crushed a rebellious agrarian South, opened the entire West to exploitation, conducted imperialistic ventures in the Caribbean and Pacific, and advanced to the third of the three phases he himself had predicted for capitalist development — from Merchant Capitalism to Industrial Capitalism to Finance Capitalism. He would certainly have pointed to the appearance of the first great corporations as the nineteenth century ended, and he would have commented on the way the Supreme Court had perverted the Fourteenth Amendment of the Constitution in order to defend these enormous accumulations of capital against legal attack. Then he would have remarked sardonically that the elaborate mansions on New York's Fifth Avenue or Chicago's Gold Coast were reserved for the few, while the many were allowed to swarm in the dirty tenements of the East or the South Side. The spectre that was haunting Europe, he would have concluded, was haunting America too.

Whether one would wish to accept Marx's interpretation of it or not, the fact is familiar beyond need of demonstration that in the second half of the nineteenth century a tremendous concentration of financial power occurred within American society. What is less well remembered is that at various times counterforces, most of them based on middle-class groups, tried to oppose or limit this development. "Small business" was a counterforce in a restricted sense. The rationale of its attack on the "trusts and monopolies" was, on the surface, a faith in the virtues of pure competition or of decentralized economic power; underneath, most small business men, then as now, were only too willing to become big if the opportunities appeared. There were the middle-class opposition forces released by Henry George's Single Tax and Edward Bellamy's Coöperative Commonwealth; but the agitation for the Single Tax was an already hopeless attempt to restore the opportunities of the free frontier, while the Nationalist Clubs that sprang up under the impulse of *Looking Backward* (1888) were a short-lived effort to achieve a form of state socialism by extending middle-class political democracy into economics. Although Bellamy's tremendously popular utopian novel became for many a first step toward further radicalism and although the term "Coöperative Commonwealth" persisted as one name for the radical goal, Nationalism itself was absorbed in the rise of the angry farmers along the Middle Border.

Agrarian discontent in the Midwest, and to less extent in the South, had erupted throughout the last three decades of the nineteenth century in a series of political parties which culminated in the Populists of the nineties. The People's Party specifically attacked Finance Capitalism as the source of the farmer's many grievances, advocated a limited amount of public ownership, particularly in transport and communications, and spoke loudly of the existence of class warfare. At the Omaha convention of 1892 revolt resounded in Ignatius Donnelly's preamble to the party's first national platform:

From the same prolific womb of governmental injustice we breed the two great classes — tramps and millionaires . . . A vast conspiracy against mankind has been organized on two continents, and it is rapidly taking possession of the world. If not met and overthrown at once, it forbodes terrible social convulsions, the destruction of civilization, or the establishment of an absolute despotism.[1]

Although the agrarian attack was the strongest to be hurled against the "Money Power" in three decades, most of its impulse was directed, like that of small business, against the "abuses" of capitalism rather than against the system itself. Goliath refused to fall before David's slingshot, and the People's Party disintegrated soon after its disastrous union in 1892 with a reformist Democracy under Bryan.

In addition to these middle-class counterforces, there was that of another class, the rapidly expanding proletariat, which expressed itself in industrial strife, the rise of the organized labor movement, and the formation of radical political parties. Although the National Labor Union, in the late sixties, and the Knights of Labor, in the early eighties, had their day and died, the American Federation of Labor, which grew out of an earlier trade union federation established in 1881, was more tenacious. The latter organization, to be sure, attempted to create a "middle class" of skilled labor; nevertheless, it became deeply involved in the industrial conflict of the times and threw up what defenses it could against the triumph of capitalism.

Defenses of any kind were needed. As the American economy steadily shifted from an essentially agrarian one in 1850 to an essentially industrial one in 1900, the number of factory workers increased more than ten times. Blocked in by a vanishing frontier, atomized by the lack of community sense in the hugely expanding cities, deprived even of the old personal relationship between employer and employee, and faced with high-speed machinery, which meant work-boredom and more frequent accidents, the factory worker steadily lost both economic and emotional security. The hopeful immigrants entering the country in accelerating millions could find only the unskilled jobs of mill and construction camp waiting for them, yet even so they were a constant pressure on those who already held jobs. Wages had, to be sure, held fairly firm during the long slow decline in prices after the Civil War, but from the mid-nineties on into the new century real wages dropped behind steadily rising prices. One indication of swelling discontent was the growth of labor union membership from less than half a million in 1897 to slightly over two million in 1904, the A. F. of L. unions gaining the greatest proportion of the increase. Another indication was the growth of industrial strife.

Sporadic bursts of localized labor "troubles" — strikes, lockouts, riots — had occurred as early as the 1820's, but after the Civil War these conflicts increased and widened, coming in the nineties to a climax which, with an occasional lull, spilled over into the early years of the present century. The first strike of national significance occurred during the depression years of the mid-seventies when, in 1877, the workers of the Baltimore and Ohio Railroad struck in Pittsburgh against a wage reduction, an act that set off spontaneous sympathetic riots in many cities across the country. The agitation for the eight-hour day brought the unrest of the mid-eighties, culminating in 1886 with the New York street-car strike, the explosion of the bomb in the Chicago Haymarket, and the ritual killing of four innocent Anarchists. After an interlude came the great strikes of the 1890's, when open warfare developed between capital and labor. In 1892 there occurred the Homestead Strike against the Carnegie Steel Company, one of the most violent in the history of the United States. There were labor troubles in the West, beginning with the Coeur d'Alene, Idaho, mine strike in 1892 and that at Cripple Creek, Colorado, where 125,000 men went out in 1894 under the leadership of the militant Western Federation of Miners. The latter year brought the great Pullman Strike in Chicago, in which Eugene Debs's American Railway Union struggled against twenty-four railroads, Federal troops, and the United States courts. Two years later came a prolonged mine strike in Leadville, Colorado, while in 1897 the United Mine Workers fought almost the whole of the soft-coal industry. As the nineteenth century ended, there were coal strikes in Tennessee, while the opening years of the twentieth brought trouble in the Pennsylvania anthracite region and again at Cripple Creek, where the entire district was placed, not for the first time, under martial law. Soldier arrayed against worker — the knowledge of it would have pleased Karl Marx.

Growing with the intensity of such open class warfare, though contributing a conscious philosophy to it only rarely as yet, came the slow dissemination of Marxist thought. The European Year of Revolutions, 1848, had, of course, produced abortive uprisings, the publication of *The Communist Manifesto*, and a push of immigration to the United States by Socialists, chiefly German, who brought their doctrine with them. Its spread here was slow, for the German Socialists remained largely isolated in their own *Vereine*, and their doctrinal literature, which was concerned with European rather than American conditions, was for long untranslated. Not until 1872 did a complete English version of the *Manifesto* appear in this country — in the sensational weekly published by the equally sensational sisters, Victoria Woodhull and Tennessee Claflin, leaders of New York Section 12 of the First International. For an English translation of *Capital* (the first volume only) the native radical had to wait for that put out under Engels' editorship in 1887 by Swan Sonnenschein, Lowrey, and Company, a London house, although an American edition of this translation was issued two years later.[2] To be sure, in 1884 there had been published Laurence Gronlund's *The Co-operative Commonwealth*, in which the Danish immigrant author explained Marxism simply and fairly thoroughly, and applied its doctrines to the situation in the United States. Gronlund's book seems to have circulated among radicals, and it helped to turn toward Socialism both William Dean Howells and Edward Bellamy, whose *Looking Backward* is clearly

indebted to it. As late as 1902, however, A. M. Simons, editor of
The International Socialist Review, could complain that the Socialist movement in the United States had produced almost no theoretical or practical Marxist literature concerned with this country's
economic conditions. Thereafter the times changed rapidly. When
Ernest Unterman's standard three-volume translation of *Capital*
was being issued from 1906 to 1909 by the Chicago firm of Charles
H. Kerr and Company, it was hailed as the first complete edition
in English anywhere and as the climax of several American triumphs in radical publishing.

Soon after the first Socialist immigrations, radical political
parties based on Marxist ideology began to appear. The first of
genuine importance, the Socialist Labor Party, was formed in
1877, to be taken over in 1890 by the brilliant and doctrinaire
Daniel De Leon, the only American Marxist theoretician for whom
Lenin appears to have had any respect. Though tiny, the party
attracted so much attention during the depression years of the
mid-nineties that the S.L.P. vote grew from about 26,000 in 1893
to 82,000 five years later. At the end of the decade, however,
splinter groups, rebelling against De Leon's arbitrary personality
and his refusal to work with organized labor, turned to the Social
Democratic Party, which Debs had recently helped to found after
being converted to Socialism while a political prisoner. In 1901,
after Debs had received nearly 100,000 votes in the presidential
election of the preceding year, most of the Left groups outside the
Socialist Labor Party joined in forming the Socialist Party.

At the time of the realignment the new party had two major
sources from which to draw its strength: first, largely foreign-born
proletarian groups in the urban East who had become class-conscious through direct ideological indoctrination; and second, native
American farmers of the West, many of whom were developing
a highly pragmatic socialism, now that the People's Party had disintegrated, as a solution to their immediate economic difficulties.
So vigorous was the combination during the strike-torn opening
years of the twentieth century that enrolled membership in the
Socialist Party rose from about 5,000 at the time of its founding to
20,000 in 1904, while in that election year the vote for Debs, again
the Socialist candidate for President, likewise increased fourfold

to a total of just over 400,000. It was also indicative of the new spirit of radicalism that in 1905 both De Leon and Debs came together in brief alliance with "Big Bill" Haywood and other leaders of the Western Federation of Miners to form the Industrial Workers of the World (the I.W.W.), a decidedly revolutionary organization which very shortly rejected politics altogether and declared that power could be seized for their One Big Union only by "direct action" — "free speech" fights, sabotage, and the general strike.

With Mark Hanna predicting that by 1912 Socialism would be America's leading issue, established society in the middle 1900's felt the ground beneath it stir and shift. "All the symptoms of a somewhat panicky state of mind have been observable, in fact, for some time, and editorials on 'The Rising Tide of Socialism' and like subjects are frequently to be seen," that dignified monthly, *Current Literature*, commented in 1906.[3] Although the commentator went on to argue soberly that "the growth of Socialism in Europe has done more than any other factor to arouse apprehension in this country," the apprehension was not denied. The feeling of the times was best caught in a book illustration, "The Hand of Fate," drawn in that year by William Balfour Ker of the old *Life*. A melodramatic story-picture, it shows, in its upper two-thirds, an obviously elegant hall filled with men and women in evening clothes beneath the flare of clustered lights and the pale gleam of familiar Greek sculptures, all the black-and-white checkered floor being upheld — this in the lower third of the illustration — by the cramped bodies of other, poorly-dressed men and women crowded into a dark cellarage. The "lesson," that starving labor supports the idle rich, is clear; even clearer is the reason why, at the moment, the wealthy men and women are neither dancing nor dining. Instead they have shrunk back against overturned chairs from a cleared space in front and are gazing, with dazed horror, at the focal point of the picture where, shatteringly, the clenched fist of one of the darkened horde beneath has burst up through the floor into the world of the rich.

III

American fiction reflected the stresses of these years. In the second edition of their study, *The Working-Class Movement in*

America, first published in 1887 after their brief tour of the United States, Edward and Eleanor Marx Aveling had asked a damning, though slightly exaggerated, question.

> And here we are tempted to ask, "Where are the American writers of fiction?" With a subject [the depressed condition of the American working class], and such a subject, lying ready to their very hands, clamouring at their very doors, not one of them touches it . . . there are no studies of factory-hands and of dwellers in tenement houses; no pictures of those sunk in the innermost depths of the modern *Inferno*. Yet these types will be, must be, dealt with; and one of these days the Uncle Tom's Cabin of Capitalism will be written.[4]

Although "the Uncle Tom's Cabin of Capitalism" was yet to be written, American writers of fiction were more aware of the "subject" than the Avelings thought. As early as 1861, to take a somewhat atypical example, *The Atlantic Monthly* had printed Rebecca Harding Davis's "Life in the Iron-Mills," a story dealing with the inferno inhabited by iron workers and even suggesting that it must lie with the men themselves to improve their lot. Elizabeth Stuart Phelps, in *The Silent Partner* (1871), had sympathetically described the stunted existence of mill workers in a New England community, while among similar novels, Amanda Douglas's *Hope Mills* (1880) and Henry Francis Keenan's *The Money-Makers* (1885) had shown concern for the victims of economic depression. The decade of the nineties, moreover, brought a flood of fiction dealing with the effects of capitalism and objecting sternly to the human cost of material achievement. Outstanding for its intensity of protest is Ignatius Donnelly's flamboyant romance of the future, *Caesar's Column* (1890), which describes a cataclysmic revolt by a world proletariat against the oligarchy which has brutally enslaved it.

This vision of disaster by one of the silver-tongued orators of the Populist movement is worth examining more closely, for it helps to establish, if negatively, the nature of the radical novel. The story is told through the device of letters purportedly written by Gabriel Weltstein, a prosperous sheepherder, to his brother in the "State of Uganda," Africa. Gabriel has arrived in the New York of 1899, a gadget paradise complete with luxury hotels, air-liner terminals, and express elevateds, although the chief method of intraurban travel still is, anachronistically, by coach and four. Having rescued a beggar from under the wheels of Prince Cabano's carriage, Gabriel is in turn rescued from the police by the beggar, who reveals himself as "Maxmilian Petion," a rich young man in disguise. Max shows Gabriel that the wealth and beauty of New York are owned by only a few people, the Plutocracy, who have achieved their present all-powerful position by forcing the great body of the people into one vast and hideous sweatshop existence. Gabriel is appalled at the Plutocracy's cruelty, but is equally distressed when he learns that Max is a leader in the Brotherhood of Destruction, a proletarian organization headed by the gigantic terrorist, Caesar Lomellini. Having learned at first hand that the Plutocracy, under Prince Cabano, plans to crush an expected uprising of the proletariat by showering the rebels with gas bombs from the "Demons" (the military airships), Gabriel argues at a workingmen's meeting for a Brotherhood of Justice to take the place of the Brotherhood of Destruction, which is planning its revolt of hatred against the Plutocracy's rule. But Gabriel's plea for a peaceful crusade against starvation and injustice is howled down by the workers, and Max tells him that the plotted destruction has long been inevitable. "One hundred years ago a gigantic effort, of all the good men of the world, might have saved society. . . No; we witness the working-out of great causes which we did not create. When man permits the establishment of self-generating evil he must submit to the effect." [5]

The revolt comes in blood and fire. Since the Demons have been bribed over to the side of the Brotherhood, the Plutocracy is destroyed and with it all civilized living. Max, who had hoped to proceed to a period of reconstruction, is prevented from his purpose by the lawlessness of the great mobs. After a quarter of a million people have been killed, both Plutocrat and proletarian, their bodies are disposed of at Caesar's order by being piled into a great column solidified by concrete. Caesar himself is dismembered by a mob even while his monument is building toward the sky; but Max, Gabriel, and their families escape in one of the Demons across a devastated Europe to Uganda, where they set up a true republic from which the world's civilization may later be restored.

As in his preamble to the Populist platform, Donnelly frequently sounds more radical than he actually was. There are, for example, echoes of Marx in *Caesar's Column*. Donnelly envisions a world ruled by a plutocracy that is separated from a progressively more downtrodden proletariat by a vast gulf, as Marx, among others, had predicted, and class warfare culminates in revolution. It is stated that the workers have long been acquainted with Marxist theories, the labor theory of value is suggested at one point, and Marx is mentioned by name, while Gabriel's "Brotherhood of the Just" may derive from the original name of the Communist League for which Marx and Engels wrote the *Manifesto*, since that organization was founded as the "League of the Just." These echoes, however, are only incidental. The Brotherhood of Destruction scarcely plays the role described by Marx for the Communist Party, the revolution ends in the ruin of society rather than in a new synthesis, and Donnelly, in his preface to the romance, has already categorically denounced class warfare as destructive of brotherhood and social justice. Throughout, the characters whom we are to admire deplore the loss of the old republican liberties. Most important of all, the welfare state outlined at the conclusion as the Uganda constitution is entirely within the Populist tradition of reform, even to such items as the creation of a flexible money supply. *Caesar's Column* is a warning, not a threat; it is part of the social-protest literature of the nineteenth century, not a radical novel.[6]

For what, after all, is a "radical novel"? To be meaningful, the term should make a distinction within the larger category of "social-protest novel," a distinction corresponding to that applicable to individual men. Among those who protest social conditions, the traditional division, of course, has been between the reformer and the radical, between one who accepts a particular socioeconomic system, believing that its faults can and should be remedied, and one who, arguing that such faults are inherent and therefore not ultimately improvable, calls for a transformation of the system itself. A radical novel, then, is one which demonstrates, either explicitly or implicitly, that its author objects to the human suffering imposed by some socioeconomic system and *advocates that the system be fundamentally changed*.

The considerable body of protest fiction brought forth in response to the Gilded Age has been mapped and analyzed by several studies, the most thorough of which is Walter Fuller Taylor's *The Economic Novel in America*. He finds, as one would expect, that the many novels classifiable as "economic" were almost entirely middle-class in origin and, more significantly, that the great majority of the novelists, though sharply critical of the evils of capitalist industrialism, inclined toward reform. Of the two minority groups making up what he calls a "middle-class Left," the novelists who followed Henry George wished merely to add some version of the Single Tax to the basic relationships of capitalism; Bellamy and his novelist disciples, on the other hand, actually desired to replace the present system with a middle-class socialism based on the nationalization of industries. Although for the needs of a professional revolutionary or a ward boss *Looking Backward* and its attendant Utopias were rudimentary in their understanding of political power, being very casual indeed about the method whereby the great transformation was to be accomplished, their insistence on a collectivized future for society undoubtedly prepared some writers and many readers for the more Marxian novels of the 1900's. Utopias based on "Bellamy Socialism" occasionally appeared after 1900,[7] but the newer novelists began increasingly to shift from projections of the future Coöperative Commonwealth to descriptions of the present conditions which made such a future inevitable and to analyses of the revolutionary dynamics whereby it might be hastened.

Marked as it was by the consolidation of capitalism, by intensified labor strife, and by a realignment of radical groups, the beginning of the century brought also the first sign of the new literary development. Early in 1901 Judge Elbert Gary, Andrew Carnegie, Charles M. Schwab, and J. P. Morgan led in the creation of the first supertrust under the name of the United States Steel Corporation; and later that same year, by a neat and not unrelated coincidence, the publishing house of McClure, Phillips and Company issued a book entitled *By Bread Alone*, with which the history of the radical novel in the present century truly begins. In some respects, though decidedly not in others, *By Bread Alone* concentrated in itself what was to come. It was no Utopia, no fantasy of the far away or long ahead; rather, the book dealt, in surprisingly realistic detail, with the here and now of a steel strike. Unlike Howells's *A*

Hazard of New Fortunes this novel did not introduce labor conflict as only one phase of the entire action; unlike John Hay's *The
Breadwinners* it revealed the author as intensely sympathetic, if
not with strikes, at least with the workers who went on strike; unlike Frank Norris's *The Octopus* (published in the same year) it
evolved a consistent theme, a whole which did not conflict with
the sum of its parts.

The book had not, of course, sprung into being simply because
conditions seemed to demand it. The author, Isaac Kahn Friedman,
had been born in Chicago in 1870 of wealthy parents. After an
education in the public schools and at the University of Michigan,
he had begun special studies in political economy, which he dropped
upon becoming interested in settlement-house work. Disturbed
by a view of the "submerged third," he was converted to Socialism late in the 1890's and proceeded to get the firsthand acquaintance with the life of Chicago steel workers which forms the background of his best book. Although he later became a foreign correspondent and eventually an editorial writer for the Chicago
Daily News, he appears to have remained a Socialist in spite of his
willingness to publish some of the presumably humorous sketches
of *The Autobiography of a Beggar* (1903) in *The Saturday Evening Post*. Besides his strike novel, he produced two other books of
long fiction: *Poor People* (1900), a sentimental local-color tale of
a Chicago tenement's inhabitants; and *The Radical* (1907), a
sequel of sorts to *By Bread Alone*, which is concerned with the
Washington adventures of a left-wing Congressman who works
in behalf of the Coöperative Commonwealth against the corrupt
combination of business and politics. These two books are marred
by their author's weakness for a self-consciously elaborate style, a
fact which makes his strike novel's relative freedom from forced
conceits even more remarkable.

By Bread Alone tells the experiences of Blair Carrhart, son of
a well-to-do Chicago grocer, who decides in college to become a
minister, but who then accepts Socialism, leaves the ministry and
goes to work in the nearby steel mills of "Marvin." The mills and,
to a considerable extent, the town are owned by Henry Marvin,
father of Blair's sweetheart, a self-reliant girl with the literary
name of Evangeline. Blair, intelligent and powerful of body, joins

the union, makes friends among the workers, most of whom are impoverished immigrants, and is promoted to increasingly skilled jobs. The long hours, the low pay, the high accident rate, the vilely crowded company houses, a shut-down — which is carried out by Henry Marvin as a stock-market maneuver — all combine to infuriate the workers, still further stirred up by secret Anarchist agitation. When a drop in the wage scales is announced, Blair, though he thinks strikes "abhorrent" because of their affinity for violence, accepts the chairmanship of the committee sent to bargain on wages with Marvin and becomes head of the strikers' Advisory Committee after the owner refuses to accept a fair compromise.

For the main events of the strike Friedman turned to the terrible struggle that had taken place at Homestead, Pennsylvania, only nine years before; and it could hardly have been lost upon him that the Carnegie Steel Company, which, through the agency of the ruthless Henry Clay Frick, had at that time destroyed the Homestead locals of the Amalgamated Association of Iron and Steel Workers, was one of the trusts just combined into United States Steel. After the strike in *By Bread Alone* has dragged on for some time, news spreads that Pinkertons, the hated strikebreakers of the Pinkerton Detective Agency, are coming to the mills by boat. (The town of Marvin appears to be situated much like Gary, Indiana, so that Lake Michigan takes the place of the Monongahela.) In spite of the Advisory Committee's protest, men, women, and children attack the mills, partially destroy them, and fight a bloody battle with a barge-load of Pinkertons. The governor at last sends in the militia to restore order, but not before Blair is wounded while trying to stop the fighting.

With the town under martial law and the men, unjustly blaming Blair for the loss of the strike, starved back to work, the Anarchists act. An attempt is made on Henry Marvin's life — as Alexander Berkman tried to kill Frick at Homestead — and a plot to blow up the mills fails only when the leading Anarchist, La Vette, rather improbably commits suicide. Evangeline and Blair leave the town of Marvin. Blair is disillusioned with organized labor as an avenue to the Coöperative Commonwealth, but not with the goal itself. As the book concludes, he has resolved to work for the Coöperative Commonwealth through political action. What he envisages is a peaceful revolution.

Since 1901 was also the year in which Leon Czolgosz assassinated President McKinley, it is interesting to note the horror with which Friedman and his hero oppose the "unnatural creed" of Anarchism. By a speech describing the form and function of the Coöperative Commonwealth, Blair at one point wins a saloon audience away from the Anarchist virago Sophia Goldstein, who had formerly escaped from St. Petersburg to New York and had, vulturelike — the figure is elaborated by Friedman — come to Chicago at the time of the Haymarket Riot. She is one of those who incite the strikers to their Luddite attack on the mill, and, after the militia has come, she villainously persuades a young Pole to attempt the assassination of Marvin. Associated with this Russian terrorist is the Frenchman La Vette, who leads a double life as head of the mill's chemical department and as conspirator. La Vette redeems himself by committing suicide when, after falling in love with Evangeline Marvin, he finds that she too will die if he blows up the steel works. Friedman, clearly a parliamentary Socialist, is careful to emphasize that the Coöperative Commonwealth cannot be attained by violence and destruction.

In addition to serving as a definition of what Socialism is not, La Vette is useful to the author as one of his several devices for juxtaposing the two nations of the rich and the poor. Early in the book a chapter entitled "The Destroyers" describes a clandestine meeting of the Anarchist band in the midst of the slums. La Vette, suave in evening clothes, stands out among the poverty-scarred conspirators huddled together in Sophia's tiny room. As the following chapter, "The Cotillon," opens, La Vette has driven directly from the meeting to a dress ball at the house of Henry Marvin. La Vette thus brings the two worlds into relation and, lest the reader miss the point, is himself struck by the "vivid contrast" of the scenes. The device of juxtaposition, which Friedman may well have borrowed from the mid-Victorian reform novelists, was to remain a standard technique in the radical novel. It is continued throughout this book in the activities of the wealthy Evangeline, who founds a settlement house in the town of Marvin just before the strike, and of course in those of Blair, who believes that he and the girl have both been acting with the "characteristic and striking tendency of our time that the hand of help [is] extended by the favored few to the unfortunate many, rather than that the hands of the few [are] uplifted beseechingly to the rich." [8]

Certainly the greatest achievement of the novel, considering the time of publication, is its dramatization for a middle-class audience of the whole intricate pattern of forces which produces a strike and is then constantly reshaped by the strike itself. The dramatization is so complete that the literary historian tends to forgive the occasional sentimentality of character or melodrama of situation, the occasional overcharged metaphor; and these defects are less important than the remarkable recreation within fictional terms of labor history and contemporary condition. Blair's experience is a detailed one, since he lives in the squalid company houses, which are all that the immigrant workers can afford on their wages, and labors beside them at their hard, dangerous trade. By means of Blair's advance through successively more skilled jobs Friedman leads the reader among the intricate processes of a steel mill, describes the usual forms of crippling accident and violent death to be found there, and demonstrates how new machinery creates technological unemployment. Even that succession of skilled jobs, which, granting Blair's abilities, might still seem an improbable manipulation of events by the author, is partly the fictionalizing of a sociological fact — the existence of a job hierarchy in the steel mills at the time, the best jobs being reserved for the native American worker, the poorer for the immigrant, whatever his skill.

Not only is the grim life of the workers in mill, saloon, and slum depicted with thorough exactness, but also the pleasanter existence of the owners, though less attention is given to the latter and the reader is proportionately less convinced. More impressive is Friedman's grasp of how the machinery of society is complexly brought to bear on the strikers. Henry Marvin, the novel's representative of capitalism. is no less able and no more unscrupulous than his prototype, Carnegie's manager at the Homestead mill. Frick's "fortification" of the steel works, his hostility to the Iron and Steel Workers and its committee, his negotiations with the Pinkerton Detective Agency well before his arbitrary breaking off of collective bargaining — these and other acts find their equivalents in Marvin's own maneuvers. In this book the police, the militia, the courts, the state governor are more forbearing than usual in the radical novel, but they all move toward the same end as they did at the Carnegie Steel Company plant — the destruction of a strike and a labor union. The author even demonstrates within his fiction how the McKinley Tariff and the election of a Democratic president in 1892 were related to the Homestead affair. Blair's ultimate rejection of direct economic action results as much from Friedman's own comprehension of how effectively political power may be wielded by a dominant class as it does from a temperamental recoil from violence.

Though it is not a forgotten masterpiece, this book is worth bringing back from oblivion as a solidly realized novel of contemporary life. Unmoved by the craze for historical romances that was seizing the American reading public, Friedman had struck a blow in the fight for literary realism and, writing as radical rather than reformer, had revealed the profound stirrings in the social abyss. *By Bread Alone* imaged powerfully new forces in America.

2.

REALISM AND REVOLUTION

THAT Friedman's novel about a steel strike was published by one of the enterprises of S. S. McClure is another indication of the sense of timeliness possessed like an instinct by the man whose *McClure's Magazine* had already been feeling its way toward a new kind of factual journalism. Since *By Bread Alone* is a conscientious exposure of certain facts of industrial life, it can be considered, despite its political radicalism, as one of the first manifestations of the "muckraking movement," which *McClure's* was about to spearhead by printing the findings of Ida Tarbell, Ray Stannard Baker, Lincoln Steffens, and other eager investigators. Participants in the great middle-class movement of reform which now gives the name "The Progressive Era" to the first decade and a half of the century, the muckrakers accepted the label hurled at them by Theodore Roosevelt in one of his spasms of political piety, and continued to dig away at the accumulated ills of the age. With relentless research articles and indignant research novels they brought to light the shame of the cities and the shame of Standard Oil, the evil-doings of railroads, life insurance companies, and patent medicine manufacturers, the self-seeking of politicos and the self-seeking of industrialists, frenzied finance in Wall Street and treason in the United States Senate.

The same editorial in *Current Literature* which had observed the public's panicky state of mind in 1906 over radicalism also noted the open worrying by press and public speakers that one result of muckraking might be "a plunge toward socialism." Certainly both the writers of exposure literature and their millions of middle-class readers were profoundly and righteously shocked at the ugly things being brought up out of the dark into the pages of popular magazines. Henry Demarest Lloyd's *Wealth against Commonwealth* had given warning in 1894 of the savage growth of Standard Oil, but Ida Tarbell's dispassionate series of articles in *McClure's* on the methods used by Rockefeller to create his near-monopoly was even more thoroughgoing and damning. Average middle-class citizens had long been aware that city administrations did not always fulfill campaign promises or fulfilled them in strange ways; yet they were hardly prepared for the extent to which these same administrations were proved to be fattening off the graft from saloons and houses of prostitution and putting public rights into private pockets. Neither had they known how many Senators of the United States were in effect retained by bankers, railroad barons, and big industrialists. Although their usual reaction to these revelations was to vote for each successive city reform administration and cheer each blow with which T.R. presumably smashed a trust, an increasing number of middle-class individuals began to feel that reform was not enough and to conclude with the muckraker Charles Edward Russell that "the only logical place for anyone dissatisfied with reciprocal rapine was the Socialist party, which did not purpose to wait for an indefinite sunrise but to remake fundamentals." [1] If no "plunge" toward Socialism was occurring, there was certainly a steadily increasing drift in that direction.

Continued success at the polls was in fact filling the Socialist Party with an ebullient confidence that the changes that they predicted for the American social structure were things soon to come. Now, after nearly half a century, this optimism appears the optimism of innocence; yet, as the first decade advanced, to more and more people of all classes the triumph of Socialism did seem inevitable. Recruits swarming to the Party from Midwest farms, the more militant trade unions, and the unorganized proletariat of factory and sweatshop met converts from indignant middle-class groups. From about 1905 on, as the Socialist leader Morris Hillquit notes in his autobiography, a growing number of new adherents, both men and women, began to appear in literary, academic, and journalistic circles, the opinion-making areas of public life. Some even among the wealthy felt the attraction, and Mr.

Dooley was not exaggerating any more than usual when he de-clared in his dissertation on Socialism that the subject "is no longer talked to ye in Platt Doitch, but handed to ye fr'm th' top iv a coach or whispered fr'm behind an ivory fan." [2]

Young college men were particularly affected. For them it was as though windows and doors were being opened throughout the land. In the immigrant-crowded cities, the settlement house — so characteristic an institution of the period that it became almost a symbol — drew university men with a fresh promise of American life and was frequently as much an informal center for Social-ist influence in all directions as it was for good works in the slums, mutual education of the classes, and sociological inves-tigation. When Ernest Poole, whose novel *The Harbor* was later to be one of the achievements of Socialist fiction, went from "museum-like" Princeton to New York in 1902 to live for an exciting year and a half at the University Settlement, he found already working there a group of bright young men: Arthur Bul-lard and Leroy Scott, who also were to write Socialist novels, and Walter Weyl, William English Walling, Robert Hunter, and J. G. Phelps Stokes, who shortly became leading intellectuals in the Socialist Party. If, for the country as a whole, the spring season of Progressivism had arrived, Socialism was helping to make the tem-perature even warmer.

II

Besides providing the basis for political organization, Socialism was a highly self-conscious educational and cultural force; and like any other relatively new movement, this one desired that an imaginative literature be created in its name even before many writ-ers had lived deeply enough into it to be able to create such a lit-erature. In the fall of 1901, just before Friedman's novel marked a new departure in fiction, a group of New York intellectuals, most of them young, brought out the first issue of a magazine designed to protest against "the miasmas of commercialism" and to affirm that a great renaissance was arriving in the name of Socialist art and literature. The new monthly, appropriately named *The Com-rade*, greeted its readers with a quotation from Whitman and a statement of purposes. "*The Comrade* will endeavor to mirror Socialist thought as it finds expression in Art and Literature. Its function will be to develop the aesthetic impulse in the Socialist movement, to utilize the talent we already have, and to quicken into being aspirations that are latent." [3] First issued under an editorial board headed by Leonard Abbott and later under the editorship of the Socialist writer John Spargo, *The Comrade* continued its attempt to unite Socialism and the arts, though it became increasingly politicized toward the end of its four-year career and was finally merged with Charles H. Kerr's *International Socialist Review*.

The art work of the new magazine, though often relaxed in form, was as a rule firmly dedicated in purpose to the cause. A feature of the second issue, for example, was the double-page illustration at the inside center, done with a Greek décor and entitled "The Race of the Nations Towards Socialism," while on the outside back cover a cartoon linked the two killers, war and capitalism. For many issues the standard front cover depicted Socialism as a handsome young woman sitting on a world globe and wearing a red Liberty cap. In its articles and book reviews the magazine called for fiction, drama, and poetry which would make use of the materials to be found in the struggles of the labor movement, though it extended a surprising charitableness toward such an "unfriendly" novel as Mary Wilkins Freeman's *The Portion of Labor*. Among other Socialist pieces, *The Comrade* printed a satire by the poet and propagandist, Morris Winchevsky (who was one of the board of editors), a short story by the novelist, Walter Marion Raymond, a villanelle entitled "The Worker and the Tramp" by Jack London, and reminiscences by Debs of his life as an agitator. An early issue carried an article by Edwin Markham predicting that the movement to emancipate American labor would bring with it a flowering of literature; in a late one, William Edlin described a powerful contemporary influence for urban radicalism in "Socialist Journalism and Journalists of the Ghetto." Through many numbers ran a confessional series by various Party notables describing the process of their conversions. Although the circulation of *The Comrade* was always meager, a very few thousand at most, it is memorable for its attempt, by publishing such mixed material, to create a meeting place between men of the arts and men of radical politics.

Many contributions to *The Comrade* remind the present-day reader that the Socialist intellectual of its time often affected the flowing tie of the painter; indeed, a tendency toward "artiness" in the magazine is best indicated by the fact that for number after number it serialized William Morris's *News from Nowhere*, complete with Pre-Raphaelite illustrations, and that the final issue consisted chiefly of a reprinting of Oscar Wilde's "The Soul of Man Under Socialism." But if a major preoccupation of the Socialist writer was with the beauty of the Coöperative Commonwealth-to-be, a complementary one was with the ugly now of capitalist industrialism. In the writer's personal history a perception of ugliness would probably have come first and readied him for his vehement response toward Socialism. Before theory came experience, some sort of collision with the enormous fact that American life was not always what parent and textbook had taught. The resulting conflict impelled the young Socialist-to-be into exploring the jerry-built squalor of the rising manufacturing cities, the chicanery and brutality of a jungle politics, the human suffering and waste that were as much products of competitive industry as were girder, plow, and locomotive. Having gained a hideous knowledge, he could not find release from its burden merely by visualizing the glories of a future society; rather he must set down ugly detail after ugly detail out of what he had learned of the present one until every shocking thing had been told. So, out of their own psychological necessity, the Socialist novelists and critics were drawn into the battle for literary realism.

Actually the Socialist literary critics arrived at realism before the novelists did and hence were of more immediate assistance to this new development in American literature by reason of their demands that it be accepted. To them, realism and Socialism were mutually implicit; one was the best way to "tell the truth" in literature as the other was the only way to tell it in politics. When *The International Socialist Review* began to appear in 1900, explicitly to combat American "Utopian" socialism with the "scientific" variety, the editor stated that the new journal would concern itself with the movement toward revolution which he saw enlivening all areas of human existence, and made a significant reference to literature.

> We shall hope to secure expression of those new tendencies in science, art, literature, education and music, which are known in the world of economics and politics as socialism . . . The movement in literature that seeks to free the mind from the control of capitalism by substituting a healthy "realism" for the corrupting productions of competition will also be represented as a correlative movement with the great economic revolt to which the name of socialism is commonly narrowed.[4]

The literary critics of *The Comrade*, if not all the other contributors, likewise held with fair consistency to this fight for realism; and Leonard Abbott, writing in the April, 1902, issue of the widely-circulated Socialist monthly *Wilshire's*, argued that art should be no "plaything," as capitalist artists had to make it in order not to reflect the intolerable ugliness of the system they accepted. On the contrary, nothing in the whole of society should be alien to the musician, the painter, the writer. Art had direct connections even with the most sordid aspects of the class struggle.

The belief that the artist's function is to reveal the true and terrible face of things beneath the capitalist mask was clearly held with great firmness by Caroline H. Pemberton, whose novel, "The Charity Girl," began to run as a serial in *The International Socialist Review* some eight months before *By Bread Alone* was published,[5] but her book demonstrates once more the truism that the road to bad literature is paved with many good intentions. This stiltedly written tale recounts how Julian Endicott, idealistic young secretary to a wealthy charitable organization, represses his love for a beautiful and compatible woman because she is already, though unhappily, married, how he tries in self-sacrifice to marry an orphan he has rescued from a gruesomely Dickensian home for unwed mothers, and how he eventually learns to return the love of yet another ward of the charity, a charming Polish-Jewish girl. Concurrently Julian moves from a faith in the efficacy of charity under capitalism to an even stronger faith in the necessity of wiping out all evils by instituting the Coöperative Commonwealth; "In place of relieving those whom society had wronged, he was to bear arms against the wrongs themselves." [6]

The author's intellectual convictions are strong enough. In her hands a meeting of the "Association for Sociological Research" becomes an attack on the snobbish, self-centered ladies of fashion who support this commercialized and basically heartless charity organization; while Julian's encounter with a prostitute is used to reveal the limitations of the mere reformer, who, as the girl says, stirs up the social mud with a stick while taking care that none gets on himself. In the climactic episodes of the book Marxist doctrine becomes explicit. When the Spanish-American War breaks out — Miss Pemberton was nothing if not contemporary — Julian volunteers in a regiment of state militia which is never shipped to Cuba, but instead undergoes epidemics and near-starvation in Southern camps because of the Government's negligence. Here a German Marxist, who with a heavy-handed attempt at symbolism is always referred to as "the Undertaker's Son," shows Julian how their sufferings as soldiers prove that the war is an imperialistic act necessitated by the inner contradictions of capitalism. To complete the conversion the Marxist lends Julian copies of Howells's *A Traveler from Altruria* and Bellamy's *Equality*, thinking afterwards that he should have started him in on Marx at once because Julian is too given already to "metaphors and daydreams" and needs "a scientific study of facts as they are." Such sequences indicate that the conscious intention of the author was doubtless to write a realistic novel, to present "facts as they are." Actually, however, she was too much bound by nonrealistic literary conventions to carry out that intention. In "The Charity Girl" Marxist attacks on the inhuman hypocrisies of capitalism are imposed on, not fused with, what is essentially a sentimental tale of romantic love. One is constantly reminded in the reading of the book that Miss Pemberton had previously been a writer of children's stories full of pathos and high morality. Such was hardly the best training for a realistic novelist.

Why the Socialist fiction writers, with the valiant exception of I. K. Friedman, did not go immediately and consistently to realism is probably best explained by the strong attractive influence of such established literary trends as that of the moral-sentimental novel. Two others were the tradition of the Utopia and the vogue of the romance, into either of which categories fall the few remaining Socialist novels to be published in the first half-decade of the century. The third and final piece of book-length fiction by a Socialist to appear in 1901 was *Beyond the Black Ocean* by Father Thomas McGrady, a Catholic priest in Bellevue, Kentucky, who had accepted Marxism a year before at the age of thirty-six and whose advocacy of it brought him a year later into a conflict with his bishop which apparently was the cause for his leaving both the priesthood and the Church. This "social romance" has a story of sorts, but the very thin thread of fanciful events is intended merely to string together what one reviewer was pleased to call "gems of socialist thought." Primarily the book is a set of radical orations delivered as an act of faith, rather than a piece with any particular literary form or merit. *Progress and Poverty* and Marxist agitational pamphlets are obviously the economic influences behind McGrady's volume; the chief literary influences appear to be — and it is a curious mixture — Jonathan Swift, Tom Moore, and Ignatius Donnelly. With much Pat-and-Mike humor the story describes the sailing of a transport of Irish soldiers in 1798 across the Black Ocean of the Polar North into the "trans-arctic" sphere. (The world is conveniently pictured as being, not one, but two globes, joined at the North Pole.) Here dwell the Ten Lost Tribes of Israel in variously named countries obviously corresponding to those of Europe, Asia, Africa, and the Americas. The rest of the book outlines the history of Toadia, which is a mirror-image of the United States, the development of a Toadian Plutocracy, and the ultimate triumph of Socialism in 1908 under the leadership of one Isaac Gilhooley, descendant of Irishman and Israelite and editor of the fearless newspaper, *The Flaming Sword*. This extraordinary exercise in Celtic imagination concludes with a brief description of the Utopia into which Toadia has been turned by Socialism.

The Utopia as a literary form was declining, but clearly was not dead, though Morrison I. Swift's *The Monarch Billionaire* (1903) could very well have killed it, for in this curious book a shallow stream of semiutopian plot at the beginning soon disappears entirely into the barren sands of doctrine. Swift, who was equipped with a tart tongue and an eclectic mind, assails the depredations of the "Pocket-Book Kings," the treachery of conservative labor leaders toward the rank and file, and the faith of the Socialists in a political

party. To fill the resulting vacuum he has two of his characters
outline for most of the book a plan designed to fuse the best features
of economic individualism and of Socialism into a variety of
syndicalism. "General ownership" (or "peopleized trusts") pro-
vides for the ownership of industrial groups by the individual
workers in them, the over-all federation of these groups to be responsive to a union of the whole people. Since any political party
is by nature a despotic institution, Swift argues, the only method by
which the people may be restored to proprietorship is that of direct
economic action. A nonviolent Universal Strike in fact brings to
heel at the end of the book the Monarch Billionaire and his Amalgamated Fish, Ship, Iron, Transportation, Coal and Steel Company.

This partially fictionalized tract is historically interesting as an
early example of the importation of European syndicalist thought,
Swift himself having been drawn to radical movements while an
American student in Germany and later editing in this country
The Public Ownership Review. More to the immediate point is a
section of the book concerned with the arts under capitalism. Contemporary literature, the author has his chief mouthpiece declare,
is trivial and false because it is produced only for profit. A true
literature, one that will be spirited and strong, can exist only when
the genius of the working class has been liberated; for then literature, art, and science will be devoted to "universal life and happiness." Unable to produce strong literature himself, as is demonstrated by his volume of short stories entitled *The Damask Girl*,
Swift in the role of critic violently rejected books that aimed only
at flattering or diverting their readers in order to blind them to the
vicious facts of competitive society.

A similar concern for the strong as opposed to the trivial moti-
vates the development of Hilda Lathrop, the leading character in
Vida Scudder's *A Listener in Babel* (1903), which is admittedly
less a novel than a series of conversations on ideas and social movements current at the turn of the century. Long before she was able,
in the author's phrasing, "at last to take the great word Socialism
with confidence upon her lips," Hilda had been a sheltered, expatriate girl dedicated to the proposition that a thing is beautiful
in exact proportion to its uselessness. She breaks away from her
ivory environment, however, returns to the United States, and

lives in a settlement house for two years, "listening." What she hears from social workers, labor leaders, Socialists, and the city's poor leads her to conclude that the opposite aesthetic is actually correct; beauty and use always coexist, and true beauty comes from the common rather than the rare. America, she decides, needs such common beauty, and she leaves the settlement house to learn how the art of handcraft may be applied to modern industry.

The Socialist literary critics continued to call for realism and particularly to deplore the fact that so many radical novels were not novels at all but simply fictional frameworks for "orations and essays" demonstrating what the author had learned concerning the evils of capitalism and the virtues of Socialism. An anonymous announcement in *The International Socialist Review* praised Walter Marion Raymond's florid *Rebels of the New South* (1904) because its characters were everyday people, and A. M. Simons thought Edwin Arnold Brenholtz's *The Recording Angel* (1905) the best Socialist novel yet, because its doctrine grew naturally out of the story. Although Brenholtz's book must be classed as another romance of the future, realism is in fact the literary creed of Charles Arndt, its Socialist hero. At one point in the tale, the author puts his protagonist on a train in order to let him converse with an acquaintance, a poet and novelist named Hubert, to whom Charles opens his mind on literary matters.

"I have almost given up reading modern fiction and poetry. And why? The poetry is beautiful, it is polished until it dazzles the senses, it is chaste and refined; but it does not report or represent the life of the world I, nor any one I know, live in. Its very polish and refinement is its bane. It does not talk a word of the worker's language." [7]

Nor does current fiction please Arndt any better and for a similar reason; it does not reflect what happens in "real life." Hubert admits that Charles is right about his own published work, for he cannot sell any realistic fiction. Even if a conservative publishing house printed it — and no prominent one will — the critics would say it was not art. Hubert has given up trying — "and now I turn out literature."

There were to be a few more such romances, and one was to be outstanding; but from about 1905 onward, as the enthusiasm for muckraking revelations drew to a climax and as their party gained maturity, the Socialist novelists turned sharply toward realism as a literary technique. An example is Leroy Scott's able novel about a labor union, *The Walking Delegate* (1905), which describes the struggle for power in the New York locals of the Iron Workers Union between Buck Foley, tough, shrewd, corrupt "walking delegate," and Tom Keating, tough, shrewd, honest rank-and-filer. Keating, enraged at Foley's open self-seeking, finally manages to build a democratic political machine that can withstand the walking delegate's use of goon squads, his stuffing of ballot boxes, and his conniving with the owner of a leading construction firm. Scott tells the rough, raw facts of the fight for union democracy, and he tells them with what appears at first to be a joy for simple revelation. His hero, Keating, is entirely a labor man. He is not a Socialist, he never mentions Socialism as a theory; yet he acts from an implicit acceptance of class warfare, and at one point, in a conversation, he confidently explains that the workers will inevitably supplant the capitalist class, at which time government will be conducted by the nine-tenths instead of by the present one-tenth. Keating is intended as a type figure of the proletarian become conscious of historical destiny, but the author carefully lets the reader perceive this intention himself. *The Walking Delegate* still preserves some air of literary sophistication to the present day.

The sympathetic use of ordinary men and women as characters and of their everyday life as the source of events, the carefully detailed physical descriptions, the reproduction of colloquial language at the various social levels, and especially the unobtrusiveness of the social doctrine — all these characteristics of Scott's novel would have delighted that temperamental radical, Clarence Darrow, who, in his essay "Realism in Literature and Art" — published in the Pocket Library of Socialism by Charles H. Kerr and Company as early as 1899 — had objected to "thesis novels" because they falsified human nature in order to teach a theoretical lesson. Darrow, whom the reporter Hutchins Hapgood remembered as being unable to appreciate any literature except that of revolt, had argued that simply by presenting the world exactly as it was the artist could not "help but catch the inspiration that is filling all the world's best minds with the hope of greater justice and more equal

social life." [8] From 1905 onward most Socialist novelists tried to
accept Darrow's requirement that they present the world exactly
as it was; but Socialism was to them a part of the world, and few
wished to deal so obliquely with it as Scott had done in *The Walking Delegate.* To do so was to run the risk of writing like the mere
muckraking novelist, and muckraking in literature, as in politics,
was not enough. Having decided to write realistic *Socialist* novels,
they at once came to a central artistic problem: how to combine
the unburdening of capitalist fact with a convincing statement, in
fictional terms, of their hope for a different future. The most
famous Socialist novel of all failed precisely at that important point.

III

Lincoln Steffens tells in his *Autobiography* of receiving a call
during the early years of muckraking from an earnest and as yet
little-known young writer.

One day Upton Sinclair called on me at the office of *McClure's* and
remonstrated.
"What you report," he said, "is enough to make a complete picture
of the system, but you seem not to see it. Don't you see it? Don't you
see what you are showing?" [9]

Having just been converted to Socialism, Sinclair was sure he
"saw it," and in the late autumn of 1905 his friend Jack London
was writing to the Socialist weekly *The Appeal to Reason* in praise
of a new book which it was serializing.

Here it is at last! The book we have been waiting for these many
years! The "Uncle Tom's Cabin" of wage slavery! Comrade Sinclair's
book, "The Jungle!" and what "Uncle Tom's Cabin" did for black
slaves, "The Jungle" has a large chance to do for the wage-slaves of
today.[10]

When *The Jungle* appeared in book form the following year, even
the conservative literary critics agreed, with certain reservations,
that at last an American was painting a picture "of those sunk in
the innermost depths of the modern *Inferno*." Part of the novel's
abrupt success among the public at large may have resulted, as
Sinclair himself was to lament, from the unintended relevance of a

brief muckraking passage on filthy meat; but no novel is read because of half a dozen pages, and this one was read internationally. The extent of the young writer's popularity is suggested by the remark of Georg Brandes, on his visit to the United States eight years later, that the three modern American novelists he found worth reading were Frank Norris, Jack London, and Upton Sinclair.

Europeans continue to read Upton Sinclair, and London as well, even if European critics on tour to the United States have long since ceased to speak of him; but it is now impossible for a citizen of the prophet's own country to go through Sinclair's work — the earlier novels as well as the present nonstop flight with Lanny Budd across recent history — without a mixed feeling of impatience and respect: impatience with him as a writer for his refusal, or inability, to make a final imaginative fusion of material and purpose; respect for him as a person, despite his curiously impersonal egoism, because of his generosity, his openness of heart, his courage, and his devotion to truth as he sees it.

The author of *The Jungle* was born in Baltimore in 1878 of a father and mother impoverished by the economic dislocations of the postbellum South, yet proud in their family ancestries. Through his father he was descended from a line of officers who had served with distinction in the British and American navies — seven Sinclairs had also been officers in the Confederate Navy — while his mother's family was a moderately wealthy one; but Sinclair's father, a liquor salesman, was one of his own best, or worst, customers, was unable to support his family, and slowly and terribly drank himself to death. Sinclair later explained in his book of reminiscences, *American Outpost*, that one of his reasons for becoming a social rebel was his psychology as a "poor relation."

Readers of my novels know that I have one favorite theme, the contrast of the social classes; there are characters from both worlds, the rich and the poor, and the plot is contrived to carry you from one to the other. The explanation of this literary phenomenon is that, from the first days I can remember, my life was a series of Cinderella transformations; one night sleeping on a vermin-ridden sofa in a lodging-house, and the next night under silken coverlets in a fashionable home. It was always a question of one thing — whether my father had the

money for that week's board. If he didn't, my mother paid a visit to her
father, the railroad official.[11]

A second influence that assisted in guiding him ultimately to
revolt was, Sinclair maintains, the Protestant Episcopal Church,
since he "took the words of Jesus seriously," envisioning himself as
a follower of "the rebel carpenter, the friend of the poor and
lowly, the symbol of human brotherhood." Although he early lost
faith in Christianity as anything more than a code of ethics, Sinclair
has characteristically continued to hold Jesus as one of his heroes.
In his own battle for Truth against Evil, he has made his life one
long saga of St. George and the Dragon. An intense, sensitive boy,
he was shocked into an ascetic denial of all indulgences by the
decline and death of his father, whom he stood by loyally and
through whose sufferings he discovered an important social fact,
that behind the saloon-keeper loomed the politicians and Big Business. Disgusted with the ugliness of the world, he turned for escape
to literature, where he found his spirit of revolt so strengthened
that he came to suppose that literature made life. Like his character
Thyrsis in the semiautobiographical *Love's Pilgrimage*, he read
Don Quixote and *Les Miserables*; he loved George Eliot and was
thrilled by the social protest of Dickens; he admired Thackeray
most of all, for Thackeray saw the human corruption which lay at
the heart of the world that he described. Significantly, the boy's
favorite poets were the blind Milton and the revolutionary Shelley.

Two elements in the education of this social rebel still remained to take effect. The first was a prolonged acquaintance with
what he later called "the economic screw." He supported himself
for a year of graduate work at Columbia by hack writing, producing thousands of words of boys' stories each week. Then he broke
away to write the Great American Novel, married the adoring
Meta Fuller, and endured with her several years of drudging poverty, desperately trying to publish his first novels and performing
more hack work in order to keep his wife and newly-born son
alive. In the autumn of 1902 he was rescued from this marginal
existence by the kindness of George D. Herron, a gentle-minded
Socialist writer and lecturer, who gave him financial support and,
equally important in Sinclair's development, helped him to discover

Socialism. Reading *Wilshire's* completed the conversion. Sinclair had more years of the economic screw to endure, but now he could gird himself for the fight with the whole armor of an economic and political philosophy.

It was like the falling down of prison walls about my mind; the most amazing discovery, after all these years — that I did not have to carry the whole burden òf humanity's future upon my two frail shoulders! There were actually others who understood; who saw what had gradually become clear to me, that the heart and centre of the evil lay in leaving the social treasure, which nature had created, and which every man has to have in order to live, to become the object of a scramble in the market-place, a delirium of speculation. The principal fact which the Socialists had to teach me, was the fact that they themselves existed.[12]

Moving his family to a tent, later a shack on the outskirts of Princeton, New Jersey, he started work on *Manassas*, the first volume of a projected trilogy based on the Civil War, while the family's poverty continued and his unhappy wife passed through long periods of black melancholy. *Manassas*, though superior to his previous novels, sold scarcely better; but it was read by the editor of *The Appeal to Reason*, who enthusiastically wrote Sinclair that, since he had described the struggle against chattel slavery in America, he should now do the same for wage slavery. With an advance payment on the new novel, Sinclair spent seven weeks in the autumn of 1904 in the Packingtown district of Chicago, where the stockyard workers had just lost a strike. Horrified by the wretched conditions under which the inhabitants of Packingtown lived and labored, he collected his evidence with the zeal and care of any muckraking reporter. He returned to Princeton, worked incessantly for three months, began serializing the novel in *The Appeal*, and finally, in February, 1906, succeeded in having it brought out by Doubleday, Page and Company, a nonradical publishing house, after an investigating lawyer sent by the company had submitted a report substantiating Sinclair's findings against the practices of the meat-packers.

The Jungle is dedicated "To the Workingmen of America." Into it had gone Sinclair's heartsick discovery of the filth, disease, degradation, and helplessness of the packing workers' lives. But any muckraker could have put this much into a book; the fire of the novel came from Sinclair's whole passionate, rebellious past, from the insight into the pattern of capitalist oppression shown him by Socialist theory, and from the immediate extension into the characters' lives of his own and his wife's struggle against hunger, illness, and fear. It was the summation of his life and experience into a manifesto. The title of the book itself represented a feat of imaginative compression, for the world in which the Lithuanian immigrant Jurgis and his family find themselves is an Africa of unintelligibility, of suffering and terror, where the strong beasts devour the weak, who are dignified, if at all, only by their agony.

After their pathetically happy marriage, the descent of Jurgis and Ona into the social pit is steady. They are spiritually and, in the case of Ona, physically slaughtered, more slowly but quite as surely as the cattle in the packing plant. Disease spread by filthy working and living conditions attacks them, they endure cold in winter and clouds of flies in summer, bad food weakens their bodies, and seasonal layoffs leave them always facing starvation. When illness destroys Jurgis's great strength, he realizes that he has become a physical cast-off, one of the waste products of the plant, and must take the vilest job of all in the packing company's fertilizer plant. The forced seduction of his wife by her boss leads him to an assault on the man and thirty days in jail. Released without money, he returns to find his family evicted from their home and Ona dying in childbirth. After being laid off from a dangerous job in a steel plant, Jurgis becomes successively a tramp, the henchman of a crooked politician, a strikebreaker in the packing plant strike of 1904, and finally a bum. Having reached the bottom of the social pit, he wanders into a political meeting to keep warm and hears for the first time, though at first unaware that he is listening to a Socialist, an explanation of the capitalist jungle in which he has been hunted. The sudden realization of truth is as overwhelming to Jurgis as it had been to Jurgis's creator. He at once undertakes to learn more about Socialism, is given a job in a hotel owned by a Socialist, and is eventually taken to a meeting of radical intellectuals where he hears all the arguments for the Industrial Republic which Sinclair wants his readers to know. Jurgis throws himself into the political campaign of 1904, the one in which the Party actually made such astonishing gains, and the book concludes exultantly with a speech first given by Sinclair himself, proclaiming the coming victory of the Socialists, at which time Chicago will belong to the people.

The "conversion" pattern of *The Jungle* has been attacked as permitting too easy a dramatic solution; however, aside from the recognized fact that many conversions have occurred before and since Paul saw the light on the road to Damascus, it should be noted that in *The Jungle* Sinclair carefully prepares such an outcome by conducting Jurgis through all the circles of the workers' inferno and by attempting to show that no other savior except Socialism exists. Perhaps a more valid objection to the book is Sinclair's failure to realize his characters as "living" persons, a charge which, incidentally, may be brought against many nonconversion novels. Jurgis is admittedly a composite figure who was given a heaping share of the troubles of some twenty or thirty packing workers with whom Sinclair had talked, and the author's psychology of character is indeed a simple one. Although in the introductory wedding scene Jurgis and the other major characters are sharply sketched as they had appeared to the writer at an actual wedding feast in Packingtown, during the remainder of the book they gradually lose their individuality, becoming instead any group of immigrants destroyed by the Beef Trust. Yet paradoxically, the force and passion of the book are such that this group of lay figures with Jurgis at their head, these mere capacities for infinite suffering, finally do come to stand for the masses themselves, for all the faceless ones to whom things are done. Hardly individuals, they nevertheless collectively achieve symbolic status.

Sinclair's success in creating this jungle world emphasizes by contrast what is actually the book's key defect. Jurgis's conversion is probable enough, the Socialist explanation might well flash upon him with the blinding illumination of a religious experience; but practically from that point onward to the conclusion of his novel Sinclair turns from fiction to another kind of statement. Where the capitalist damnation, the destruction of the immigrants, has been proved almost upon the reader's pulses, the Socialist salvation, after its initial impact, is intellectualized. The reader cannot exist imaginatively in Jurgis's converted state even if willing, for Jurgis hardly exists himself. What it means to be a Socialist is given, not through the rich disorder of felt experience, but in such arbitrarily codified forms as political speeches, an essay on Party personalities, or the long conversation in monologues about the Coöperative Commonwealth which comprises most of the book's final chapter. *The Jungle* begins and lives as fiction; it ends as a political miscellany.

The fact that Jurgis's militant acceptance of Socialism is far less creatively realized than his previous victimization is indicative of how Sinclair's outraged moral idealism is attracted more to the pathos than the power of the poor, and suggests his real affinity for the mid-Victorian English reform novelists. More specifically, *The Jungle* is reminiscent of the work of the humanitarian Dickens, whose social protest had "thrilled" the young rebel. There are frequent resemblances between the two writers in narrative method, in presentation of character, in the tendency of both to intrude themselves with bubbling delight or horrified indignation into the scene described. Whole paragraphs on the wedding feast of Jurgis Rudkus and Ona recall, except for the Lithuanian, the manner of Dickens with the Cratchits' Christmas dinner, and Madame Haupt, fat, drunken, and filthy, might have been a midwife in Oliver Twist's London. Finally, the temper of Sinclair's protest is curiously like that of Dickens. Where the latter urges only the literal practice of Christianity as a remedy for the cruelties he describes, Sinclair, to be sure, demands the complete transformation of the existing order of things by the Socialist revolution; yet the revolution that the orator so apocalyptically envisages at the conclusion to *The Jungle* is to be accomplished by the ballot and not by the bullet. Sinclair's spirit is not one of blood and barricades, but of humanitarianism and brotherly love.

Both in life and in writings Sinclair has attempted, as did Dickens, to be the persuading intermediary between the contending classes. With admirable sweetness of temper, considering his lack of success, he has continued to argue that the owning class should perform a revolution by consent, that the capitalist should give up his profits and power in exchange for citizenship in an industrial democracy. But in the novels that he has so prodigally brought forth year after year since the publication of *The Jungle*, the lamb of his Christian spirit has rarely been able peacefully to lie down with the lion of his Marxian vocabulary. As a result, although Sinclair is the only one of the Socialist novelists who continued, and after a fashion continues, to write Socialist novels, his is the classic case among them for unresolved discrepancies between his fictional structure and the "message" that he is trying to convey. The formal flaw of *The Jungle* represents one such failure; other novels have others, and always the total effect of the fiction is weakened. *King Coal* (1917), to take only one of his better-known earlier novels, illustrates the point with a damning simplicity.

Like most of his fiction, *King Coal* is what Sinclair calls "a novel of contemporary life." This time Sinclair is exposing the conditions which led to the great Colorado coal strike of 1913–14. In a style reminiscent of his early hack-written boys' stories, he narrates the experiences of Hal Warner, a wealthy mine-owner's son, who has decided to work for a summer in a Colorado coal camp under an assumed name in order to supplement with practical experience what he is being taught at a college endowed by the chief mine operator of the state. What the coal camp teaches him is not the symmetry of classical economics, but the sprawling wretchedness of King Coal's prisoners and the brutal reality of the class struggle. North Valley turns out to be another Jungle, and the once-blithe college boy eventually leads a movement for honest weighing of the miners' output, gets a taste of class justice, and then heads an unsuccessful strike against the coal company after a mine explosion has resulted from company carelessness.

Perhaps the squalid camp is most effectively described through the opening eyes of a representative of the owning class, although it is certainly absurd to express the strike almost completely in terms of the young man's adventures, which are of the very best Rover Boys variety. The author is also psychologically accurate in returning the enlightened Hal to his own class. But Hal goes back expressly to convert his class to the Truth, and here the discrepancy between fictional structure and political message gapes wide; for the young man, in spite of a rare opportunity which Sinclair affords him, has been unable to convert any of his wealthy friends during the course of the mine disaster and strike. The reader is left, not converted to Sinclair's implied solution, but rather, intensely aware of the disparity between the author's hopefulness of a "revolution by consent" and the hopelessness of the novel's events, which have demonstrated only the inevitable continuation of class warfare. The optimism of the book is simply irrelevant to the situation it describes.

Despite his artistic limitations, however, Upton Sinclair has built up over half a century a body of work which is a whole tradition in itself. The outstanding Socialist novelist of the first two decades, in the lonely twenties he almost *was* radical American literature. In the thirties the young Leftists, when they were not damning him as a "social fascist" in accordance with some current "Party line," admitted that his novels and tracts had been and still were instrumental in teaching them the facts of capitalist life.[13] But Sinclair's work, from *The Jungle* onward, had always pushed out from radical circles into the wide ranges of the whole reading public to inform them of the social and personal irresponsibility of capitalists, the disruption of the middle class, the struggle of labor to organize, and the martyrdom of radicals. In the forties his moderately Socialist tales of Lanny Budd and a stricken century sold to hundreds of thousands of American citizens, who found them the easiest way to learn what historical events had prepared the Second World War and were preparing the "Peace." If Sinclair has never been a great creative novelist (what is Lanny Budd beyond a mirror of history?), he has been something else of value — one of the great information centers in American literature. Few American novelists have done more to make their fellow citizens conscious of the society, all of it, in which they live.

IV

When Sinclair, who has never yet abated his zeal for new propaganda devices, conceived and helped to organize the Intercollegiate Socialist Society in 1905 because he had been able to go through college without learning of the existence of Socialism, the already famous Jack London became its first president; and in October of that year London, with a soft-collared red shirt and a Korean valet, set off by Pullman to lecture in the cities of the Middle West and the East on the coming revolution. The newspapers had already found that the "Boy Socialist" was good copy at any time. They now raised a storm among the women's clubs and clergy by announcing London's precipitate marriage to Charmian Kittredge on the day after the divorce from his first wife had been granted; but headlines and editorials grew even more violent over his lecturing, particularly when he spoke on "Revolution" before what must have been nearly the entire population of Yale University. Broad-shouldered and handsome, London stood up to tell the undergraduates: "Seven million revolutionists, organized, working day and night, are preaching the revolution — that passionate gospel, the Brotherhood of Man. . . The capitalist class has been indicted. It has failed in its management and its management is to be taken away from it. Seven million men of the working-class say that they are going to get the rest of the working-class to join with them and take the management away. The revolution is here, now. Stop it who can." [14] The New York *Times* misquoted London as saying, "To hell with the Constitution," Sinclair as usual wrote a letter to the editor, and the young revolutionist himself went back to California satisfied that he had "rattled the dry bones some."

Unlike Sinclair's, London's conversion to Socialism had resulted almost entirely from his experience with the pressure of the economic screw. To be sure, he was not of the proletariat by birth, in spite of what overexuberant radical critics have longed claimed; on the contrary, the late T. K. Whipple has brilliantly demonstrated London's origin in and relationship to the lower middle class, whose sporadic outbreaks of violence have been so characteristic a phenomenon in the development of modern Fascism.[15] Nevertheless, since his stepfather — Jack was the illegitimate son of an astrologer father and spiritualist mother — was unsuccessful as grocery-store proprietor and as farmer, London's boyhood in and near Oakland was mostly one of work and poverty. He sold papers, did odd jobs, worked in a cannery until the long, hard hours drove him to the exciting life of an oyster pirate, served for a year in the equally dangerous job of a deputy for the Fish Patrol, and shipped out on a sealing ship for a seven-months' cruise off the coasts of Japan and Siberia. He returned to an Oakland struck down by the panic of 1893 and learned what it meant to work ten hours a day in the jute mills. Then, after having unknowingly performed two men's jobs shoveling coal for the Oakland Street Railway, he set out east over the mountains in the spring of 1894 to catch up with Kelly's Army of the unemployed, one of the "petitions in boots" marching to join Coxey's Army in Washington, D. C. He deserted from the "main push" of Kelly's Army, went on the road as a tramp, did thirty days for vagrancy in Buffalo, and at last, vividly picturing himself slipping toward the bottom of the Social Pit in the struggle for existence, rode the freights back to the West Coast, determined to make money by exploiting his brains rather than his powerful body. Back in Oakland, where he entered high school to prepare himself deliberately for a career as a writer, he began reading books, among them *The Communist Manifesto*, which had been recommended to him when he was on the road, in order to discover "what manner of thing" his experiences had made him.

I was already It, whatever It was, and by aid of the books I discovered that It was a Socialist. Since that day I have opened many books, but no economic argument, no lucid demonstration of the logic and inevitableness of Socialism affects me as profoundly and convincingly as I was affected on the day when I first saw the walls of the Social Pit rise around me and felt myself slipping down, down, into the shambles at the bottom.[16]

In 1895 he took out his red membership card in the Oakland branch of Daniel De Leon's Socialist Labor Party.

After a semester at the University of California at Berkeley, London left in order to support his parents, endured the wage-slavery of a laundry, and quit that job for the lure of the Klondike. Alaska made his fortune, although he brought out no gold, because here he found the material for the stories which first brought him fame and for, in fact, a good part of his best writing. Back from the Klondike in the summer of 1898, he drove himself to study and write nineteen hours a day, resolved that he would be one of the fit who survived in the struggle for recognition. By January, 1900, his battle with the magazine editors had begun to run definitely toward victory, and from that year until his death in 1916, he published forty-three books, a tremendous output when one considers the several posthumous volumes and the many uncollected stories, essays, and articles, to say nothing of his other activities as lecturer, war correspondent, adventurer, and landed gentleman.

A search for the creative sources of London's work leads most clearly to that important, germinal moment in his life when he viewed "as vividly as though it were a concrete thing" the picture of the Social Pit, wherein he saw himself "hanging on to the slippery wall by main strength and sweat" not far above the shambles at the bottom. That moment does not "explain" Jack London; it was not the traumatic experience of the Freudian biographers, but it did stand as a central, generative image in the shaping of both his attitude toward society and his literary imagination. From the crammed reading of his apprenticeship years — the Darwin, Spencer, Nietzsche, Marx, and, particularly, the Spencerian popularizer Benjamin Kidd — he picked out that which explained or reinforced his vision of society as a struggle in the Pit, as the conflict of man against man, as the domination of the weak by the strong. When reading *The Communist Manifesto* after his return from his adventures on the road, he had underlined the concluding sentences.

The Communists disdain to conceal their views and aims. They openly declare that their ends can be attained only by the forcible overthrow of all existing social conditions. Let the ruling classes tremble at a Communist revolution. The proletarians have nothing to lose but their chains. They have a world to win.
Working men of all countries, unite!

He enthusiastically accepted the social analysis of the *Manifesto* precisely because it was stated as a manifesto. He was drawn to Marx partly by the Marxian vision of a better world, where, London usually agreed, the strong would support the weak instead of thrusting them downward; but even more was he drawn by the violence of the class war and of the developing revolutionary struggle which Marx predicted. The struggle of the workers against a capitalist class forced by history to attempt to enslave them was for him a reproduction on world scale of his own intense drive to struggle upward lest he drop into the shambles at the bottom of the Pit, into what the *Manifesto* called "the social scum, that passively rotting mass thrown off by the lowest layers of old society." Thus his own fear and his consequent drive to power, which was the fear's positive reaction, were expressed through a not very profound synthesis of Darwin, Nietzsche, and Marx. His Socialism was always interpenetrated by his individualism, a condition which explains how both he and his writings could at once combine racism, the glorification of the superior individual over the mass, a fascination with brute force, and a warm-hearted sense of the brotherhood of man.

Having chosen a writer's career as the way to make money and become top dog, London had to acquiesce to the fact that there was little market for revolutionist stories. As a result, the amount of his fiction which is consistently Socialist in intention is relatively small, part of his reputation as a radical writer being based on the essays collected in *War of the Classes* (1905) and *Revolution* (1910), and on the muckraking study of English slum life, *The People of the Abyss* (1903). The radical fiction is confined, with the exception of parts of novels, to half a dozen short stories and that amazing romance of the future, *The Iron Heel* (1908), which has become a minor revolutionary classic.

Like *Caesar's Column*, but far superior to it, *The Iron Heel* foretells a lengthy Iron Age of Fascism before the ultimate Socialist triumph. Influenced in its conception by events in the Russian Revolution of 1905 and by W. J. Ghent's study of capitalist society, *Our Benevolent Feudalism* (1902), this romance is written in the form of a personal account of the events in the United States between the years 1912 and 1932, a Foreword stating that this document, the "Everhard Manuscript," is now published seven centuries after being written because it describes the first of the many revolts that swept the world before labor at last overthrew the brutal power of the Iron Heel (the capitalist Oligarchy) which had enslaved it. The foreword is dated from the "Brotherhood of Man" Era, but London's concern, as always, is with the struggle for the better world rather than with the new world itself. Avis Everhard begins her story by telling how she met her future husband, Ernest Everhard — whom she significantly describes as "a blond beast . . . aflame with democracy" — at a dinner in the home of her father, a physicist at the University of California in Berkeley. Ernest challenges the friendliest of the guests, Bishop Morehouse, to investigate the conditions existing in the working class and to call publicly for the literal application of Christianity. Avis he challenges to find the facts of a recent industrial accident. In her subsequent investigation she learns that terrible accidents are fre-

quent in industry, that the law sides with the employer in cheating
the injured of compensation, and that the newspapers will not
print the truth; her fine clothes, as Ernest has said, are stained
with the blood of the workers. The truth having set Avis free, she
of course agrees to marry Ernest.

When Ernest is invited to speak before the exclusive Philomath
Club, he enrages his upper-class audience by charging them with
incompetence and telling them that the working class is determined
to take over the management of society. He ends with words like
those of London's own address at Yale: "This is the revolution, my
masters. Stop it who can." After the angry protest has died down,
one of the capitalists makes a cold, and grandiloquent, reply: "In
roar of shell and shrapnel and in whine of machine-guns will our
answer be couched. We will grind you revolutionists down under
our heel, and we shall walk upon your faces. The world is ours, we
are its lords, and ours it shall remain." [17] Ernest's own reply is a
quiet declaration that such violence will be met by superior force
from the working class.

Bishop Morehouse's experience illustrates the corruption and
futility of the Church. When he indignantly speaks against the
oppression of the workers, he is committed to an asylum. The dis-
missal of Avis's father from his university post shows the rising
capitalist Oligarchy's control over still another social institution.
Ernest fruitlessly warns a meeting of middle-class businessmen and
farmers that the Marxist theory of surplus value is operating to
break down capitalism and that they must unite with the workers
to achieve Socialism lest all be crushed by the "iron heel" of the
Oligarchy. Meanwhile the Oligarchy has already begun its march
toward total power. A general strike led by the Socialists prevents
a war for markets between the United States and Germany; but
the Iron Heel learns its lesson and sets up hereditary labor castes
of favored unions over the mass of unskilled workers, expropriates
the farmers, liquidates their Granger Party, imprisons the fifty-two
Socialist Congressmen elected in 1912, and declares open war on
the Socialist underground organization. Ernest and Avis become
agents provocateurs in the service of the Iron Heel in order better
to carry out their work as leaders of the underground in planning
for the abortive First Revolt. When the Oligarchy learns of the

revolt, it prepares to inflict a terrible punishment on the underground by provoking a premature rebellion in Chicago alone.

The concluding chapters in which Avis describes the revolt in Chicago and its destruction by the Mercenaries reveal how the picture of the struggle in the Social Pit pervaded London's literary imagination. Although one of the chapters is entitled "The Chicago Commune," there is no description of the kind of government ("the better world," so to speak) that the Socialists would supposedly, judging by the chapter title, attempt to set up; instead, Avis expressly states that her experiences were confined to the unorganized inhabitants of the labor ghettos. London focuses his climax on "The People of the Abyss" — H. G. Wells's phrase now appears as another chapter title — on the shambles at the bottom of the Social Pit, the hideous, raging, "Roaring Abysmal Beast."

The next moment the front of the column went by. It was not a column, but a mob, an awful river that filled the street, the people of the abyss, mad with drink and wrong, up at last and roaring for the blood of their masters. . . It surged past my vision in concrete waves of wrath, snarling and growling, carnivorous, drunk with whiskey from pillaged warehouses, drunk with hatred, drunk with lust for blood — men, women, and children, in rags and tatters, dim ferocious intelligences with all the godlike blotted from their features and all the fiendlike stamped in, apes and tigers, anaemic consumptives and great hairy beasts of burden, wan faces from which vampire society had sucked the juice of life, bloated forms swollen with physical grossness and corruption, withered hags and death's-heads bearded like patriarchs, festering youth and festering age, faces of fiends, crooked, twisted, misshapen monsters blasted with the ravages of disease and all the horrors of chronic innutrition — the refuse and the scum of life, a raging, screaming, screeching, demoniacal horde.[18]

The people of the abyss are slaughtered, the premature revolt of the Socialists is bloodily put down, and the Iron Heel begins the work of searching out the revolutionaries who have burrowed into its structure. Here the manuscript purportedly breaks off, and the book ends.

If *The Iron Heel* is an example of London's ability to produce "strong" fiction, it is not because of character portrayal or story construction. Ernest and Avis Everhard are little more than walking phonographs, and the action gains momentum very slowly, the first half of the novel being only an animated pamphlet. The "strength" is in the second half where it appears in the convincingly circumstantial detail with which London shows that It Can Happen Here, and in his description of the nightmarish uprising and slaughter of the people of the abyss. His creative imagination always functioned increasingly well the more it was able to disintegrate the fabric of social life or the civilized responses of the individual personality, reducing that life, that personality to its simplest level, a condition of complete violence. His concern is with the struggle, which horrifies and fascinates him, rather than with the achievement; and hence, though there are sections in his other novels where this power to communicate violence is turned momentarily to what might conceivably have been radical ends, his shift in that direction is always, consciously or unconsciously, deflected.

"Unconscious deflection" may have operated while he was writing that superb yarn, *The Sea Wolf* (1904), and the semi-autobiographical *Martin Eden* (1909). Although London later maintained that both were attacks on Nietzschean individualism from a radical point of view, the assertion does not convince. The author's sympathy is manifestly with Martin in his struggles to succeed as a writer and to escape middle-class domination; it would have to be, for many of them were too intimately his own. As for *The Sea Wolf*, the fascination of the book lies irresistibly in the brutal magnificence of Wolf Larsen, and the author is too busy playing devil's advocate to bother with a prosecution. In such late novels as *Burning Daylight* (1910) and *The Valley of the Moon* (1913) London's radicalism is consciously deflected from its expected conclusion. The first half of the latter book, for example, contains some sharp pictures of strike violence in Oakland, but soon Billy and Saxon Roberts, the working-class hero and heroine, set out to go back to the Land. (A "blood and earth" motif is established when the heroine's name is explicitly connected with Anglo-Saxon supremacy.) They bewail the retreat of the "old stock" like themselves before the incoming foreigners, meet a couple who are clearly the author and his wife, and, as London had in actuality done, settle down in the Sonoma Valley (The Valley of the Moon) to become landed proprietors, leaving the class struggle to take care of itself.

Upton Sinclair once said that London could never make up his mind whether to be a great revolutionary writer or a landed gentleman. In order to struggle upward away from the nightmare at the bottom of the Social Pit and to live in the grand style of the American Dream, London was committed to making money as fast as he could by means of writing, an occupation which he came to loathe. What is perhaps most admirable in his contradictory personality, therefore, is his willingness to put a considerable amount of energy, money, and writing into the Socialist cause at the risk of his reputation and his royalty checks. Up until the last year of his life he never failed to proclaim his faith in Socialism; and when he did resign from the Socialist Party nine months before his death, he went on public record, whatever his confused private reasons, as leaving because the Party had become too respectable to insist on the class struggle. The generations of radicals who came after him preferred to forget *The Valley of the Moon* and to remember *The Iron Heel*. They were proud that it had been written by a man who had himself openly prophesied revolution, a man who had worked ten hours a day with his hands before he became the creator of fast-selling novels with two-fisted heroes. However mistaken they might be as to his true class affiliation and his self-contradictory ideology, they came to view him as incontrovertible proof that a "proletarian" could be a radical and also a successful writer. In their eyes, Jack London, whatever his shortcomings, had made good for the Revolution.

3.

VIEW OF AN ERA

WHEN *The Jungle* was published, it was an immediate best-seller, became one of the most discussed books of its year, and even influenced the nation's political history directly, if slightly, by helping to excite the furor over unsanitary meat-packing which forced the Pure Food and Drug Act of 1906 through the Senate. Jack London's *The Iron Heel*, however, was received joyously only among the revolutionary I.W.W. and the extreme left wing of the Socialist Party. Whereas Sinclair's book was frequently reproved by otherwise pleased reviewers for its outspoken use of realistic detail — one not-entirely-unfriendly commentator called him a "buzzard genius" with "a natural taste for what is vicious, indecent and revolting" [1] — London's radical romance was condemned, except among the Far Left, for both unpleasant detail and unpleasant doctrine. The more conservative Socialist leaders, who controlled the Party, were annoyed by London's coupling of Socialism with violence, and John Spargo, writing in *The International Socialist Review*, censored the novel for its support of the "cataclysmic theory" of social change. Success at the polls and a large increase in middle-class membership were just beginning to give the Party an aura of respectability which the leaders wished to preserve.

Despite the fact that the less fiery Party chiefs, Morris Hillquit and Victor Berger, felt uneasy over his emotion-charged radicalism, Eugene Debs held the loyalty of the Party rank-and-file, the obscure "Jimmy Higginses" of the movement, and was for three times more their presidential candidate. After conducting a coast-to-coast speaking campaign that nearly killed him, Debs in the national elections of 1908 succeeded in adding only about 20,000 votes to his previous total of 400,000, chiefly because the Republican Taft was expected to carry on Roosevelt's presumably liberal policies and because the Democrats had once again nominated Bryan, the Great Commoner. Yet in the next four years the Socialist message was taken so industriously to the people and so colored the nation's cultural climate that in 1912, when Roosevelt rode to Armageddon under the banner of the New Nationalism and Woodrow Wilson declared in cool ecstasies for the New Freedom, Debs more than doubled the Socialist record by polling just over 900,000 votes, or approximately 6 per cent of the total vote cast, a record percentage for an American radical party.

Quite as significant were Socialist triumphs in state and local politics. Made curious by the frequency of newspaper editorials on "The Rising Tide of Socialism," Robert F. Hoxie, professor of economics at the University of Chicago, dispassionately analyzed the 1911 local elections and stated that there was now a verified minimum of 435 Socialist office-holders, including a representative in Congress and a mayor in Milwaukee. Contrary to popular assumption, most of these came, not from large urban areas, but from small industrial cities, towns, and agricultural communities, the centers of voting strength being the Middle West, particularly the state of Wisconsin, the mining regions of the Rockies, and the Pacific Coast. Though Hoxie did conclude, correctly enough, that "the actual political power of the party is as yet exceedingly light," [2] there was a noteworthy jump the following year in the number of Socialist members in state legislatures, from the 6 of 1908 to 21.

Meanwhile the Party was expanding in size and was making its influence felt in the trade unions. When in 1912 Max Hayes, a Socialist lawyer from Cleveland, ran against the permanent Samuel Gompers for the leadership of the American Federation of Labor, then numbering nearly 2,000,000 unionists, he received one third of all votes cast. Equally spectacular was the increase in the Party's dues-paying membership from, approximately, the 20,000 of 1904 to 40,000 in 1908 and 60,000 in 1910. Within two more years it had again doubled, standing at 120,000 in the year of Debs's greatest success. This rapid growth was clear indication that the Revolution had at last become "Americanized." As a matter of fact, a Party census in 1908 had demonstrated that 71 per cent of its members were native American citizens, which was a higher ratio than for the country's population as a whole, while in 1912 this percentage stood at approximately 87. New York and Chicago held the highest single concentrations of members, but other groups were scattered through cities, towns, and farm areas across the entire nation.

What produced this rapid spread of radicalism appears to have been a combination of forces and influences. These years saw the climax of muckraking and also its sudden collapse about 1910 under the attacks of alarmed vested interests. Here seemed to be proof that the Socialists offered the only sure opposition to the "money powers," and disillusionment with the major political parties increased correspondingly. The Panic of 1907, though brief, had been one of the most disastrous in the country's history and had particularly dramatized the vulnerability of Finance Capitalism, leaving a residue of suspicion toward the "System" in the minds even of political moderates. Accompanying the continued decline in real wages came, after the Panic, the beginning of a concerted attempt on the part of employers' associations to destroy labor unions by retaining bands of strikebreakers, agitating publicly for the "open shop," and lobbying against the passage of legislation favorable to labor. Not surprisingly, these measures touched off further industrial strife, which culminated at the turn of the decade in such spectacular struggles as the "Great Revolt" in the garment trades and the successful textile strike led by the I.W.W. at Lawrence, Massachusetts. The most immediate influence of all toward radicalism during these years of unrest was, of course, an extraordinary outpouring of all forms of Socialist theoretical and agitational literature.

The year 1912 brought the Socialist Party to its highest point of power and prestige; yet, paradoxically, in the same year its decline began. At the Indianapolis Convention in May, by a vote of 191 to 90, a new section was written into the Party constitution requiring the expulsion of any member who opposed political action and advocated "crime, sabotage, or other methods of violence as a weapon of the working class to aid in its emancipation." The amendment was obviously aimed at the antipolitical I.W.W. and its most colorful leader, "Big Bill" Haywood, who had been elected in the previous year to the National Executive Committee of the Socialist Party. Early in 1913, despite the protests of Max Eastman, Walter Lippmann, Helen Keller, and many other contemporary Socialists, Haywood was recalled from the Committee and expelled from the Party, taking with him a number of militant left-wingers.

The steady decline in Party membership after 1912 was by no means due alone to the expulsion of Haywood and his sympathizers. The main cause was the all-consuming conflict of World War I, which demonstrated the collapse of the Second International before the bloody fact of European nationalism and set up strong psychic tensions in the United States between those who favored American neutrality and those who desired participation on the side of the Allies. In 1916, the Socialist Party, whose membership had now declined to 83,000, adopted an antiwar resolution; but just after the United States declared its belligerency in the following year, an emergency convention split over the issue, the very large majority under Hillquit and Berger voting to continue its stand. Some of the majority were probably influenced, if unconsciously, by national origins. The considerable German–American strength of the Party undoubtedly felt that the marching of the Fatherland's armies was not without provocation, while the Russian Jewish element had no reason to love the Czar, now on the side of the Allies, since his government had countenanced the persecutions from which they or their parents had fled. As conscious Socialists, however, the majority faithfully maintained the Marxist opposition to capitalist wars. A minority group, holding that a German victory would be disastrous even for the working classes of the defeated countries, bolted the convention; and a number of the Socialist intellectuals, among whom were J. G. Phelps Stokes, Charles Edward Russell, William English Walling, and Upton Sinclair, went over to Wilson's New Freedom, which had now become the War to End Wars.

Immediately after the close of the emergency convention, Socialist headquarters were raided in many localities and a number of leaders arrested as one phase of the wartime persecutions of the Left. Debs himself was imprisoned the following year after he had deliberately made antiwar remarks in a speech in Canton, Ohio. Although its opposition to the war relaxed somewhat after the October Revolution in Russia and the publication of Wilson's

Fourteen Points, the Party had been seriously weakened by defections and by attacks from the government. When the war ended, Party membership swelled abruptly to nearly 110,000, but the increase was largely in the so-called foreign-language federations, chiefly the left-wing Slavic ones. The final stroke that brought the Socialist Party down occurred in 1919 when the civil war between the Left Wing (which ultimately became the Communist Party) and the Right Wing nearly destroyed the parent organization. Deb's winning of nearly a million votes in 1920, when he made a final campaign from his cell in the Atlanta Penitentiary, demonstrated merely a desire by many citizens to protest the Government's current subversion of civil liberties. By the following year Party membership had melted to 13,000. Since that time, except for an alliance with the LaFollette Progressives in 1924, the Socialist Party has had at most only a peripheral influence on American politics and society.

II

During the years from the middle of the century's first decade to the end of World War I enough Socialist novels were published, not to make up a literary movement, for they were only one part of the whole movement of critical realism in American literature, but at least to form a definite literary development. Contemporary critics and reviewers showed, indeed, a tendency, not discouraged by the Socialists themselves, to find more radical fiction than there actually was. One literary investigator, writing at the end of 1906 in the sober *Charities and the Commons* (later renamed *The Survey*), exclaimed over the frequency with which "socialistic novels" were being written and concluded that within the last two years at least fifteen such books had appeared.[3] Her choice of six worthy to be discussed is illuminating: Richard Whiting, *Ring in the New;* Upton Sinclair, *The Jungle;* Bart Kennedy, *Slavery;* Ernest Poole, *The Voice of the Street;* John Ames Mitchell, *The Silent War;* H. G. Wells, *In the Days of the Comet.* Three — the volumes by Whiting, Kennedy, and Wells — are of course English productions and are only another reminder that American Socialism was part of an international movement. Of the three American books only *The Jungle* is a Socialist novel in any real sense: that is, a novel which, as one of its primary purposes, explicitly or implicitly advocates some form of Socialism. The reviewer admitted that the novel by Poole, who was about to join the "liberal wing" of the Party, expresses no specific social doctrine; while *The Silent War*, which makes use of Socialism in a not-unkind but highly inaccurate fashion, has a non-Socialist millionaire hero. Furthermore, its author, the highly respectable editor of the old *Life*, expressly indicates in a preface that his book is to be taken as a warning that democracy must become enlightened or the nation's ills will be cured by more drastic methods.[4] Clearly, during the decade and a half when the Party was a power the solid body of Socialist novels was surrounded by a penumbra of "socialistic" ones shading out into the whole large sphere of social-protest fiction.

If claims by earlier literary critics need to be examined almost as carefully as those of present-day ones, the actual Socialist influence on literature was nevertheless strong. A chronicler for *The Bookman* concluded in 1908 that "Socialism is indeed so much in the air that it is becoming the topic of discussion not only in political circles, but also in the highways of literature," [5] and went on to cite as evidence the current novels of London and Sinclair along with two expositions of aspects of the political movement and two widely read analyses of society by the Christian Socialists, Walter Rauschenbusch and R. J. Campbell. The appearance of radical novels in fact parallels fairly closely the fortunes of the Party, as a glance at the Appendix of the present volume will indicate. Within a span of nineteen years at least forty-nine radical novels were produced, almost all of them Marxian Socialist in outlook. Whereas ten such books had appeared from 1901 through 1906, nearly three times that number, or twenty-seven, were published during the next seven years, 1907–1913. In a third period from the year in which World War I broke out through 1919, when the Socialist Party splintered apart, twelve more were produced. Interestingly enough, the incidence of Socialist novels was greatest during two periods of particularly intense Party activity — nine in 1907 to 1908 and twelve in 1910 to 1912. Why only four should have been published in that last exciting year remains unexplained; perhaps the discrepancy is best taken as a reminder that politics and creative literature, though they may have strong ideological connections, do not by any means bear a direct one-to-one relationship.

The most significant single feature of the entire body of Socialist long fiction is the fact that almost without exception it reflects the faith of the Party's moderate majority in a peaceful transformation of society. The exceptions are chiefly the two revolutionary romances, *The Iron Heel* and C. A. Steere's *When Things Were Doing* (1907). The latter book, also unusual as a humorous Utopia, tells in dream form the events of a bloodless but extralegal revolution in which the five million Socialists of the United States overthrow the government and seize power because the capitalists have prevented change by ballot. The President, in whose characterization Steere seems to be more a precursor of Groucho Marx than a follower of Karl, gives up his office out of sheer impotence, the Coöperative Commonwealth is established, first in America and then in the European countries, and even the Russian tyranny is crushed, though there the small Socialist Party has to destroy the many representatives of an oppressive church and state with quantities of *sizmos*, a powerful explosive invented by an American Socialist. But Steere's book is distinctly of its own kind. Ordinarily these novelists, following Friedman's lead in *By Bread Alone*, ascribe violence to either capitalists on the one hand or Anarchists on the other. At least a third of them either introduce Anarchist characters in order to make the point clear through dramatic action or contrive that a Socialist character shall spell out the official sentiment in favor of parliamentary methods of change.

If *When Things Were Doing* has a few amusing moments of burlesque, it is on the whole a rather sophomoric production, as even the radical critic John Spargo recognized; however, the assumption in almost all the other Socialist novels of a nonviolent revolution certainly bears no necessary relation to their literary excellence or, as is much more frequently the case, their lack of it. What is important is how they demonstrate that the premises assumed by a radical novelist concerning the implementation of his political theory may powerfully, and not always consciously, shape his creative design. Three books taken at random illustrate this point variously.

A radical novel was only one of the many lunges at self-realization made by George Cram Cook, who later became the unifying instinct behind the Provincetown Players and subsequently died of drink and fever in Greece. After being abruptly converted from Nietzsche to Marx by the youthful Floyd Dell when they were both living in Davenport, Iowa, Cook published a Socialist novel, *The Chasm* (1911), the scene of which is laid partly in Moline, Illinois, and partly in Russia after the Decembrist Revolt. The "chasm" of the title is partly objectified in the conflict faced by a wealthy American girl between the philosophy of Nietzsche, as represented by her husband, an aristocratic Russian landowner, and that of Marx, as represented by her father's handsome young Socialist gardener. Both Socialism and true love of course triumph when, after an unhappy year in Russia, the girl divorces her husband, aids a group of Russian revolutionaries, and returns to America to "be on [her] side of the world-fight." The triangle situation enables Cook to argue the inferiority of Nietzsche to Marx with the drama of dialogue and action, even though the two male characters rarely come out from behind the philosophies respectively assigned them. By setting the story in the two different countries the author can depict Nietzscheanism as having its logical end in both the heartlessness of American capitalists and the tyranny of the Russian aristocrats, whereas Marxism is revealed as producing the international idealism of both American Socialist and Russian revolutionary. Furthermore, the device very neatly gives him the opportunity to advocate terrorism — and employ Graustarkian melodrama — in despotic Russia, while urging — with literary realism — nothing more violent than a Socialist victory at the polls in the United States. In this way the author has his constitutional cake and eats it too.

In *Comrade Yetta* (1913) violence and its alternatives become keys to character. Arthur Bullard, a radical social worker, who, with Ernest Poole, Leroy Scott, and Charles Edward Russell, had labored to build the Socialist daily newspaper, *The Call*, recounts in this novel the career of one of the New Women, a girl from the New York East Side who experiences the facts described by Socialism before she learns the theory. When her immigrant father dies, young Yetta Rayefsky is forced to work in a garment sweatshop until she is taken up by the head of the Woman's Trade Union

League, leads a spontaneous strike, is jailed briefly for hitting a detective while defending a fellow picket, and helps to form a union among the "vest workers." After deciding to join the Socialist Party, she works on a struggling party newspaper — *The Clarion* is the name used here for *The Call* — and eventually consents to marry the editor, whose doctrinaire Socialism has been humanized by his long-continued love for her. Together they devote themselves to the Cause.

It is noteworthy that Yetta, the working-class girl, becomes a Socialist, for she is in part attracted to the antipolitical syndicalism of the I.W.W., an ideology which here for one of the first times in American fiction receives serious attention. Bullard in fact uses her attitude toward this extreme left-wing organization as a means of explaining Yetta's psychology of revolt.

At first Yetta was confused by the conflicting organizations which were struggling for support from the workers. There was the American Federation of Labor, to which Mabel [the head of the Woman's Trade Union League] gave her allegiance. Its organizers were practical men, interested first, last, and all the time in shop conditions. Effective in their way, but their cry, "A little less injustice, please," seemed timid to Yetta. Then there was the Socialist party. Their theories were more impressive to her — they went further in demands and seemed to have a broader vision. But of all the Socialists she knew, Braun [the editor] was the only one who interested himself actively in the organization of the workers. The rest seemed wholly occupied with political action. There was also the Industrial Workers of the World. They cared very little for either firmly organized unions, which were Mabel's hobby, or for the party in which Isadore [Braun] put such faith. They placed all their emphasis on the Spirit of Revolt. In a more specific way than the other factions they were out for the Revolution. They appealed strongly to that side of Yetta which was vividly touched by the manifold misery she saw about her, the side of her personality which had struck out blindly at Pick-Axe [the detective]. She recognized that it had been a blind and dangerous impulse. It was not likely to come again. But this phase of her character, although she feared it, she could not despise. It was not dead, it was only asleep. And she knew that the same thing was present in the hearts of all the down-trodden people — her comrades in the fight for life and liberty.[6]

Rejecting the "blind and dangerous impulse," Yetta breaks with the undisciplined philosopher Walter Longman, who inclines toward

the "direct-actionist" position of the I.W.W., and instead marries
the Socialist, who is working for change by constitutional methods.
As a result of his heroine's choice, Bullard ends *Comrade Yetta*,
not with the wild upheaval of a general strike, but with the more
staid enthusiasms of an International Socialist Congress.

Class war and the revolutionary spirit of syndicalism create the
context of events in the best Socialist novel of all, Ernest Poole's
The Harbor, a book which appeared so happily at the height of
the Wilsonian Era that it went to twenty-two editions within a
few months after its publication in February, 1915, and stood eighth
on the best-seller list in fiction for that year. Billy, the central
figure of this novel, tells the story of his life, showing how it has
been bound up with his changing attitudes toward the harbor of
New York ever since, as a child, he thought Henry Ward Beecher
a "chump" for saying in a sermon that a harbor was a place of
refuge. To the boy, the harbor has already begun to symbolize
Change. As he grows up and prepares to be a writer, he first sees
his surroundings through the eyes of his father, a stern man of
business, who still hopes to bring back the day when American
sailing ships cut the oceans of the world. Billy's worship of Art and
his hatred for the ugliness of the harbor in the new age of iron
ships, the "factories" of the sea, are slowly changed by an engineer
who has been employed by financiers to rationalize the facilities
of the entire port. Billy's love for and eventual marriage to Eleanore
Dillon, the engineer's daughter, helps to remake his view of the
harbor, and he now sets up Efficiency as a god to worship.

While he is writing the "glory stories" of the harbor and describing the lives of the heroes of big business, he meets again with
Joe Kramer, a former college friend, who has been a muckraking
journalist, foreign correspondent, and ship's stoker, and is now
one of the organizers for an approaching general strike of the port
of New York. Shocked by the glimpses which Joe gives him of
the hideous world in which the stokers and dockers are forced to
live, Billy sides with the workers when they tie up the harbor, acts
as publicity man for the strike, and builds in his own mind out of
the wreck of the god of Efficiency "a huge new god, whose feet
stood deep in poverty and in whose head were all the dreams of all
the toilers of the earth, [a god who] had called to me with one

deep voice, with one tremendous burning passion for the freedom of mankind." [7] The strike is broken bloodily by the men in the towers of Efficiency, and the products of the world flow again through the harbor; yet Billy feels that his latest god is not dead, but sleeping, waiting until it has gained strength to reopen the struggle.

As his autobiography, *The Bridge*, reveals, Poole transmuted many of his own experiences and beliefs into those of his hero; Billy is, in fact, just as much as and no more "revolutionary" than his creator was himself. Some years before Poole began work on *The Harbor*, he had become a member of the Socialist Party after Morris Hillquit had overcome his scruples about joining "churches" by making "the creed to which I must subscribe so very broad and liberal that my objections were swept away." [8] Like his creator, like so many of the young intellectuals who were attracted to Socialism, Billy is the middle-class American with a conscience. He first worships beauty as against ugliness, then efficiency as against confusion, and finally the power of the workers to order the world humanely as against the cold rule of the engineers and big finance. During the course of the strike, the parabola of which Poole describes vividly in a series of movielike scenes, Billy carries on his education in the class war with all the hesitations, reticences, and impulsive actions of which a person of his background is capable. The strike over, he does not go off with Joe Kramer to organize, dangerously (and illegally), among the soldiers now fighting each other in Europe, but — quite sensibly and believably in his case — stays home with Eleanore to write a book about his experiences, perhaps to be entitled *The Harbor*.

Billy has sided with Joe only in general, not in particular, for upon their leave-taking he accuses the syndicalist organizer of being tied to an inflexible creed. As he returns from saying goodby to Joe, who is stoking on a liner to get to Europe, Billy passes immigrants in the crowded tenement street and wonders if the giant spirit of the strike can be reborn out of them. "Could it be that the time was near when this last and mightiest of the gods would rise and take the world in his hands?" [9] Despite these uncertain questionings, the book does end affirmatively, but the affirmation is vague as well as vast. As the great liner, in the bottom of which

Joe Kramer is shoveling coal with the black gang, moves like a microcosm of civilization out of the harbor, its whistle blast seems to Billy to be saying:

"Make way for me. Make way, all you little men. Make way, all you habits and all you institutions, all you little creeds and gods. For I am the start of the voyage — over the ocean to heathen lands! And I am always starting out and always bearing you along! For I am your molder, I am strong — I am a surprise, I am a shock — I am a dazzling passion of hope — I am a grim executioner! I am reality — I am life! I am the book that has no end!" [10]

This is not Marx's *Manifesto*, nor even a strike call; it is the exalted voice of Wilson's New Freedom. The highest god of all is not Revolt, but Change. From such an ending, the reader could start anywhere, could voyage, for example, as far as the stormy thirties, where Ernest Poole — reporter of two Russian Revolutions and erstwhile Socialist novelist — might be seen, sheltered in the lee, writing for *The Saturday Evening Post* and grumbling mildly about the New Deal of Franklin Roosevelt, Wilson's spiritual inheritor.

III

Besides their confidence that a nonviolent revolution will come, inevitably and soon, to shatter the crystallized social structure of America, the three novels — *The Chasm*, *Comrade Yetta*, and *The Harbor* — have another feature in common: in each the leading character comes toward the revolution after an education in social reality has shaken him (or her) loose from an unthinking acceptance of the status quo. Whether a member of the proletariat itself or of some layer of the middle or upper classes, he learns in each case by experience that his country is a class society ruled by the owning class and that he can help to establish, or often reëstablish, democracy in the United States only if he throws in his lot with the movement which is struggling to free the workers. So obvious a dramatic plan is this, in fact, that the history of a character's "conversion" to political radicalism easily dominates in a classification of Socialist novels according to major types of subject matter used, for approximately a third of all the novels employ this particular story material. No doubt the shock and hurt endured by these (largely) middle-class writers upon realizing the disparity between story-book America and the real thing, their relieved joy at discovering in Socialism a resolution to the conflict, would lead them consciously to cast their experiences into some literary equivalent as a guidebook for other possible converts.

If the favorite subject of these novels is an individual's introduction to and acceptance of the Socialist position, the next most popular "matter" is that of the actual coming of Socialism, usually to America. This is the subject of the revolutionary romances, ten of which appeared during the century's first two decades, all of them, if George Allan England's contributions are excepted, being confined to the 1900's. Of the romancers England is the most prolific, however, and it is for this reason alone that he is worth considering at any length. This army chaplain's son, who began a career as editor and free-lance writer after graduating from Harvard and who in 1912 ran as Socialist candidate for Governor of the State of Maine, published his three books of radical fiction, one of them a trilogy, in the years from 1914 to 1916. A literary disciple of Jack London and Ignatius Donnelly, he possessed neither the former's compulsive fascination with violence nor the latter's flair for darkly powerful melodrama, but he did have a lurid fancy that responded to their visions of future catastrophe. In all his adolescent tales of wild adventure some upheaval shatters American capitalist society and makes possible its reorganization in more or less Socialist form, the upheaval or its immediate aftermath always receiving far more space in the book then the reorganization itself.

The three romances grouped in sequence under the general title of *Darkness and Dawn* (1914) recount at length the fantastic adventures of a brawny engineer and his beautiful secretary who, awakening from a centuries-long trance in a ruined New York skyscraper, find themselves apparently the last man and woman left alive on earth after a cosmic convulsion, who discover a "race" of American survivors at the bottom of an enormous abyss where most of the Midwest used to be, and who lead these people back to the surface to construct a proper coöperative society. In *The Golden Blight* (1916), an early example of modern science fiction, a physicist whose sympathies are with the proletariat in their opposition to World War I invents a machine which from any distance can reduce gold to ash. Despite the villainous attempts of the capitalists and their kept government to prevent him, he eventually attacks even the gold in the United States Treasury Building in his effort to bring a stop to the war. When the financiers of the world gather in the Treasury's vaults to observe, as one of them has predicted, the reconstitution of the ash back into its original form, the transformation indeed occurs; but the great resultant heat melts the metal, kills the financiers, wrecks the Treasury Building, and leaves for wiser posterity a Caesar's Column of gold, bodies, and masonry. Freed of their servitude to gold, which, as the physicist explains, represents capitalism, the people of the world immediately declare peace and vote in the Coöperative Commonwealth.

Although in these volumes England bases his denunciations of capitalism on Socialist theory, it is only in *The Air Trust* (1915) that the destruction of the outmoded social system results from actual class warfare. In this yarn, a billionaire conceives the notion of controlling the distribution of the air itself as the keystone monopoly in his trust of trusts. Having made the Federal Government subservient to his will, he has the Socialist Party outlawed, sets up a great Air Trust power plant at Niagara Falls, and prepares to put his scheme into action. Since peaceful legislative methods of change are denied the Socialists, they form an underground resistance and put at its head the book's radical hero, Gabriel Armstrong, who leads a successful armed assault against the Air Trust plant. The billionaire dies with suitable horror in the general destruction, and his daughter, long since converted to Socialism, falls into Gabriel's embrace, while the burning plant lights up the sky in promise of "the Great Emancipation." But though England at one point has the billionaire's daughter say of the Air Trust's dictatorship that "London didn't put it half strongly enough" in *The Iron Heel*, he carefully dissociates himself from his master's prediction of an inevitably violent overthrow of capitalism. In order that the reader should know that his interest in violence is purely for the sake of story excitement, England includes a foreword which expressly asserts his belief in political, not "direct," action. Only if all political rights are suppressed will he accept revolution by force. Hence it is not surprising to find Gabriel describing Socialism in terms that recall the fact that the author of *The Air Trust* was the son of an ordained minister as well as a literary follower of Jack London: "[Socialism] explains life, points the way to better things, gives us hope, strengthens the weary and heavy-laden, bids us look upward and onward, and constitutes the most sublime ideal ever conceived by the soul of man!" [11] If England liked his events to be strenuous, he was as eager as any missionary to make them moral as well.

In addition to the novels centered either on a conversion or the coming of Socialism to America, a third, somewhat smaller, body of fiction is primarily concerned with the struggles of militant labor. Only Leroy Scott's *The Walking Delegate* shows extensive acquaintance with union affairs, and novels in which the main action is the course of a strike are few; *By Bread Alone*, James Oppenheim's *The Nine-Tenths* (1911), and *King Coal*, though the latter two can also be classed as conversion stories, exhaust the list of strike novels. As Comrade Yetta had discovered, the Socialists tended to concentrate on political action, and the newly radical novelist, because of his middle-class background, was more likely to feel at home in a political party than in a labor union. Nevertheless, Socialists were accustomed to giving organizational help to strikes, and approximately ten of the novels of the conversion type introduce a strike as one element in the education of a radical.

The frequency with which strikes appear as events in this fiction makes them worth examining more closely. More than half of the strikes are placed in New York City, although "labor troubles" in Chicago and the state of Colorado are also well represented; and very often the strike appears to be a fictionalization of the actual labor conflict that helped to precipitate the author's own conversion to Socialism. Easily the most popular strike for fictional treatment is that first full-scale battle of the five-year "Great Revolt" in the garment industries which became known as "The Uprising of the Twenty Thousand." On November 22, 1909, after preliminary skirmishes between hard-driving employers and workers made desperate by a depression in the industry after the Panic of 1907, a general strike of shirtwaist makers and dressmakers was dramatically voted at a mass meeting in Cooper Union on the appeal of a young girl striker. Because almost all of the strikers were girls and because they held their picket lines throughout most of the ensuing winter in spite of assaults from thugs hired by the employers and the hostility of the police and the magistrates, the conflict attracted much public sympathy. After nearly three months the girls won a limited but definite victory. It is this strike in which Comrade Yetta is jailed for defending a fellow picketer against a detective's brutality, and it also seems to have contributed to the conception of the city-wide strike that climaxes Florence Converse's *The Children of Light* (1912).

The most nearly complete fictional account of the Uprising appears in James Oppenheim's *The Nine-Tenths*. The first third of the book describes the reaction of Joe Blaine, owner of a printing business, to a sweatshop fire that starts in his plant. (The fire is clearly based on the actual disaster at the Triangle Waist Company on March 25, 1911, in which 146 workers, chiefly girls, burned to death because the sweatshop exits were locked. A similar fire at the "Circle Waist Company" occurs in Zoe Beckley's *A Chance to Live* [1918].) Horrified by what had proved his greater devotion to property than to human life, Joe vows to give his life to the dead girls, goes to live among the poor of Greenwich Village, and establishes a prolabor weekly paper named *The Nine-Tenths*. The author then reverses the sequence of historical events by having Joe actively support the Uprising — here "Of the Thirty Thousand" — after the workers at Cooper Union, as was actually the case, have taken as one mass the old Jewish oath: "If I turn traitor to the cause I now pledge, may this hand wither from the arm I now raise!" Although the strikers are of course ultimately victorious, an interview with a ruined sweatshop owner turns Joe away from his recently acquired theoretical view of society as a "sharp twofold world of the workers and the money-power" to a practical view of a corrupt world "of infinite social gradations," all sharing in the guilt for the world's corruption. Thus specifically rejecting the Marxist dialectic, Joe ends in a pragmatic hope for a many-faceted (and vague) movement which will create out of New York "a city of five million comrades." Oppenheim was clearly a very latitudinarian Socialist, any Marxism he may have acquired being overwhelmed by ecstatic surges of brotherly love.

Both the Triangle Fire, which figures in some of the nonradical fiction of the period, and the Uprising became, in effect, *causes célèbres*. Two other events in the history of labor and its struggles received special treatment. Strictly speaking, *The Cage*, published in 1907 by Charlotte Teller, journalist and niece of a Colorado senator, is a conversion novel; but its scenes describing the awakening of a young Chicago woman to the worker's cause through her love for and marriage with a Hungarian Socialist are climaxed by the Haymarket Bomb, the panic-stricken reactions of city officials, press, and public, the endeavors of the husband, despite doctrinal differences, to aid the condemned Anarchists, and the hanging of the men after "all the traditions of justice and all the forms of law had been put to one side." [12] The martyrdom of the Anarchists is overshadowed at the end, however, by a reconciliation between husband and wife after an estrangement that is the last step in the woman's journey toward self-realization. Like the workers, she too must break out of the "cage" in which society attempts to keep her captive.

One other novel is organized, if that be an accurate word in this case, around the most famous *cause célèbre* in the labor history of the century's first decade. In 1907 Walter Hurt, at the time on the staff of *The Appeal to Reason*, published *The Scarlet Shadow*, subtitled "A Story of the Great Colorado Conspiracy," which purported to be "a new experiment in realistic story writing, in that all his characters are real persons." [13] In this case the persons were those involved in the death by bombing on December 30, 1905, of ex-Governor Steunenberg of Idaho and the subsequent trial of three men influential in the Western Federation of Miners — Bill Haywood, Charles Moyer, and George Pettibone. A Federation member, one Harry Orchard (who died on April 13, 1954, after serving a life sentence), confessed to the killing, claiming in his confession that these men had hired him for the purpose. Thereupon the three were kidnapped in Denver and taken with scant legality into Idaho, where over a year later Haywood went on trial, with the young William E. Borah as prosecuting attorney and Clarence Darrow for the defense. Debs himself wrote one of the most revolutionary editorials of his life for *The Appeal*, calling for armed resistance to any attempt at judicial murder, the radical press violently protested Haywood's innocence, and parades and mass meetings sprang up across the nation. All three men were eventually acquitted, Haywood after an eleven-hour summing-up by Darrow, but the affair remained for several years a catalyst for radical sentiment.

Written in the highly charged style of a Sunday Supplement, *The Scarlet Shadow* — the title refers to the shadow of the gallows over the defendants — is so much a melodramatic omnibus of radical ideas and attitudes that it almost becomes an unintentional parody of the Socialist novel. The central theme of the bombing and trial is linked with the adventures of two ace reporters, Shoforth and Dick Walton, both of whom are in love with the daughter of Daniel Melnotte, wealthy head of the Mine Owners' Association and key conspirator against the Western Federation of Miners. Shoforth, a sound antiviolence Socialist,[14] wins the girl after converting her to the Cause; whereas the rich and suave Walton turns out in the end to belong to the "Terrorist wing of the Russian revolutionary party." A neat and thoroughly fantastic explanation of the bombing is given when Walton commits suicide, leaving a note that declares that he himself killed Steunenberg because the latter was the son of "Detective MacFarlane," who stands for the real James McParlan. This famous Pinkerton operative had not only obtained Orchard's confession, but years before in the mid-1870's had helped break up the Molly Maguires, a workers' terrorist organization of the Pennsylvania coal fields. The suicide note further reveals that Walton's motive was revenge for the death at "MacFarlane's" hands of the reporter's father, who had been one of the Mollies.

As though there still were not enough ingredients in his literary stew, Hurt adds many subplots. There are several chapters in which Debs is made to appear a kind of revolutionary Rover Boy. A few sections deal with the Socialist attempts to prevent dishonest voting in the state elections of 1906, in which Judge Ben Lindsey, here named, ran for the governorship. Other chapters are concerned with the careers of Hoostman, military adventurer, and Antonio Boccarini, inventive genius, who plan to capture the city of Washington with the help of a powerful explosive and who are blown up with their own bombs. Mingled with these sequences are quite unrelated glimpses of Denver newspaper and Bohemian life and editorials by the author on the control of Colorado politics by the mine owners. Despite the publisher's insistence that the story violates nothing in the history of the affair, the reader is left to marvel how much is fiction disguised as fact, rather than fact disguised as fiction.[15]

At one point in *The Scarlet Shadow* the author comments in his own person on what it means to be a Socialist. The Party button, he rather smugly writes, stands for "social order, proper public deportment and clean personal living"; and he continues: "The *sans-culotte* no longer consists of the rabid rabble, but with a newer significance of name it comprises the more intelligent laborer, the self-respecting mechanic, the professional man who has learned to think, the small tradesman, the litterateur and the artist, the scholar and the philosopher, often the man of large means and equally large mentality." [16] Although the Socialist Party maintained its basically proletarian composition, Hurt was correct in listing as many middle-class groups of adherents as he did; and at least in their writings the Socialist novelists, because most of them had been brought up to respect the virtues he named, added a middle-class animus to their knowledge of Marx when they found these virtues particularly lacking in the rich. Although censure of the rich naturally runs as a consistent motif through the novels, enough of them are sufficiently directed toward exposing the moral deficiencies of this class that they form a fourth type in a classification according to subject matter. In *The Metropolis* (1908), a weak sequel to *Manassas*, Upton Sinclair cries out upon the foibles and sins of New York society, while the young enthusiast's second novel of the year, *The Moneychangers*, attacks the moral corruption as well as the financial chicanery of the bankers and speculators whose struggling had precipitated the Panic of 1907. Considerably more subtle both in conception and presentation is Abraham Cahan's *The Rise of David Levinsky* (1917), in which the device of first-person narrative, used so effectively in Robert Herrick's *The Memoirs of an American Citizen*, reveals the increasing human loneliness and spiritual aridity which overtake a young scholar of the Talmud when he immigrates to the United States from the Russian Pale, deserts orthodox ways, and unscrupulously builds a fortune in the New York garment trade.

One of the most startling illustrations in the century's first decade of the extent to which Socialism attracted, temporarily, the sons and daughters of the bourgeoisie itself was the taking out of a

Party membership card by the son of the man who at that time published the Chicago *Tribune*. Joseph Medill Patterson was only twenty-four when he was elected a Republican representative to the Illinois House. Two years later, after he had helped to elect a Democratic mayor in Chicago, he was appointed the city's Commissioner of Public Works; and in 1906 he resigned from that position with the announcement that he had become a Socialist since real reform was impossible under capitalism. For a liberal magazine, *The Independent*, he elaborated his position in "Confessions of a Drone" and then retired for four years to write fiction and plays for the Cause, to say nothing of compiling the *Socialist Campaign Book for 1908*. It is an extraordinary comment on the mutability of men's faith that the Joseph Medill Patterson who later became copublisher of the Chicago *Tribune* and eventually publisher of the equally reactionary New York *Daily News* was the author in that election year of a Socialist novel entitled *A Little Brother of the Rich*. Appearing near the peak of Debs's campaign, it went through four printings within two weeks.

Patterson, whose love for ironic contrast was often stronger than his ability to create it effectively, interweaves in his novel the stories of Sylvia Castle and Paul Potter, once sweethearts in a small Indiana town. When Sylvia's father fails financially, Paul, who has gone to Yale and fallen in with a wealthy set, decides not to marry her and instead uses his university connections to obtain a place in a brokerage firm. While the chaste Sylvia supports herself by working in a department store and finally by touring with a theatrical company, Paul becomes a successful broker because of his ability to adapt protectively to the wastrel ways of the leisure class, receiving one of his most profitable market tips by helping the father of his friend, Carl Wilmerding, force Carl into giving up a working-class girl he loves. Sylvia comes to New York as a nearly famous actress, rejects Paul after being momentarily attracted to him again, and makes a triumphant debut in an English version of a play called, significantly, *L'Oeuvrière*. When by accident they meet once more, Paul confesses that he is about to marry a brewery heiress for her money and that he cannot break away from a life which he knows to be rotten. Sylvia serenely says goodby to him, for her life and her art have become one. "Humanity, realism . . . is the future of the drama," she concludes elsewhere. "Romanticism, like other lies, must go." [17]

Through still other sets of contrasted characters and situations, ingeniously though stiffly worked out, the author expands his attack on the empty and vicious lives of a leisure class made possible only through the wealth-creating activities of the workers. Occasionally he enters in person to give a jeremiad. When at a "Watteau fete" for the Anti-Vivisectionist Society of Boston a dilettantish Brahmin reads Chaucer with Middle English accent, Patterson comments scathingly that the Brahmin's hands are kept soft and white by the labor of children in his mills in South Carolina. Throughout a chapter describing a yachting cruise the dissolute pleasures of the rich passengers are contrasted in an ironic counterpoint with the labors of the crew, and a similar intention appears in such narrative passages as the summary of the yacht trip taken by Carl Wilmerding and Paul Potter from Newport, Rhode Island, to New York.

Before morning a full gale was blowing, but it blew harmlessly by the strong, graceful vessel, conducted by forty-five sea experts — navigators, engineers, quartermasters, able-bodied seamen, deckhands, oilers, stokers. The forty-five fought the gale all through the night, and the next afternoon their labors fruited, for little Carl Wilmerding was landed safely on the wharf of the New York Yacht Club.[18]

Irony enters even into the chapter titles. The Watteau fete comes in a chapter called, heavy-handedly, "Suffer, Little Children," and "The Oldest Profession" describes the devices whereby Katherine Dunbar, socially acceptable though without income, snares a rich and, at the moment, quite drunk young man as husband.

If the accusation of general moral viciousness among the rich is frequent throughout these novels, a specific concern in several with the sexual behavior of the capitalist male makes it possible for prostitution to be listed as a fifth type in the classification of Socialist fiction according to subject. Two books, Reginald Wright Kauffman's *The House of Bondage* (1910) and Estelle Baker's *The Rose Door* (1912), deal entirely with prostitution, considerable attention is paid it in *The Scarlet Shadow*, and it is involved in one of the several major sequences of events in James Hattan

Brower's *The Mills of Mammon* (1909). (In addition, the related matter of the effects of venereal disease is the "problem" in James Oppenheim's *Wild Oats* [1910] and Sinclair's *Sylvia's Marriage* [1912], two novels written by Socialists, though not primarily concerned with advancing specific Socialist doctrine.) The fact that all of these novels, except Hurt's, are grouped at the end of the century's first decade and the beginning of the second indicates how responsive the radical novelists were, not only to Marxist theory, but also to the current preoccupations of the American public, for it was during these years that clamor was loudest over the "social evil." In 1908 the United States formally adhered to an international treaty aimed at checking the "white-slave traffic," and from 1907 to 1910 the Immigration Commission investigated the "Importation and Harboring of Women for Immoral Purposes," one of the results of the investigation being the passage of the Mann Act in 1910. Vice commissions had already been organized in many cities; within the next five years, forty-five states passed laws direced at preventing financial gain from prostitution by third persons; reports of "committees of fourteen," sociological analyses, and muckraking articles and novels poured forth. The Socialists noted these earnest discussions and added to them their own interpretations.

With the assistance of lengthy quotations from *The Social Evil*, a monograph which had recently been published by a Socialist doctor, Estelle Baker attempts in *The Rose Door* to define prostitution as merely one more competitive business, buying cheap, selling dear, and stimulating demand for goods. The life stories of three different girls who eventually are established at a house called "The Rose Door" in San Francisco are credible enough as case histories, but when the author attempts to weave together the fortunes of the girls and those of the upper-middle-class men who have visited them, her fictional structure collapses into a rubble of awkwardly related scenes designed to show that the wages of capitalistic sin is death. Far more impressive is *The House of Bondage*, which was so much *the* novel of prostitution that it went through sixteen printings in less than two years and helped to popularize Socialist theories in general.

Besides being more skillful than Estelle Baker as a storyteller, though quite as melodramatic, Kauffman was a more thorough research worker. A publisher's note, placed at the end of the book partly in its praise and partly, perhaps, in self-defense, states that the novel gives facts which can be duplicated from court records, the findings of investigatory bodies, and volumes of sociological research; and for good measure is appended the Report on White Slave Traffic filed by a Grand Jury (John D. Rockefeller, Jr., Foreman) in the County of New York on June 29, 1910. Kauffman had in fact been a newspaperman and journalist for several years — his experience had ranged from a four-year associate editorship of *The Saturday Evening Post* to the managing editorship in 1909 of *Hampton's*, the leading muckraking magazine — and he and his wife had lived for a while in a tenement on New York's East Side in order to study the conditions of prostitution. In *The House of Bondage* he correlated his wide knowledge by the device of tracing the career of a girl in such a way that it exposed, not only the machinery of prostitution, but all of its intricately related causes.

As young Mary Denbigh is lured by a "cadet" from her harsh, impoverished home in a Pennsylvania industrial town to New York, becomes a prisoner in a house run by Rose Légère, escapes with the help of one of the customers, a lawyer for the Tammany machine, as she tries to hold various jobs in kitchen service, and ultimately is forced down into streetwalking, Kauffman illustrates through her degradation how prostitution is enmeshed and imbedded in the oppressive wage relationships, the corrupt operations of capitalist society, how it stands, indeed, as a frame of reference for capitalism itself. Prostitution, as a profitable, though not legalized business, is part of the underworld and is linked with law enforcement through the payment of "protection" money to the police, the same graft being involved in the corruption of the lower courts and the city government by political machines that carry out the wishes of the business community. These are only the more obvious connections, however; eventually the whole of society is involved, for it is the industrial system itself that produces prostitution as a necessary by-product. In a variety of episodes, starvation wages are shown to be the major reason that girls turn to prostitution for a living, and the point is made explicit by a German Socialist, who befriends Mary and who concludes, after a Marxian survey of the economic and political framework of prostitution, that there is only one real solution to the social evil.

"For de single time badness makes poverty, ninety-nine times poverty it makes badness. Do avay vith poverty. Reorganize de whole of de industrial system; gif effery man und voman a chance to vork; gif effery man und voman effery penny dey earns. So only you do avay vith unhappy and discontented homes and unhappy und discontented people, und so only you do avay vith badness." [19]

Prostitution is, then, simply one more form of slavery under capitalism, which is the real House of Bondage: " . . . the slaves of Rose Légère were as much slaves as any mutilated black man of the Congo, or any toil-cramped white man in a factory." Since an inhuman system mostly produces inhuman results, Mary Denbigh at the end of the book returns voluntarily, diseased and worn out, to Rose Légère's house as a last device for staying alive; and Rose's genial refusal to take her back stands as an epitaph for all the victims of a competitive society: "It wouldn't be good business. You see, the life's got you. . . You're all in." [20]

Although the author did not reveal his purpose until it had been effected, *The House of Bondage* was the first in a cycle of four novels projected in 1909 and completed in 1913. What unified the group, as Kauffman explained in an introduction to the final volume, was not plot or characters, for each novel was conceived as an independent entity; rather the cycle was held together by a particular view of life — "that the superimposing of one human being's will, or the will of any group of human beings, upon any other's is the Great Crime." *The House of Bondage* had clearly been attacking the compulsion of the capitalist economic system though it dealt ostensibly with one of its effects. The next two novels continued to analyze aspects of sexual conduct; but the emphasis was placed so exclusively on the conduct that economic causes faded into the background, and conservative reviewers professed shock at the author's "salacity" rather than his Socialism. In *The Sentence of Silence* (1911) Kauffman denounced the imposition upon youth of an unrealistic code of sexual morals, derived ultimately from the economic system, a code that produced the hypocrisy of the double standard and the tragedies of sex ignorance. *Running Sands* (1912), the poorest of the four books, described the effects of the compulsion of women within marriage. For the final volume, *The Spider's Web* (1913), he turned to a direct analysis of the coercive institutions of modern society, and he carried that analysis to a surprising ultimate.

The "web" of the novel's title is the intricate set of all capitalist relationships which is gradually explored by young Luke Huber, law school graduate, who begins his career as assistant to the newly elected District Attorney of New York, a reform Republican. As his knowledge of the city grows, Luke becomes aware of the omnipresent influence of an unnamed Man, whose position as head of a group dominating American industrial, financial, and political life was no doubt suggested to Kauffman by that of J. Pierpont Morgan. The Man is given a stylized description and a set of stylized actions that indicate that he is the "spider" of the novel's title. An intensely honest young conservative, Luke begins to be disillusioned after he comes into possession of two letters which prove the Man's culpability for a disastrous train wreck. When the District Attorney wants to use them for selfish political reasons, Luke resigns and appears melodramatically before the Man and his lieutenants to demand that they repair the railroad's faulty equipment as a price for the return of the incriminating letters.

The remainder of the novel's action details the various methods resorted to by the Man's hierarchy of underlings to get the letters away from Luke. One strong thread of the web runs down from the financier's skyscraper office in Wall Street through legal representatives and law enforcement officials to the underworld, but Luke manages to retain the letters in spite of those particular machinations. Because of his personal integrity and his opposition to the political corruption that his experiences are laying bare, he becomes the Municipal Reform League's candidate for mayor; but even reform is caught in the spider's web, and the League hastily withdraws his name from their ticket after Luke openly denounces the Man and his Money Powers in a speech at Cooper Union. Meanwhile Luke has fallen in love with Betty Forbes, daughter of the owner of an independent clothing factory, in which Luke has invested an inheritance and which is struck by the men under I.W.W. leadership in order to bring the wages up to those of a Money Power monopoly launched to ruin Luke financially. During the strike the Man dies. Thereupon the churches praise his life, and Luke rejects them as another institution subservient to capital's web. He now throws himself into fighting his workers with strike-breakers and troops until, after a pitched battle in which the strikers are routed, he abruptly sees that what the Man had been to him, he has been to the men. There are many spiders, not just one, and they as well as the flies are helpless in the web. Finally comprehending "the present wrong and the future impotence of churches and laws, of politics, governments, and property," he resolves to give up Betty and to join the oppressed. Even as he makes his resolution he is shot down by a hired gunman of the Money Power, and he dies cursing all the institutions of capitalism and singing the I.W.W. song of the strikers: "Hallelujah, I'm a bum. . . " If the web of coercive relationships remains unbroken as yet, Luke has at least found a personal salvation before his death. Others can perhaps do the same before so late.

Kauffman admits in the introductory "Explanation" to this most sweeping of the radical condemnations of society that he "did not want to produce the effect of a work of Art," but rather "to produce conviction of truth." Yet what has happened to many other radical (and liberal and conservative) novelists here happens to him: the failure to produce the effect of art precludes conviction of truth. *The House of Bondage* convinces, where it does, because it keeps its realistic framework intact, but *The Spider's Web* is an incomplete attempt at fusing two forms, fable and realistic state-ment. For the first it is too topical, for the second too schematized. The stylization of the Man as spider is an obvious but acceptable allegorical device, but the reader balks at the author's demand that Luke's continued possession of two letters, even incriminating ones, be considered sufficient cause for the rather formalized set of events which follow; it is simply too weak a push to release upon the hero all the complex machinery of capitalist society beneath which he is crushed.

Most of the Socialist novelists, however, must have rejected *The Spider's Web* for political as much as artistic reasons. It was all very well to attack the institutions of capitalist society, but Kauffman attacked all institutions, including Socialist ones. Such doctrine led even beyond the I.W.W.-ism at which Luke Huber

appeared to have arrived at the moment of his death. It led ultimately to Anarchy.

IV

Besides the five major subject matters with which the Socialist
novels are concerned — conversion, the coming of Socialism, labor
struggles, the decadence of the rich, and prostitution — there are
others treated by one or two novels at most. Elias Tobenkin, for
example, is concerned with the fate of immigrants in *Witte Arrives*
(1916); Friedman's *The Radical* is the sole instance of a realistic
political novel; in *Jimmie Higgins* (1919) Upton Sinclair writes
a war story with a pacifist ending. Varied as all the Socialist novels
are, however, in subject matter, artistic form, and literary value,
they are united, not only by their mutual advocacy of Socialism,
but also by certain "motifs," themes which recur from novel to
novel and which are sometimes common to all of them. The disso-
luteness of the rich, for example, besides being the major subject of
several novels, is illustrated by some character or single event in
many others. The brothers of Evangeline Marvin in *By Bread Alone*
are portrayed as irresponsible woman-chasers, the capitalist in *Rebels of the New South* gets an orphan girl with child and then deserts
her, the aristocrats of the Russian court in *The Chasm* are almost
without exception weak-willed but arrogant sensualists.

It is significant that Reginald Wright Kauffman, after concerning himself explicitly in the first three novels of his cycle with
sexual relationships, weaves into *The Spider's Web* the story of
Luke Huber's self-thwarted love for Betty Forbes, whom at the
climax of the novel Luke, maddened with anger, almost rapes after
saving her from the mob of strikers. Luke restrains himself from
such an act as part of his sudden realization of the evilness of all
compulsion. This explicit linking together of economic relationships in society as a whole and individual sexual relationships is only
one instance of the tendency among Socialist novelists to view the
Revolution as the destroyer of all outworn systems, particularly the
complex of law and tradition which held women in an inferior
status to men. It should not be assumed that these novelists were
more "daring" in their opinions on man–woman relationships than,

say, the Dreiser of *Sister Carrie* or the David Graham Phillips of *Susan Lenox*. They were not. Although willing to attack sex ignorance, prostitution, and venereal disease as aspects of an archaic social system, proudly ignoring the epithet of "salacious" in their devotion to Truth, they were almost unanimously unwilling, at least in their books, to condone a sex relationship outside the marriage bond. Out of all these novels there is only one, Arthur Bullard's *A Man's World* (1912), in which a man and woman live together without benefit of clergy and with the full approval of the author. Except for the partially successful, thoroughly honest experiment of Bullard's hero, free love is for Anarchists, and capitalists. Most of these writers would have subscribed to the words of young Lucian Emery in Florence Converse's *The Children of Light* when he writes to the heroine: "If ever there were a system that insisted upon restraint, and discipline, and law, as concomitants to liberty — or rather as inherent in liberty, and evolution — that system is Socialism. . . " [21] Nevertheless, these novelists did not add a love story to the attacks on a competitive society simply to conform to literary convention or to make their books sell by sweetening the bitter pill of doctrine. They earnestly wanted to discover, even when they became sentimental or unrealistic, how men and women should get along with each other in the twentieth century.

This exploration of relationships usually results in a prophecy of, in part a reflection of, an emergent social phenomenon of the time: the New Woman. Appearing as Evangeline Marvin in *By Bread Alone*, who establishes a settlement house in the slums around the steel mills in order to extend her social and intellectual horizons, the New Woman is also Hilda Lathrop of *A Listener in Babel*, who seeks knowledge of the world as a means to knowledge of herself, and Ruth Barton of *The Walking Delegate*, another wealthy girl, who nevertheless becomes a business secretary in order to be self-supporting and who eventually assists Tom Keating in his fight for a democratic labor union. The New Woman is as courageous and self-reliant as her literary prototype of the 1890's, and far more curious about the world in which she lives. If physically she appears at first to be cold toward men, her emotional potentiality is shown by her deep, generous warmth toward ideals. Occasionally she comes from the proletariat, but more often from at least an upper-middle-class family, so that her manners are proper. Whatever her class of origin, she always awakens to self in proportion as she awakens to the promise of the new society. Such a person is Sally Heffer of *The Nine-Tenths*, who, however, is already self- and class-conscious when she enters the story.

> A new kind of woman! . . . Sally was of the new breed; she represented the new emancipation; the exodus of woman from the home to the battle-fields of the world; the willingness to fight in the open, shoulder to shoulder with men; the advance of a sex that now demanded a broader freer life, a new health, a home built on comradeship and economic freedom.[22]

Seeking emancipation and equality herself, the New Woman instinctively aligns herself with the movement for industrial democracy. As George Cram Cook says of his heroine in *The Chasm*, "It was probably this in her — the approaching revolt of the Woman — which gave her sympathy with that other world-revolt — of the Worker." [23] In the New Woman the radical hero finds a strong mate to bear his children, a brave comrade to share his work for the Cause, a free individual to stand beside him as a first-class citizen of the Coöperative Commonwealth.

Considering the valuable support that the Socialist Party actually gave to the movement for Woman Suffrage, it is not surprising to find of the novelists that in proportion as they admire the comradely woman, they dislike the merely feminine one. Joseph Medill Patterson devotes an entire Veblenesque chapter and many other passages to attacks on the conspicuous consumption, both material and emotional, indulged in by leisure-class women; while one of the prostitutes in *The Rose Door* insists that the meek conventionality of "good" women keeps "bad" women bad and perpetuates the double standard. Even the gallant young Virginian Socialist of *Rebels of the New South* rejoices that his sweetheart is a courageous, though tender, revolutionary rather than a timid conservative like so many of her sex. Only in one novel is there any serious questioning that full equality for women will automatically help to regenerate society. The focus of Henry Berman's searching novel, *Worshippers* (1906), is the relationship between Katherine

Bronski, the dissatisfied wife of a well-to-do druggist of the Philadelphia Jewish colony, and Alexander Raman, an idealistic and popular young Socialist poet and journalist. Katherine's thwarted desire to be a great actress convinces her that she is in love with Raman, and Raman falls in love with her out of his ignorance of women. Deserting her husband, she goes to live with Raman in New York, where he encourages her in her career though doubtful of her ability. When she fails to get the hoped-for parts in plays, her self-centered desire to be worshiped more than the poet turns her into a subtle destroyer of his happiness and talent, until, under the influence of a feminist aunt, she deserts him as well. Failing as an actress in summer farce, however, she returns self-pityingly to her husband. Although this Ibsenesque study stands at the borderline between the Socialist and the "socialistic" novel, the values upheld by the author are those which inform Raman's radical idealism. Understanding, respect for others, generosity of the heart — these are equally relevant for both sexes. Woman should be emancipated, but she must not expect to use independence as a means to retaliate by establishing her own tyranny.

The concern shown by the characters of these novels for honest and practicable man–woman relations is quite often linked to another "motif," involving more general relationships, the wide recurrence of which indicates its tremendous importance to the writers. This motif is the failure of traditional Protestant Christianity to practice what it teaches or even to preach what Christ had taught. Although clerical characters not infrequently point the moral in some fashion themselves, more often nonclerical characters are brought into situations that constitute indictments of institutionalized religion. Thus, in *A Listener in Babel* when Hilda Lathrop goes to talk with Dr. Wilkinson, pastor of a wealthy church, he refuses to face the facts that Hilda states concerning hunger among the poor in a current depression. Poverty, says the pastor, is a sign of immorality, and he describes instead the woes of businessmen. As Hilda angrily leaves the rectory, she stops at his church and hears words of Christian brotherhood and humility being sung and spoken before a richly dressed congregation. The ironic contrast is sharp, both for her and the reader: "She was aware that the young priest in the pulpit was knocking great words about sin and atonement against each other till they sounded hollow." [24]

Formal Christianity is almost invariably stigmatized as conservative and antidemocratic. *My Brother's Keeper* (1910) opens quite appropriately during a service in a wealthy Chicago church, where the philosophic adventurer Herford Rand, who has escaped from a prison stockade in a Colorado labor war, hides out from the police and comments satirically to himself on the congregation of overdressed women with selfish faces. To take at random another example, Katie Jones, the heroine of Susan Glaspell's conversion story *The Visioning* (1911), teases her uncle, an Episcopal bishop, rather caustically for his practice of living well, preaching against democratic "excesses," and being disturbed about the spread of Socialism into the American Army. Most churches, in short, have become merely part of the ideological camouflage developed by ruthless business enterprise, which professes to accept the teachings of Jesus while acting with un-Christlike selfishness, cruelty, and greed. One of the few sections that come to life in Brower's *The Mills of Mammon*, which through most of its five hundred pages sounds as though it had been written on a soapbox by Harold Bell Wright, is the narrative, only casually related to the action, of the Reverend Mr. Smiley's difficulties when he helps to get a reform administration into city office and then continues his muckraking after the reformists, illustrating Lincoln Steffens's formula, have given up or themselves become machine politicians. His congregation ultimately removes Smiley from his pulpit when he opposes the continued collection by wealthy parishioners of rents from buildings which they know to be houses of prostitution.

Almost never does the attack on institutionalized Christianity go beyond it to include the religion itself. *The Spider's Web* stands practically alone in this respect. To be sure, in the Coöperative Commonwealth visualized in *When Things Were Doing*, there are no churches, simply because no one is ignorant enough to wish to build them, and Sunday services have given way to lectures on a materialistic "cosmic evolution"; but most of the Socialist novelists reveal in their attitude toward religion the carry-over effects of a middle-class upbringing. Although they did not adhere to Christian Socialism as such, they were here influenced by the "New

Theology" and the Social Gospel more than by Marx. In their novels, the churches are an opiate of the rich, Christianity a hope of the masses, for its spirit is held to be simply brotherly love. The true Christian is the one who goes to the poor, who takes the side of the workers in the struggle for economic democracy. Because of its belief in coöperation, it is Socialism, in fact, which will realize on earth the teachings of Christ. In mentioning Christ himself, who is often referred to as the "first Socialist," these writers emphasize, not his divinity, but his carpentry. To them he is a revolutionary worker.

Yet another illustration of the opposition of the Socialist novelists to dogmatic Christianity is their assumption, and Marx's also, that human nature is essentially good, that the first private ownership of a means of production, not the apple of forbidden knowledge, brought sin into the world. If the competitive social structure of capitalism is replaced by the coöperative one of Socialism, love rather than hate will rule. Hence these writers are basically environmentalists, for they argue that it is environment which is responsible for shaping both character and personality. Crime they tend to regard as a blind reaction against social injustice, while prisons are often accused of producing, not reforming, criminals. A very few of the writers accept heredity as being of equal importance with environment, but the German Marxist in "The Charity Girl" asserts that those who insist on heredity are trying to justify their conservatism; and Walter Hurt voices the majority belief when he has a Socialist philosopher tell the reporter hero: " . . . human nature is much the same in all men. It can improve only under improved conditions. In order for man to evolve to greater excellence of character we must remove the incentive to injustice and the opportunity for oppression." [25]

That man will evolve is unquestioned; the scientific evolution of man is inextricably interwoven with the economic development of society, and characters in these novels frequently come to an acceptance of scientific evolution as part of the broadened intellectual horizon brought them by conversion to the new political doctrine. Acceptance of evolution, however, involves adopting an attitude toward the theories of Darwin, which are reduced in the several novels that directly discuss them to the formula, "the survival of the fittest." Commonly this popularized version of Darwinism appears in the speeches of characters who are themselves capitalists or adherents of capitalism and who use it to support their belief in competitive individualism. Thereupon a Socialist character refutes the speaker, usually with some adaptation of Christian ethics. The doctrine of "survival of the fittest," the Socialist is likely to say, and that of might making right may very well apply to the beasts of the jungle or among savage tribes, but civilized persons have already evolved to the higher ethic of brotherly love and all of society will do so when coöperation becomes universal.

In a very few instances the popularized form of Darwinism is actually accepted as not being in essential conflict with Socialism at all. A tired radical in *Worshippers* flares up momentarily with his old fire and declares that the upper-class intellectuals who are making much of "Darwinistic Pessimism" do not realize how unfixed are all present-day institutions, nor how important the very numbers of the proletariat are in the struggle for class power; while in *When Things Were Doing*, the leader of the Russian Socialists suggests that the strong may voluntarily discontinue the struggle for survival when the Coöperative Commonwealth plentifully furnishes the necessities of life to all. The most extended discussion of the Darwinian problem, however, is contained in the chapter of Brower's *The Mills of Mammon* which records the speech on ethics by John Bulman, Socialist, before the "Ethical Study Club," a group of wealthy reform faddists. Here the refutation is based, not only on Christian ethics, but also perhaps on the observations concerning cooperation among species made in Prince Kropotkin's *Mutual Aid: a Factor of Evolution*, which Brower could have known through the American edition published in 1902 by McClure, Phillips and Company. Too aroused to be bothered by mixed metaphors, Bulman denies that capitalist ethics are founded on altruism.

"I contend that your 'ethics' today are but the ethics of the jungle, the law of tooth and claw, half hidden under the thin, white enamel of a spineless Christianity. The only 'ethic' you know, the only one the world has known since the days when Christ attempted the founding of a 'world-ethic,' has been made to fit 'property rights' in labor, and the products of labor. As a Socialist, I contend that the human family will not be lifted out of the degradation of ignorant sinning against the fixed laws of life until society shall give to the weakest individual among us the protection of its strong arm — shall institute a world democracy and take up the task of deodorizing present day 'ethics.' " [26]

Being writers rather than economists, the Socialist novelists ultimately came to grips with capitalism less on the economic grounds that it is inadequate than on the moral grounds that it is unjust. They were less concerned with analyzing the theory of surplus value than in showing what they considered to be its results. The city slum, the home of the "submerged third," forms a familiar background in these novels, and in most of them there is some description, direct or indirect, of inhuman working conditions. Whether it is a foundry being depicted, as in *Toilers and Idlers* and *The Mills of Mammon*, garment sweatshops, as in *Comrade Yetta* and *A Chance to Live*, the killing beds in *The Jungle* or the stokeholes of *The Harbor*, the reader is always informed of the long hours, the low wages, the filth, the racking clatter of machinery, the accidents without compensation, the domination of foreman or manager, their large and petty methods of graft or terrorization, the job insecurity, the "yellow dog" contract and the blacklist, the semi-imprisonment of those who have nothing to sell but their strength. Particular attention is paid to the extensive use of child labor, usually by church-going employers. Children supply a large part of the working force in the Alabama textile mills of *My Brother's Keeper*, and Bruce McAllister, left-wing Congressman in Friedman's *The Radical*, makes the greatest fight of his career on behalf of his Anti-Child Labor Bill.

It is into this jungle of tenement and factory that the immigrants come, hopeful in the thought of the New World stretching far and wide behind the Statue of Liberty. Since fourteen-and-a-half million immigrants actually did enter the United States in the first two decades of the century, a majority of them pouring into the already swollen cities, it is no wonder that their fate is one of the most frequently mentioned single problems in the Socialist novels. In this fiction there is little of Mary Antin's Promised Land, and the Americanizations are rarely like Edward Bok's. Occasionally, as in Zoe Beckley's *A Chance to Live*, the radical writers admit that the immigrants, particularly the Jews from the Russian

Pale, may have found freedom from the pogrom or from immediate political terrorization, but beyond that their outlook is a somber one. Yetta Rayevsky's father, who had come to New York from the Ghetto of Kovno, talks always of a kindly Democracy, but, the author states, old Rayevsky knows nothing of "the modern Plutocracy, which is everywhere in a life-and-death struggle" with it. Freda's Socialist husband in *The Cage* often speaks to her "of the pathos in the fact that these children of the nations had high hopes and great trust in American principles and did not realize that they were entering the prison house of the age to be worn out and flung aside with greater disregard than in their native places." [27]

The two novels which have most to say about the lot of the immigrant are hardly more optimistic. In one of the "imaginary conversations" of *A Listener in Babel*, Vida Scudder antedates Randolph Bourne's concept of "Trans-America" by having one of her characters argue that the materialistic civilization of the United States needs to be enriched by the gifts of other nationalities. If these gifts were encouraged to develop freely, America could become the most richly complex nation in the world's history. Unfortunately, the speaker concludes, the newcomers can expect only deadening work and sorrow. The single Socialist novel devoted wholly to the story of an immigrant, with the exception of *The Rise of David Levinsky*, does indeed describe the successful Americanization of its hero. Tobenkin's *Witte Arrives* traces the life of Emil Witte from his arrival as a child at the old Castle Garden entry station, predecessor of Ellis Island, through his studious boyhood to a career, first as newspaper reporter and finally as a youthful editor on an established liberal weekly. Yet Witte sees that caste lines have formed in his adopted country, the masses are gripped by the terrible fear of joblessness, and he himself must face religious discrimination as a Jew. His first success comes to him when, as a Socialist, he writes what he consciously considers to be an *Uncle Tom's Cabin* of wage-slavery.

Against the workers, both native and immigrant, stands the corporate power of capitalism, a system which, as novel after novel insists, not only creates war as a means to market its surplus products, but is itself a state of war. The deaths and injuries of men and women in industry are the steady attritional casualties. There are no noncombatants; war is carried to the young and old of the slums in the form of poverty and disease. Strikes are the open fighting, and when these occur, capitalism throws off all pretense of benevolence and brings naked oppression to bear on the workers.

No capitalist institutions are credited in these novels with being of any significant help to the working class in the long war. The politics of democracy, which should mean the rule of the many, has become the tool of the few, since politicians at all levels, from ward leader to state governor to congressman, respond to capitalist domination. Thus, in *The Scarlet Shadow* the same powerful economic forces that are seeking the judicial murder of the radical Bill Haywood are also corrupting the ballot boxes by which the citizen of Colorado presumably governs himself. Bruce McAllister in *The Radical* fights at the level of the House of Representatives and the Senate of the United States against the power of Anthony Wyckoff, "father of the Trust of Trusts," who moves Congressmen and cabinet members about like pawns. As Blair Carrhart rejected economic action in *By Bread Alone*, McAllister in that book's "sequel" comes to reject the political action of the two major parties, resigns his Senate seat, and leaves Washington to take to the people his case for the Coöperative Commonwealth.

The whole apparatus of the law is equally corrupt, for it is designed, not to produce justice, but to protect the property rights of capital against the human rights of labor. The Supreme Court in *The Radical* nullifies the Anti-Child Labor Law because it infringes on the employer's freedom of contract; and Dyker, the Tammany lawyer of *The House of Bondage*, protects the gangsters, madams, and pimps who are loyal to the political machine by methods which, the author points out, "far from being unusual, are merely a daring extension of the methods that, within the last decade, have increased in popularity among the seemingly more respectable practitioners":

Evidence is manufactured or destroyed, according to immediate needs; favorable witnesses are taught favorable testimony; postponements are secured until a politically indebted judge is on the bench. There follows a formal bellowing against what are called invasions of inalienable personal rights, and then there comes a matter-of-course acquittal.[28]

When the attritional warfare of industrialism flares into a strike, the class nature of law and the courts can no longer be concealed. If an antilabor injunction cannot by chance be issued, individual labor leaders can be railroaded on flimsy evidence. In these novels, judges almost invariably resemble that real Magistrate Olmstead who, in sentencing a girl picket during the Uprising of the Twenty Thousand, perpetuated himself to fame by shouting: "You are on strike against God and Nature, whose law is that man shall earn his bread by the sweat of his brow. You are on strike against God." [29]

Even during a period of relative industrial "peace," and of course much more so during open war, another capitalist institution, the "free" press, is usually pictured as being irresponsible and venal, for the "money power" owns most of the newspapers outright. When Yetta Rayevsky climaxes a brief career as columnist for a yellow journal by trying to put into a column facts that would embarrass an advertiser, her piece is refused and she resigns. The stories in capitalist papers on the Haywood Trial in *The Scarlet Shadow* twist the truth out of recognizable shape, though the author does not blame the reporters themselves, for they have to eat. Since no hero of a Socialist novel believes what he reads in the ordinary papers, it is not surprising that a number of leading characters are at some time connected with a radical journal devoted to telling the truth, journals always with titles like *The Torch, The Clarion, The Flaming Sword.*

All attempts at class collaboration between proletariat and *grande bourgeoisie* are usually held to be fruitless or to be smoke screens set up by capital to conceal the deployment of its forces. There is, of course, charity, but John Bulman, the Socialist in *The Mills of Mammon*, finally persuades a wealthy girl to give up the practice of it on grounds acceptable to all the novelists: it is degrading to the poor and corrupting to the rich, who hope to free their consciences of blood guilt by giving back to labor a pittance out of the surplus wealth it has created. Bulman's argument is expanded, but not changed, in both "The Charity Girl" and Mary Marcy's *Out of the Dump*, the two novels in this fiction which are mainly devoted to attacking organized charity. There is also the settlement house, and the novelists are less in agreement on the instrumentality of this institution. Those in the opposition classify it with charity, insist on its futility, and argue that the settlement house increases the workers' frustration by infecting them with the hopeless desire to rise from their class. Those who favor the institution, like Clara Emery, heroine of *The Children of Light*, point to its value, not in "uplifting" the masses, but in educating the middle- and upper-class inhabitants of such houses to the facts of working-class life and of Socialism. Even Clara, however, admits to herself that the settlement houses "do not improve the conditions of the working people; indeed, that they cannot improve those conditions." They are merely tactical devices in the class war.

Ultimately the workers can be helped only by themselves; and the novelists of Socialism agree with the "Firebrand," the girl organizer in *A Chance to Live*, when she cries to the well-bred, well-to-do audience at the Carnegie Hall memorial meeting for the girl victims of the tragic sweatshop fire: "I tell you if we [workers] are to get even the simplest human rights we must get them without you. Yes — in spite of you!" [30] For class war is the real condition of capitalist society; everyone must choose sides, and peace can come only after the working class has triumphed.

v

An appalling case might seemingly be made out to prove that the typical Socialist novel is really an inverted variation on the pattern of the Horatio Alger tale, that legend which continued to channel the imagination of American youth for years after its author's death. In the variation the hero's male parent is not only living, but financially comfortable, so that the young man must begin as rebel against a father rather than as sole support of a widowed mother. To be sure, both kinds of heroes go to the city, but the Alger youth goes from a small town, the other from college, and once there the one who is to attain radical, instead of business, success must observe the thousands of men who cannot make good rather than the dozens who do, must learn the necessary human expense of the system rather than its possible material profit, must decide to help free a class rather than to gain power over it. The wealthy, kindhearted old gentleman who gives the Alger hero his first working capital is metamorphosed into the Party organizer who gives the young radical-to-be his first Marxist insights, and a shrewd business deal becomes instead a successful blow for the Coöperative Commonwealth. Finally, if the young Socialist does marry the boss's daughter, as sometimes happens, she goes with him willingly to a flat in Greenwich Village rather than to a mansion on Park Avenue, and they spend the rest of their days striving to put ideas into workers' heads rather than gilt-edged securities into safe-deposit boxes.

Fortunately for the worth of some of these novels the suggested parallel has no more relation to actual literary fact than the mythological chimera had to nature, both being constructed by joining quite unrelated parts of books or creatures. Besides having been written for boys according to the fixed pattern that Frederick Lewis Allen has amusingly described, Alger's stories are now read only by students of literary history or by whimsical antiquaries. The Socialist novels were written for adults, though not always sophisticated ones, and their subject matter is highly varied; they all describe approaches to a political doctrine, but the approaches are similar only in the most general of terms. Some of these books are indeed fantastically bad. *The Rose Door* is surpassed in narrative competence by any one of the Ragged Dick series; *The Mills of Mammon* is as melodramatic and sentimental as *The Winning of Barbara Worth* or its own title; the Reverend Dubois H. Loux's *Maitland Varne: Or the Bells of De Thaumaturge* ranks with the feeblest examples of the English "Silverfork" School, from which base ancestry it appears to have descended. Nevertheless, a significant number of them are still readable, a few very much so. Although a study of the Socialist writers does not change present judgment as to the leading novelists of the century's first two decades, at least five volumes — besides Sinclair's well-established *The Jungle* — continue to hold up as effective, if minor, pieces of literature, often awkward in technique by comparison with the present average book-club selection, but possessed of life: *By Bread Alone, The Walking Delegate, Worshippers, The Harbor,* and *The Rise of David Levinsky.* These five also achieve the most successful solutions to the chief artistic problem of the radical novelist, for in each case "message" is integrated into fictional structure.

Sales popularity, taken by itself, is hardly a dependable criterion of value, but it is worth recalling that both *The Jungle*, despite its pamphlet conclusion, and *The Harbor*, boyish in spirit, but within its limits complete, were among the ten best-sellers in fiction for their respective years.

Besides these half-dozen leading novels, there are others that are memorable by virtue of individual scenes, such as the birth of the child in *Love's Pilgrimage* and the destruction of the people of the abyss in *The Iron Heel*, or because of the author's intellectual boldness in attempting, as in *The House of Bondage*, to dramatize an enormously complex set of socioeconomic relationships. But the big, plain, awkward fact is that a majority of the writers were Socialists first, novelists second, had something to say before they had a way of saying it. For them art was means, not end or, what is of course best, means-and-end. Hence the greater part of this fiction is of more interest now to the historian than the critic. Here the interest is considerable; for however crude and inept many of the writers are as writers, they all faced up to the very real economic, social, and political problems of their times — the growth of corporate industry, the centralization of finance, the tremendous rate of urbanization, the changing status of women, the flood of immigration, the development of the city boss and the nationwide pressure group, the domination of government by business, the struggles of the middle class to be politically effective, of labor to organize, of radicalism to create a power base in American society. As a result of devotion to or miscomprehension of Socialist theory and practice, this novel or that may reveal exaggeration, one-sidedness, perhaps plain ignorance of fact in stating its fictional case; yet on the whole the writers attempted to see these problems honestly, not through the eyes of the many whose needs and desires the socioeconomic system did partially or wholly satisfy, but through the eyes of the many more on whose failure the success and well-being of the others rested. No society can be understood by examining a single layer of it. The great contribution of the Socialist novelists was that they earnestly assisted in the detailed exploration of layers which many more popular writers were still observing casually, desultorily, or superciliously, and these layers were statistically the largest ones in society. During the first two decades of the twentieth century more inhabitants of the United States knew a marginal existence in mill, sweatshop, tenement, and rural slum than lived with any marked degree of comfort.

Despite their somber subject matter, despite the inevitable defeats for the working class which some record, the spirit of the Socialist novels as a whole is one of curiously innocent joy. The details of oppression which crowd their foregrounds bulk so black because they stand, not under the night of endless tyranny, but against the golden dawn of the new day. Already on the horizon shine the rising cities of the classless society; here and now is being realized the American Dream. These novels remind us that the twentieth century once was young.

4.

FROM MOTHER EARTH TO THE MASSES

F ROM the beginning of the century up to World War I, the history of the Socialist Party was in one sense a history of its slowly increasing acceptance into the American scene, but the groups clustered at the extreme red end of the political spectrum continued to glory in the name of social outcast. Of these the two most influential and most widely feared were the Anarchists and the Industrial Workers of the World, the I.W.W.

There had been small scattered groups of Anarchists in the United States, most of them of the philosophic variety, even before Josiah Warren, offended by the mismanagement of Robert Owen's utopian ·community at New Harmony, began writing, printing, and publishing *The Peaceful Revolutionist*, which lived and died in 1833; and Thoreau's essay on Civil Disobedience gave support to the spirit, if not the name, of generations of these intransigeants. Communist Anarchism became prominent only with the arrival in America in 1882 of the German radical Johan Most, who was at that time fiercely preaching "the propaganda of the deed" and who in the next year helped to found the International Working People's Association at Pittsburgh. The explosion of the Haymarket Bomb, the *attentat* upon Henry C. Frick by Alexander Berkman during the Homestead Strike, and the assassination of President McKinley by Czolgosz, all contributed to popularizing the cartoon image, loosely based on Most, of the Anarchist as a darkly whiskered, evilly crouched man holding pistol or smoking bomb, an image which colored the characterization of Anarchist figures in the Socialist novels, and which newspapers so illogically yet effectively transferred to the Bolsheviks after the Russian Revolution that it was for long a stereotype in the American mind. Actually, just as Most repudiated Berkman's deed, so Berkman himself repudiated that of Czolgosz. Excepting some use of dynamite in labor conflicts, such as in the disastrous McNamara Affair of 1911, terrorism was rarely practiced by the Anarchist in this country. To the inquiring Hutchins Hapgood, who examined its philosophy in *The Spirit of Labor* (1907), Anarchism was not a creed of violence, but rather the proletariat's aesthetic ideal, a way of life aimed at the greatest fulfillment of the individual personality.

From the last years of the nineteenth century to the end of World War I, the outstanding exponents of Communist Anarchism in this country were the dynamic Emma Goldman and, after his release from prison, her companion Alexander Berkman, their deportation to the Soviet Union late in 1919 being one important cause for the swift decline of the movement. During the period of their greatest influence, in the 1910's, there were a group of adherents in San Francisco, where Berkman briefly published a magazine called *The Blast*, and others in Chicago, Boston, and Philadelphia; the most important one, however, centered ultimately in New York around the Ferrer School, named after an executed Spanish Anarchist, and around Emma Goldman's own periodical, *Mother Earth*. According to her later declaration, this magazine, which appeared monthly from March, 1906, until its suppression by the Federal Government in April, 1918, had the double purpose of supporting any unpopular cause and of bringing together art and the revolutionary movement, particularly that part of it characterized by the basic Anarchist doctrines of individual sovereignty and voluntary coöperation. The regular circulation appears to have been slight, for a special wartime edition of 20,000 copies was considered to be unusually large; but because the Goldman-Berkman group as individuals had, on the one hand, close informal ties with militant labor and, on the other, contacts with the literary and Bohemian worlds of New York, *Mother Earth* and the circle about it were of definite, though unassessable, importance in introducing literary people to radical ideas. Yet with the exception of Emma Goldman's vigorous autobiography, *Living My Life*, not written until late in the twenties, Berkman's classic in penology, *Prison Memoirs of an Anarchist* (1912), the impassioned but stiff poems and short stories of Michigan-born Voltairine de Cleyre, some of which were collected into a single volume, or the poetry and short fiction which appeared from time to time in *Mother Earth*, Anarchist literature was limited to the critical, the philosophical, and the polemical.

There were two known attempts by Anarchists to write extended pieces of revolutionary fiction, but both came to nothing. In a biographical introduction to Voltairine de Cleyre's *Selected Works* (1914), the Greenwich Village radical Hippolyte Havel states that the subject of his sketch and her companion, Dyer Lum, began a radical novel but never finished it. Again, Berkman writes in his *Memoirs* that during the early part of his imprisonment in the Western Penitentiary of Pennsylvania he expanded a short story called "Story of Luba" into a novelette about life among revolutionaries in New York. Although this was smuggled out of the prison to Emma Goldman, it was never published. "Story of Luba" may very well have been one of the manuscripts intended for book publication which were seized, along with typed copies of Emma Goldman's six lectures on American literature, in a Federal Agents' raid on the *Mother Earth* office in June, 1917, and, if so, doubtless still rests in the extensive archives of the Department of Justice. Hutchins Hapgood also attempted to create a sympathetic literary "photograph" of the personalities and histories of two highly typical radicals, Terry and Marie, in *An Anarchist Woman* (1909); but Hapgood's study is not actually fiction despite the assertion in his autobiography, *A Victorian in the Modern World*, that he was creating art according to Aristotle's theory of it as a copy of nature, and he of course accepted individual Anarchists rather than their philosophy.

Considering that Hapgood's various writings and the memoirs of both Berkman and Goldman have much to say of the usual Anarchist's interest in and sensitiveness to literature, it is not at all clear why the movement should have produced no novels. One can only suggest a combination of possibilities: absorption in labor struggles and the task of propagandizing, the lack of an amenable publisher — there was, to be sure, the active Mother Earth Publishing Company — or the Anarchist "temperament," which expended itself more readily in personal reminiscence, critical analysis, short poems, and long arguments. Whatever the reason, the nonexistence of such novels emphasizes by contrast the domination of radical fiction at that time by the Socialist writers.

Quite as outspoken as the Anarchists in their opposition to established society, but far more powerful in numbers, organization, and effectiveness, the Industrial Workers of the World rose during the 1910's to dominate the Far Left and to cast into the uneasy imagination of middle-class America the same shadow of terrified revulsion that the Communist Party does now. Organized in 1905, by a widely assorted group of radicals and labor leaders, among whom were Daniel De Leon, Eugene Debs, and William D. Haywood, the I.W.W. was intended as the economic counterpart of political Socialism, "a labor organization builded as the structure of socialist society, embracing within itself the working class in approximately the same groups and departments and industries that the workers would assume in the working-class administration of the Co-operative Commonwealth." [1] In its very conception it was bitterly opposed to the conservative craft unionism of the American Federation of Labor, for its founders considered the latter a naïve device to combat the employers, now themselves organized by industries in their developing search for world markets. Instead, the I.W.W. called for the uniting of all the workers of an industry into a "vertical" union, the resulting industrial organizations to be in turn parts of a "One Big Union" of international labor, which would "build the new world in the shell of the old" and, ultimately dispropriating the owning class by a climactic general strike, emerge full-formed as the Coöperative Commonwealth.

Since the American Federation of Labor already was the controlling force among skilled workers, the industrial unionism of the I.W.W. made its greatest appeal among unorganized, unskilled migrant and immigrant workers, particularly among the hands of harvest fields and construction camps, the longshoremen, the seamen, and the lumberjacks, or "timber beasts," of the South and the Pacific Northwest. Such men had then even fewer stable ties with organized society than they do now; they were, in fact, practically outside society. They were usually young, had no families, were for the most part voteless because of their wanderings from place to place, and were treated with harsh suspicion or worse by the citizenry of settled communities. Declaring in its "Preamble" that the "working class and the employing class have nothing in common," the I.W.W. became a focal point for the rebellion of these footloose men against the established order of things.

For a number of years the growth of the organization was slow because of internal dissensions and struggles for power. At the annual convention in 1908, Haywood and the "direct-actionists," the migratory workers who were opposed to any political activity, won out over the parliamentarians. De Leon was ousted with his Socialist Labor Party representatives, and Debs, alienated by the new policy, allowed his membership to expire. The following year, however, the Wobblies — they had made this nickname their own — began to attract attention with a series of "free-speech fights" which crowded jails from New Bedford to San Francisco; and in 1912, they burst into national prominence when two of their organizers, Joseph Ettor and Arturo Giovannitti, helped to lead the spontaneous strike of unskilled, foreign-born textile workers in Lawrence, Massachusetts, to an unconditional victory. From that time on, the names of their strikes and fights for free speech were like the names on the land. In 1913, the year that Haywood was expelled from the Socialist Party, he, Elizabeth Gurley Flynn, and Carlo Tresca conducted the Paterson silk strike, which the young John Reed helped to dramatize in the famous labor pageant in Madison Square Garden. The year 1915 brought a great surge in membership, particularly among farm laborers and harvest hands, and the movement began to develop momentum. That momentum, which pushed membership to a peak of 100,000 in the summer of 1917, ran head-on into the barrier of a nation at war.

The Wobblies had always needed their hard-bitten sense of humor, for the communities into which they swarmed for strikes or free-speech fights had struck at them with whatever legal or extralegal methods could be contrived. Joe Hill, "The Wobblies' Troubadour," had been executed by the State of Utah on November 19, 1915, after a trial which attracted international attention and is even yet a subject of dispute;[2] a number of I.W.W.'s were killed outright by a sheriff's posse at Everett, Washington, on "Bloody Sunday" in 1916; while in the following year the organizer Frank Little was lynched at Butte, Montana. Now the I.W.W.

stand against the war and its continuation of strikes in wartime brought attacks from both the local vigilante committees and the Federal Government. After a protracted trial in Chicago on the charge of "spoken and written denunciation of war," Judge Kenesaw Landis sentenced nearly a hundred of the Wobbly leaders to prison terms which, according to Ralph Chaplin, one of the defendants, totaled more than eight hundred years. Democracy having been made safe to this extent, the remainder of the I.W.W. became fair game for mobs, whose lawless violence was abetted by the authorities. The prison sentences, later commuted by President Harding after President Wilson had refused to do so, factional conflicts with the Communist Party during the early twenties, and a fission in the organization in 1924 destroyed what little the vigilantes had left. The I.W.W. is now carried on, chiefly for the sake of tradition, by a handful of old-timers.

Being for the most part tough migratory workers, deeply suspicious of intellectuals and all the superstructure of capitalist society, the Wobblies produced a species of folk literature rather than an artistically sophisticated one.[3] Arturo Giovannitti, to be sure, published a volume of dithyrambic poetry entitled *Arrows in the Gale* (1914), and Ralph Chaplin's book of prison poems, *Bars and Shadows* (1922), appeared while he was still serving his sentence in Leavenworth; but "the real Wobbly stuff" is almost entirely contained in the *Little Red Songbook*, still available in its twenty-eighth edition at the I.W.W. headquarters in Chicago. These songs, usually written to popular or hymn tunes by men like Joe Hill, Covington Hall, "T-Bone Slim," and again Ralph Chaplin, author of "Solidarity Forever," are occasionally soft and sentimental. More characteristic, however, is the lean-jawed humor of "The Preacher and the Slave," "The Popular Wobbly," and "Casey Jones." One of the few radical movements ever to possess a sense of humor, the I.W.W. was also a revolution with a singing voice.

Fiction on the scale of a novel was another thing. A number of novels have appeared which include Wobblies among their characters, the best known being John Dos Passos's *The 42nd Parallel* (1930) and one of the most recent being Wallace Stegner's *The Preacher and the Slave* (1950), which works out in fictional terms the author's conclusion after much investigation that Joe Hill probably committed the crime for which he was executed. Such books as Max Eastman's *Venture* (1927), James Stevens's *Big Jim Turner* (1948), and Matthea Forseth's *The Color of Ripening* (1949) are very sympathetic toward their I.W.W. characters, but only two novels appear to have been written by actual Wobblies on revolutionary themes. Strictly considered, the first of these, Charles Ashleigh's *Rambling Kid* (1930), belongs to English literature, for the author came to the United States from England as a youth in the early 1910's and returned there early in the twenties; during the interval, however, he joined the I.W.W., became an organizer, was a defendant in the trial of the Chicago Wobblies, and eventually became one of those who left the One Big Union in favor of the Communist Party.

Rambling Kid, an unpretentious novel in the realist tradition, quite clearly contains much autobiographical material. After receiving a small inheritance the Crane family moves from London's East End to a farm on the South Dakota prairies and then disperses after the farm's mortgage is foreclosed. Young Joe joins the I.W.W. in Minneapolis, follows the "harvest circle" northwest across the plains, rides the freights to San Francisco, becomes a street speaker, evades Federal Agents when World War I comes, and accepts the offer of a left-wing Socialist group to go to the Soviet Union to work for the Comintern. The interest of the novel lies less in the character of Joe, a shadowy young man through whose eyes the action is seen, than in its picture of the life of the migratories, scorned by the solid citizen, whom they scorn in return, brutalized by the police, whom they outwit or fight when the odds are fair, and preyed on by the criminals at the bottom of the Social Pit into which many of them are forced. A novel concerned with the violence of life at the lowest levels of the working class, it is nevertheless curiously passive, an effect which perhaps results from the fact that, with the exception of his street speaking, Joe is a learner rather than a teacher and a follower rather than a leader. Typical is his reading modern literature on the advice of two older Wobblies, listening to their arguments over Dreiser, Sandburg, and Sherwood Anderson, and concluding with the more talkative one that these writers are merely men in blind revolt rather than revolutionaries who know how to set the working class in motion. Quite suitably,

Joe is sent to work for the Comintern, not because he is any more than adequate as a soapboxer, but because while still a farm boy he had been taught by a neighbor to be an expert taker of shorthand.

In *Rambling Kid* one of Joe's "teachers" has left a bourgeois college, where he found neither sound minds nor sound bodies, in order to obtain a real education among the working class. The hero of the second I.W.W. novel, Harold Lord Varney's *Revolt* (1919), is likewise a young college man. After being tricked into acting as a strikebreaker, he falls in with two Wobblies, who immediately start to reëducate him properly. Convinced of his errors by their arguments, he helps them in an attempt to break the strikebreaking, goes to jail, and, upon release, travels about the country with his two friends in true Wobbly fashion, learning what life in the working class is like. He also learns how strong are the oppressive powers of capitalism, and eventually goes to Russia, where he helps in establishing the Soviets during the Revolution.

As the radical critic Floyd Dell pointed out in a review of *Revolt*, the significance of the book lies in the fact that "the bourgeois hero learns from the working class how not to be bourgeois — and only upon these terms becomes one of their leaders." [4] Varney's hero learns his lesson more quickly and permanently than did the author himself; for Varney's subsequent career, after his seven years as member and officer of the I.W.W., might well have justified the Wobblies in their suspicion of intellectuals. Early in the year following the publication of *Revolt*, evidently with an indictment hanging over his head for his membership in a convicted organization, Varney repudiated the I.W.W. and, presaging a more recently familiar pattern, savagely attacked his former associates. His change of heart must have been drastic. During Harding's presidential campaign that summer he was in charge of labor publicity for the Republican National Committee, while in the thirties he turned up at the head of the Italian Historical Society, a propaganda agency in New York for the then Fascist state of Italy.

The powers of capitalism are indeed strong. In one way or another, by temptation, social pressure, indifference, or cruelty, they broke the challenge of the I.W.W. as they broke that of the Anarchists and the Socialists. With that destruction went, for a decade, any chance to maintain the radical novel as a significant form in American literature.

II

Much more extensive than the amount of radical fiction and poetry published during the first two decades of the century was, of course, the subliterary material — theoretical writing, editorial comment, exposé story, personal narrative, polemic, and the like — which poured forth in floods from the radical press. One of the great fountainheads of this material was the publishing house of Charles H. Kerr and Company of Chicago, which is still in existence. Although it has now for a long time been owned by a tiny radical group known as the Proletarian Party, the career of this company reflects with considerable accuracy the history of American radicalism for three crucial decades.

Established as a coöperative publishing business in 1886, it had at first issued mainly books on "free thought" until in 1891 it began to publish literature for the People's Party. As that decade advanced, Kerr next became one of the chief publishers of the Utopias. In 1899 the company's officials determined to put out only material concerned with the international Socialist movement and began publishing the Library of Progress, a series chiefly devoted to inexpensive reprints of the classics of Marxism, and the Pocket Library of Socialism, a series of pamphlets covered in transparent red paper and made small enough to fit into a worker's pocket. An indication of the company's zeal for its newly adopted cause was the fact that within two years nearly 300,000 copies of these pamphlets had been printed, and the zeal did not abate. By the early summer of 1908, when Debs had already begun his third campaign for the Presidency, Kerr could boast: "Nearly two thousand socialists are now coöperating through our company to bring out the books that the socialist movement needs. We do not yet publish all; we shall add to our list as fast as more capital is subscribed. But we already have at least two-thirds of the socialist books published in the English language that are worth reading." [5] So great were the efforts of the coöperative, indeed, that four years later it had to be cleared by the Party's National Investigating Committee of charges that it had effected a monopoly over the literature of Socialism.

Interestingly enough, the major publisher of Socialist novels was not a radical firm at all, but rather the Macmillan Company, which issued *The Iron Heel*, *A Man's World*, *Comrade Yetta*, *The Harbor*, *King Coal*, and *A Chance to Live*. In addition, Macmillan was Jack London's regular publisher, and in 1904 it brought out W. J. Ghent's *Mass and Class*, which the Kerr Company hailed as the first Socialist work on the class struggle to be issued by a capitalist publishing house in the United States. Charles H. Kerr, however, was close behind Macmillan's in the publishing of Socialist novels, though its literary taste was considerably weaker, for it brought out *Beyond the Black Ocean*, *Rebels of the New South*, *The Recording Angel*, *When Things Were Doing*, and *The Rose Door*, along with *The Rebel at Large* and *Stories of the Struggle*, collections of short fiction respectively by May Beals and Morris Winchevsky. If the coöperative did not publish more than a small number of the Socialist novels, which actually appeared from a variety of "capitalist" and radical presses, it did have other triumphs. Of these Ernest Unterman's complete translation of *Capital* was of course the greatest, but another was Marcus Hitch's *Goethe's Faust: A Fragment of Socialist Criticism* (1908), a brief 127-page study by one of the coöperative's directors, which has the distinction of being the first extended piece of Marxist literary criticism by an American to be published in this country. More tolerant than some of his critical successors on the Left, Hitch admitted admiration for Goethe's poetry, but he insisted that *Faust* was a class product, that it reflected the dominance of bourgeois property concepts, and hence that it was sharply limited in its attempt to portray "universal" human nature.

Besides being the source of many Socialist books and pamphlets, Charles H. Kerr and Company issued the monthly *International Socialist Review*, the first number of which appeared on July 1, 1900. Under the scholarly editorship of A. M. Simons it was largely devoted to discussions of Marxist theory designed to educate a Party intelligentsia, which would then presumably pass its knowledge on down to the Jimmie Higginses, but the magazine also con-

tained notes on international Socialism, news of the labor movement, book reviews, and an occasional short story. Circulation
fluctuated between three and six thousand, and the magazine ran
at a small but permanent deficit. Finally, early in 1908 Simons was
dismissed, Charles Kerr himself took over the editorship briefly,
and a new policy was adopted. Although the purpose of the
Review remained to educate, it was now increasingly oriented
toward the industrial working class, was gradually enlarged to
twice its former size, and began to take on the format of the popular magazines, at the same time becoming increasingly more radical
in tone. One of its first acts was to serialize *Out of the Dump*, that
blast at organized charity by the thoroughly revolutionary Mary
Marcy. By 1912 the *Review* was the voice of the I.W.W. and the
extreme left wing of the Socialist Party, and its circulation had
leaped from 3,000 to 50,000. It praised John Reed's Paterson Strike
pageant, bitterly attacked the authorities responsible for the Ludlow Massacre in 1914, printed articles and poems by Joe Hill,
Charles Ashleigh, and a Socialist poet named Carl Sandburg, and
urged in every issue that the United States keep out of the conflict
which had begun to rage in Europe.

If 1912 marked the Socialist Party's greatest triumph at the
polls, a very considerable part of that success belonged to the
Party's press, of which *The International Socialist Review* was only
one representative; for in that year alone 323 papers and periodicals
with policies of various shades of red were devoted to Socialism.
Five English and 8 foreign-language dailies, 262 English and 36
foreign-language weeklies, 10 English and 2 foreign-language
monthlies were creating an audience receptive to radical ideas.[6]
Because the rebels who had originally left De Leon's Socialist Labor
Party to form their own political organization knew from experience how the S.L.P.'s National Executive Committee had been able
to dictate policy partly through its control of a single official publication, the Constitution of the Socialist Party provided that its own
National Committee should "neither publish nor designate any
official organ." Out of the 262 English weeklies only one, *The
American Socialist*, with a circulation of 60,000, was actually
owned by the Party. The most important periodicals by virtue of
the size of their distribution were the monthly *Wilshire's Magazine*

(400,000) and two weeklies, *The National Rip-Saw* (200,000) and *The Appeal to Reason*. *The Appeal*, which had serialized *The Jungle* at a circulation of about 200,000, ran off three million copies of a single "Moyer-Haywood Rescue Edition" in 1906; while in 1912 its regular circulation went over 500,000, and for the ten weeks before the election it put out special editions that averaged slightly over a million a week. Periodicals were not lacking with which to state the Socialist case, but there was still room for a monthly magazine of a quite different sort.

Of all the left-wing magazines published during this period, the most gifted, the most varied, and the most iconoclastic was *The Masses*, which, taken with its worthy but less brilliant successor, *The Liberator*, was not only of artistic and political value in its own right, but appears now as an extremely important link between the rebel generations of the first two decades and that of the late twenties. None of its contemporaries on the Left — and few on the Center and Right, for that matter — remains so readable, and viewable, today, so capable of evoking the ferment of those awakening years in American literature and life.

The idea for a new monthly magazine originated with Piet Vlag, an excitable Dutchman, who ran a coöperative restaurant in the basement of the Rand School of Social Science, which had been established in New York in 1906 as a center for Socialist education. Under the editorship of Thomas Seltzer — later of Vlag himself — and with financial backing from a Socialist vice-president of the New York Life Insurance Company, *The Masses* first appeared in January, 1911, announcing its intention to be "a general ILLUSTRATED magazine of art, literature, politics and science" [7] with the special mission of propagandizing for the coöperatives movement. Quite logically, it was coöperatively owned by a group of artists and writers — among them being John Sloan, Art Young, Louis Untermeyer, and Mary Heaton Vorse — and was published on a nonprofit basis.

Besides advertising Karl Marx Cigars and carrying on a relentless attack upon the Boy Scouts as a quasimilitary organization, the new magazine serialized Zola's *Germinal* and published short stories, articles on Socialism, illustrations, and anticapitalist cartoons. In the second number Seltzer recognized the existence of a left-wing literature with an editorial entitled "Socialism and Fiction," which excoriated the artificiality of most American fiction, but argued that Socialist writers should reject the thesis novel in favor of an impartial realism, lest "a crude attempt to make a minute part of life equivalent to the whole of Socialism, which is the whole of life . . . make that particular exposition of Socialism ridiculous and in so far harmful." [8] Taking likewise unextreme political sides, *The Masses* became involved in the factional disputes within the Socialist Party, at the time of the 1912 convention coming out for the parliamentarians and against the "direct-actionists." The magazine's Socialism was of a conservative "yellow" rather than an advanced "red," and its format was equally staid. Although claiming a circulation of 10,000, it began to suffer from the usual financial diseases. Death came quietly with the issue of August, 1912.

In December, however, *The Masses* was brought back to life after the artist and writer owners had unanimously elected Max Eastman editor with "no pay." Eastman, the son of parents who were both Congregational ministers in upstate New York, had done graduate work under John Dewey at Columbia and had taught a class in poetics at that university before leaving early in 1911 to write his first book, *Enjoyment of Poetry*. Under his editorship the political orientation of the magazine swung abruptly from right-wing to left-wing Socialism; for Eastman, who had joined the Socialist Party in February, 1912, had already written to the New York *Call* that, although he endorsed the Party's positive program, he also advocated sabotage and violence if necessary to the workers' struggle against its capitalist oppressors. His first lead editorial, "Knowledge and Revolution," stated that the magazine now intended to work for a thoroughgoing revolution, although admitting that the event itself need not inevitably be a bloody one. A second editorial was in defense of Ettor and Giovannitti, the I.W.W. leaders who were currently on trial on a trumped-up murder charge growing out of the Lawrence strike. There was to be no suspicion that the resurrected magazine lacked fight.

A more inclusive statement of policy, composed by Eastman from a first draft by the restless John Reed, appeared in the issue of January, 1913, and was carried in all succeeding numbers just under the masthead like a war flag.

A Free Magazine

This magazine is owned and published co-operatively by its editors. It has no dividends to pay, and nobody is trying to make money out of it. A revolutionary and not a reform magazine; a magazine with a sense of humor and no respect for the respectable; frank, arrogant, impertinent, searching for the true causes; a magazine directed against rigidity and dogma wherever it is found; printing what is too naked or true for a money-making press; a magazine whose final policy is to do as it pleases and conciliate nobody, not even its readers . . .

The Masses was to be modeled after the foreign satirical journals like Simplicissimus; nothing but the free spirit of inquiry and of revolution was sacred. "We shall have no further part in the factional disputes within the Socialist Party; we are opposed to the dogmatic spirit which creates and sustains these disputes. Our appeal will be to the masses, both Socialist and non-Socialist, with entertainment, education, and the livelier kinds of propaganda."[9] Under these colors, which were never struck, The Masses began its brash, rollicking, and intransigeant career.

Unlike the usual radical periodical, the new magazine combined its firm and outright revolutionism with aesthetic values and a hilarious sense of humor. Its pages contain some of the best cartoons and drawings, both political and nonpolitical, published in any American magazine during the 1910's; in fact, as Eastman has suggested in his autobiography, Enjoyment of Living, its most successful revolution was in magazine format. Several of its features — the "bled" drawing on the front cover, the cartoon on the back — had already been used by its precursor, The Comrade, but it developed others of its own. As far as possible, the text of stories and articles was not distributed among advertisements in the back pages, and the cartoons and drawings were given importance by careful space arrangements. One highly successful device, though it had already been developed by Puck as far back as the 1880's, was the double-page cartoon in the center of the magazine. For the first of these two-page spreads, Art Young depicted the daily press as a whorehouse with the madam ("Editor and Proprietor") receiving a wad of bills from a generous gentleman friend labeled "Big Advertisers." After such a beginning, it was possible to be unsympathetic toward The Masses; it was not possible to ignore it.

The new magazine, the circulation of which usually fluctuated between 15,000 and 25,000, though it once rose, by Art Young's account, to 40,000, continued its coöperative form of ownership and its practice of not paying for contributed items; yet a large number of the artists and writers, many of them now established in their fame, joyfully sent in things that they felt could not be published elsewhere. Although it has become a commonplace to characterize *The Masses* in terms of the names of these individuals, in no better way can the magazine's inclusiveness be indicated. Such a list, indeed, reads like an inventory of the personnel in the artistic and literary worlds of the time. The first issue named as contributing editors: Literature — Eugene Wood, Hayden Carruth, Inez Haynes Gillmore, Ellis O. Jones, Max Eastman, Horatio Winslow, Thomas Seltzer, Mary Heaton Vorse, Joseph O'Brien, Louis Untermeyer; Art — John Sloan, Arthur Young, Alice Beach Winter, Alexander Popini, H. J. Turner, Charles A. Winter, Maurice Becker, William Washburn Nutting. With the January, 1914, issue Floyd Dell, Socialist and former editor of the Chicago *Evening Post's* Friday Literary Review, became permanent associate editor, his first contribution as literary critic being appropriately an enthusiastic review of Charles Beard's *An Economic Interpretation of the Constitution*. Other artists — Cornelia Barnes, George Bellows, Glenn O. Coleman, Stuart Davis, H. J. Glintenkamp — became contributing editors; while the list of contributing editors for Literature included at some time or other John Reed, William English Walling, Howard Brubaker, Frank Bohn, and Arthur Bullard. Contributions were published from, among many others: William Rose Benét, Witter Bynner, Susan Glaspell, Harry Kemp, Ernest Poole, and Wilbur Daniel Steele. Eastman lists even more who at one time or another appeared in the magazine's pages.

Others not then so well known published some of their earliest work in *The Masses*: among them, Sherwood Anderson, James Oppenheim, Djuna Barnes, Helen R. Hull, Arthur Bullard, Mabel Dodge, Vachel Lindsay, Alice Duer Miller, Sara N. Cleghorn, Leslie Nelson Jennings, Phillips Russel, Amy Lowell, Norman Matson, William Carlos Williams, Konrad Bercovici, Randolph Bourne, Babette Deutsch, Elizabeth Coatsworth, Philip Littell, and George Creel. We received contributions from Romain Rolland, Bertrand Russell, Maxim Gorky, and letters from our enthusiastic reader, Bernard Shaw. The painters Maurice

Sterne, Arthur B. Davies, Randall Davey, Morris Kantor, Mahonri Young, John Barber, Eugene Higgins, Abraham Walkowitz gave us drawings. The cartoonists Robert Minor and Boardman Robinson came in and made *The Masses* their own.[10]

By no means were all these individuals Socialists, let alone of the Party's left wing, though many were radicals of various sorts and degrees. Much of the art and most of the literature which appeared in the magazine showed no concern for politics, a good part of it, in fact, being what a sterner generation came to dismiss as "escapist." But if *The Masses* as a rule saw no necessary connection between aesthetics and revolution, it fought consistently in editorials and articles for its interpretation of society in terms of the class struggle. John Reed, who was listed as a contributing editor beginning with the issue for March, 1913, learned how far free speech extended when he was jailed in Paterson later that spring for investigating the silk strike; and his subsequent article, "War in Paterson," was one of the first steps that led to his organization of the Madison Square Garden strike pageant. In the following year, Eastman went to Colorado to cover the Ludlow Massacre and published the facts concerning one of the most brutal acts by organized authority in the labor history of this country. As its pages testify, *The Masses* stood on the side of the working class in every important labor battle which occurred during the five years of its lively existence.

Being so highly charged, it naturally attracted trouble from within a wide magnetic field. When, for example, Eastman and Art Young discovered in 1913 that the Associated Press was not reporting the labor side of what amounted to civil war in the West Virginia coal fields, the editor wrote a biting editorial, and the artist drew a cartoon entitled "Poisoned at the Source," showing a figure labeled "The Associated Press" emptying vials of "Suppressed Facts," "Prejudice," and "Lies" into a reservoir below which lie sleeping cities. The Associated Press brought a lawsuit for slander which was welcomed with ridicule by the editor and the cartoonist. The suit hung fire for two years and was then quietly dismissed, evidently because the Associated Press feared what evidence against itself a court trial might reveal. *The Masses* continued its crusades. In December, 1913, appeared a Special

Christmas Number which from front cover to back was one blast at the hypocrisy and venality of the modern Christian Church. The issue for October–November, 1915, was a Woman's Citizenship Number, dedicated to the cause of the New Woman and Suffragism. But inevitably the magazine at last attracted more trouble than it could handle.

Along with scores of other Socialist periodicals, *The Masses* opposed from the very beginning America's entry into World War I. When, after April 6, 1917, it continued to attack social injustices still existing in a nation pledged to make the world safe for democracy, and when it indicated its opposition to the Draft Act by outspokenly sympathizing with conscientious objectors, it met a fate similar to that of *The American Socialist*, *The Call*, *The International Socialist Review*, and so many others. First, its issue of August, 1917, was barred from the mails because of alleged violations of the Espionage Act. The September issue was allowed to pass, but in October *The Masses* was denied its second-class mailing privileges. Then Max Eastman, Floyd Dell, Art Young, and the business manager, Merrill Rogers, were indicted under the Espionage Act, brought before a grand jury in April, 1918, and charged with conspiracy to obstruct the Draft. When the jury disagreed as to the evidence of conspiracy, a mistrial was declared. In September of the same year, Eastman, Dell, Young, and now John Reed, who had returned from observing the Revolution in Russia, again stood trial. Again the jury was divided, several jurors holding that conspiracy might be only too likely among foreign immigrants but not among obviously American-born young men. The case was dropped.

But the war had shut in, and the savage hunt for radicals was in full cry. The day of *The Masses* was gone. Even before the trials Max Eastman and his sister Crystal, with very much the same group of contributing editors, had begun publishing *The Liberator* as a more circumspect successor to the original venture. Yet *The Masses* had fulfilled its function. Far more influential than *The Comrade* had ever been, it had existed as a common ground between artists, writers, the intelligentsia on the one hand and the left-wing labor movement on the other, enabling a significant number from the first group to come in contact, not only with the spirit, but also with the actuality of labor revolt against monopoly capitalism. For all of this group it had been an education; for the younger ones, notably for two youthful critics, Michael Gold and Joseph Freeman, *The Masses* had proved an informal college of radical arts. It was through some of these writers that the spark of revolutionary literature was kept alive during the twenties so that it could burst into flame in the Depression Decade.

5.

THE YEARS BETWEEN

THAT the end of World War I marked the coming of age of American capitalism can be shown by many different sets of statistics, but one will be sufficiently suggestive. While in 1900, Americans had held half a billion dollars in foreign investments, in 1914 the figure had advanced to over three-and-a-half billions, although this sum was offset by twice that amount in foreign investments in the United States. The necessity of financing their war efforts compelled European nations to liquidate holdings in this country; American foreign investments continued to increase, and by 1927 these investments stood at $25,000,000,000, of which $11,000,000,-000 was in war debts.[1] The war years had completed the emergence of the United States from its earlier status of a debtor nation which exported a predominantly agricultural surplus. Possessing a vastly increased industrial plant forced into being by the war, yet not damaged by it, the nation now in the twenties poured forth goods for its own use, exported a surplus of manufactured products, sought markets in every country, and was creditor to the world.

The war had only accelerated an inevitable development in material affairs, but it brought no equivalent increase in social values; indeed, by 1919, these were undergoing devaluation in almost reverse ratio. Already in the war's, and his, last autumn, that stubborn pacifist, Randolph Bourne, had seen the destruction of his hopes for a freer American society composed of richly varying cultures and had written with bitter directness: "War is the health of the State."

The State ideal is primarily a sort of blind animal push towards military unity. Any interference with that unity turns the whole vast impulse towards crushing it. Dissent is speedily outlawed, and the Government, backed by the significant classes and those who in every locality, however small, identify themselves with them, proceeds against the outlaws regardless of their value to the other institutions of the nation, or to the effect their persecution may have on public opinion. The herd becomes divided into the hunters and the hunted, and war-enterprise becomes not only a technical game but a sport as well.[2]

In its impulse toward military unity the American State had crushed, among other elements of dissent, the organizations, the publications, and the individuals of a Left which had become, as Bourne put it, changing the figure, "like sand in the bearings" of the State's "great herd-machinery," nor did the impulse stop on Armistice Day. Collective emotions had been stirred too profoundly to subside at once, and even when they did, the herd-machinery turned from sheer momentum.

Among the first to feel the power of this machinery was organized labor, which had for the most part coöperated in the prosecution of the war and was now feeling its own strength. In 1900, union membership had stood at only 833,600, or somewhat over 5 per cent of the nation's total number of wage and salary workers. For the next decade and a half there had been a steady growth in unionization, and the war had of course started a membership boom which reached its peak in 1920 with 4,961,000 union members, representing 17.6 per cent of the total number of workers.[3] The first postwar year, 1919, brought industrial reconversion and tremendous labor unrest. Among other "troubles," Seattle was held for five days by a general strike, 1100 policemen walked out in Boston, and the Great Steel Strike, involving 367,000 workers, began its four-month career. Big business, working partly through such direct powers of the government as the court injunction, partly through the "herd-machinery" of the community, moved quickly to put labor in its place. Hired thugs, strikebreakers, the police, the courts, the churches, the press backed the employers; the strike wave receded.

After the dislocations of the reconversion to "normalcy," a normalcy that included the sharp recession of 1920–21, began the boom times of the twenties. Caught between the drive for the "American plan" (that is, the open shop) on the one hand and, on the other, the astute use by business of the company union, employee stock-sharing, and other employer welfare practices, organized labor was weakened and confused. By 1925, union membership had shrunk from its historical peak of five years before to only 3,400,000. Despite rising prices, labor's militancy was reduced still further through the twenties by steadier employment and increased wages. Even less than in the prewar years did organized labor afford a power base from which radicals could work.

There remained, to be sure, little that could still be considered a radical movement. At one blow the I.W.W. had lost almost its entire leadership in the mass trial held at Chicago in the spring of 1918, while the headless body continued to writhe under the attacks of lawless superpatriots; Emma Goldman, Berkman, and lesser figures from the tiny Anarchist groups in American cities had been imprisoned during the war, and the groups were permanently disrupted by the wholesale deportation of radicals late in 1919; Socialists, having lost many members on the issue of American participation in the war, were still further split by what became known as the "Great Schism." Fired by the formation of the Third (Communist) International in March, 1919, the left wing of the American Socialist Party had begun an attempt to take over party machinery. At the Emergency Convention in Chicago at the end of August, the Socialist Party leaders retained control of the organization by expelling the left wing, which constituted a majority of the delegates. The foreign-language federations, led by the Slavic ones, which felt that the occurrence of revolution in Russia proved them to be the only true Bolsheviks in the United States, thereupon formed the Communist Party; while a group primarily composed of native-born delegates, headed by John Reed and Benjamin Gitlow, organized the Communist Labor Party. Reed subsequently went to Russia late in September in order to affiliate the latter group with the Communist International, and never returned. At the end of 1919, both Communist parties were driven underground by Attorney General Palmer's "Red Raids."

During the ensuing period of "revolutionary romanticism," the underground organizations quite unrealistically called on the American workers to "seize the streets" in open revolt; the American workers, however, did not hear, and for two years Communist factions warred with one another and agitated in a vacuum. Finally, in December, 1921, the Workers' Party of America was formed as the legal "above ground" counterpart of the underground — the two parties had by now united — but the underground organization was not finally dissolved until April, 1923.

The history of the Communist Party [4] between 1922 and 1929 is one of bitter internal dissensions and of increasing isolation from organized labor. For the first five years of this period, the chief factional disputes took place between Charles E. Ruthenberg, the Secretary of the Party, and William Z. Foster, head of the Trade Union Educational League, which attempted with decreasing success throughout the decade to "bore from within" the American Federation of Labor. When Ruthenberg died in 1927, the internal struggles of the American party began clearly to reflect the Stalin-Trotsky-Bukharin struggle for power in the Soviet Union. With Trotsky defeated, the "left-wing deviation" of Trotskyists was expelled from the American party in 1928. In the following year the Lovestoneites — so-called from the name of their leader, Jay Lovestone — were expelled for a "rightist deviation," this majority group having argued the doctrine of "exceptionalism," that is, that the United States was an exception to the rule that world-wide revolution was imminent. Although leader of the minority faction in the latter conflict, Foster was supported by the Communist International, since, paradoxically, Stalin had now assumed part of Trotsky's argument for world revolution in his successful struggle against the more cautious Bukharin. Hence in 1929 Foster became the head of the Communist Party of the United States.

The intraparty fighting had been costly in terms of membership. Where the total number of Communists in all factions had been perhaps 35,000 in 1919, the number had dropped by 1925 to about 16,000, while the expulsions at the end of the decade reduced the total to a bare 7,000.[5] For the first time in its history, however, the Party, though diminished, was at last united and obedient to one discipline. Meanwhile, in October, 1927, Party headquarters and the office of *The Communist*, the Party's monthly "Magazine of the Theory and Practice of Marxism-Leninism," had been moved from inland Chicago to seaboard New York. The move indicated a symbolic as well as actual shift in polarization. Native radicalism, such as it had been, was in eclipse. The view now was not outward on the heartland of America, but eastward to the land of the Soviets.

The fact must be emphasized. Whatever has been the *exact* nature of the relationship between the American Communist Party and what is loosely called "Moscow," it can readily be observed that the American organization has never long deviated knowingly from Comintern (or Cominform) policy. When, for example, the First Congress of the Communist International, meeting in March, 1919, proclaimed immediate world revolution, the Communist underground in the United States, declaring that a revolutionary situation existed here, called for a workers' uprising. In line with the more conciliatory policy enunciated at the Third Congress of the Comintern in the summer of 1921 — Lenin was at that time initiating his New Economic Policy — the American Communists formed the legal Workers' Party and soon dissolved their underground organization. The Sixth Comintern Congress in July–August of 1928 reverted to a technique of noncoöperation with capitalist countries and of world-wide "revolutionary extremism" in defense of the Soviet Union. The ensuing year in the United States brought the expulsion of the Lovestoneites and the initiation of an aggressively anticapitalist program. Likewise in 1929, Foster's Trade Union Educational League, which had been unsuccesfully attempting to "coöperate" with the American Federation of Labor, changed its name to the Trade Union Unity League and began to build rival unions. This correspondence of policies is important, for only by recognizing that the American Communist Party faithfully followed the policy of the Comintern can one understand fully the course of the radical novel after the lean years of the 1920's.

II

The reasons why so little radical fiction was produced in the postwar decade are not in themselves simple, though their sum is obviously so: the immediate conditions for such writing did not exist. Certainly there was subject matter enough, for not all layers of American society were invited to what Scott Fitzgerald was later to call "the gaudiest spree in history"; but the orientation of both authors and audiences had changed. Every literary history of the twenties now dutifully, and quite properly, records the shattering impact made on unprepared sensibilities by a bloody war and by a peace that did not keep to promises. Such an impact might have helped to drive many young writers toward radicalism had there been, as there clearly was not, a powerful Left or even a militant labor movement to pull them into its wake. On the contrary, the far superior attractive force was American business itself, which had profited by the war and, as the twenties advanced, seemed to be establishing a "permanent plateau of prosperity." In this frustrating situation the choice for most writers, whether potentially radical or not, lay between living with disillusionment or surrendering to circumstance: with T. S. Eliot they could look out upon their world as a waste land, with H. L. Mencken they could regard it as a zoo, or with any writer for *The Saturday Evening Post* they could accept it as an enormous stock market.

Three novels by three "tired radicals" are illuminating here, though the first is perhaps a special case. Dorothy Day, who in the thirties was to become cofounder of the Catholic Worker Movement, published her chatty autobiographical novel, *The Eleventh Virgin*, in 1924, midway in her progress, as she was to put it, from Union Square to Rome. A lower-middle-class Chicago girl awakened to an emotional radicalism in part by *The Jungle* and Jack London's books, she had joined the Socialist Party in 1914 when only sixteen, had subsequently worked in New York on the Socialist *Call* — where "Everyone at the city desk was writing a play or a book" — and had assisted Floyd Dell on *The Masses* for the last six months of its existence. *The Eleventh Virgin*, episodic and jerkily organized, indicates that its author had responded chiefly to the exciting color of life as a Bohemian radical; *The Masses* is accordingly renamed *The Flame*, while the most memorable portrait in the book is of Dell ("Hugh Brace") in the days when he appeared the quintessence of Greenwich Village. It is perhaps revelatory of the author's own gradual dissociation from the radical movement after the war that in her novel, which otherwise closely follows the personal events indicated by her actual autobiography, *The Long Loneliness* (1952), she does not let her heroine actually join any organized left-wing group, but merely has her get excited over them all simultaneously. The excitement, however, does not hold out after *The Flame* is extinguished by Government action, for the heroine works as a probationer nurse in a New York hospital during the last months of the war and then demonstrates her emancipated womanhood by entering upon an intense but impermanent free-love relationship that deflects her completely from radicalism. As the book concludes, the heroine states the unexpected lesson of her life: women really want their new freedom, not in order to transform society, but rather to accomplish an old purpose, to gain a man, a marriage, and motherhood. Although Miss Day later renewed her own radicalism, her novel is an example of how "Back to Normalcy" was operating in the sphere of the emotions.

A more profound though no less awkward book is A. J. Barr's *Let Tomorrow Come*, which did not appear until the last year of the decade. This volume is a novel only in the widest sense, being more precisely a loosely related series of impressionistic sketches, often horrifying in content but compassionate in tone, of life in, first, a jail and then a "Bighouse," or penitentiary. Although the inmates and the unnatural pressures on them are seen through the eyes of a "federal" prisoner — apparently the writer had been an I.W.W. member — the viewpoint is curiously apolitical. For all his sensitiveness the author reveals the nightmare passivity of one who can observe but no longer act, whether he describes in his oblique, imagistic prose a prisoner so crazed at the approach of each long night that he can only moan constantly, "Sundown — let tomorrow come," or a banker so overwhelmed by shame at his conviction for embezzlement that both body and personality slowly collapse into shapelessness, or a young social rebel who harangues his cellmates as though from a corner soapbox until an uncomprehending tough knocks him down with a blow on the mouth. The short concluding section of the book gives the clue to this passivity. An interior monologue subtitled, "You're Away from All That Now," this section indicates that the author has been released and has found employment as a newspaperman. He has only two wants now — to keep his job and to remember as little as possible of prison experience. The book, then, is an act of psychological catharsis, an attempt to exorcise even his bad dreams; and in sweeping away the past he has swept away also any desire toward that radicalism which brought upon him the personality-crippling imprisonment.

The blocking of the will to write radical fiction is most clearly revealed by the career of Clement Wood, which in its essential aspects typifies that of many young men who might otherwise have become left-wing novelists. Born in Birmingham, Alabama, in 1888 of a well-to-do family, Wood went to the state university and the Yale Law School. When he returned to Birmingham in 1911, he became a Socialist and took on law cases with equal impetuousness, served briefly as magistrate of the Central Recorder's Court until he was removed for "lack of the judicial temperament," came out second in a mayoralty campaign, and departed for New York to become a writer, while continuing Socialist agitation as secretary to Upton Sinclair. After publishing two volumes of poetry, he brought out in 1920 the semiautobigraphical *Mountain*, a novel that is of more documentary than literary value.

Pelham Judson, the hero of the story, is the son of a rising real-estate and mine owner who controls the iron ore mountain on the outskirts of Adamsville (Birmingham). Pelham goes to the Sheffield School at Yale, where he studies mining engineering and exhibits class loyalty by acting as a scab in a local street-car strike. Back home in Adamsville, he helps his father exploit the mine and eventually meets a young social worker, a New Woman named Jane Lauderdale, who introduces him to Socialism. His conversion is so thorough — H. G. Wells's *A Modern Utopia* completes what Jane has begun — that when a mine strike breaks out, he sides with the workers against his father. During the course of the hard-fought strike, he runs for the office of sheriff on the Socialist ticket, but is defeated, whereupon he and Jane are married and go off on a honeymoon. Scenes of the melodramatic violence that brings the strike to a head now become interspersed with others showing Pelham's dissatisfaction over home life and his postmarital philandering. The climax of the strike and the book is a raid on the workers' tent village by deputies and by troops of the National Guard. When the chief labor organizer is killed by a Negro who has been expelled from the union as a spy, the strikers' resistance collapses. With remarkably little soul-searching for one who is described as having accepted the official Socialist position on the European conflict, Pelham departs for Washington to take up wartime duties with the Federal Mining Commission after being reconciled with Jane. The final words of the reunited pair form a lofty duet on the necessity of building a New World in the hearts of men; yet, while this interchange cannot be read otherwise than as a straight-forward statement of Wood's own hopefulness, the last scene of the book, as if escaping from its author's conscious control, returns to Adamsville for one more glimpse of Pelham's father, who has at last reached his highest ambition for wealth and political influence. The power of the iron mountain has passed to him rather than to the workers, nor can any New World be built in such a heart.

Judging by what one can gather of Wood's own life and opinions from the bumptious Foreword to *The Glory Road*, his "auto-biography in verse," he was apparently drifting away from Social-ism even while writing *Mountain*, and in partial explanation of the novel's ending it should be noted that during World War I he became a Quaker. Besides the contradictory conclusion, however, yet another structural flaw in the book suggests that his creative imagination may have been impaired by the limitations on his radicalism. Since Wood evidently was a "Jim Crow" Socialist, his Negro characters, except for one, are of the Uncle Remus variety. The curious exception is the man who becomes a labor spy. Al-though he is introduced in the character of a Negro proletarian hero, a prototype of similar figures in the fiction of the thirties, the author arbitrarily sacrifices him to plot mechanics. When he next appears, he is depicted as a shiftless ne'er-do-well. It is a minor but revealing point, too, that *Mountain* contains one of the very few puns on Marxist ideology made in radical fiction in the author's own person. When Pelham and Jane, ignoring the fact that the strike still goes on, leave Adamsville by train for their honeymoon, the engine is described as commanding the wheels to "take up their proletarian revolutions." That this gratuitous, and pointless, play on words follows only three pages after grim references to the course of the strike indicates that Wood, obviously a volatile person, lacked not only the judicial temperament, but the revolu-tionary as well. Indeed, he very soon forsook the Socialist cause and wrote no more novels based on radical experience, turning his rather gaudy talents instead to detective stories, historical romances, verse, or anything else for which a free-lance writer could expect payment. Like many other aging young radicals, he forewent revolution in favor of his daily bread, and became a casualty of prosperity.

In observing some of the effects of the war and its aftermath, however, it should not be forgotten that the literature of the twenties, taken as a whole, is permeated with a sense of antagonism toward contemporary society, particularly as that society manifested qualities considered to be "bourgeois." True, most of the creators of this literature did not use the term "bourgeois" in its specifically Marxian sense, but loosely, as a synonym for "Philistine," one whose money-grubbing smugness has made him impervious to the demands of art. True also, their fierce opposition was usually directed against the surface manifestations of an acquisitive society — its coarseness, its stupidity, its obvious spiritual drought — rather than against its basis in economic injustice. Again, the antonym of "bourgeois" was not "worker," but "artist," and the remedy that these writers offered was less frequently to do battle than to make individual escape to Greenwich Village, Paris, or a Land of Poictesme — to the Left Bank and not the Left Wing. Nevertheless, with an astonishing unanimity postwar writers of any consequence opposed the values of what they conceived to be the dominant class in their society. This phenomenon was later to be of importance.

There was even considerable exploration of the class structure of America and of class conflict, although at the level of pragmatic observation rather than of politically radical analysis. Perhaps Sinclair Lewis should be disqualified here as an ex-Socialist, but it is significant that his George F. Babbitt gets into really serious difficulty in Zenith only when he sides with striking labor against the business community.[6] Theodore Dreiser, not yet within the Communist orbit, had turned his ponderous attention from financiers, titans, and geniuses, the superior individuals at war with society, to the fate of the very average lower-middle-class boy, Clyde Griffiths, who is goaded on by the American Dream — once independence and self-improvement, now become simply social and financial success — only to be defeated by the American reality of class stratification. When Clyde brings about the death of Roberta, a farm girl turned mill worker, in an effort to rise into the owning class by marrying the wealthy Sondra, he is trapped by a legal process to which the author clearly gives overtones of class justice.[7] Even Scott Fitzgerald, the golden boy, stated a theory of the leisure class in *The Great Gatsby*, while illustrating through Gatsby's own career the degradation of the American Dream into the American success story. His attack, moral rather than economic and qualified by his attraction toward the object of his disgust, still is destructive. Because of their wealth, the very rich have the means for living graceful lives, but they are a decadent class because they lack individual and social responsibility. Disintegration and disaster hang over their ornate lives as over the Rome of Petronius Arbiter; as Rome fell, so shall their grandeur perish.

The writers of the twenties were not the "irresponsibles" that, at the beginning of another world war, they were said to have been by one of their number, who perhaps had overlooked the fact that to describe one's experience as truly as possible is the real responsibility of any serious artist. If they rather enjoyed viewing themselves as a "Lost Generation," they as frequently felt that, like the story of the Indian in the woods, what was lost was actually the camp rather than the hunter, the society rather than the writer. It is emphasis that counts in a paradox. They themselves were not lost; they simply did not know where to go. One possible direction, however, that toward the political Left, was for most of them temporarily eliminated.

III

Contrary to what might be expected from the previous discussion, the radical novel did not die out in the twenties, but it barely kept alive. Where half a hundred such volumes filled the years between 1900 and 1919, the ten scattered through the postwar decade have an isolated appearance in the literary scene. One picks his way from book to book as though following a poorly marked trail, or no trail at all, for the only obvious continuity is given by the lonely but indefatigable figure of Upton Sinclair. To these years belong, besides two fanciful tales, his grimly ironic *100%: The Story of a Patriot* and his two best novels after *The Jungle. Oil!* is memorable for its introductory scenes of a boy's automobile ride with his father across the mountains of Southern California, perhaps the best descriptive passage Sinclair ever achieved, and it is of interest as prefiguring, in the character of Bunny Ross, the Lanny Budd of the later series; while *Boston* is a detailed and highly dependable account of a trial that was soon to exert tremendous influence on American intellectuals. Aside from Sinclair's fiction, however, only four other novels, each by a different author, continued anything like a radical tradition: Elias Tobenkin's *The Road* (1922), Samuel Ornitz's anonymously published *Haunch Paunch and Jowl* (1923), Max Eastman's *Venture* (1927), and M. H. Hedges' *Dan Minturn* (1927).

With the exception of the first, all of these novels share in the liveliness, the joyful response to the world of the senses, the communicated excitement over mere existence which too rarely appear in the prewar radical fiction and which mark so much writing of any kind in the 1920's, although none of them achieves the intensely finished art which in the postwar decade so many writers struggled to produce. *The Road* alone makes dull reading; but it too at least *reflects* excitement over new attitudes and new ideas, and it is the only one of the four which makes any use of the most obvious subject matter of all — life in the newly-created Soviet Union.

Like his first novel *Witte Arrives*, Tobenkin's second, *House of Conrad* (1918), had dealt with the Americanization of immigrants, though it ploddingly recounted the progression of three generations of Conrads away from, not toward, organized Socialism. *The Road* returns in form to the conversion novel and even employs an epigraph, as is not uncommon among the prewar Socialist novels, from Walt Whitman. In a self-conscious determination to sound contemporary, however, Tobenkin opens his books with the thoughts of a young girl, Hilda Thorson, who has just given birth in a New York hospital to an illegitimate son and who resolves to keep the child with her in an unsupported struggle for existence. Certainly one of the themes of the novel, the interrelation between economic revolution and the full emancipation of women from all the bonds of bourgeois convention, is of the 1920's in the extremity to which it is pushed; a free-love relationship between two European radicals is held up for praise, while Hilda herself ultimately rejects an offer of marriage by her well-to-do lover on the grounds that present law and society unjustly restrict women's right to motherhood and that her own independence is sufficient to warrant that her son proudly bear her own last name. Her independence has been established by self-support as waitress and sweatshop laborer. After being converted to Socialism by a woman friend, who dies in yet another version of the Triangle Fire, she becomes a social worker and then devotes herself to the fight waged by a semi-Wobbly friend, Frank Hillstrom, against the copper bosses of Vulcan City (Bisbee?), Arizona.

Still intent on contemporaneousness, Tobenkin kills off Hilda's child with influenza and brings her back to a war-mad New York where she and Hillstrom, still determined pacifists, join the Red Cross in order to get to Europe. In the Epilogue Hillstrom has already entered the Soviet Union, is managing a great locomotive repair works on Stakhanovite principles, and is eagerly awaiting Hilda's arrival. Another such ending was not to appear until the next decade.

Tobenkin's faithfulness to current social history even leads him to include a Greenwich Village party, a sober one to be sure, where gather young people interested in a mixture of art, social uplift, and radical politics; yet the book is dated in technique despite the liberal use of three dots in the passages reproducing the characters' thoughts. *Haunch Paunch and Jowl*, on the other hand, while concerned with life in New York's East Side from the 1880's to the early 1910's, is far more of the twenties in spirit because of its unconventional form and its enveloping irony. Subtitled "An Anonymous Autobiography," it makes a destructive foray against capitalist society by purporting to be the revelations of one Meyer Hirsch in his rise from poverty-twisted East Sider and brains of a boy's gang to shyster lawyer, crooked politician, and corrupt judge. Quite probably Ornitz had found the inspiration for his narrative device in Abraham Cahan's *The Rise of David Levinsky*, published only six years before, but the more serious David has little of the gusto with which Meyer describes both the dirty underparts of "The System" and the richly human life of the East Side.

Meyer's dead-pan revelation of his own rascality — it was he, he says, who invented the racket of "protection money" and first employed gangsters in strike conflicts — is reinforced by his account of the career of Uncle Philip, ex-Talmud scholar, who, resolving to be top dog in the heap, decides that the road to wealth leads over the backs of the workers, builds through sweatshops a dominant place in the garment industry, and climbs high in moneyed society. But out of the Ghetto's welter come both ward heeler and settlement worker, capitalist and Socialist, cynic and idealist, and even the unscrupulous Meyer admits to his lyric moments. Among the several minor figures standing in opposition to the ironic defence of the American success story is Avrum Toledo, a Spanish Jew, who goes from job to job across the country in order to educate migratory workers toward one big union. By the end of the book, Uncle Philip has died of cancer, induced by his concentration on business success, while the grotesqueness of capitalism appears concentrated in a Meyer grown so monstrously fat that the radical press lampoons him as "Haunch Paunch and Jowl." His political career ended by a private scandal, he himself rests secure in his appropriately titled position as Judge of the Superior Criminal Court; nevertheless he admits that the Socialists have developed real political power on the East Side, where is growing up a new generation devoted to art, science, and a more idealistic politics. As a final ironic comment on those things to which capitalism is devoted, Meyer waddles out of the book toward another rich meal.

Just as much as *Haunch Paunch and Jowl*, Max Eastman's *Venture* has the verbal bounce so characteristic of the twenties, but the objects of Eastman's enthusiasm must have seemed, even in 1927, those of a past and more golden age. Set like the two preceding novels chiefly in New York, *Venture* details the development of a fresh, eager young man from innocence to experience via Greenwich Village Bohemianism and the radicalism of the I.W.W. Jo Hancock, whose prototype is clearly John Reed, comes from college to the Village in the early 1910's, supports himself as a "portrait poet" and is successful in love among the gifted and the wealthy. Like the central figures of "Jig" Cook's *The Chasm* and

Ernest Poole's *The Harbor*, however, Jo soon finds himself caught between antithetic ideologies. Much impressed by the young Nietzschean business genius, George Forbes, he has started to work out a scheme to distribute freshly roasted coffee with the morning milk, a scheme which in actual life had been the creation of Eugene Boissevain, the future husband of Edna Millay. But the Wobbly-led silk strike of 1913 breaks out in Paterson, New Jersey, Jo goes over from the Village to see the excitement, is drawn into the struggle as John Reed was, and falls in love with Vera Smirnov, the Russian-born "Sweetheart of the I.W.W."

For all Eastman's sophistication, the story from this point onward develops as adventuresome a plot as that of, say, an Upton Sinclair novel. Inevitably Jo must choose sides. He does so by giving up his chance to save the coffee scheme and by telling Forbes, in a final face-to-face clash of ideologies, that he has declared allegiance to the revolutionary working class instead of to a business elite in a hierarchical society. Eastman himself had admired the Wobblies in the day of their hope, but, after a brief membership in the Communist Party early in the 1920's, he was already drifting away from organized radicalism. Possibly Jo's hero-worship of Haywood and Tresca is a literary substitute for his author's continued admiration for Trotsky, exponent of the permanent revolution. At any rate, *Venture's* declaration for the cause of the I.W.W. as though the organization were not in fact almost dead makes the novel seem to have been published ten years after its proper time.

Unlike the other three novels, Hedges' *Dan Minturn* is set in Minneapolis–St. Paul, which had been for years a sort of staging area for Wobblies moving out to the great harvest circle of the Plains and the Northwest, and, though the others are all concerned with American radicals, the very geography of this book helps it to express more clearly than they the spirit of native radicalism. Equally to the point is the fact that the novel, like the rank-and-file Wobblies themselves, is not very explicit in its brand of ideology. Furthermore, though it belongs to an unusual form in American radical fiction, the political novel, and though it deals with a classic type in all revolutionary movements, the young rebel who sells out to the system which he once had fought, occasional reference to it by other writers of the late twenties suggest that the book had fixed for them, in its minor way, a definitive image of the fate of American radicals under the Boom.

When the book opens, Dan Minturn, whose room in a working-class home contains a portrait of Mazzini, some law texts, a few Marxist pamphlets, and novels by H. G. Wells and Upton Sinclair, has just been elected to the Minnesota House of Representatives with labor's backing and the canvassing help of plain, faithful Alice Miller. When the book ends, he is machine candidate for state governor and husband of beautiful, wealthy Agatha Morreson, niece of a political boss. In between occur the events which chart his political success and his personal degeneration. From their first meeting Agatha is repelled by Dan's lack of breeding, attracted by his force; he is repelled by her moneyed attitudes, attracted by her beauty. Dan slowly yields before both the "grace and mobility" of the rich and the allurement of established power until he sells out his constituency on a key vote that would have brought about public control of a private utility.

Like the young Dan Minturn, the novel is sometimes crude, but it is forceful. If Hedges descends to caricature in the presentation and even the naming of the machine politician "Senator Goodnite," he can also effectively suggest the whole process of Dan's corruption through his descriptions of the harsh cold of a Minnesota winter or the scrubbiness of a proletarian home on the one hand and on the other the warm luxury of a resort hotel or the smooth acceleration of an expensive automobile. The revolt in this book is not only against politics as a system of business power, but also against the seductive influence of a merely materialistic civilization. With a sure stroke the author places a concluding scene to balance unobtrusively against the description early in the novel of Dan's boyhood home. While staying at a fashionable hotel on Lake Superior's Northern Shore, Dan ponders over a letter received from Rakov, a former friend, who, bitter against America's machine civilization, has gone off to India to escape it. Clearly Rakov is not a mask for the author, but his letter does point the scene. Dan has succumbed to *things*. Sitting in the comfort of the hotel, the future governor tries to write to his friend, but gives up the attempt. He cannot bring himself to admit to Rakov what he knows to be true — that his apostasy from rebellion has raised him to the show of power and has utterly emptied him as an individual.

Thus *Dan Minturn* became an astringent comment on the Cinderella myth of America and, if only half-consciously, caught the frustrated revolt of a decade.

IV

The complex of causes which brought about an eclipse of the radical novel in the twenties had, of course, a similar effect on the media available for radical literary expression. Possibly the regular commercial firms which had published a majority of the Socialist novels grew cautious after the war about accepting other such manuscripts in the face of a hostile or indifferent market; most certainly the radical press in all its forms swiftly declined in size and influence until there was little apparatus left for the publishing of even nonliterary work. The Charles H. Kerr Company of Chicago, the Socialist coöperative that had been the leading radical publishing house before the war, now began retrenching, evidently for financial reasons, and confined itself mostly to reissuing Marxist classics. In 1924, International Publishers was founded by Alexander Trachtenberg, who was also, according to Benjamin Gitlow, representative of the Comintern Publishing Department in the United States. This became the one firm in the country issuing new Marxian books, but its list was chiefly nonliterary. Most of the left-wing magazines too had disappeared. *The Masses* had been a war casualty, and its successor possessed a less flamboyant personality. Still, *The Liberator* was a successor, and it deserves a brief discussion at this point since it is one link in a thin chain stretching across the twenties to another generation of radicals.

In February, 1918, while the editors of *The Masses* awaited trial, *The Liberator* made its appearance with a defiant statement of its devotion to the revolutionary cause and its hostility to "dogma and rigidity of mind." If this challenge was modified by Eastman's endorsement of the war aims proclaimed by both "the Russian people" and President Wilson, the new monthly nevertheless asserted itself by publishing a series of dispatches ("Red Russia") from John Reed, who was on his way back to the United

States to stand trial with the other *Masses* editors. Later issues printed reports on that trial and the trial of the Chicago I.W.W., on the Spartacist Revolt in Germany, the Béla Kun government in Hungary, and the deportation delirium in the United States.

Just as the politics of the new magazine, now owned solely by Max and Crystal Eastman, were on the whole still those of the extreme Left, so the literary policy remained unchanged from that of the coöperatively owned *Masses*. "THE LIBERATOR," Eastman wrote, "will be distinguished by a complete freedom in art and poetry and fiction and criticism." [8] Such freedom apparently meant a continued schizophrenia within the magazine, for the fiction and poetry which it printed tended, like that of its predecessor, to be more radical in form than in ideological content. During the summer of 1921, however, Eastman conducted a running fight with Van Wyck Brooks, then literary editor of *The Freeman*, over the relation of the writer and artist to the Communist Party, a fight in which Eastman argued simultaneously for intellectual guidance of the creative artist by the Party and yet his complete freedom from its official control. In its way, then, *The Liberator* continued to serve as a meeting ground for political radicals and literary people. Many of those who had contributed to *The Masses* contributed to its successor, and new names appeared, from John Dos Passos and William Gropper to William Ellery Leonard and the Bohemian Maxwell Bodenheim. The magazine's influence among intellectuals is suggested by the fact that for some years it attained a circulation of 50,000 copies.

The Liberator made yet another contribution to literary history: in the issue for February, 1921, it published Michael Gold's dithyrambic article, "Towards Proletarian Art," the first attempt in America to formulate a definition for what was to become the most important critical term among radical literary groups of the early thirties — "proletarian literature." * Gold, originally named

---

* In Section I of Chapter Seven appears a discussion of the various meanings assigned to the adjective "proletarian" as used specifically in relation to the radical novel, but a brief history of the word in left-wing literary criticism is relevant at this point. Attempting to find historical sanction for the equation of "proletarian" with "radical," Joseph Freeman, in his introduction to the anthology, *Proletarian Literature in the United States*, published in 1935, states that the term "proletarian poet," meaning a working-

Irwin Granich, had been born in 1894 into a Romanian immigrant family on New York's East Side. He went to work at the age of twelve and for a number of years held various unskilled and semi-skilled jobs in New York and Boston. While in Boston, he reported the Plymouth cordage strike in which one Bartolomeo Vanzetti took part. He joined the I.W.W. briefly, became a Socialist, worked as a copy reader on the New York *Call*, contributed sketches and stories to *The Masses*, and sided with the Communists in the Great Schism. When his article appeared, he had just been made a contributing editor of *The Liberator*.

"Towards Proletarian Art" is a rhapsodic credo which, in its characteristic combination of intense expression and diffuse idea, reflects its author's brooding emotionalism. (In this same issue of *The Liberator* appeared the not surprising announcement that Gold had suffered a nervous breakdown.) Beginning, "In blood, in tears, in chaos and wild, thunderous clouds of fear the old economic order is dying," it continues with several paragraphs of dark ecstasy over the beauty and horror of Life, and then reaches the writer's point. Up to the present artists generally have considered themselves aristocratic solitaries, aloof from mankind. Aloofness from "the people" has become contempt for them, with the result that artists are now incapable of faith and are spiritually sterile. The new artists of the people, on the other hand, will learn what Life is from their solidarity with the eternal, yea-saying masses. Since the

---

class poet, appeared by 1901 in *The Comrade*; but it is clear from an examination of the files of this literary periodical that the adjective was used in its restricted sense and that when contributors wished to speak of a *radical* work, they most frequently employed the adjective "Socialist." Apparently the use of "proletarian" to mean "radical" was slow to develop, for Floyd Dell still felt the need for further qualification when, in his review, "Three Leaders of Revolt," in *The Liberator* for July, 1919, he described Harold Lord Varney's *Revolt* as "the best example so far produced in America of a significant new kind of fiction — the Novel of Proletarian Revolt, which seems to me the destiny in which the political novel will find its fulfillment." Gold, whose literary attitudes had been formed in part by association with Dell, is thus the first to make "proletarian literature" synonymous with "radical literature." Although this definition was not widely adopted in literary circles until the early 1930's, it had some currency in the twenties. In an article, "Literary Politics," in *The New Republic* for February 1, 1928, Edmund Wilson, not yet a student of Marxism, could refer to a group of "social revolutionary" playwrights as "the apostles of proletarian literature."

Social Revolution is the religion of the masses and the fullest expression of Life, "The Revolution, in its secular manifestations of strike, boycott, mass-meeting, imprisonment, sacrifice, agitation, martyrdom, organization, is thereby worthy of the religious devotion of the artist." To fix in a creative work even the least moment of such a manifestation expresses Life more deeply and permanently than to compose out of "some transient personal mood." The prophet of the new art has been Walt Whitman, for despite the fact that he had been deceived by his faith in merely political democracy, he had drawn his strength from the masses.

But now, at last, the masses of America have awakened, through the revolutionary movement, to their souls. Now, at last, are they prepared to put forth those huge-hewn poets, those striding, out-door philosophers and horny-handed creators of whom he prophesied. Now are they fully aware that America is theirs. Now they can sing it. Now their brain and heart, embodied in the revolutionary element among them, are aroused, and they can relieve Walt, and follow him in the massive labors of the earth-built proletarian culture.

The method of erecting this proletarian culture must be the revolutionary method — from the deepest depths upward.[9]

Ten years later Gold was to admit that his had been "a rather mystic and intuitive approach." "Towards Proletarian Art" called for an identification of the artist with the workers in the class struggle and listed certain possible subjects for creative activity; beyond these pronouncements it pointed nowhere in particular. *The Liberator's* other contribution to a discussion of the writer's relation to revolution was less rhetorical, but no more helpful as a guide. Floyd Dell's series of articles entitled "Literature and the Machine Age" (published in book form in 1926 as *Intellectual Vagabondage: An Apology for the Intelligentsia*) is, as he himself later wrote, "a kind of Marxian essay in literary criticism [and] the first attempt in America to apply a particular principle of historical criticism to any wide range of literary productions."[10] This "Spiritual Autobiography" is a description of the literary and social influences which had produced in his time, he believed, a generation of intellectual vagabonds, a deracinate group pushed to the boundaries of society by its inability to find a place in or come to terms with a machine civilization. "The literature of the early twentieth century, so far as it influenced us, did so chiefly by an unconsciously adroit emphasis upon the incidental beauty of the essentially homeless and childless and migratory life to which capitalism had largely condemned us." [11] Nor, in the concluding chapter of *Intellectual Vagabondage* (not contained in the serial publication), does Dell see much probability that his generation of the intelligentsia will polarize around the doctrines of political revolution; for, he insists, the intellectuals are still in revolt against the imposition of order on society whether by Bolsheviks abroad or business men at home. *Intellectual Vagabondage* ends with an elegy for Dell's generation — he was thirty-nine when the book appeared — and with the expressed hope that the younger intellectuals, by recognizing the sober possibilities and promise of the Russian Revolution, will live not only more joyously, but more responsibly as well.

Dell had earlier, in 1921, resigned his editorship, although his name still was listed on *The Liberator's* masthead, in order to devote himself to a literary career, which was soon to take him out of active participation in the radical movement. In his excellent first novel, *Moon-Calf* (1920), he had drawn an autobiographical character sketch of a very young young man who happens, as part only of his intellectual development, to join the Socialist Party. It was not a radical novel at all, in the usual sense, but a shrewd psychological study of an intellectual vagabond. His later novels were likewise psychological studies, for he had become deeply interested in Freudian theories. Although he avowed a continued support of the Russian experiment, he more and more detached himself from immediate political situations until he finally became a perpetually convenient target for attack as a deserter.

John Reed, who had been an editor of *The Masses*, had resigned from the staff of *The Liberator* as far back as 1918 because of its conciliatory position toward the war. Strictly as a literary man, Reed has no place in this volume; for neither his poetry nor his short fiction — he of course wrote no novels — can be called politically radical; indeed, his best work is to be found in the nonfictional books where he brought reporting almost to an art form, in *Insurgent Mexico*, *The War in Eastern Europe*, and the classic *Ten Days That Shook the World*. Unable to reconcile the occupations of poet and revolutionist, he resolved the conflict by pouring his immense energy into propagandizing the Russian Revolution, and soon lay dead near the Kremlin wall.

Particularly during the thirties there has been much sterile dispute over the question whether, had John Reed lived longer, he would have repudiated Communism, or at least the Russian variety; the point of course is that he did not live longer. The legend of John Reed, however, did live, and within only a few years after his death this legend had become fixed. Standing for the prototype of the adventurous young American intellectual who refused to be simply a vagabond, who gave up all his middle-class advantages for solidarity with the working class, and who even sacrificed his life to the Revolution, Reed became one of the chief ideographs employed by the Communist Party to combat the picture in the American mind of the bomb-throwing Bolshevik. References to Reed's career occurred frequently in the few left-wing periodicals of the twenties, a full-scale biography appeared in 1936, and when groups of young radical writers began to band together in New York City and elsewhere during the early thirties, these organizations called themselves John Reed Clubs. As far as his influence on the literature of the Left goes, Reed's death was his greatest achievement.

The generation of Eastman and Dell and Reed was passing. Younger men, Michael Gold and Joseph Freeman,[12] were taking over the literary duties on *The Liberator*, which circumstances were making of less and less importance. When Eastman left the magazine in April, 1923, to go to the Soviet Union, Robert Minor, cartoonist turned Communist organizer, assumed the editorship. The associate editors were divided into the categories of "Political" and "Art," the "Political" editors including the leaders of the new Workers' Party. The magazine was now officially a Communist organ, and during the last year of its existence its contents showed a steadily decreasing concern with art in any form. The final issue of *The Liberator* appeared in October, 1924, with the announcement that it was combining with *The Labor Herald* and *Soviet Russia Pictorial* to form *The Workers Monthly*, the "Official Organ of the Workers Party of America," under the editorship of Earl Browder. An era had ended.

The gap left by the death of *The Liberator* was only partially filled by *The Modern Quarterly*, the first number of which, under the editorship of V. F. Calverton, appeared in March, 1923.[13] During the late twenties and the thirties this periodical was to become identified with the "Trotskyists" and certain non-Party Marxists, but until 1928 the literary Communists welcomed its support despite its tendency to combine psychoanalysis with Marxism. *The Modern Quarterly*, however, was almost entirely concerned with literary criticism and socioeconomic analysis; in fact its existence indicates that there were in the twenties more critics to invoke the need for radical novels, and other literary forms, than there were novelists to write them. Typical of Calverton's approach was an essay, "Proletarian Art," one of a series published in 1924 and collected a year later into *The Newer Spirit: A Sociological Criticism of Literature*.[14] Here he declares that the future lies with "proletarian literature," a literature which will be undecoratedly realistic in form, comprehensive of all experience in content, and permeated with the sense of the collective as opposed to the individual. The vagueness of Calverton's definition is shown by his inclusion of Frank Norris, Stephen Crane, and David Graham Phillips as "continuators" of a trend which he traced back to Whitman.

Despite the optimism of *The Newer Spirit*, only a year later Calverton was sadly asking in his magazine, "Where are our literary radicals of today?" Almost the only relief he could point to in the bleak contemporary scene, and that a much qualified exception, was *The New Masses*. When *The Liberator* had gone under, there had no longer been any magazine available to the creative writer who, even during the triumphal days of American business, might wish to see literature and revolution at least associated if not fused. *The New Masses* was the somewhat imperfect answer to that need. After more than a year of discussion and argument among its founders, the first number appeared in May, 1926, under the editorship of Egmont Arens, Joseph Freeman, Hugo Gellert, Michael Gold, James Rorty, and John Sloan. At the beginning this magazine, unlike the more definitely committed *Masses* and *Liberator*, was intended as the organ of a "popular front" of liberals and radicals, and the list of contributing editors contained the names of individuals ranged from the lightest to the deepest red in political belief.[15]

For the first two years of its existence, however, *The New Masses*, much like its predecessors, continued to combine radical political comment with literature that, as a rule, had no direct radical purpose. The initial issue of May, 1926, may be taken as typical. In it appeared Robinson Jeffer's passionately brutal "Apology for Bad Dreams" as well as a sympathetic article by Mary Heaton Vorse, a skilled labor reporter, on the textile strike currently being fought out in Passaic, New Jersey, the first big strike of the twenties to be led entirely by Communists. (The second number of the new magazine contained a collection of reports by some of the three hundred New York intellectuals of liberal or radical belief who visited Passaic "to show their solidarity with the workers.") Likewise in the first issue were published a short story by William Carlos Williams, drawings by William Gropper, Adolph Dehn, and Wanda Gág, and, almost symbolically on opposite pages, poems by Witter Bynner and a young man named Whittaker Chambers. Mere iconoclasm stood side by side with radical protest: the artist I. Klein satirized William Jennings Bryan for his part in the Scopes Trial at Dayton, Tennessee; while Michael Gold impressionistically and Scott Nearing more soberly attacked the civilization of America and praised that of the Soviet Union, where, apparently, they were ordering things better.

Perhaps most significant of all from the standpoint of literary criticism was a dialogue by M. H. Hedges entitled "The War of the Cultures," in which a magazine editor favoring "the capricious cynicism" of the "modern school" is opposed by a writer who upholds serious art composed with a radical purpose. To save himself from emptiness, argues the writer, the artist must forsake his ivory attic in Greenwich Village and make contact with the masses, who are nearest to reality. The fact that a good part of the dialogue is concerned with "proletarian art" is evidence that by the midtwenties the term "proletarian," when used with reference to literature by left-wing writers, was taking on the meaning of "class-conscious radicalism." The way was being prepared for the radical novel of the thirties.

The search which *The New Masses* maintained for "proletarian literature," more often in article and book review than in actual

story or poem, had a notable characteristic: its almost complete
lack of knowledge about, or at least acknowledgment of, the tradition of prewar Socialist fiction which the present volume has already described. True, many of these novels had been brought out
in small editions by ephemeral presses and had small circulation
even in their day; yet except for occasional references to Sinclair
and London one would hardly learn from the critics and reviewers
of *The New Masses* that a sizable number of novelists with a conscious orientation toward Marxism had published books during the
century's first two decades. Doubtless the decline of the Socialist
Party as a political force and the fierce antagonism of the Communists toward non-Communist radicals helped the critics and reviewers to forget or overlook most of the native pioneers in the art of
which they wrote. Thus in "What There Isn't and Why Not" in the
issue of *The New Masses* for February, 1928, the young poet Robert
Wolf could ascribe the supposed lack of "proletarian literature" in
American literary history to two causes: first, the nonexistence of
a *contemporary* revolutionary situation in this country; and second,
the fact that out of the whole *Communist Party* membership,
which he sets optimistically at between ten and twenty thousand,
"less than 3,000 speak English."

. . . the same problem that has been hitherto the despair of the revolutionary organizer in America has prevented the growth of a proletarian literature. It has been quite simple — there was no one to write
it for, and so it didn't get written at all.[16]

Wolf's argument that radical literature is read only by radicals is a
highly dubious one, as a later chapter in this book will attempt to
show, but of far greater importance here is his underlying assumption that a concern for such literature originated in 1919 with the
birth of American Communism. It is indicative of a tendency to
repudiate the American past which characterized the Communist
Party until the second half of the 1930's.

    If writer and revolutionary remained imperfectly united in the
early *New Masses*, so did the uneasy popular front between the
liberal and the radical members of the executive board, who clashed
frequently on the question of the magazine's political orientation.
Early in 1927, for instance, after the liberals had voted to remove

Gold from the editorial staff, the radical faction managed to gather a sufficient number of proxies to reinstate him. Finally, in the following year, Eastman, now disillusioned with the Russian Experiment by his visit to the Soviet Union, resigned from the staff of contributing editors, Michael Gold became sole editor, and *The New Masses* began to be pulled more closely into the orbit of the Communist Party, particularly into that of the Foster-led "Stalinist" faction. According to Joseph Freeman, the men who had previously tried to remove Gold left the magazine for the advertising and publishing jobs that opened at the peak of the prosperity boom.

From the time of its reorganization until the Boom broke so catastrophically late in 1929, *The New Masses* went through a period of decline in size, income, and number of readers. Gold nevertheless continued his appeals to young writers to "Go Left" and find their materials in the experience of class-conscious workers. With a subsidy from the American Fund for Public Service, the so-called Garland Fund, the magazine managed to scrabble along financially. When the Crash of '29 did come, therefore, there was in existence on the American scene a literary publication which boasted, if somewhat as a pretender, of a long revolutionary pedigree, which gave an ever-increasing allegiance to the newly purged Communist Party, and which was self-consciously prepared to act its role as a catalytic agent for the combination of literature and revolution.

v

One more event must be recalled from these years, one involving the lives of a good shoemaker and a poor fish-peddler to whom justice was denied in Massachusetts. The Sacco-Vanzetti case probably stirred the world as did no other event between the end of World War I and the beginning of the Great Depression; and although it no longer lies at the surface of our consciousness, its impact still reverberates obscurely within the American social organism.

As early as the summer of 1921, when the two men were convicted in the Dedham trial, intellectuals were being drawn into the case; but it is nothing more than a widely held superstition, Louis Joughin points out in *The Legacy of Sacco and Vanzetti*, "that from the beginning a horde of poets, novelists, and miscellaneous writers were actively engaged in writing on behalf of the men." [17] John Dos Passos, "the first major American writer to be deeply concerned," did not enter the case until December of 1926, about nine months before the execution. Even in the following spring, when there was a tremendous surge of excitement — caused by Felix Frankfurter's summation of the evidence in the March issue of *The Atlantic Monthly*, the subsequent publication of his book, and the imposition of sentence upon the two Anarchists — the only other leading American writer actively to join the defense was Upon Sinclair.[18] Nevertheless, many writers had publicly committed themselves, and during the last two weeks they did somewhat more.

On August 8, 1927, the Sacco-Vanzetti Defense Committee sent out an appeal to the "leaders and rank and file of labor, letters, art, science, education and social reform" to participate in a peaceful demonstration in Boston on the tenth, the day originally set for the execution. During the twelve days of the reprieve, intellectuals all over the country were aroused. A number of writers — Dos Passos, Michael Gold, Ruth Hale, John Howard Lawson, Grace Lumpkin, Edna St. Vincent Millay, Dorothy Parker, Katherine Anne Porter, and Lola Ridge — went out on the picket line in Boston and were arrested for exercising their constitutional right of free assembly. On the tenth, ninety-three artists and writers signed an appeal to Governor Fuller for a reprieve; [19] while other literary figures joined the Citizens' National Committee for Sacco and Vanzetti, an emergency organization formed by Robert Morss Lovett, Glenn Frank, and David Starr Jordan, the purpose of which was to bring pressure upon the Federal Government to open the files of the Department of Justice for evidence bearing on the case. One of their appeals was a telegram to President Coolidge urging a stay of execution pending examination of the Department files. Among the signatures of various intellectuals appear the names of the following literary people: Fannie Hurst, Zona Gale, Upton Sinclair, Paxton Hibben, Horace Liveright, Vida Scudder, Ida M. Tarbell, Ralph Cheney, Lucia Trent, John Dos Passos, John Howard Lawson, Joseph Wood Krutch, Carl Van Doren, Genevieve Taggard, Katherine Anne Porter, Floyd Dell, F. E. Faragoh, Margaret Marshall, Egmont Arens, Dudley Digges.[20] The roll call of American citizens becomes inspiring, but names could not save the two victims. There was no second reprieve.

So many intellectuals had become so bitterly involved in this American tragedy that the news of the execution reached them with an overwhelming shock. Whatever causes lay behind the failure of justice — radical, liberal, and conservative intellectuals of course disagreed on this point — the fact of the failure had to be faced; and Robert Morss Lovett, in his scornful article "Liberalism and the Class War," burst out with a statement of the event and its consequences which no doubt voiced a widespread reaction.

It may seem at first sight a far cry from the great international conflict to the execution of two obscure Radicals, yet it is perhaps true that since the War nothing has happened to stir public feeling so intensely and unanimously throughout the world; and it is certainly true that no event since the War has so shaken the Liberal's belief in the working for equal justice of free institutions, in the application of intelligence to correct the short-comings of system, and in the possibilities of educating public opinion and making its control effective over the instruments of government. The Sacco-Vanzetti case resulted in a defeat for the three cardinal principles of Liberalism, and for every man and woman who holds them as articles of faith.

It is no longer possible to deny the existence of the Class War in the United States. Its opening may be dated from the decision of the Liberal administration, which took the country into the War, to sacrifice protestant groups to their economic oppressors. Sacco and Vanzetti were among the first victims; their long trial was the first battle. . . Now that the war is on and cannot be ignored, Liberals will be compelled to choose between the arrayed classes.[21]

Writers, the seismographs of social shock, recorded — and still record — the profound disturbance. In his discussion of the literature based on the event, Louis Joughin demonstrates that, while this poetry, fiction, and drama has by no means all been written by "extreme radicals," it "becomes particularly noteworthy that . . . the literary verdict is unanimously sympathetic to the executed men." The best literary uses of the case — if we except some of the more eloquent letters of Sacco and Vanzetti themselves — have been made by a Socialist and by one who wrote as an independent rebel; for in both Upton Sinclair's *Boston* and John Dos Passos's *The Big Money* the dignity of the event is matched by the author's passion and understanding. But the important point is that the whole intellectual community, of which writers are a part, was eventually dislocated by the shock, a shock with extreme repercussions. After the execution was over, writes Malcolm Cowley, people stopped talking about it.

Yet the effects of the Sacco-Vanzetti case continued to operate, in a subterranean style, and after a very few years they appeared once more on the surface.

It was during the second year of the depression that everyone began talking about a new phenomenon. The intelligentsia was "going left"; it was becoming friendly with the Communists; it was discussing the need for a new American revolution. All sorts of people tried to explain this development in all sorts of contradictory fashions, some of which were partly true. Almost nobody mentioned the obvious fact that, whatever else it might be, it was also a sequel to the Sacco-Vanzetti case, a return to united political action. This time, however, the intellectuals had learned that they were powerless by themselves and that they could not accomplish anything unless they made an alliance with the working class.[22]

Thus, in a manner already prophesied by Lovett, the event assisted markedly in the political polarizations of the thirties. Whether the Sacco-Vanzetti case was interpreted as a battle in the class war or, as Joughin himself more convincingly argues, an outstanding incident in "the continuing warfare between the forces of democratic and undemocratic action," one judgment began to seem inescapable for many sensitive Americans shortly after midnight on the morning of August 23rd, 1927:

America our nation has been beaten by strangers who have turned our language inside out who have taken the clean words our fathers spoke and made them slimy and foul

their hired men sit on the judge's bench they sit back with their feet on the table under the dome of the State House they are ignorant of our beliefs they have the dollars the guns the armed forces the power-plants

they have built the electricchair and hired the executioner to throw the switch

all right we are two nations [23]

Sacco and Vanzetti did not have to live out their lives talking on street corners to scorning men. Their deaths were their most compelling deeds; their agony was their triumph.

6.

CLASS WAR

Late in the year 1928, *The Modern Quarterly*, which the Communist Party was to assail in the next decade as a "Trotskyite organ," voiced for many radicals the frustration engendered by their defeats and failures during the twenties. In his editorial section entitled "The Pulse of Modernity: The American Scene," V. F. Calverton looked out despairingly on a wealthy nation and a political waste land.

Perhaps nothing so clearly reflects the superficiality of the American mind as present politics. In the presidential campaigns this year, this superficiality is tragically conspicuous. With the dominant parties there are no significant issues at stake, and with the minor parties what issues there are have been either weakened by compromise or obscured by an unfortunate, although courageous, denial and defiance of reality. Nowhere is there light or hope. The radical movements of Europe have little meaning or application on American soil. American radicals are isolated from the American scene.[1]

Yet ever since World War I, destructive economic forces had been at work everywhere, tunneling the foundations of the social structure. Even in the United States, which was now dazzled by the last speculative boom of the stock market, such phemonena in that "New Era" election year as the long-term stagnation of agriculture, the declines in construction and industrial production, the steady growth in unemployment, and the ballooning of credit, all were preparing the judgment days in October, 1929, when the prestige of the American business man began dropping as decisively, if not so suddenly, as the quoted price of stock in American Telephone and Telegraph. Then, almost by displacement, the prestige of the Left at last began to rise once more.

In the midst of a nearly universal depression, one more far-reaching than any which Marx had analyzed, the collapse of American capitalism was spectacular; for the decline in the industrial production of the United States surpassed that of the world as a whole and, in fact, that of any other country except, barely, defeated Germany. Where, from 1929 through 1932, production in the United Kingdom declined about 18 per cent, in France just under 30, and in the whole world (exclusive of the Soviet Union) just over 36, in Germany and the United States it catastrophically dropped almost 50 — 46.7 per cent for the former, 46.2 for the latter. The three years following the October crash were the most disastrous which this country's economy had ever seen.

National income dwindled from eighty-one billion dollars in 1929 to less than sixty-eight in 1930, then cascaded to fifty-three in 1931 and hit bottom in 1932 with forty-one. Correspondingly, the country's estimated wealth over this span shrank from three hundred and sixty-five billion to two hundred and thirty-nine, a loss representing diminished values in real property, capital and commodities. Much of the nation's physical plant, of course, rusted in idleness and disrepair. These three years took a toll of eighty-five thousand business failures with liabilities of four and a half billion dollars and the suspension of five thousand banks. Nine million savings accounts were wiped out, and wage losses upwards of twenty-six billion dollars sustained.[2]

To the average citizen of the United States, the Depression was not a set of statistics but an immediately personal matter of wage cuts, restricted family budgets, loss of job, business, or market for crops. It meant for him the forfeiting of luxuries, the paring of necessities; it meant intense concern, not simply over the operation postponed or the children's teeth allowed to decay, but over whether he and his family would actually have food to eat, a place to sleep, something to wear. As the economy slowed almost to a stop, human rust and erosion equaled that of machines and the land, the latter by a double curse now entering a cycle of drought.

Along with the rest of the middle class, the professional groups were badly hit, hundreds of thousands joining the great masses of unemployed workers, which at the bottom of the Depression in 1932–33 reached a total variously estimated at from thirteen to sixteen millions but certainly amounting to one quarter of the country's entire civilian labor force. The colleges and universities, their endowments and operating funds seriously reduced, retrenched sharply in many ways; nevertheless, student enrollments remained steady — perhaps a degree would get one a job — and many new teachers, doctors, lawyers, architects, scientists, and engineers were graduated, usually after financial struggles of their own, only to find that there were not even jobs available for the technically trained. The depreciation of human skills was one of the many great unmeasurable wastes of these years. Similarly the writers found that, whether they liked the fact or not, their livelihoods had been dependent on the business prosperity which they had fled, laughed at, or acquiesced to in the postwar decade. Although the circulation of magazines generally dropped only slightly during the early thirties, payments for articles and stories frequently became smaller; while the younger writers discovered that the repatriated expatriates, because they were already established in their fame, were taking up much of the available magazine space. Conditions were even worse for the writers of books. "The book trade, severest sufferer in the publishing field, saw its total production of new titles fall from nearly a quarter-billion copies in 1929 to slightly more than a hundred million in 1933. . ." [3] Books, after all, could be borrowed without charge from the public libraries, although these institutions too were cutting budgets drastically. The New York *Times* for February 10, 1933, announced that the New York Public Library would buy that year, not the normal number of 250,000 books, but only 50,000, most of these being replacement copies of already standard books.[4]

Thus, large numbers in those groups usually included by the term "the intellectuals," felt the full weight of the slump. The industrial worker, faced with frequent lay-offs and arbitrary discharges even in boom times, had always been more aware how precarious was the life led by the majority of people in a relatively uncontrolled capitalist society and was psychologically better prepared to meet periods of unemployment. The intellectuals, however, drawn for the most part from the various strata of the middle class, and therefore more susceptible, even when they consciously rejected it, to the myth of the American success story, were singularly ill-equipped for what now happened. As the Depression deepened through 1930 and 1931 into its darkest pit in 1932–33, the intellectuals thrashed desperately about to find firm ground in the encompassing quicksand of unemployment and deprivation. They did not turn at once — and of course a majority of them never did — to the far political Left. (The notion that the thirties can properly be called the Red Decade has been satisfactorily demolished recently by Granville Hicks's *Where We Came Out* [1954] and Murray Kempton's *Part of Our Time* [1955] — though the absurdity of the term as an all-inclusive description of the period should be obvious to anyone who cares to consider it for a moment.) Some, mostly literary academics, took temporary refuge in Humanism, which reached the status of an intellectual fad during 1930 and 1931, while others, chiefly engineers, were fascinated by the later craze of Howard Scott's Technocracy; perhaps most found satisfaction ultimately in the pragmatism of the New Deal. Nevertheless, significant numbers, in these years of the locust, did begin to examine the Communist position.

A gigantic fact helped to impel that new interest. In an economically disrupted world, one part, comprising a sixth of the world's area in fact, seemed markedly more coherent than the rest. While in the teeter-board American economy, industrial production dropped and unemployment headed for the sky, the Soviet Union was successfully completing its first Five-Year Plan and ever demanding more workers and technicians.[5] Statistics comprehensible even to a literary man seemed to be confirming Lincoln Steffens's famous pronouncement that he had seen the future and that it worked. Quite as palpably, the American present did not.

Many intellectuals, in their tormented search for answers to the malfunctioning of capitalism, began to investigate Marxism because of the Russian success at social engineering, but there were other reasons for their gravitation toward this body of doctrine. Marxism described the nature of the immediate capitalist crisis; it was an explanation, which, unlike those filling the newspapers and magazines over the signatures of industrialists and financiers, really could explain why unemployed men went hungry in New York while farmers burned wheat in Kansas. Marxism represented itself, furthermore, as a coherent, unitary explanation of all phenomena; it satisfied the intellectuals' desire for logical consistency and completeness. Marxism predicted a future classless society as the inevitable result of an inevitable historical process; hence it was a spiritual refuge, a rock of hope in the shifting waters of despair. Marxism emphasized that at present health, life, progress were in the hands of a particular economic class rather than in those of individuals; therefore it provided a sense of unity, of togetherness, for an intellectual who felt isolated and exposed in a chaotic society. There was, to be sure, a party dictatorship in the Soviet Union; but, as any Communist would elaborate, there was a class dictatorship in the United States, one which was utterly incapable of providing for a third of the nation and for another third could provide only inadequately. The true answer to the failure of capitalism seemed to reside in a Soviet America, and intellectuals began to look to the Communist Party, which presumably embodied the explanation, the refuge, the sense of unity, and the hope.

The new enthusiasm was reflected by certain manifestations in the publishing world. Between 1929 and 1936, three new editions of *Capital* appeared, two of them being in inexpensive series running to large issues — The Modern Library and Everyman's Library. In addition, Max Eastman, now a confirmed "renegade," edited for The Modern Library in 1932 an abbreviated version, while Hugo Gellert's *Karl Marx' 'Capital' in Lithographs* was published in 1934. One may speculate on how many of the new converts got beyond or through the first volume of Marx's monumental work; doubtless many of them acquired their knowledge of Marxist theory from the more available, and readable, *Communist Manifesto*, from the handbooks and commentaries on Marxism which began to appear in increasing numbers, from such works by Lenin as *State and Revolution*, from pamphlet and magazine article and conversation with more politically advanced friends. At any rate, some illuminating figures are available concerning the expansion of International Publishers, the Marxist publishing company, during the early part of the Depression. In 1935, *The New Masses* gleefully stated:

In five years time, from 1929 to 1934, its [International Publishers'] distribution increased from 50,000 to 600,000 pieces of literature annually. . . 80,000 copies of Stalin's *Foundations of Leninism* have been distributed in two months. An edition of 4,000 copies of [R.] Palme

Dutt's *Fascism and Social Revolution* has been exhausted in a few months and a new edition of 5,000 copies, with the price reduced to $1.55 is being issued. No wonder writers and intellectuals in general stream to the revolutionary movement where intellectual health is good, where alone a vigorous and alert public can be discovered.[6]

Meanwhile the Communist Party, U.S.A., began to feel that it had come into its own. Speaking in May, 1929, only a few months before the stock market crash, Stalin had addressed a statement to the American branch of the Party on the matter of expelling the Lovestoneites for their "exceptionalist" error that a revolutionary situation was not developing in the United States. Quite to the contrary, he had prophesied, a revolutionary crisis was imminent, and he had demanded that the American Communists be ready to assume leadership in the coming struggle for power. The Party hastened to carry out manifest destiny. In 1930, Earl Browder replaced Foster, under whose leadership the Communist Party, U.S.A., had been finally united, and in that year the Party's Seventh Convention examined at length the "major problem" before the American Communists: the necessity of developing "from a propaganda sect into a revolutionary mass Party of action . . . of extending and anchoring the base of the Party in the factories, shops and mines." [7] The American Communists continued to follow undeviatingly the "line" set by the Sixth Congress of the Communist International in 1928, the line of revolutionary activity in all countries in defense of the Soviet Union. In the United States, that meant implacable opposition to capitalism, not only to the rugged individualism extolled by the unhappy President Hoover, but also to the improvisations of President Roosevelt's New Deal when they began in the spring of 1933. It meant revolutionary militancy on the labor front. The policy of boring from within the American Federation of Labor was discarded, the name of the Trade Union Educational League was changed in 1929 to the Trade Union Unity League, and the latter, under the leadership of Foster, began a strenuous but not very successful attempt to organize rival unions, one of their chief targets being the Southern textile mills. This latter campaign, as will be seen, formed the background and provided the action for a whole group of radical novels.

Although it is impossible to estimate how many of the intellectuals joined the Communist Party under the impact of the economic slump, its membership in general grew steadily. At the Party's Eighth Convention in April, 1934, Browder announced a rapid increase from about 9,000 dues-paying members in 1931 to nearly 25,000 at the present, while a year later a total of 31,000 was being claimed. The Party accepted intellectuals into its ranks only after a considerable period of testing, and many of them were probably content to remain, in the exact sense of the abused term, "fellow travelers"; that is, they accepted Party policy but not Party discipline. Certainly a significant number of intellectuals did become Communists, but a much greater number simply revolved within the Party orbit.

Besides its claim of being the legatee of Marx and the revolutionary vanguard of the proletariat, the Communist Party had a more immediate attraction for the intellectuals. In the early years of the Depression, when President Hoover was attempting to meet an unlimited crisis with distinctly limited measures or bickering with an unfriendly Congress, the Communists were "doing something." While the unemployed sold apples or stood in breadlines or swarmed into Hoovervilles, waiting for Congress and the President to act, the Communists were organizing discontent into local demonstrations for relief or into hunger marches on Washington. One Communist writer, insisting on the direct literary results of politics, in fact dated the beginning of the upsurge of proletarian literature from the mass unemployment demonstrations which took place under the coördination of the Party in a number of American cities on March 6, 1930.[8] Any action was an improvement over ineffectiveness or lethargy in high places.

In addition to guiding the Unemployed Councils that sprang up, the Communists agitated on behalf of "class-war prisoners," such as Tom Mooney and the nine Negroes in the Scottsboro Case. The memory of Sacco and Vanzetti now reasserted itself within a context of class conflict, and those intellectuals who were turning to Marxism began to interpret cases of injustice and oppression, not as isolated errors, but as parts of a vast, brutal pattern. In order to channel protest in these cases, a group composed primarily of writers formed, in the spring of 1931, the National Committee for the Defense of Political Prisoners, with Theodore Dreiser as chairman, Lincoln Steffens as treasurer, and with such literary figures as John Dos Passos, Waldo Frank, Josephine Herbst, and Sherwood Anderson among the committee members. One of their first acts was an investigation of the violence in Harlan County, Kentucky, an account of which they published under the title of *Harlan Miners Speak: Report on Terrorism in the Kentucky Coal Fields* (1932). Writers were beginning to find that if they needed conflict to write about, all they needed to do was to open their eyes.

An important point may here be missed. The accusation by ex-Communists that the Party defended such social victims to further its own ends rather than to redress specific injustices can doubtless be substantiated, but one should not make the mistake of assuming that the leftward-moving intellectuals of the thirties were impelled by a similar cynicism. Rather they responded to a quite opposite motive — an intense idealistic indignation that such victimization could occur and was indeed occurring in American society. They had little sense of joining a conspiracy; they had a great sense of joining a crusade.[9] This fact is a partial explanation for the iron vein of anger which runs through the left-wing writing of the decade.

The leftward movement among writers became so pronounced that there was published in *The New Masses* for September, 1932, a symposium with the evangelical heading, "How I Came to Communism." Besides — of course — Michael Gold, contributors were Waldo Frank, Clifton Fadiman, Granville Hicks, Sherwood Anderson, and Edmund Wilson, men whose names gave this new development intellectual prestige. Wilson's confession of faith had already appeared in *The Nation* as "What I Believe," and despite the fact that his independence of mind soon led him away from the Communist Party as such, his example helped to interest writers in Marxist theory. An even more powerful and widespread influence toward radicalism in general was exerted by Lincoln Steffens's *Autobiography*, which was published in 1931. Although the final chapters presented Communism, Fascism, and Fordism as equally possible ways out of the liberal impasse, the book did document with thoroughly American evidence Steffens's argument that capitalism and political corruption were inevitably complementary, that business enterprise and "good government" were antithetical, that any solution must be revolutionary rather than reformative. The popularity of the *Autobiography* — and it was immensely popular — cannot be explained solely by the fact that Steffens seemed to have gone everywhere and known everyone; the sales of the book and the temper of the period actually interacted remarkably.

The radicalized intellectuals now wished to make public commitment. In October, 1932, at the peak of the presidential campaign, a group of fifty-two writers, painters, teachers, and other professional workers, who had already declared themselves for the Communist candidates, now organized the League of Professional Groups for Foster and Ford, and issued *Culture and the Crisis*, a pamphlet which excoriated all other parties, analyzed the effect of the Depression on the professions, and called on their fellow intellectuals to vote Communist in November.

Why should we as a class be humble? Practically everything that is orderly and sane and useful in America was made by two classes of Americans; our class, the class of brain workers, and the "lower classes", the muscle workers. Very well, we strike hands with our true comrades. We claim our own and we reject the disorder, the lunacy spawned by grabbers, advertisers, traders, speculators, salesmen, the much-adulated, immediately stupid and irresponsible "business men". We claim the right to live and to function. It is our business to think and we shall not permit business men to teach us our business. It is also, in the end, our business to act.

We have acted. As responsible intellectual workers we have aligned ourselves with the frankly revolutionary Communist Party, the party of the workers.[10]

Significantly, the percentage of writers among the individuals who signed the call was very high, and the literary historian will notice that the object of attack is not unfamiliar. It is George F. Babbitt, now become as much villain as fool. With weapons blessed in the name of Art, writers had fought in the twenties against a *bourgeoisie* conceived as a dominant group seeking to impose meretricious "business" values on the creative individual. Sophisticated as they may have been in aesthetic matters, most of these writers were as yet naïve in economics and politics; and it was easy for them to confound their vague, abusive use of the term "bourgeois" with the more descriptive use of it made by Marxism. They were, of course, assisted in this transference by the fact that Marx and his modern followers were themselves quite willing to utilize the emotional connotations of the word. So the writers found that they could fight with weapons blessed in the name of Politics against their old enemy, now conceived as a dominant class seeking to keep down the creative masses. From this new standpoint, Flaubert, who had counseled that hatred of the *bourgeoisie* was the beginning of virtue, was not contradicted by Marx, but transcended by him. Through the Marxist view of world history, individual hatred could be enlarged into class antagonism, victory by rebellion into victory by revolution. Communism answered both the writer's negative recoil from things as they were and his positive desire for things as they should be.

II

All such reasons for a leftward movement among American writers — the economic collapse, the example of the Soviet Union, the clarification and comfort offered by Marxism, the championing of the underdog by the Communists, the opportunity for a new angle of attack against the *bourgeoisie* — were exploited by elements of the Left itself which were attempting to meet and speed onward those writers coming in their direction. While the "proletarian novel," the name assigned by its practitioners to the radical novel of the thirties, can hardly be called the creation of the Communist Party or even of Communist literary critics, it is clear that the latter particularly made a deliberate, though not always successful, effort to plan and guide a whole literary "movement" in which the novel had a very large part. Certainly the immediate substratum of ideas for this new school of novelists was prepared by a conscious "apparatus," the two basic components of which were *The New Masses* and another institution known as the John Reed Clubs.

With an almost too appropriate historical irony, it was in October, 1929, that there gathered in the office of *The New Masses* a group of writers and artists, many of them contributors to that magazine, who formed themselves into an organization designed to "clarify the principles and purposes of revolutionary art and literature, to propagate them, to practise them." [11] Accepting as fact what was in reality only part of the legend, that John Reed had combined his poetry and his politics, they adopted Reed's name as symbolic of the group's purpose. Unlike a short-lived Proletarian Artists and Writers League created in 1926 by some of these same Americans, while in Moscow, for writers in the United States, the John Reed Club thrived for several years because of the more favorable environment of the early thirties and because of a more skillfully planned strategy, one which was closely coördinated with radical politics.

Both the John Reed Club, which soon had over fifty members, and *The New Masses* were represented at the Second World Conference of the International Union of Revolutionary Writers, held in Kharkov in the Ukraine from November 6 to November 15, 1930, and attended by delegates from twenty-two countries.[12] A report of the conference, which appeared in *The New Masses* for February, 1931, gives considerable information concerning the events and also enumerates the specific obligations imposed on the club and the magazine by resolution of the entire conference and accepted by the American delegates. Having listed an eight-point "political platform for America which must be accepted by the John Reed Club and *The New Masses* before they can be affiliated to the International Bureau" — the most important plank is adherence to the struggle to defend the Soviet Union — the report gives the "concrete Program of Action for the United States." Of the ten points included, the first and tenth are perhaps the most relevant.

1. The widening of the activity of the John Reed Club and the *New Masses* in two directions: a) extending the proletarian base of our movement by drawing in new proletarian elements; b) winning over of radicalized intellectuals.

10. The strengthening of the *New Masses* by the election of a cooperative editorial board (this had already been done) and the improvement of its contents by connecting it more organically with the struggles of the workingclass and making it in every respect the cultural organ of the class-conscious workers and revolutionary intellectuals of this country. . .[13]

Though some of the American delegates, and those of other countries, were given posts in the organizational structure of the International Union of Revolutionary Writers, control lay firmly in the hands of the Russians; for the I.U.R.W. was a literary counterpart of the Comintern. Henceforth the John Reed Club and *The New Masses* were pledged to work under the more than eagle eye of the Union and its official new publication, *Literature of the World Revolution*, the task of the latter being flatly designated as "not only to supply information about international literary problems, but also to guide the world revolutionary literary movement." [14]

The John Reed Club undertook very seriously its obligation to expand by encouraging the formation of similar clubs in other American cities, some having already sprung up spontaneously. These centers particularly attracted young writers, embittered by the disparity between what they had been taught to expect at school or college and the iron facts of blocked opportunity and unemployment, which afflicted youth more than any other segment of the nation's manpower. Clubs appeared in Chicago, Detroit, Philadelphia, Boston, Cleveland, and even Chapel Hill, North Carolina. By May, 1932, there were thirteen such groups, and in the following month, under the stimulus of a National Organizing Conference, six more came into existence. This conference, held in Chicago from May 29 to May 30, was attended by thirty-eight delegates representing a total membership of approximately 800 writers and artists. The delegates organized their clubs into a federation under the "general supervision and direction" of an eleven-man National Executive Board with a national office in New York City,[15] and membership in the clubs was declared open to any artist or writer who accepted the articles of faith set forth in the Preamble of the Constitution: that the class war exists and that artists and writers should side with the working class in this struggle.

Encouraged by the success of the Organizing Conference, the John Reed Clubs continued to spread, particularly in the cities of the East and Midwest, until by January, 1934, there were nearly thirty of these nuclei, about which revolved, according to Alan Calmer, at one time their National Secretary, the Communist movement's "cultural front." [16] Their activities were varied. They held open meetings for the discussion of proletarian literature, arranged exhibits of revolutionary art, wrote strike pamphlets, organized local conferences against war, Fascism, and imperialism. A number of the individual clubs, in the years from 1932 to 1934, published little magazines, with remarkably similar names, devoted to radical literature and criticism, among them being *Partisan Review* (New York), *Leftward* (Boston), *Left Review* (Philadelphia), *Left Front* (Chicago), and *The Partisan* (Hollywood, Carmel, and San Francisco). Of these only *Partisan Review*, the most important, survived through 1935 — combining early in 1936 with *Anvil*, a magazine for proletarian short stories, and undergoing a political metamorphosis in 1937 to reappear as the present periodical; however, these little magazines served the purpose, not only of agitating among literary people, but also of providing outlets for expression to many young writers who were dissatisfied with the literary policies of the established magazines or whose manuscripts were rejected. The publications were training ground for potential proletarian novelists. Nevertheless, the John Reed Clubs were doomed.

In October, 1934, a Second National Conference of the federation was held, to which somewhat over 40 delegates were sent by a total membership of about 1,200; and immediately Orrick Johns of the New York club reported in *The New Masses* the conference's significance: ". . . that it represented a high level of revolutionary consciousness; that it was made up of new writers and artists just beginning to be heard; and these writers and artists had created — since the last conference — their own periodicals and mediums through which they could be heard." [17] Yet in sessions chiefly devoted to "self-criticism" it was agreed that the gathering did not truly represent the ferment of the times. None of the revolutionary pioneers of the twenties and few of the proletarian writers of the early Depression years were present, while the number of both delegates and members was inadequate. The sense of the meetings was for widening the area of left-wing influence. For example, Alfred Hayes, a poet from the John Reed Club of New York, insisted in one of the opening addresses that the cultural movement must be less rigid in demanding ideological orthodoxy of its members so that more of the American intellectuals could be won over. It may be noted that Hayes was an editor of *Partisan Review*, which since its inception early in 1934 had been opposing doctrinal extremism, or "sectarianism," as it affected the writing of revolutionary literature, and his argument for widening the cultural "front" doubtless had literary as well as political motivation. When the official political word from the Party was spoken, however, it was of the same tendency. In order to "strike a blow at the growing fascist enemy, the rapidly developing White Guard and fascist criticism, and the Roosevelt-fostered national-chauvinist art," as well as to "organize American revolutionary culture against the imperialist war plans," it was proposed by Alexander Trachtenberg, representative to the Conference from the Communist Party's Central Committee, that a National Writers' Congress of the largest possible attendance be held within the next eight months.[18] Recalling that the First All-Union Congress of Soviet Writers had only recently been held in Moscow with great publicity, the delegates enthusiastically endorsed Trachtenberg's proposal. But they endorsed more than they apparently knew, for within the eight months the John Reed Clubs themselves had ceased to exist. What their death implied will be seen in Chapter Eight, where it will be related to the ultimate decline of the proletarian novel.

Meanwhile *The New Masses* had been laboring, with slower success, to fulfill its share of the program laid down at the Kharkov Conference of 1930. Nearly a year before Kharkov, Michael Gold had proposed that the members of the John Reed Club's literary section attach themselves to the various industries, learn them thoroughly over several years, and become a group of correspondents sending in to the magazine in a variety of literary forms their reports about current industrial developments. The printed replies to this proposal had been for the most part thoroughly negative. Now, in spite of such improvements as an increase in size from twenty-four to thirty-two pages each monthly issue and an attempt to publish more revolutionary literature and art, the work of the magazine for the year following the Kharkov Conference was humiliatingly censured by the Secretariat of the International Union of Revolutionary Writers as containing a number of serious defects, the basic one being its "insufficient politicalization," its lack of a militant "line." Since *The New Masses* was "the central organ of the IURW in the U.S.A.," the Secretariat was "compelled to state that the magazine has not worked sufficiently at leading the revolutionary fellow-travelers in the U.S.A. or at securing a mass basis for the American proletarian movement by mobilizing cadres of worker correspondents around the magazine." [19] The editorial board "enthusiastically approved" this resolution, thus demonstrating an interesting lack of confidence in its own editorial abilities, and plunged again into the struggle; but the problems were not solved immediately.

The basic problem, it is now clear, was one familiar to any periodical of any, or no, political belief: the problem of audience. As far as making up the magazine went, there was no impassable difficulty presented by the demand of the I.U.R.W. that *The New Masses* become the revolutionary cultural organ of *both* proletariat and intelligentsia. The class-conscious worker, struggling to articulate his experience as literature, and the radicalized intellectual, struggling to make literature articulate revolutionary experience, could equally well be published. Who, however, would buy and read? Under such editors as Michael Gold and Walt Carmon, the policy in the early years of the decade continued to emphasize the proletarian approach, with the result that the literary contents often seemed artistically crude and the circulation remained numerically unimpressive. Protest against this policy developed slowly and as slowly took effect. Joseph Freeman had joined the editorial staff in the early part of 1931 on the condition that the magazine be aimed at a higher level of intelligence as part of a general plan to attract the leftward-moving intellectuals more strongly; yet as late as November, 1932, he was lamenting a continued shortage of manpower for directing the "cultural front" and was pointing to the necessity for still more changes in its chief class-conscious organ in order to increase its revolutionary efficiency.

We are faced with an unprecedented problem, a problem I have raised time and again at various meetings: how to guide the "cultural front," how to do it not through individuals but through organizations, not through personal gossip and abuse but through political and literary thought and action. We have agreed on this principle. . . We said we must have basic literature; we must have more people active in this field; we must have a definite policy; we must get people who can raise money for this work; we must have a professional John Reed Club secretary; we must have a NEW NEW MASSES with a NEW staff; we must not permit our fellow-travelers to drift about without guidance.[20]

In September, 1933, when *The New Masses* last appeared as a monthly, its circulation had reached a total of only 6,000. After a brief period of reorganization, the magazine reappeared as a weekly with a new board of editors in order to keep step, according to its announcement, "with our rapidly moving revolutionary epoch." The editors, the new Literary Editor being Granville Hicks, declared that the magazine would be addressed primarily to the radicalized sections of the middle class; and the first issue, dated January 2, 1934, sold 9,500 copies. The right formula seemed to have been hit upon at last, for by the end of a year circulation had leaped to 25,000 and the editors were appealing to the readers for an expansion fund. The magazine had found its audience, but, significantly, less among the "class-conscious workers" than among the "revolutionary intellectuals of this country."

Another indication of success was the appearance in April, 1934, of the first of several forty-eight-page "Quarterly Issues," this one containing a Book Supplement which included the initial article of a series by Granville Hicks entitled "Revolution and the Novel." Throughout these years, of course — a fuller discussion of the magazine's critical policies has been reserved for Chapter Eight — *The New Masses* had continued to be the chief critical exponent of all proletarian literature. This series by Hicks marked at last a kind of institutionalization of the proletarian novel, which, with the encouragement of the John Reed Clubs and *The New Masses* critics themselves was entering, in 1934, on the climax of its fame.

III

As the Depression Decade opened, then, a highly self-conscious — if not always efficient — subliterary apparatus was in the process of development by the Left for the guidance of the radicalized intellectuals, particularly the writers. Already a few novels with a radical orientation were appearing, though still as isolated expressions of revolt. In 1929, Agnes Smedley had published her semi-autobiographical *Daughter of Earth*, the crude but magnificently bitter narrative of one "Marie Rogers," who is born into the poverty of a northern Missouri farm, grows up in the midst of labor struggles in the coal fields near Trinidad, Colorado, is discharged

from her schoolteaching position because she has become a Socialist, and opposes World War I as a rich man's war and a poor man's
fight. While working in New York as a reporter on *The Call*, she
is imprisoned in the Tombs for having given assistance to a Hindu
plotting to free India and is released without trial at the end of the
war, whereupon she leaves the Socialist Party, joins the I.W.W.,
and later turns all her energy into the movement for the freedom
of the colonial peoples of Asia, whose subjection she considers to
be "one of the chief pillars of world capitalism." *Daughter of Earth*
links political revolt with personal revolt against "bourgeois" sexual
morality, as Floyd Dell would have linked them; but unlike *Moon-
Calf*, this book is the story of the education, in part the self-educa-
tion, of a hardened fighter in an international revolution. It points
forward to a decade of hunger and anger rather than backward to
a decade of disillusion and compromise. The radicalism of Marie
Rogers–Agnes Smedley may approach hysteria, as in the final section of the book; it never comes anywhere near being tired.

A radical "novel" that attracted far more attention than *Daughter of Earth*, however, was Michael Gold's *Jews Without Money*,
which went into eleven printings between February and October
of 1930. *Jews Without Money*, which is perhaps more accurately
characterized as a book of personal reminiscence rather than a
novel, describes the swarming life of New York's East Side, where
the author's childhood and youth were spent. In a series of related
sketches, Gold attempts to convey directly to the reader's nerves
the crowded clamor of tenement and street where, night and day,
life "exploded like fireworks"; in fact, Gold's chief talent is the
ability to tell brief tales in the rhetoric of intense emotion, an emotion that is always on the verge — and frequently well beyond the
verge — of diving into sentimentality. Here are the stories of the
David Levinskys who did not rise from the poverty and filth of the
Ghetto, from the religious and social hatreds of conflicting nationalities piled one on top of the other, from the brutalities and brutalized living which made whores out of excitement-desiring girls
and gangsters out of boys banded together for self-protection. Here
are also the occasional joys and the frequent generosity of the very
poor toward the very poor in the midst of stinks, diseases, sexual
frustration and perversion, crooked politics, and the degrading

inhumanity of Organized Charity. Throughout these passionate, high-pitched sketches, the dominant motif is the disfigurement of human character by poverty and fear, by sweatshop and job hunt. The weak go under, the honest are their own enemies, the strong exploit labor or, as another kind of criminal, exploit society.

Gold was criticized by reviewers on the Left for his "nationalistic vehemence" in defense of his people and for the relatively little attention which he paid to the unionization of the garment industry that was developing during his childhood years; he was criticized by conservative critics for the abruptness of the "conversion ending." But he was merely telling the truth about his own life. Adult responsibility came to him early in spite of the labors of a brave and idolized mother. By the age of twelve, he was committed to the hunt for unskilled work, moving from one badly paid job to another. The years of his adolescence were, as he describes them, blind drift — until the sudden, chance illumination (on the last page of the book) from a man on a soapbox, preaching the word of revolution.

I listened to him.
O workers' Revolution, you brought hope to me, a lonely, suicidal boy. You are the true Messiah. You will destroy the East Side when you come, and build there a garden for the human spirit.
O Revolution, that forced me to think, to struggle and to live.
O great Beginning! [21]

In so far as the book is a novel, the hope of revolution does come too much like a god from the dialectical machine; but in so far as the book is personal narrative, the ending-beginning is psychologically accurate. Only obliteration could subdue the jungle of the East Side, and complete revolution must have seemed more possible to a work-drugged boy than that less spectacular palliation, the Jacob Riis Houses. At any rate, the abrupt ending of the book may have taught later proletarian writers to demonstrate more exactly how, through acquiring revolutionary knowledge, their characters passed from the kingdom of necessity to the kingdom of freedom.

The year 1930 was Gold's marvelous year. Writing in *The New Masses* for September, he recalled that he was, he believed, "the first writer in America to herald the advent of a world proletarian literature as a concomitant to the rise of the world proletariat," for it was ten years since his article "Towards Proletarian Art" had appeared in *The Liberator*. At that time he had been "feeling [his] way," but now he could triumphantly declare that "the little path has since become a highroad." [22] In this second proclamation, Gold proceeded to outline the characteristics of a new form, that of "Proletarian Realism," which he felt was evolving to meet the new circumstances. "Proletarian Realism" would deal with working-class characters and their experiences; it would describe precisely the technical skill of their work; it would always embody a social theme and be filled, not with pessimism, but with "revolutionary elan"; it would do all this in swift, unadorned language and without resort to melodrama, for "life itself is the supreme melodrama."

Many subsequent proletarian novels were to fulfill this so-called "new" form even down to that last evasively worded dictum, but a successful book and a prophecy — to say nothing of a first visit to the Soviet Union and the news that three of his stories had been translated into Japanese — did not complete Gold's triumph for the year 1930. As nearly as any single literary event can be pointed to as the "beginning" of the new school of radical writing, this honor must go to Gold's review, "Wilder: Prophet of the Genteel Christ," which appeared — perhaps "exploded" is more accurate — in *The New Republic's* Fall Literary Section. The basic argument in this onslaught against four of Thornton Wilder's books was that their author, though claiming to be a spiritual teacher, actually had nothing to say to Americans facing the tragic realities of American life, that the "human heart" of which Wilder spoke was only the heart of a small, sterile, and superficial leisure class. The argument should have been supported by a critical analysis; instead, Gold took a club to his victim.

Mr. Wilder wishes to restore, he says, through Beauty and Rhetoric, the Spirit of Religion in American Literature. One can respect any writer in America who sets himself a goal higher than the usual racketeering. But what is this religious spirit Mr. Wilder aims to restore? Is it the crude self-torture of the Holy Rollers, or the brimstone howls and fears of the Baptists, or even the mad, titanic sincerities and delusions of a Tolstoy or Dostoievsky?

No, it is that newly fashionable literary religion that centers around Jesus Christ, the First British Gentleman. It is a pastel, pastiche, dilettante religion, without the true neurotic blood and fire, a daydream of homosexual figures in graceful gowns moving archaically among the lilies. It is Anglo-Catholicism, that last refuge of the American literary snob.[23]

Like most of Gold's writing, this review gives the appearance of having been thought out somewhere in its author's bowels. Certainly its demand for "nativism" and its appeal to Veblen were not characteristically Marxist; nevertheless, *The New Republic* received an unprecedented rush of mail, some of it defending the reviewer, but much more of it attacking Gold for applying the standards of Communist economics to Wilder's works of art. The tempest raged for weeks in the Correspondence section of the astonished *New Republic*, and outside in the literary world, until the magazine was forced, two months later, to refuse to print any more letters on the matter. Though the dispute was confused and frequently comical, Edmund Wilson was later to note its significance in focusing wide attention on the whole question of the relation between Marxism and literature.

Yet there is no question that the Gold-Wilder row marked definitely the eruption of the Marxist issues out of the literary circles of the radicals into the field of general criticism. After that, it became very plain that the economic crisis was to be accompanied by a literary one.[24]

What this affair represented was a divide — although by no means a continental one — in American literary life, the split into pro-Gold and pro-Wilder factions leading further into polarizations of pro-Left and anti-Left. A professional decision was demanded which many writers viewed as involving the larger problems of economic and political allegiance. The contribution of the controversy was that it made more immediate the time when these writers had to ask themselves, in the hymnlike refrain of the old strike song: "Which side are you on? Which side are you on?"

IV

As the economic and spiritual crisis deepened in that decisive year 1930 and as intellectuals felt increasingly the need of choosing sides, it was particularly fortunate for the literary radicals that they could point to the achievements of an established writer who was, or often seemed to be, one of theirs. If *Daughter of Earth* had been artistically crude and *Jews Without Money* sentimental, *The 42nd Parallel*, published only a few days after Gold's book, was neither; in fact, what made John Dos Passos's fifth novel so impressive was in large part its combination of technical brilliance and sardonic objectivity. Here was concrete, published proof that when a writer "went Left," he did not need to sacrifice his art, but on the contrary could strengthen and intensify it. Furthermore, Dos Passos's own experience was comprehensible to the middle-class writer. Where Agnes Smedley and Mike Gold had made articulate their harsh proletarian lives, Dos Passos was of a more recognizable type, the intellectual from the well-to-do home who voluntarily sided with the oppressed. So important an influence in the thirties was Dos Passos, the artist and his work, that both deserve closer consideration. They require attention too, despite the possibility of digression at this point, for the special paradox which they present — that they often sounded and were almost always made out to be more radical than they actually were.

By birth Dos Passos was, he insisted, of the middle class, though certainly of its upper layer. His father was a well-known corporation lawyer, Dos Passos grew up in comfortable, rather protected surroundings, and after his birth in 1896 the parents continued their custom of traveling for months at a time in Mexico and Europe. Dos Passos was taken along on their travels, had a year at an English public school, and completed his formal education at Choate and Harvard. Before going to college he had read widely, the author of most significance for his later writing being Walt Whitman, whom he "read . . . a great deal as a kid." [25] At Harvard, where he spent a restless four years, he found his bible, not in the work of Karl Marx, who looked forward to conflict and victory, but in that of Gibbon, who looked backward, in subject at least, to disintegration and decay. Although it is easy to overestimate the effects of certain reading, even on such bookish persons as the young Dos Passos, Gibbon's influence was apparently as great as Whitman's. The ironic detachment of the eighteenth-century historian and his sense of structural design are paralleled in *U.S.A.*; in *The Ground We Stand On* Dos Passos was to make explicit his continued sympathy with the values of the Enlightenment; and he

has defined the novelist as being solely an "architect of history."
He did not read Marx until the late 1920's and then by no means
completely. In college or soon after, however, he discovered
Veblen, read him and absorbed him, attracted by the elaborate
irony and the destructive attack on capitalism's institutional facade.

The sheltered environment and the books were still awaiting
catalysis with experience when Dos Passos graduated from Harvard
in 1916. Not yet an "architect of history," he had decided to become an architect in actuality and went off to Spain to study for
this profession. He was not a student long, however, for World
War I bulked too large to be ignored by a young American in
Europe; he had to see it "before the whole thing went bellyup."
What he saw as a driver in the American Volunteer Ambulance
Corps and later a private in the Medical Corps of the A.E.F. sick-
ened him with anger that such things could be. The catalysis, a
violent one, had taken place. Out of the war came directly his first
two histories of our time.

One Man's Initiation — 1917, published in England in 1920,
has received a full share of critical abuse for its cloudily impressionistic prose and its hero's daydreams of aesthetic withdrawal. It was
a first novel and not a particularly good one, but the fragile daydreams of Martin Howe have too readily been accepted as the
complete mental content of the author. In an illuminating preface
to an American edition, published in 1945 under the title of *First
Encounter*, Dos Passos compared the illusioned generation that
fought the First World War with the disillusioned one that
fought the Second. The former, finding "war and tyranny abhorrent," easily accepted the illusion "that by a series of revolutions
like the Russian the working people of the world could invent out
of their own heads a reign of peace and justice." Thus the radical
conversation of the Frenchmen in Chapter IX, though the Dos
Passos of twenty-five years later found it unsatisfactory, was
allowed to stand in the American edition in order to show the san-
guine hopes of young men in the year of the October Revolution.
The book's rejection of "the brutalities of war and oppression,"
then, is not only aesthetic, but politically radical; and in fact Dos
Passos has elsewhere stated that the war drove him toward radicalism by way of pacifism.[26]

Dos Passos's second novel, *Three Soldiers*, has also been criticized for aestheticism; the arrest of the deserter John Andrews and the consequent loss to the world of his projected symphonic work is made to appear, it is argued, the major tragedy of the war. One can hardly deny that the author must have felt particular kinship with his sensitive musician, but the usual argument ignores the function in the novel of the two other soldiers, Fuselli and Chrisfield, who are decidedly not artists and who are also destroyed by the gigantic machine that is the Army. For it is the Army as system rather than the War as combat which is the destroyer, and the peculiarly bitter quality of this antimilitarist novel can be explained only if the Army is seen as standing for any society organized on a basis of oppression and hence antagonistic to the individual, no matter whether he revolts or accepts.

The relation of the individual to society has consistently been the key problem for Dos Passos, both as writer and citizen; and his conviction that individual freedom was being lost within a steadily congealing social organism attracted him from the very beginning of his career to any expression of revolt. The revolt could be aesthetic or social, but preferably both simultaneously. That Dos Passos was not himself split between aesthetic and rebel, that he did not see art and politics as antitheses, but as facets of a unified whole, was demonstrated at once in the way the explosive social doctrine of *Three Soldiers* was presented through verbal and structural experimentation. Another demonstration was the fact that in *Rosinante to the Road Again*, the first of his several travel books, he devotes a whole chapter to Pio Baroja, the Spanish "Novelist of the Revolution," with whom he is revealingly sympathetic. The Spaniard's Anarchism, Dos Passos argues, is "an immensely valuable mental position." A middle-class man, Baroja lacks the community felt by workers because of their common relation to the machine, and hence his mission in writing is solely a destructive one — "to put the acid test to existing institutions, and to strip the veils off them." Yet he is never a propagandist and only occasionally allows himself "to hope that something better may come out of the turmoil of our age of transition." It is as though Dos Passos were describing his own work, and it may be noted that he was writing *Three Soldiers* while traveling in Baroja's Spain.

The historian, the artist, and the middle-class rebel are fused in *Manhattan Transfer*, which attempts to compress into a single book the New York of the twentieth century. Though the book is not derivative, certain "artistic" influences are obvious — Joyce's *Ulysses* and the documentary movie for structure, Dos Passos's own interest in painting for the impressionistic color of the prose. The prolific sense for detail, furthermore, owes much to Walt Whitman, who had also rejoiced in the swarming pavements of his city of the Manahatta. But where Whitman is expansively optimistic, where he is always aware of the city's natural beauty, the "dumb beautiful ministers" glimpsed daily from the Brooklyn Ferry, the modern Manhattan, glittering and water-girt though it is, has become sign and symbol of a mechanized society. Dos Passos the middle-class rebel puts this society's institutions to the acid test, and Dos Passos the historian records that, as the character Jimmy Herf concludes, New York's inhabitants are doomed more surely year after year to a treadmill of sex and money. The book is corrosive, but the author does not propagandize. Even the radicals, the Anarchists or Communists who appear occasionally in these pages, are trapped. Marco, the old waiter, exhausts his anger at exploitation by upholding Anarchism before a future shopkeeper and a future big bootlegger; while Anna Cohen — garment worker, striker, taxi-dancer, and scab — daydreams half-heartedly of the Revolution and awakes to her horrible burns in a flash fire in a dress shop.

Radical critics of the twenties and thirties objected to the ending of *Manhattan Transfer* as lacking in "militancy"; yet when Jimmy Herf walks out of New York into an indefinite future, his act is positive as well as negative. He has made a conscious rejection of an antiindividualist society, and he is willing to go "pretty far" in search of something better. That Dos Passos's sympathy remained, like Baroja's, with "the oppressed and the outcast," but that he would make his own search on his own terms, is indicated by the part he played in the Sacco-Vanzetti Case, the historical event which, except for World War I, had the greatest effect on him. As one of his contributions to the work of the Defense Committee, which he joined in 1926, he published a long pamphlet entitled *Facing the Chair: Story of the Americanization of Two Foreign-*

born Workmen (1927), which passionately proclaimed that: "If they die what little faith many millions of men have in the chance of Justice in this country will die with them." On the other hand, the pamphlet's conclusion, though it may be in part a propaganda technique, urges persuasion rather than revolution as a method for social change.

The conscience of the people of Massachusetts must be awakened. Working people, underdogs, reds know instinctively what is going on. The same thing has happened before. But the average law-admiring, authority-respecting citizen does not know. . . All that is needed is that the facts of the case be generally known.[27]

Sacco and Vanzetti had become identified in Dos Passos's mind with the fate of the individual in society. When the execution of the two Anarchists revealed how crushing a force could be brought to bear on the dissenter, he turned his outraged sympathy even more toward the side of the "working people, underdogs, reds." So toward the end of the twenties and into the early thirties Dos Passos's name became associated with various radical organizations close to the Communist Party. He was a member of the New Playwrights, a left-wing group including Michael Gold and John Howard Lawson, which from 1927 to 1929 struggled to create a public for drama that was expressionistic in form and revolutionary in content.[28] He served with the National Committee for the Defense of Political Prisoners, investigated and wrote about the terrorization of miners in Harlan County, Kentucky, and signed the manifesto of the League of Professional Groups for Foster and Ford. He occasionally contributed to *The New Masses*, both *The 42nd Parallel* and *The Big Money* were offered at various times as a premium for a *New Masses* subscription, and in that magazine a review of the latter volume, even as late as 1936, was entitled with the single word "Greatness."

At the same time Dos Passos was maintaining a position of astonishing independence. Sympathy for Communism as a dissolvant of a too-rigid society was not commitment to it as a system of power. On a trip to the Soviet Union in 1928, where he first read volume one of *Capital*, he admired the social ferment and sense of a new civilization being built, he did not admire the dark suggestions of terror which he encountered, and when he left, he was unable to state categorically whether he accepted or rejected the Soviet experiment. In 1930 in the midst of his closest relation to the Communists he openly anounced himself as being, not a "radical," but a "middle-class liberal," [29] and two years later he spoke his mind on the new "proletarian literature" in his answers to a questionnaire entitled "Whither the American Writer," printed in Calverton's *Modern Quarterly*. Here he maintains, on the one hand, that American capitalism is doomed and that the American writer should side with the producers; but on the other hand, he insists that the novelist should not become a member of the Communist Party, that he should write what he feels regardless of the Party's philosophy, that Whitman is more revolutionary than any Russian poet, and that good writing is good writing under any social system. And he concludes with a statement which, read in retrospect, is clearly prophetic of his later work.

It seems to me that Marxians who attempt to junk the American tradition, that I admit is full of dryrot as well as sap, like any tradition, are just cutting themselves off from the continent. Somebody's got to have the size to Marxianize the American tradition before you can sell the American worker on the social revolution. Or else Americanize Marx.[30]

As the thirties continued, Dos Passos repeatedly revealed that while he had a temperamental affinity with revolt and was willing to work with radicals because they too opposed the drift of American capitalism toward "centralized plutocracy," he retained his faith in persuasive techniques for social action. For example, on February 16, 1934, a mass meeting was held under the auspices of the Socialist Party in Madison Square Garden to protest the siege and slaughter of the Viennese Socialist workers in their apartment houses by the Dollfuss Government. When Communists attempted to gain control of the meeting, it broke up in disorder. Dos Passos and several other former signers of *Culture and the Crisis* now signed "An Open Letter to the Communist Party," which blamed the Party for the breaking up of the meeting. *The New Masses* replied in kind and suggested that Dos Passos was "growing away from" the Revolution. Since the novelist had never claimed to be anything more than, in his words, a "camp-follower" of the Revolution, he felt that the Revolution was growing away from him.

During these same years, of course, the volumes which would constitute the trilogy, *U.S.A.*, were appearing. Here again, though on a vaster scale, the historian, the artist, and the social rebel are fused. The trilogy is an acid analysis of thirty years of American capitalism, an analysis that envisages the country as split between the exploited and the exploiters; yet none of the fourteen characters important enough to carry the interwoven stories in their own names comes from other than the working class or the lower or middle layers of the middle class. What Dos Passos is concerned with is the efforts of ordinary people to survive in a business civilization and the disintegrative effect that such a civilization has upon them through their experience of economic injustice, war, and financial boom. The class analysis undoubtedly owes something to Marx, but the spirits of other men preside more powerfully here. As the trilogy develops, one sees that it is the history of the rise and incipient decline of yet another empire, chronicled with the ironic detachment of a twentieth-century Gibbon who happens also to be a novelist. More importantly, when one reaches *The Big Money*, the basis of Dos Passos's economic criticism becomes at last almost explicit, for it is in this third, climactic volume that he places the key "biography," that of Thorstein Veblen, whom he had read so much.

he established a new diagram of a society dominated by monopoly capital,
etched in irony
the sabotage of production by business,
the sabotage of life by blind need for money profits,
pointed out the alternatives: a warlike society strangled by the bureaucracies of the monopolies forced by the law of diminishing returns to grind down more and more the common man for profits,
or a new matteroffact commonsense society dominated by the needs of the men and women who did the work and the incredibly vast possibilities for peace and plenty offered by the progress of technology.
These were the years of Debs's speeches, growing laborunions, the I.W.W. talk about industrial democracy: these years Veblen still held to the hope that the working-class would take over the machine of production before monopoly had pushed the western nations down into the dark again.

War cut across all that: under the cover of the bunting of Woodrow
Wilson's phrases the monopolies cracked down. American democracy
was crushed.[31]

Sometimes in *U.S.A.* the producing class confronts the hired
agents of the owning class, but the central opposition in these
volumes is between "production" and "business," that division of
function which is so basic to Veblen's thinking. Max Lerner has
pointed out that the most clearly Veblenian character is Charley
Anderson, the engineer who is trapped and broken by the power of
business as though he were a "footnote" to *The Engineers and the
Price System.* If one accepts the fact of Dos Passos's reliance on
Veblen more than on Marx, it likewise becomes clear why there
are no major characters from the owning class; they would simply
be in the way of the author's intent. It is sufficient for his purpose
that Charley Anderson's destruction should come when he attempts
to shift from productive technician to unproductive tycoon, and
that J. Ward Morehouse and the smaller parasite Dick Savage lose
their integrity, create nothing of social value, and win the big
money. As for the blankly beautiful Margo Dowling, the finest
flower of this civilization, her apotheosis in the movie "industry" of
Hollywood is a legend of conspicuous consumption, a living proof
of the theory of the leisure class. Even Mary French, who sides
with the class-conscious working class and would therefore be
granted a fuller life by a Marxist writer, is affected by the social
dry rot and doomed to sterile frustration.[32]

Because of its dependence for ideological basis on Veblen's
bitter drink, *U.S.A.* seems a somber and negative book; yet it contains a tentative affirmation. The positive hope of *U.S.A.* comes
from Walt Whitman, of whose revolutionary quality Dos Passos
wrote in answering the *Modern Quarterly* questionnaire. Even
more than in *Manhattan Transfer* one sees that Whitman's love of
the American spoken word lies behind Dos Passos's own colloquial
style in the stories, and like the poet, the novelist has tried to include, not just New York, but all America in his work. Equally
important, Dos Passos looks for the cure of his sick country, not to
a dictatorship of the proletariat, but to a restoration — the word is
significant — of the democratic vista. In Number 46 of the auto-

biographical Camera Eye sequences, the author presumably makes a soapbox speech in Union Square, trying to "talk straight" yet clutching quickly at the easy slogan:

you suddenly falter ashamed flush red break out in sweat why not tell these men stamping in the wind that we stand on a quicksand? that doubt is the whetstone of understanding is too hard hurts instead of urging picket John D. Rockefeller the bastard if the cops knock your blocks off it's all for the advancement of the human race while I go home after a drink and a hot meal and read (with some difficulty in the Loeb Library trot) the epigrams of Martial and ponder the course of history and what leverage might pry the owners loose from power and bring back (I too Walt Whitman) our storybook democracy [33]

Although a class struggle exists, the outcome envisaged by the author is not a new and historically determined synthesis, but rather the hoped-for overthrow of usurping owners and the *re*building of a democratic society. Thus the Sacco-Vanzetti Case stands as whatever climax the trilogy is allowed to have, and the next to the last two Camera Eye sequences shift to that brutal act on the part of America's owners in order to reveal the extent of their arrogance and their usurpation.

how can I make them feel how our fathers our uncles haters of oppression came to this coast how say Don't let them scare you how make them feel who are your oppressors America
rebuild the ruined words worn slimy in the mouths of lawyers districtattorneys collegepresidents judges without the old words the immigrants haters of oppression brought to Plymouth how can you know who are your betrayers America
or that this fishpeddler you have in Charlestown Jail is one of your founders Massachusetts? [34]

To rebuild the words spoken at Plymouth and Paumanok, words like "liberty" and "democracy," is for Dos Passos the answer, the only answer, to the corrupt rulers of present-day America. If this be Marx at all, it is surely Marx "Americanized."

After the publication of *The Big Money*, with its corrosive sketches of a bureaucratized Party, the myth of "Comrade" Dos Passos could not be maintained much longer. But back in 1930 young writers going Left found in him what they wanted, what they needed to find — a real sympathy for "the oppressed and the outcast" and a hard anger against the oppressors, both expressed skillfully by a man accepted internationally as a major novelist. So when they talked revolution in eager communion far into the night or when they struggled to put into words their own new vision of the U.S.A. or when, occasionally, on picket lines they sang that song with its hymnlike refrain, "Which side are you on?", then they could warm themselves with the happy, if inaccurate, conviction that Dos Passos too was with them all the way.

7.

"ART IS A CLASS WEAPON"

A FAVORITE charge hurled by hostile literary critics against American radical novelists during the thirties — and one which is still routinely made in newspapers and literary histories — is that they were, in the striking phrase used by Max Eastman to describe Soviet writers, "Artists in Uniform." The applicability of this epithet to the American novelists should be examined. As the present and following chapters will attempt to establish, the radical writers especially of the first half of the Depression Decade did show marked *uniformity* of outlook, and the new direction taken by radical writing in the second half of the thirties was indeed essentially a response to a major shift in Communist political strategy; but to charge that the American writers were *in uniform*, in the necessary sense that they all wrote exactly alike and obediently to whatever arbitrary command, is to exaggerate for the sake of polemics.[1] Admittedly the warlike nature of the metaphor is apt, for the Americans, like the Russians, enjoyed thinking of themselves as fighters and their books as weapons. The proper comparison, however, is less to a regiment of infantry trained to automatic response than to a detachment of irregulars, outfitted in a pied combination of civilian and military equipment and decidedly fractious in discipline. One proof of the accuracy of the latter image is the disagreement that persisted both publicly and privately among the Left over the definition of the term "proletarian novel," the name by which the radical novel came to be universally known in the first half of the thirties.

The word "proletarian" had had no such special literary application among Socialist writers in the United States, and its immense popularity in the early thirties with the American literary radicals certainly reflected the fact that while the Russian Association of Proletarian Writers (RAPP) was "mobilizing" authors during the First Five-Year Plan, from 1928 to 1932, "proletarian literature" was in effect the official literary strategy in the Soviet Fatherland.[2] This was, of course, the term employed in 1930 at the Kharkov Conference of Revolutionary Writers, to which *The New Masses* and the John Reed Club had sent delegates, and was used constantly in *Literature of the World Revolution* (published as *International Literature* beginning with the summer of 1932), the official periodical of the International Union of Revolutionary Writers; but the amount of Soviet criticism published in this magazine was insufficient to give its readers in the United States a clear and thorough understanding of Russian literary theory, let alone to dictate their literary practice. What the term actually meant in the capitalist country of America, then, had to be determined by Americans, and they did not determine it at once.

On the face of it, "proletarian" would seem to describe fiction written by a member of the working class about, presumably, working-class characters and experience; and some left-wing critics did argue that subject matter, the expression of proletarian existence, was the chief characteristic distinguishing the proletarian novel from the usual "bourgeois" one.[3] Other critics polarized around what was, in terms of tradition in the American radical novel, a more usual definition. They maintained that the only important consideration was the conscious ideology of the author, whether he attempted, whatever his class origin, to work out in his fiction a Marxist analysis of society. Both groups agreed that the proletarian novel was the wave of the future which would soon sweep entirely over "bourgeois" fiction, but the dispute over subject matter versus viewpoint continued into the middle thirties.

At times it seemed that every radical critic laid down his own law. In 1932, V. F. Calverton, editor of *The Modern Quarterly*, published *The Liberation of American Literature*, the first of the very few whole books in the thirties attempting a Marxist analysis of literature. Rejecting his own earlier definition by subject matter, Calverton now stated that the one necessary distinction between proletarian and bourgeois writers was the adherence of the former to Marxist ideology, no matter what their class origin: "They are writers who have adopted the revolutionary point of view of the proletarian ideology, and who try to express that ideology in their work." [4] Among the opposition to Calverton's view was E. A. Schachner, radical journalist and editor, whose all-inclusive essay, "Revolutionary Literature in the United States Today," was one of the events of left-wing literary life in 1934. As an announced member of the Communist Party, he presumably spoke with more authority than Calverton, who had for long been charged with whoring after the false god Trotsky, and his definition of the proletarian novel was juxtaposed to that of another, the "revolutionary novel," with considerable doctrinal care. Revolutionary fiction was that which "consciously supports the movement for the revolutionary destruction of Capitalism," while the proletarian merely "reflects the life of any typical cross section of the proletariat and need not be more revolutionary than the proletariat itself is at the time the novel is written." Since, however, revolutionary ferment is now characteristic of the working class, the contemporary proletarian novel must reflect it; in fact, "the revolutionary novel and the proletarian novel tend to lose their respective identities as a revolutionary situation approaches." [5]

A situation, though not a revolutionary one, had approached close enough by April, 1935, so that there could be held the first of the three American Writers' Congresses which convened during the second half of the 1930's. At that Congress, next to the dangers of Fascism and of imperialist war, the chief subject of the papers read and discussed was proletarian literature, particularly the proletarian novel, its nature and its function. The published record [6] clearly indicates the lack of critical unity on the Left even during this period of the proletarian novel's greatest popularity.

At the first session of the Congress, in an address entitled "Values of the Revolutionary Writer," Waldo Frank — who was to be unanimously elected chairman of the League of American Writers, the Congress's continuing organization — maintained, as had Calverton in 1932, that the ideology of the author alone determines whether a work be proletarian or not.

There is much confusion among us as to "material" and "subject." The subject of a book is a mere label or container; it may mislead or be empty. Our poet or proseman, by his loyalty to the working class (whether born in it or not) and by natural selection of strong, expressive subjects, will write more and more of the struggles of farmer and worker. But if his vision be sound, it will make — *whatever his subject* — the material for revolutionary art. The term "proletarian" applied to art should refer to the key and vision in which the work is conceived, rather than to subject. It should be a qualitative, not quantitative, term. A story of middle-class or intellectual life, or even of mythological figures, if it is alight with revolutionary vision, is more effective proletarian art — and more effective art for proletarians — than a shelffull of dull novels about stereotyped workers.[7]

A definition similar to Frank's was employed by Edwin Seaver when, at the second day's session, he read a paper on "The Proletarian Novel," whose creators, he affirmed, had made "the most valuable contributions to the American novel during the last several years." The resolution of the problem, he contended, lay not in aesthetics, which were "an individual concern" of the artist himself, but in politics.

In the last analysis, it is not style, not form, not plot, not even characters, nor even the class portrayed that are fundamental in differentiating the proletarian from the bourgeois novel.

. . . it is the present class loyalty of the author that is the determining factor, the political orientation of the novelist, and not the class origin, or the class portrayed.[8]

The discussion concluding the session at which Seaver's paper was given reads like a warm one; at any rate it brought into immediate opposition the two contending definitions: viewpoint versus subject matter. A member of the audience, one Martin Russak, who was writing a novel about weavers and who some years previously in *The New Masses* had praised Jack London as a worker speaking to workers, objected to Seaver's definition and argued flatly that the proletarian novel is simply one that deals with the proletariat. Thereupon, an extensive rebuttal was made by Michael Gold, by then the grand middle-aged man of American left-wing literature, who had been introduced at the first session of the Congress as "the best loved American revolutionary writer." He opposed the "primitivism" of the attitude for which Russak was a spokesman and upheld Seaver's emphasis on political orientation, while at the same time he warned his listeners against the danger, because of the latitude this definition gave to the novelist, that "our literary movement" might become petty-bourgeois. Gold's reputation and the fact that his remarks appear in the final position in the printed discussion suggest that his stand was the more popular one, although this did not deter Malcolm Cowley, one of the ablest of the left-wing critics, from compounding the problem at the last session of the Congress by his insistence on both a revolutionary viewpoint *and* proletarian materials.

Actually the weight of evidence taken from the proceedings of the Congress, from book reviews in such publications as *The New Masses*, and from critical articles by various radicals clearly indicates that the definition of the "proletarian novel" most frequently accepted in both theory and practice was the one stated variously by Calverton, Frank, Seaver, and Gold. It is, in short, once more the novel written from a Marxist viewpoint.* This fact could be asserted as final by Alan Calmer, former National Secretary of the John Reed Clubs, when his "All Quiet on the Literary Front" appeared in *Partisan Review & Anvil* for March, 1936:

> . . . critics define proletarian literature as *by* or *about* workers, although Marxists point out that it is the present outlook of the author and not his subject matter, characters or class origin which determines whether his work is proletarian or not. . .

But a very sharp ideological distinction marks off the proletarian fiction of the thirties and the earlier Socialist novels, a distinction clearly resulting from the divergence in the dominant political attitudes of the two parties. Where almost all of the Socialist writers had expressly rejected violence in favor of parliamentary methods of change, almost all of the proletarians insisted that the coming struggle for power between capitalist and working class would be of the "cataclysmic" nature described in their favorite handbook of revolution, *Toward Soviet America*, published by

---

* Just as most of the proletarian novelists were not actual members of the Communist Party, but rather were within its orbit as fellow travelers, so they were less Marxists than within the Marxian orbit, though they did have access to more of the fundamental writings than had the Socialist novelists. The Marxism of many consisted chiefly in adherence to the current Party line. A few, like Sherwood Anderson and Waldo Frank, made a conscious rejection of much Marxist doctrine, but remained for shorter or longer periods in sympathy with the Party.

William Z. Foster in 1932. The end of capitalism was both inevitable and immediate, but capitalism would not abdicate its power
peacefully. Now in its death frenzies it was lashing out at the
proletariat with desperate brutality and forcing upon it the use of
violence in self-protection. Such violence would of necessity carry
the workers into dictatorial power, after which they could set
about establishing the classless society. And just as literature during
the years of capitalist domination had reflected bourgeois values,
had attempted, while reassuring the middle classes, to disarm the
worker and alienate him from his class, so the new literature would
reflect proletarian values, would bring the worker to class-consciousness, steel him for the coming revolution, prepare him for
the role he would play in the next stage of history. Art was a form
of politics; it was a weapon in the class war.

II

If literature were as direct and immediate a by-product of economics as was claimed by some of the more dogmatic Marxist
critics of the thirties, the proletarian novel should have sprung
forth full-armed as soon after October, 1929, as any work of that
size could be written, printed, and published. Actually the relationship between art and economics is somewhat more devious. As late
as the end of 1932, one *New Masses* reviewer stated that the whole
radical literary movement "in this country is at present very weak";[9]
and despite the skirmishes over art and propaganda which the early
examples of the form set off, it was not until 1934 that the advance
of the proletarian novel developed from a series of border incidents
into a full-scale attack. In that year, *The Saturday Review of Literature* indirectly admitted that the revolutionaries had captured
strong positions when it gave one of the two lead articles in its
Tenth Anniversary Number to H. L. Mencken, who laid down a
noisy, and ineffective, barrage against the proletarian ranks. At
last, in the issue of *The New Masses* for January 1, 1935, Granville
Hicks could jubilantly review the revolutionary triumphs achieved
over the forces of reaction during the preceding twelve months.

It has been a good year, an exceptionally good year, a year to put
the Menckens, Hazlitts and Soskins on the defensive. Before 1934 it re-

quired some understanding of literary and social processes to recognize the promise of revolutionary literature, but now even a daily book reviewer has to blindfold his eyes to ignore its achievements and its potentialities.[10]

The rise, and also the decline, of the proletarian novel in the thirties is best indicated by figures drawn from their listing by year in the Appendix of this volume. During the decade seventy examples of the form were published, fifty of them, a significantly large majority, appearing between 1930 and 1935. These fifty came chiefly in two waves, a preliminary one in 1932 — eleven books — and a larger and more extended one in 1934 and 1935 — thirteen and fifteen books respectively. The year 1933, with only four novels, marks a low possibly explained by the economics of Depression publishing and the draining off of the energies of writers into the 1932 Communist political campaign; while the sharp drop on the other side of 1935 to no more than six in any of the last years of the decade represents the decline, the reasons for which will be discussed in the following chapter. A total of seventy novels over a period of ten years or even fifty over six does not represent a genuine literary *movement* even though it is greater in quantity and more concentrated in time than the prewar Socialist output; and it certainly does not lead to the conclusion that, during a time when, despite economic stagnation, an average of nearly 1900 fiction titles was published annually, Communism had "taken over" American writing. Nevertheless this body of work does represent an area of our literature worth exploring — extrinsically because it was the occasion of great furor at the time and intrinsically because it was by no means entirely given over to "desolate wastes," as it is now customarily labeled on the literary maps.

A preliminary survey of this disputed terrain to determine, so to speak, its soil types, shows that most of the novels can be fitted fairly easily on the basis of content or subject matter into four main groups: (1) those centered about a strike; (2) those concerned with the development of an individual's class-consciousness and his conversion to Communism; (3) those dealing with the "bottom dogs," the lowest layers of society; and (4) those describing the decay of the middle class. Obviously these groups are not mutually exclusive; for example, development of class-conscious-

ness and conversion frequently come by way of a strike or a series
of strikes, while in the novels of middle-class decay, a countertheme
of development-conversion in one or more characters usually appears. There are even, as will be noted, subdivisions within the four
major categories. This preliminary classification is, however, both
valid and useful.

Where Socialist writers had much preferred to describe a conversion to radicalism rather than a strike, the "proletarians," especially in the first half of the decade, show an almost equal fascination with both subjects. The reasons for interest in the novel of
labor conflict are several. Since the Trade Union Unity League,
in its attempt at the turn of the decade to organize a group of revolutionary unions, was relying on the old I.W.W. formula of
striking early, often, and unexpectedly, it would be quite possible
for many middle-class writers to gain their first vivid experience
with radical action from observing or participating in a strike. A
strike, after all, was clearly a battle in the class war; in such a battle,
the abrupt Marxian clash of capitalist class and proletariat was
most nearly imaged, without the everyday blurring of distinctions
made inevitable by the existence of sizable middle-class groups in
society. Edmund Wilson has shrewdly noted that one of the "literary" qualities of *Capital* is this same melodramatic confrontation
of the two extreme classes, who are pictured as being continuously
and directly locked in conflict. Certainly a strike afforded enough
drama, or melodrama, for a shocked ex-bourgeois to describe.
Finally, the trajectory of the usual strike presents a curve of action
aptly designed for artistic expression. The storm gathers, the initial
clash occurs, the struggle veers back and forth, producing suspense
as the advantage goes now to this side, now to that; the climax is
reached when the strike succeeds or is broken, and the action
thereafter drops swiftly. A strike, in short, possesses a basic rhythm
not unlike that which underlies almost any piece of literature.

One labor conflict in real life produced a notably large fictional
response. In carrying out its self-imposed task of organizing the
unorganized textile workers of the country, the Trade Union Unity
League had reached by 1929 the third step of its strategy, which
had begun with the Passaic, New Jersey, strike of 1926–27, the
one that had briefly attracted the three hundred New York intel-

lectuals, and with the New Bedford, Massachusetts, strike of 1928. The ambitious third step was a statewide set of strikes in North Carolina. Now the activities of the T.U.U.L. in the Southern textile mills were to become widely known through the particularly violent events at Gastonia in that state in the spring and summer of 1929. Since before World War I, cotton textile mills of New England had of course been moving to the South, attracted by low taxes, nearness to raw materials, and the abundant supply of cheap labor. Workers had been drawn to a considerable extent from among the mountain people, who came down to the factories because of the promise of, to them, high wages and the glamour of town life after their isolation. They soon found, however, that rents and prices were as high as the wages, that even with several members of a family working the family could hope to earn only enough to live from day to day. Independent because of their former way of living, they gradually became discontented and began turning to the established and not highly militant A.F. of L. textile union. This explosive situation suited the developing strategy of the T.U.U.L., which had in 1928 created a rival Communist-headed union, the National Textile Workers, and which now sent Fred E. Beal, leader of the New Bedford Strike, to help organize for the N.T.W. in North Carolina. Beal prepared his key strike in the Manville-Jenckes Company's Loray Mill at Gastonia, one of the leading textile cities of the South.

Soon after the strike broke out, the union headquarters and the strikers' relief store were demolished by a masked mob. A second headquarters was erected on union-owned land along with a tent colony to shelter strikers evicted from company houses. When police attempted to enter the new union hall without a warrant, a fight ensued in which Police Chief Aderholt was fatally shot and four of his men wounded. Thereupon the tent colony was terrorized by the "Committee of One Hundred," a vigilante group. After a trial noted for anti-Communist histrionics on the part of the prosecution lawyers, Beal and six other strike leaders were sentenced to long terms in state prison.[11] Yet another act of violence by the community, while the trial was going on, was the shooting of the "ballad woman" and strike leader, Ella May Wiggin.

These events form an important part of the dramatic framework of six of the earliest strike novels: Mary Heaton Vorse, *Strike!*; Sherwood Anderson, *Beyond Desire*; Fielding Burke (Olive Tilford Dargan), *Call Home the Heart*; Grace Lumpkin, *To Make My Bread*; Myra Page, *Gathering Storm*; and William Rollins, *The Shadow Before*, this last making use also of events from New Bedford. *Strike!* is primarily a fictionalized account by a labor journalist; while *Beyond Desire*, which is perhaps the poorest of Anderson's novels, makes use of the strike to bring about the death of the chief character, a puzzled young American named Red Oliver, who is attracted toward Communism and killed by another puzzled young American wearing the uniform of the National Guard. *Call Home the Heart*, *To Make My Bread*, and *Gathering Storm*, the first being the most proficiently written, are in effect local-color fiction performed with a radical purpose. All three are concerned for the most part with the movement of the mountain people to the mills, but all culminate in the events which occurred at Gastonia. In *The Shadow Before*, the strike, described through a number of experimental devices, occupies most of the book and gives it whatever dramatic quality it possesses.

Besides Gastonia, and the industrial South in general, a second geographical locus for the strike novels is the Pacific Northwest, evidently because of the region's long history of struggles between the lumber barons and the I.W.W.[12] Of the sixteen novels that are particularly concerned with one or more "class battles," [13] the best from most points of view is Robert Cantwell's *The Land of Plenty*, which deals with a spontaneous strike in a wood veneer factory situated in a coastal city of the State of Washington. The overtones of I.W.W.-ism in the book come to some extent out of the author's experience; for Cantwell was born in 1908 in the town of Little Falls (now Vader), Washington, south of that Centralia where the Wobbly, Wesley Everest, was hideously lynched in 1919,[14] and his childhood was spent in towns that saw free-speech fights and syndicalist-led struggles for industrial democracy. Having graduated from high school in Aberdeen, the city where his novel is set, Cantwell spent one unhappy year at the University of Washington, worked from 1925 to 1929 as a "plywood factory veneer clipper operator" in Hoquiam, and held an assortment of part-time jobs. *Laugh and Lie Down* (1931) was a pessimistic first novel about disillusioned middle-class youths. In 1931, he moved to New York, married, and began a career in journalism, finally joining the staff of *Time* in 1935. Cantwell was, then, a middle-class writer who had had experience as a wage worker. Some years later he stated that his main reason for wanting to write had been the one announced by a character in a novel by Malraux: " . . . in order to give working people a sense of their own dignity."

The Land of Plenty ably conveys that sense of dignity. The title is, of course, ironic, for the land Cantwell describes exemplifies that peculiarly unnerving capitalist contradiction, deprivation in the midst of potential wealth. The book is divided into two approximately equal parts. As Part One, "Power and Light," opens, the lights in a veneer factory on night shift have just gone out. Carl Belcher, the company's new efficiency expert, being unable to find his way about the mill in the dark, flounders helplessly; but the workers automatically shut off their switches so that the machines will not be injured when the current returns, and from long acquaintance with their place of work they move easily about among the hazards. The reader soon understands that Cantwell is utilizing this failure of power and light, not only to show how capable the workers are of handling the factory's operations without management's help, but also to suggest the failure of capitalism itself. It is Hagen the worker who must check the factory, determine that the cause of the stoppage was in the powerhouse supplying the plant, find the dazed efficiency expert, and advise him what to do.

Like Carl and Hagen, the other chief characters are each introduced in sections which are labeled with their names and which overlap in time. (The entire first part, occupying slightly over half the book, takes place within a space of not much more than an hour.) The men come together in groups, separate, coalesce once more; and from their thoughts and conversation the reader fits together the reasons for dissatisfaction — the long hours, the speedup, the vacillations of the management, the present overtime work on the night before the Fourth of July, and cuts in the already too small pay. Some of the men drift toward one end of the mill, drawn by a community sense of the accident which occurred when the power stopped and a huge log swung soundlessly in the dark against an inexperienced hoist-man's leg. MacMahon, the aging manager of the mill, has come down from the town to see what is wrong. He and Carl get lost under the mill, wander out — a little too clownishly, it would seem — into the bushes on the surrounding tide-flat, and sit down to wait until they can see to find their way back. Meanwhile, Hagen and other workers have managed to get the hoist-man free; but when the lights come on again, Carl, furious at the slowness with which the men are returning to work, fires Hagen and the half-breed Winters. The men crowd around MacMahon, arguing that Hagen had not been at fault for the power failure and that he had, furthermore, engineered the rescue of the hoist-man. On their insistence, MacMahon rescinds Carl's order and sends everyone home early. The workers leave with a strange new feeling of solidarity, for "they had their first sure knowledge of their strength." The title of Part One has now assumed a new meaning. As the "power and light" of capitalism fail, power in a different sense shifts to the hands of the workers; the light is now their new understanding of what they hold.

Part Two, "The Education of a Worker," is primarily concerned with Hagen's young son, Johnny, who cannot go to college since his wages are needed by the family. Over the Fourth — patriotic display is ironically contrasted with economic injustice — the night-shift workers drift together and talk about striking, for they have heard that Carl is going to fire Hagen and Winters after all. Few of the men except Vin Garl, an ex-Wobbly, have had any strike experience; yet when they go back to work the next day and find that twenty men from the night shift have been fired, both day and night shifts spontaneously "go out." Johnny feels the emotional pull of this act of defiance.

That was the beginning. Nothing else ever gave him the same strange feeling of excitement and strength, and all during the next week he treasured the memory, calling on it like some powerful charm to help him in the moments of despair. At home he used it most, making himself remember when the wrangling in the house got too bitter and when the disorder and the lack of any quiet wore on his nerves, but he used it every day on the picket line when the waiting got tiresome or when someone got caught and was hauled off by the cops; he called on it when Sorenson and Dwyer had a fight and when, after the third day, a part of the factory began to run with scabs who came from nowhere. In a week it had lost its strength for him, for in the bitterness of defeat and in all the misery he lived through nothing, for a while, could give him any hope. But then that feeling died too, and years later he could call up the memory of the afternoon when the machines began stopping, when the day shift raced out to join them, when the girl danced along beside him as they went around and around the office.[15]

As the strike holds, Johnny receives his education. He learns what being on a picket line involves — the misrepresentations made in the newspapers, the hardness of a policeman's club, the enmity of the townspeople — but the strike is disciplining him into manhood. During a sudden fierce rainstorm, the strikers enter the factory for protection and, after driving out the scabs and the police, hold it all night. During this night of possession, Johnny has his first sex experience with the girl Ellen, with whom he has fallen in love, thus becoming a "man" in another way. His education in the class struggle is completed on the following day when the strikers fight a pitched battle with the police, his father is shot, Ellen is chopped down by a policeman's club, and he himself is forced to hide out by the harborside with Vin Garl and an injured worker. The book ends somberly.

The rain fell hard, drenching them while they waited, not like rain but like some new and terrible weapon of their enemies. He tried to crowd under the driftwood and Vin Garl put his hand on his shoulder. "Come on, son," he said gently, "don't cry," and then they sat there listening to him, their faces dark with misery and anger, listening and waiting for the darkness to come like a friend and set them free.[16]

Shortly after *The Land of Plenty* was published, Cantwell announced that he had written the book as "quite simply, a work of propaganda." It was important, he felt, that both novelists and their critics attack strike problems, for in this way " . . . we can work out, in our own imaginations, some of the problems the working-class must face in actuality; we can fight out on paper some of the real battles that are coming and so be a little better prepared for them." In his own book, he had been wondering what would be the result if workers seized a factory; " . . . I couldn't imagine clearly what would happen, and the novel suffers as a result." [17] Since it was still two years before the embattled workers at the Goodyear plant in Akron were to put in motion the great wave of sit-down strikes of 1936–37, Cantwell may be forgiven for not being able to blueprint the result of such a technique in the hands of a group of unorganized workers. Dispossession by force could have been, in fact, a very possible outcome; but so could a negotiated settlement, since, as Vin Garl himself argues in the novel, the men would have had strong support from other labor elements in town. What is most significant here is not that Cantwell published a book the ending of which he felt to be inadequate, but that he chose to have his workers crushed in spite of their fair chance for a moderate victory and that he dissolved the ending in violence. Obviously there are two possible resolutions for the radical strike novel. The strike may be won, in which case the victory becomes a direct portent of the approaching working-class revolution; or the strike may be lost, in which case the reader is assured that the workers have at least been educated, have learned solidarity, and are better prepared for the next battle in the class war. Yet one suspects it is not by chance that in a large majority of these novels the strike is broken under the vicious onslaught of the police or other forces of capitalist "law and order."

One may argue, as did Malcolm Cowley, that the strikes which the T.U.U.L. was then waging and which the writers heard about or observed were being conducted in such dangerously antiunion areas as the textile towns of the South, but such an argument should not necessarily apply to any except the Gastonia novels where the evidence of defeat could not be changed. A less literal and more profoundly operating explanation is suggested by the important fact that a very large proportion of these writers were middle-class in origin. When the shock of the Depression dislodged them from a relatively secure economic place in society, they were brought for the first time into angry awareness of social instability, of widespread suffering, and of the violence of industrial dispute, which exists for the middle-class individual chiefly in newspaper headlines. Out of this unprepared-for awareness developed a fascination with violence, a fascination far more obsessive than that felt by the earlier Socialist writers. The latter too had felt the compulsion to write of suffering and horror, but more typically they had observed rather than participated, had deliberately gone toward from the outside rather than found themselves involuntarily caught within, had written *of* rather than *out of*. For the young radicals of the

Depression Decade the fascination was with violence as such. Actually this preoccupation with violence for its own sake beyond even such terrible events as those of Gastonia became for the proletarian writer a mode of psychological self-defense. The phenomenon may be observed in many nonradical novelists of the decade, one variant of it being imbedded in the work of Ernest Hemingway, whose prose tones occasionally echo in this fiction. The physical and spiritual injuries inflicted on young writers by society could, in a sense, be exorcized if they themselves outdid these injuries, if they were able to create in their art the very worst fate that could happen. Indeed, the created work would be a kind of introverted retaliation by the innocent victim upon offending society. So they wrote novels about violent strikes and in the end compulsively sent their workers toward defeat.

Paradoxically, these literary lost strikes in a decade marked by massive labor victories indicate a core of uncertainty in the writers' minds as to whether the proletariat ultimately would win or not. An even clearer case than *The Land of Plenty* is the ending of Clara Weatherwax's *Marching! Marching!*, the book which won the *New Masses*-John Day Company contest for the best manuscript of a proletarian novel submitted between June, 1934, and April 1; 1935. This book is likewise laid in Aberdeen, Washington, and likewise details the development of a strike. When finally the leaders are tried on fraudulent assault charges, the strikers, now class-conscious and united, gather for a demonstration march. The last chapter consists of alternating, movielike "shots" showing on the one side National Guard troops setting up machine guns, fixing bayonets, adjusting gas masks at ready; while on the other side is seen the steadily advancing vanguard of the unarmed marchers. And so the book ends, with the strikers marching toward the troops, the machine guns, the rifles, the bayonets, the gas, marching and singing:

> Hold the fort for we are coming;
> Workingmen be strong! . . .

Such an ending would seem to support, not Marx's theory of the proletarian revolution, but Freud's postulate of a universal death-wish. Cantwell himself saw the point in "A Town and Its Novels," his review of *Marching! Marching!* He noted that of the three proletarian novels based on labor conditions in Aberdeen — Louis Colman's *Lumber*, his own novel, and *Marching! Marching!* — all described strikes that were lost. In actuality, he continued, there was a general lumber strike in that city in 1935 which labor won "hands down," and he concluded:

The novelists insensibly patronized the workers they wrote about. They knew that the masses were on the move, but they did not know where they were going; and in their hearts they feared that the militant working class, its ranks solid and its morale high, was marching, marching! smack against a stone wall.[18]

From the Party's viewpoint perhaps the Communists were wise in encouraging these middle-class writers to be fellow travelers only.

A strike and its accompanying violence were of course not the only material for literary creation. Since his discovery of Marxist theory was usually the most illuminating intellectual event in his recent experience, the proletarian novelist turned as frequently to a consideration of the process whereby a worker becomes class-conscious or a middle-class individual comes to identify himself with the proletarian masses. Like a strike, "conversion" furnished so appropriate a curve for dramatic action that eighteen novels use it for their central theme.[19] This group readily subdivides into two smaller groupings: those with actual proletarians as protagonists, and those in which the leading character comes from some layer of the middle class. Unlike the case with Socialist fiction, the former grouping is somewhat larger, because critical discussions of the novel did so often emphasize the need to write of proletarian life and because, where the Socialist writer thought of himself as primarily joining a political party, the radical author of the thirties imaged himself as plunging into the surge of a mass movement.

Each grouping tends to follow a characteristic pattern. For the proletarian hero, the developmental process is a slow awakening to the injustice of capitalism as it operates within his own limited experience. The worker often attempts to rise from his class, only to find that his struggles are thwarted by his lack of money or his predilection for honesty. He blunders along, painfully puzzling out such questions as why he is periodically laid off, why men injured by machines are given no compensation or are cheated of it, why strikes are sometimes sold out by corrupt union officials, why police brutality has always to be expected. When, therefore, a Communist agitator or organizer begins to make the protagonist generalize from his experiences, the agitator's words are like a match applied to an already laid fire, which then blazes up in the red flames of revolt. Such a development may be seen in James Steele's *Conveyor*, a crudely fictionalized report on working conditions in Henry Ford's River Rouge Plant. Jim Brogan, an "average worker," who votes for Hoover and hates the Reds, at first quits his auto plant job because of the speed-up, but is unable to find other work. After he and his wife lose the company house that they have been buying at exorbitant interest rates, they both go to work. Jim finds that the "River Rohte" Plant puts out its production under the pressure of a frantic speed-up of the assembly line, disregard of safety regulations, and strict surveillance by the "servicemen" (labor spies). When the men in Jim's room spontaneously rebel, the servicemen beat them up, Jim being injured so badly that he is taken to the hospital. Upon leaving, he decides that he must help the Communist who has been quietly organizing an auto union. Jim's conversion has come the hard way.

The conversion of a middle-class protagonist consists usually in his being shaken out of his bourgeois lethargy by the effects of the Depression. Declassed, he is forced to earn what he can through the sale of his labor power, discovers how precariously the proletariat lives, is drawn into a strike or radical demonstration wherein his middle-class faith in capitalist justice is shattered, and thereupon throws himself wholeheartedly into the class struggle on the side of the workers. In somewhat this fashion does ex-private William Hicks receive his education in Thomas Boyd's *In Time of Peace*, a sequel to the author's bitter war novel, *Through the Wheat*. Hicks, who is pictured as a sincere and unsophisticated, "naturally" moral man, leaves his exhausting nightshift job as a turret-lathe operator in order to get a white-collar position on which to be married. Slowly he loses his naïveté by working as a reporter on various cynical or double-dealing newspapers, attempts unsuccessfully to keep up with Prosperity in the late twenties, and, after the Market Crash, tries to become a machinist again.

Turned away at the gate of Victory Motors, he joins a Communist demonstration for jobs, helps lead it against police opposition, and is wounded in the resulting clash. *Through the Wheat* had ended with Private Hicks numbed by the horrors of battle; Civilian Hicks has now learned that in time of peace, one must prepare for class war.

Lying on the pavement, he [Hicks] gasped from sheer disbelief. He was an American citizen protesting against intolerable conditions into which he had found himself being forced. No more than that. And he had been clipped by a machine gun bullet when there was no chance of his fighting back. If he had had a gun he could have understood it, but he had been shot down by a man he had never threatened, by a man he had never seen before. It was as murderous as when, after St. Mihiel, an Illinois roughneck in his battalion had killed two unarmed German prisoners. He had that same sense of mute horror now.

Then the numbness left. Pain rushed with the air into his wound — hot, exquisite stabs of self-pity. But no, by God! Back of the guards stood the police, back of the police the politicians, the Libbys [owner of Victory Motors], and behind them all the sacred name of Property. In the name of property men could be starved to death, and if they even so much as raised their heads, there was war. Hicks gritted his teeth. If it was war again, he was glad to know it. He at least had something to fight for now.[20]

More than half of the conversion novels have New York City as a setting, probably for the obvious reason of New York's primacy as a center of both radical and literary activity. Again for a rather obvious sociological reason, those novels involving skilled-worker or middle-class protagonists usually have a single city or locality for background, since such individuals in actual life tend to show less geographical mobility than unskilled or semiskilled workers. One of the features of the conversion group, however, is the occasional appearance of a "picaresque" novel, in which the hero, an unskilled or semiskilled laborer, wanders about Ulysses-like past all the Circes and Scyllas of the American land. Such an episodic structure underlies Jack Conroy's *The Disinherited*, which has the further distinction of being one of the relatively few proletarian novels written by a working-class author. Conroy, who was born in 1899 at Moberly, Missouri, had grown up in poverty similar to that described in this first novel, had drifted from job to job about the Middle West, read widely, and, it is reported, taught himself Latin and mathematics in order to attend the University of Missouri. Intermittent periods of unemployment, he later asserted, had meanwhile made him anticapitalist. He formed the group known as the Rebel Poets and was coeditor of their anthology *Unrest*, which appeared annually from 1929 through 1931. Later he edited *Anvil*, the first magazine devoted to proletarian short stories.

His novel, dedicated to "the disinherited and dispossessed of the world," opens with the childhood of Larry Donovan at Monkey Nest Camp, a tiny coal community in Missouri, where the dump from the mine tipple "dominated [the] . . . camp like an Old World cathedral towering over peasants' huts." First one older brother, then another, is killed by the mine; and strikes, led by Larry's father, keep the family constantly in debt until, when the father dies from a poorly placed dynamite shot, the mother is forced to take in washing in order to keep the two surviving children alive. At the age of thirteen, Larry goes to work in the railroad repair shops of a nearby city, tries to supplement his irregular public schooling with night school and correspondence courses so that he may rise in the world, goes out on strike after World War I with the rest of the railroad maintenance men, and sees the strike systematically broken with the help of the militia and crooked union leaders.

From that time on he becomes a drifter. He works in a steel mill until he is fired for trying to save a "bolshevik" from a beating, and then takes a job in a rubber factory, where he meets Hans, who had deserted from the German army and fought after the war as one of Karl Liebknecht's Spartacides. Hans tells him to read Marx, but Larry's more immediate interest is to make love to the lunchwagon girl. Moving on to Detroit by freight car, he begins a series of jobs in the fast-growing automobile industry of the twenties, gradually giving up his ambitions for a white-collar job and, like his cynical friend Ed, spending his money on bootleg liquor and women. When the bottom drops out of the Great Bull Market, Larry and Ed are left to the hard mercies of soup line and flophouse to get them through the first winter of the Depression. In an automobile trek matched only by that of the Joads, the two

men work their way back to Monkey Nest Camp, to find that the
Depression has struck the surrounding farming areas as hard as the
cities. After working at construction jobs through freezing winter
and burning summer, Larry at last succeeds in identifying himself
gladly with the rest of his class.

I no longer felt shame at being seen at such work as I would have
once, and I knew that the only way for me to rise to something approx-
imating the grandiose ambitions of my youth would be to rise with my
class, with the disinherited: the bricksetters, the flivver tramps, boom-
ers, and outcasts pounding their ears in flophouses. Every gibe at any
of the paving gang; every covert or open sneer by prosperous looking
bystanders infuriated me but did not abash me. The fat on my bones
melted away under the glare of the burnished sun, and the fat in my
mind dissolved, too. It dripped in sweat off the end of my nose onto the
bricks, dampened the sand. I felt weak as from the loss of blood, but
also resigned. I felt like a man whose feet have been splashing about
in ooze and at last have come to rest on a solid rock, even though it lay
far below his former level.[21]

When, therefore, Hans reappears as a Communist organizer, Larry
readily helps him gather a crowd of farmers to block the sheriff's
sale of a mortgaged farm by buying it back for the farmer at a
price of ninety-nine cents. As the book concludes, Larry and Ed
have both set off with Hans to help organize agrarian discontent
into "a mighty blaze." As they drive along, Ed speaks to Larry:
" 'Another hard Winter comin' on,' he said. 'But I won't mind it
like the others. I'm beginnin' t'get some kick out of livin'. You
and me both got a different spirit.' " [22]

In writing *The Disinherited*, Conroy probably committed every
error known to the self-taught novelist. His style mixes partially
successful attempts at reproducing the slangy speech of workers
with stretches of the most painful "fine writing"; his characters,
even the semiautobiographical Larry, are little more than grouped
reflexes; he starts scenes only to wander off into narrative; and the
ending of the book is scarcely more emphatic than that of any
other of the loosely-strung-together episodes. For all its rambling
structure — it was originally a series of sketches — the book has a
driving vitality, and the combination of these two contradictory
qualities, whether consciously on the part of the author or not,
gives the reader a sense of the active but undirected life of migra-

tory laborers. Conroy also shows convincingly what it feels like to work in the racket of a steel mill or through the night shift, where one's stomach turns sick from sleepiness, and there are memorable passages, such as the description of his mother, "of the nights she sweated over the irons or the days she bent over the steaming wash tub." If the novel is not a good one artistically, it at least springs from authentic experience, harsh experience which makes the conversion ending credible in its flatness.

In the strike and conversion novels, the proletarian writer, with some exceptions, tends to make his message explicit: the working class will move forward under the leadership of its revolutionary vanguard, the Communist Party. In the relatively few novels concerned with the "bottom dogs" of society,[23] the message tends, again with exceptions, to be implicit only. For the most part refusing the assistance of slogans, resolutions, and other revolutionary gestures, these novelists ambush the reader from behind a relentlessly objective description of life in the lower depths. Here is the vast area of failure, of have-not, of down-and-out. In *Bottom Dogs*, Edward Dahlberg created a name for the genre when he described Lorry Lewis's life at an orphanage, his careless drift from job to job, his hoboing experiences while riding the freights, and his viciously directionless life in Los Angeles. As the book ends, Lorry has had intercourse with a dance-hall girl and is wondering whether he has caught a venereal disease. He realizes "the monotonous dead level he had been in for months. . . Something had to happen; and he knew nothing would. . . " Nelson Algren's fascinatingly hideous novel about America's homeless boys, *Somebody in Boots*, has epigraphs taken from *The Communist Manifesto* at the head of each section to counterpoint the action; but the story itself is confined to the bleak life of Cass McKay, who grows up in a filthy, brawling home in a West Texas border town, goes on the road, spends nineteen days in jail for vagrancy, and finally arrives in Chicago.[24] Here he lives with Norah Egan, a sweatshop worker, falls in with a Negro Communist, and is beaten up by a former friend for associating with Negroes. Norah leaves him, and when he loses his job, he sets off again, never knowing that he could have helped build a better society than the scabrous one he inhabits.

Of this group the outstanding one and, in the opinion of the present writer, the most distinguished single proletarian novel is Henry Roth's *Call It Sleep*. Far more complex in conception, far firmer in execution, than any usual first novel, *Call It Sleep* is a full record of approximately two years (from the age of six to eight, from 1911 to 1913) in the childhood of a Jewish immigrant child in Brownsville and the Lower East Side of New York. David Schearl is the sensitive and timid son of a generous, loving mother and a truculently egotistical, almost paranoiac father, whose wild bursts of anger prevent him from holding any job or friend for long. The child identifies various parts of the two tenements in which the Schearls successively live with feelings of terror, revulsion, security, release; and these places, as they are refracted through David's mind, become for the reader a complex and powerful system of symbols concerned with human consciousness. In the Brownsville tenement, the cellar is a source of terror to David because its darkness is inhabited by rats and by the grotesque shapes of horrified imagination. On the East Side, "cellar" becomes synonymous with bodily corruption, with stinking toilets and adolescent sex. Since it is to his mother that he turns from the terrors of the cellar and from the turbulent harshness of ordinary street life, the top floor of the tenement where the family lives naturally represents refuge, whereas the roof of the tenement holds release through friendship and emotional growth.

When David is sent to Hebrew school, he impresses the filthily dressed Reb Yidel Pankower with his "iron wit," that is, his ability to read Hebrew. David is fascinated one day to hear the rabbi translate a passage describing how an angel touched the lips of Isaiah with a fiery coal that the prophet might speak in the presence of God. The passage becomes a shaping concept which ultimately brings together the disunified elements of David's experience — the cellar, the street, the tenement apartment, and the roof. A preliminary but incomplete attempt at unification comes when three young hoodlums catch David at Passover — anti-Semitism has an organic place in the plot; it is not introduced self-consciously for "propaganda" purposes — and force the child to drop a strip of zinc into the crack between the streetcar tracks where the power line runs. Terrified at the flash produced when the metal strikes the electric current, David runs back to Hebrew school, where he begins to ponder on darkness and God's power. Darkness brings to his child's mind the cellar, where coal is kept in bins. Then, by association, he thinks that God's "coal" is down in the "cellar" of the crack in the streetcar tracks and that the flash produced by the metal was such a coal as Isaiah saw. When he tells this to Reb Yidel, the rabbi laughs at him.

To give himself courage, he goes up to the roof of the tenement, where he meets the adolescent, Leo.[25] In order to gain Leo's friendship, he helps him to lure Esther, the stepdaughter of his aunt, into a cellar so that Leo may "play bad" with her. David's complicity is discovered, and his father, already crazed by a mistaken conviction that the boy is not his own son, begins to beat him. David runs from the house to the streetcar track, hysterically pushes the ladle of a milk can into the slot of the power line, and is shocked unconscious. While reviving, he has a vision that finally unifies the disparate elements of his consciousness and makes him capable of accepting even terror and revulsion.

Since Michael Gold's *Jews Without Money* is likewise concerned with life in the East Side Ghetto at roughly the same historical time, it is instructive to compare his book with *Call It Sleep*. Though Gold's intentions were — to be fair — somewhat different from Roth's, the comparison shows the difference in result between the operations of the Coleridgian "fancy" and "imagination." Gold's book is that of a man with strong impulses and sympathies, but without, as the very sketch form of the book suggests, the capacity for sustained artistic vision. Roth's impulses and sympathies are strong also, but he has the ability, essential for the first-rate writer, to express them fully while simultaneously remaining in control of them, shaping them into the most effective form for transmission to the reader. Though the presence of an actual plot in *Call It Sleep* may seem contrived to some, the real force of the author is revealed in the intricate strength of his symbolic pattern. Both men, moreover, write with respect for their characters, even the hopelessly twisted ones; but Gold's people are simplified literally into sketches, while Roth's are given all the tangled complexity of human beings. Gold's pictures of the Ghetto are frequently blurred by a warm rush of sentiment or jarred out of focus by a kind of hysteria; Roth's view of the same life has the dizzying intensity of the mystic who sees all things at once, even the most minute, in utter clarity. Finally, they approach the problem of writing a proletarian novel quite differently. When Gold introduces a conversion at the end of his book to make his point clear and to provide some sort of climax for his sketches, one may accept it as logically possible, given the preceding circumstances, but not as psychologically or artistically necessary. Roth's ending, on the other hand, is organic with what has gone before, and hence what he is saying is artistically more compelling. The reader of *Jews Without Money* has enlarged his information; the reader of *Call It Sleep* has enlarged his imagination.

Despite the much greater frankness of dialogue and incident in *Call It Sleep* — too frank, most reviewers felt — Roth, unlike Gold, is mostly content with an implied criticism of capitalist society; yet there are a few points at which the revolutionary purpose juts close to the surface. In a remarkable passage just before David drops the ladle, Roth brings together snatches of the typical conversations that could have been heard within the vicinity. Among these voices one stands out:

"They'll betray us!" Above all these voices, the speaker's voice rose. "In 1789, in 1848, in 1871, in 1905, he who has anything to say will enslave us anew! Or if not enslave will desert us when the red cock crows! Only the laboring poor, only the masses embittered, bewildered, betrayed, in the day when the red cock crows, can free us!" [26]

In the coda of speech fragments which Roth introduces at the moment when the ladle connects David with the power line, the street agitator's words are the culmination over the banal and obscene:

To a red cock crowin'. Over a statue of.
A jerkin'. Cod. Clang! Clang! Oy! Machine! Liberty! Revolt! Redeem!

> *Power*
> *Power! Power like a paw, titanic power,*
> *ripped through the earth and slammed*
> *against his body and shackled him*
> *where he stood.*[27]

At the conclusion of the book, David is brought home safe to a repentant father and a grief-stricken mother who put him to bed.

His last thoughts before he goes to sleep imply, although very obliquely, that the vision which unified his past will give him the courage to shape his later life toward the masses.

He might as well call it sleep. It was only toward sleep that ears had power to cull again and reassemble the shrill cry, the hoarse voice, the scream of fear, the bells, the thick-breathing, the roar of crowds and all sounds that lay fermenting in the vats of silence and the past. It was only toward sleep one knew himself still lying on the cobbles, felt the cobbles under him, and over him and scudding ever toward him like a black foam, the perpetual blur of shod and running feet, the broken shoes, new shoes, stubby, pointed, caked, polished, bunyiony, pavement-beveled, lumpish, under skirts, under trousers, shoes, over one and through one, and feel them all and feel, not pain, not terror, but strangest triumph, strangest acquiescence. One might as well call it sleep. He shut his eyes.[28]

As might be supposed, the appearance of a book in which revolutionary ideology played so little explicit part produced an altercation on the Left. *The New Masses* dismissed the book with a generally unsympathetic, one-paragraph review, concluding: "It is a pity that so many young writers drawn from the proletariat can make no better use of their working class experience than as material for introspective and febrile novels." [29] In the following issue, however, the magazine published a letter from one David Greenhood, who on political grounds strongly demurred from the reviewer's judgment.

But *Call It Sleep* is about the working-class bottom, written by one of its own naturals who became articulate long before he wrote the novel, and who while he wrote it was engaged, as he has never ceased to be, in the one struggle that counts.[30]

It remained for Edwin Seaver to settle the controversy, or at least have the last word, by sensibly considering the character of the book within its own terms. He pointed to the obvious facts that David is in the "pre-political" period of childhood and that the time of the book was not the present.

Elsewhere . . . I have reviewed Roth's novel at length and attempted to speak of the very genuine experience his book gave me. What I wish to point out here is the manner in which the author shows how his hero surmounts the fearful obstacles on his road to life, with the result that when we close the book we honestly feel that such a childhood can mature into a revolutionary manhood. If there is a better, a more purposeful rendering of an East Side proletarian childhood than that contained in *Call It Sleep* I have yet to see it. What better use could Roth have made of his working-class experience as a child than to have shown honestly and greatly exactly what that experience consisted of? Should little David Schearl have joined the Young Pioneers, a nonexistent organization? Should David's working-class father have been a socialist when he wasn't? Should the author himself have turned Jehovah and moved history forward to satisfy his critic? [31]

Criticism based on the number of revolutionary gestures per book was likewise aimed occasionally at representatives of the fourth major group of proletarian novels, those concerned with middle-class decay; but most were spared this blind fate because they employed counterthemes of revolutionary development as a method of emphasizing and offsetting the central theme. A well-known example of this device occurs at the conclusion of James T. Farrell's *Judgment Day*, the final volume of the *Studs Lonigan* trilogy. Although the life of Lonigan himself is as drab and flat as most of the Chicago terrain where the story is laid, the architectonics of the trilogy have a massive regularity similar to that city's street plan; and the death of the degenerated Studs is balanced by scenes from the Communist parade which the uncomprehending father, Paddy Lonigan, witnesses. Despair and hope, death and life perform a counterpoint in class terms: the middle class is decaying, the power of the proletariat is being born.

The only other proletarian trilogy [32] is likewise concerned with the decay of the middle class and likewise utilizes the theme of revolutionary development in some characters as contrast to a narrative of disintegration. The author, Josephine Herbst, was born at Sioux City, Iowa, in 1897, her parents having come west from Pennsylvania in the late 1880's. She writes that she "was brought up on my mother's nostalgia for the East; and her admiration for those members of her family who had ventured, often to their downfall, dramatized for me my entire conception of American life." [33] After attending four different colleges — she graduated from the University of California in 1919 — she held various writing jobs in New York, lived for three years in Europe, published her first story in *The Smart Set*, and, in 1925, married an expatriate named John Herrmann. From that time on, she lived in the United States except for travel abroad as a correspondent. During the Depression, she visited the drought areas and was in Cuba at the time of the general strike in 1935, events which she later made use of in the last volume of her trilogy.

While in Europe, she had been influenced by the expatriates, and her first novels — revealingly titled *Nothing Is Sacred* (1928) and *Money for Love* (1929) — dealt in the approved disillusioned manner with the lives of spiritually dry people. When she subsequently turned to the tracing of her family's history, therefore, she was at first neatly adjusted to simply a saga of decline; but with the advent of the Depression she had been drawn to Marxism, and her attitude underwent a subtle reorientation. If the decay of a family were seen as a tiny part in a dialectical process of world history, a story of disintegration could affirm as well as deny; for indications of capitalism's decline might be matched by indications of a future collective society in the same way that her new interest in Marxism contrasted with the attitudes of the other members of her family. In a sense, then, her own mental development and the development of values in her trilogy show a one-to-one relationship.

The first volume, *Pity Is Not Enough*, traces the lives of the various members of the Trexler family from 1868 to 1896, the three chief characters being linked, evidently with the author's conscious intention, to three outstanding socioeconomic developments of those years. The elder son, Joe, goes to Reconstruction Georgia, involves himself in the political manipulations of the Western & Atlanta Railroad, is made the scapegoat when the fraud is exposed, and flees to the West, where he becomes insane after participating in the Black Hills gold rush. Anne marries Amos Wendell and goes with him to the farmlands of Iowa and to poverty; while David, the astute and self-centered youngest child, begins his climb toward a Robber Baronetcy by profiteering in government flour. In order to give depth to this family chronicle, the author establishes a double chronology by inserting from time to time brief selections showing the four daughters of Amos and Anne Wendell growing up and, in the last insert piece, defending the unions in the Seattle General Strike of 1919.

The second volume, *The Executioner Waits*, takes the Trexler descendants from 1902 to 1929. Here the major historical developments considered are the rise and fall of the I.W.W., the First World War, and the Boom. The action centers mainly around David and his two nieces, Rosamund and Victoria Wendell. For David, the World War is a blessing. He "made money before the day the European nations went to war, but after that date, his money bred money, the stuff was fertile as a grain field in good growing weather." Rosamund marries Jerry Stauffer before he leaves for France as a soldier. Upon his return, they struggle along with very little money until she is killed in an automobile accident. Jerry regains the spirit he lost in the war by joining workers in a strike. Victoria goes to New York, where she lives with the young intellectual, Jonathan Chance, until his well-to-do parents force them to marry. The insert pieces in this volume are still advanced in time, consisting of short scenes from various parts of the United States which show the ground swell of revolt in the years of 1932 to 1934. These indications of the collapse of the middle class and the developing class war are brought to a culmination in the last scene of the book where the ill and aging David goes to visit a grave in a cemetery, only to overhear the speeches at the burial of a dead striker.

> "*Don't mourn. Organize*," said the voice, the body leaning toward them, the hands out, then dropped quietly. A deep silence followed the words.
> David Trexler shivered on the ignored edge of the crowd but when the yellow lumps of earth began to fall, he shuddered as if they were falling into his own grave, upon his own unprotected flesh.
> The crowd stood tight, a hard nucleus like a fist that would never open, and he looked toward it appealingly for sympathy for David Trexler, the little orphan, but it was staring at the grave and did not see him.[34]

This obviously symbolic juxtaposition of the dying middle class and the proletariat in a field of graves is the pivot of the trilogy. *Rope of Gold*, which covers the thirties up to the sit-down strikes of 1937, describes the later life of Victoria and Jonathan. Jonathan, now a Communist, is trying to organize the farmers in the section of Pennsylvania where the couple is living.

After their baby dies, Victoria has an affair with a German refugee Communist, and she and her husband begin to drift apart. She travels through the drought areas of the Midwest writing articles on the agrarian unrest, goes to Cuba to cover the general strike, and finally splits with Jonathan on personal rather than political grounds. The other central character of the book is Steve Carson, a farm boy from South Dakota, who takes a job in Detroit. Finally realizing that he must stand by his fellow auto workers, he joins the sit-down strike; and the trilogy ends with the class lines drawn on an actual barricade, strikers inside and National Guard troops outside a high factory wall.

One suspects that it may have been partly their major theme which bleached out to colorlessness the prose style of most novels in this last major group. It would certainly have been difficult for these writers to chronicle with zest and passion the slow downward spiral of what they considered both a dull and ideologically unimportant class; and only James Farrell succeeded, because setting down the minutely detailed degradation of Studs Lonigan represented for him an angry act of catharsis. Like the autobiographical Danny O'Neill, one of the counterweights to Studs, he "wanted to purge himself completely of the world he knew." Possibly, too, the prose in this group of novels suffers from the authors' tendency to schematize — evidences of middle-class decline to be set off at regular intervals by indications of proletarian growth. But despite heavy prose and mechanical structure, the over-all scheme, even if one rejects the doctrine, lends a certain dramatic power to these books. That scheme is clear enough. The middle class, which so long obscured the actual operation of Marxian laws in American capitalism, is fast disintegrating between the hammer and the anvil of the two great antagonistic classes. The lines are now drawn. Class war is out in the open for all to see.

Besides the four major subject matters of the proletarian novel there are a number of minor ones. For example, the problem of anti-Semitism, intensified though it was in these years by the malignant rise of German Nazism, was given full-length treatment only in Edward Dahlberg's *Those Who Perish*, which examines the effects in America of the Nazi pogroms and the widespread menace of Fascism. Unfortunately, the despairing hysteria of Regina Gordon — who comes to believe that Communism is the hope of the future, yet poisons herself because she is too much of the decaying old world — is matched by a semihysterical, synesthetic style that dissolves what is being said in the manner of saying it.

The important "matter" of our American dilemma, Negro–white relations, is frequently introduced as a minor theme in these novels and is the central concern of five. Guy Endore's *Babouk* is chiefly interesting as an excursion into economic history, for it details the conditions which, in 1791, at last pushed the slaves of San Domingo into bloody revolt against the white planters. Grace Lumpkin's *A Sign for Cain* deals with the contemporary suppression of Negro rights in the American South through economic exploitation, Jim Crow, and lynchings; while John Spivak's *Georgia Nigger* [35] details the results of its author's documented observation of the horrors in Southern chain gang and prison camp. In order to show that the Negro was oppressed in North as well as South, Scott Nearing in *Free Born* has his colored hero become a Communist after witnessing both a lynching in Georgia and the 1919 race riot in Chicago, and be railroaded to a Pennsylvania prison for his part in a coal strike. *Free Born*, subtitled "An Unpublishable Novel" because presumably no commercial publisher would accept it, has the distinction of being, as the scholar Hugh Gloster states, "the first revolutionary novel of Negro life," [36] and is further at least noteworthy for containing probably the most ghastly lynch scene in American literature. These four books, it should be noticed, were by white writers. Despite the conditions under which American Negroes must still live in the middle of the twentieth century, the fact is now established that the Communist Party has influenced remarkably few members of the race, although throughout the late twenties and the thirties it set as one of its major tasks that of organizing Negro workers and "peasants" and of drawing them into Party activity. Additional evidence of the almost complete rejection by Negroes of the Communist appeal is that the proletarian school could genuinely claim no Negro novelist until Richard Wright's book of four novellas, *Uncle Tom's Children*, appeared in 1938, after Wright had broken with the Communist Party.[37]

Four novels may be considered as taking their themes from special aspects of American history. Melvin Levy's *The Last Pioneers*, although it might also be considered a novel of middle-class decay, is particularly concerned with the development of "Puget" (Seattle) from a wide-open lumber town through the years of the I.W.W. and World War I to the city of the Prosperity Decade and the 1929 Crash. In *Strange Passage*, Theodore Irwin quietly chronicles the lives of two aliens who meet on a "Deportation Special" train traveling the reverse of the pioneer route, from Seattle to Ellis Island. Finally, William Cunningham, who in the middle thirties was teaching Marxist theory at Commonwealth College in Mena, Arkansas, contributed two novels. *The Green Corn Rebellion* — the incident is so named in the War Department Archives — describes the armed uprising, in August, 1917, of a number of Oklahoma farmers who intended not only to seize power in the state, but to march on Washington, force an end to the war, and establish a coöperative commonwealth. *Pretty Boy* is an attempt to present the life of the gangster "Pretty Boy" Floyd in terms of the economic conditions that forced him to act outside the laws of capitalist society.

Cunningham's first book could also be included with the anti-war novels, of which there are two others, one at each end of the decade. Charles Yale Harrison's *Generals Die in Bed*, originally serialized in *The New Masses*, adds only a few suggestions of revolutionary sentiment to the picture of World War I made familiar in the disillusioned fiction of the twenties. Despite his use of an impressionistic first-person narrative consistently in the present tense, Harrison's book no longer has the powerful impact still residing in Dalton Trumbo's tour de force of 1939, *Johnny Got His Gun*. Here, told solely through the mind of the sufferer himself, is the story of how a "basket case" from World War I reëstablishes contact with the world about him even though the shell explosion that cost him his limbs also tore away his face, leaving him without taste, smell, sight, or hearing. Having communicated out of the dark prison of his crippled body, he asks to be exhibited to people everywhere as a protest against all future wars. His request is denied, for the men who make the wars do not wish the truth to be known by the working people who have to fight them;

and the book ends with the assertion of the sufferer that next time the people will turn the guns which they have received, not against the "enemy," but against their own masters. Ironically in the perspective of history, *Johnny Got His Gun* was published only six days after German Panzer divisions roared into Poland and ignited World War II.

Almost all of the proletarian novels kept to subjects that were located in the American present or near past. In spite of the fascination exerted by the Soviet Fatherland, most of these authors never traveled there bodily, and only one novel has a Russian setting. Myra Page's journalistic *Moscow Yankee* tells the story of how an average un-class-conscious American worker leaves the production line at Ford's for the production line of the Red Star truck plant in Moscow, gradually acquires the spirit of the Five-Year Plan, falls in love with a Russian girl of the new generation, marries her, and settles down in the Soviet Union to assist in building a workers' society.

One final theme, so obvious a one that again lack of detailed knowledge on the part of middle-class writers can alone explain its neglect, was the life and experience of a Communist Party member. According to *The New Masses*, which published it in October, 1931, the first piece of fiction concerning "life and activity in the American Communist movement" was the short story, "Our Comrade Munn." The author of this pioneering effort, it is now interesting to note, was Whittaker Chambers, who in the preceding March issue had published a "revolutionary classic" entitled "Can You Make Out Their Voices" [38] about rebellious farmers in the drought area. Communists appear as characters in a number of the novels, of course, and all the Gastonia novels contain a figure based ultimately on the strike leader, Fred Beal; yet none of these is a full-length portrait or is even particularly successful as character creation. For example, Larry Marvin in Rollins's *The Shadow Before* is inconsistently conceived. Although Marvin is at first presented as "neurotic" — this is the author's own subsequent description — his basic feeling of insecurity seems later to be contradicted by the author's insistence on personal mannerisms indicating thorough self-assurance. Without sufficient motivation, Marvin slips into insecurity again just after the battle resulting in the police chief's death, only to be given back his self-assurance almost immediately.

Thomas Boyd had intended to complete his William Hicks trilogy with a novel describing Hicks's experiences in the Communist Party, but Boyd died of a cerebral hemorrhage early in 1935 before he could even begin the project. Two books about the life of radicals appeared in 1936, but for opposite reasons neither qualifies as the study of a Communist. The central figure of Martin Delaney's *Journal of a Young Man* is a convinced Marxist and Party member, becomes in fact treasurer of his unit, takes part in a street demonstration and even completes a proletarian novel, which is finally rejected by a friendly, nonradical publisher on the grounds that a " 'revolutionary novel should be more cheerful, more hopeful. . . ' " The focus of this presumably autobiographical novel, however, is on Danny Kerry's tormented and hopeless love affair with a girl who dislikes his radical activities. On the other hand, Dave Houston, the protagonist of *Red Neck* by McAlister Coleman and Stephen Raushenbush, is a labor leader committed to class war but opposed to Communists because of a Socialist background. Although McAlister Coleman himself was a Socialist — this book and the novels of Upton Sinclair are the sole *Socialist* contributions to the radical novel in the thirties — Dave's later career is rather surprisingly shown as a decline through continued compromise and sell-out until he becomes simply another "porkchopper," or labor bureaucrat. He is now too empty a man to state openly his continued belief that capitalist violence must be met by violence from the workers, and control of his original union finally passes to the "reds" in a vigorous rank-and-file movement. *Red Neck* may best be thought of as a *Dan Minturn* of the labor world.

The one proletarian novel centered on a Communist's Party activity to appear in the thirties, therefore, was Edward Newhouse's *This Is Your Day*, published in 1937. A lively earlier novel, *You Can't Sleep Here*, had recounted the conversion to Communism of Gene Marsay, unemployed newspaperman and product of the Depression Generation. Since this first book seems to be semiautobiographical, it may be assumed that, like the central figure of *This Is Your Day*, Newhouse had had some experience with Party organizing. That the author wants his hero, Gene Marsay again, to be considered only human may be shown by the fact that the novel opens with a scene in bed between Gene and the girl he plans to marry, and then gets down to business. The larger part of the book is given over to Gene's experiences while organizing farmers in an upstate New York community, but for contrast there are also scenes revealing the hypocrisy of Marsay's brother-in-law, who pretends to himself that he too is working for the Cause while actually being a careerist teacher at a New York City university. Instead of being positive propaganda for Communism, however, *This Is Your Day* [39] would seem best calculated to frighten any writer away from active participation in radical affairs; for the novel's looseness of organization, the flat style — despite the presumably clever wisecracks — and the complete collapse of the slight dramatic structure at the end give the reader a sharp sense that he is reading the work of a man almost totally exhausted by the large and petty crises of day-to-day agitational duties. The writer's very imagination seems lifeless with fatigue. The book suggests, in fact, that the diversion of creative energy into nonliterary activity was a contributing cause for the swift decline of the proletarian novel in the second half of the thirties.

III

Late in 1937, when the second and last wave of proletarian fiction had long since receded, Sinclair Lewis, ex-radical, complained with characteristic exaggeration that young writers should examine the infinite variety of America rather than go on producing a class of novels as standardized as the automobiles that roll from an assembly line at Ford's.

But a surprising number of new talents plod up the same dreary Communist lane, and produce, all of them, the following novel: There is a perfectly nasty community — mining or pants-making or sharecropping — but in it one Sir Galahad who, after a snifter of Karl Marx, rushes out, gathers the local toilers into an organization of rather vague purposes, and after that everything will be lovely, nobody will have hay fever again, nor the deacon ever wink at the widow.[40]

That the complaint is based only on a half-truth at most should have been illustrated by the foregoing discussion of proletarian novels grouped by subject matter. Taken as a whole, this body of fiction is considerably less stylized than the prolific results of the "boy-meets-girl" formula, and any of the major groups permits as much variety as that type of novel of the twenties and thirties, the revolt of the sensitive youth against Philistia, a type that in the forties was refined into an interminable study of the artist's "alienation." Rather, what is patterned about the proletarian novels is a frequently too self-conscious intrusion of their Marxist frame of reference. As in the earlier Socialist fiction, a number of "motifs" or themes appear in so many of these novels that they soon become predictable from book to book. The writers still could not be considered as "in uniform," but like the volunteer irregulars that they were they all bore common insignia. By their signs one could know them.

Since the economic contradictions and the exploitative social relationships of capitalism are the chief object of attack, these novels, like the Socialist ones, attempt to expose all manifestations of capitalist evil — to reveal that business ethics are the ethics of the jungle and that the comfort of the few rests heavily on the misery of the many. Police brutality, such as is unleashed against the strikers in *The Land of Plenty*, appears often, for the police are the immediate agents of class domination. A blow from a policeman's club, however, is only the result of a whole long series of impulses. In these novels, it is always demonstrated to the reader in some way that the chain of authority runs back behind the police, behind the strikebreakers, the hired thugs and private detectives, the citizens' committees and vigilantes, to institutions which capitalism has set up to protect and preserve itself. Capitalist justice is always class justice; if property relationships are endangered, the whole legal apparatus is brought to bear against the offender. When strikers are brought into the courts, as in the Gastonia novels, no really fair trial can be expected by either striker or reader. The jury, usually composed of petty-bourgeois individuals, is prejudiced, the prosecution lawyers exploit the unsanctified attitude of radicals toward God and country, the defense lawyers may very well be in cahoots with the prosecution, and the judge either consciously or unconsciously responds to the dominant economic pressures of the community. Hence "justice," as is recognized by Aline in Leane Zugsmith's *A Time to Remember*, should properly be conceived, not as an absolute for all men, but as a conspiracy of one class against another.

But *we* know now, she thought. The faintest-hearted among us know. We've gone to school and in less than four weeks, we have learned a lesson that we'll never forget. We've seen the propertied elements of the city join together in a union to fight us because we belong to a union. We've seen commercial competition put aside while the merchants help Sig and Art Diamond [owners of the struck department store] to defeat us. The police and the courts and the city officials are the servants of the Chamber of Commerce and the Board of Trade. We used to think they were the servants of the people; but perhaps we aren't people. We know that these few weeks of opposition have cost Diamond's more, with their five-dollar-a-day guards and their bribes to corrupt public officers, than it would cost them to meet our wage demands for six months. There was a time when we would have said it didn't make sense; but we know the sense of it now. We've seen police ride us down and crack sticks on our heads. Sometimes I think I'll die when they shove me. I was brought up to say "How dare you!" But that was another country.[41]

Although all parts of the business community are depicted as being united in their resolve to impose capitalist justice, the newspapers come in for particularly heavy attack from these novelists, as they had from the Socialist writers. The reporter friendly to labor finds that the stories he sends in are censored or bring about his discharge; the unemployed man, settling to sleep on the park bench, covers himself with papers, the headlines of which shout that prosperity has returned; demonstrators discover that their slogans have been twisted; strikers read, first with amazement and then with anger, how facts have been distorted against them so that actual police violence will be interpreted by the public to have been "mob" violence. At the conclusion of *The Land of Plenty* two burly reporters even help the police by methodically slugging a striker, while a whole chapter in *Marching! Marching!* is given to describing strike events through the device of printing in parallel columns the divergent news stories from a local representative of America's free press and from the union's own paper. Quite unlike the heroes of the older Socialist novels, however, few proletarian protagonists feel it necessary to found their own radical newspapers, possibly because in actual life *The Daily Worker* was firmly established as an official organ of the Communist Party and because proletarian authors were more interested in bringing out little magazines of a politico-literary nature.

Various other representatives from the institutional superstructure of capitalism come under almost as bitter fire as do the gentlemen of the press. Bankers, it goes without saying, are anathema, and politicians, both local and national, are often attacked as being at best the mere creatures of capitalism or at worst ruthless schemers with native fascist goals. Although there are no political novels such as were popular among the Muckraking School,[42] the novelists had carefully learned, and constantly try to teach, Lincoln Steffens's lesson, that a competitive economics begets political corruption. In accordance with the Party line, as set forth unremittingly in *The Communist* from spring of 1933 until fall of 1935, considerable antagonism is directed against the "social fascism" of the early New Deal. Maxwell Bodenheim's *Slow Vision*, for example, makes a special point of showing how the codes established under the National Recovery Act were used to the disadvantage of labor. It should be kept in mind, of course, that *Slow Vision* and *Marching! Marching!*, which also attacks the New Deal at some length, were written before the People's Front policy of supporting President Roosevelt was adopted by the Communist Party. Along with politicians are lumped the great majority of established union officials in the American Federation of Labor, who are usually portrayed as the corrupt leaders of a Labor Front for capitalism. Such officials, being interested only in money or personal power, are as ready to break a strike as any hired gun thug. On the other hand, since the Communists did contribute to the formation of the Congress of Industrial Organizations and did help to spark its great organizing strikes in the second half of the thirties, later proletarian novels, like John Hyde Preston's *The Liberals*, often include praise for the C.I.O. and its policy of industrial, as opposed to craft, unionism.

Characters who are professional people are usually portrayed as conservatives or as more of Preston's "liberals," the "summer soldiers" who talk of social justice but who in a crisis demanding action always reveal their basic psychological dependence on a capitalism however brutal. Considering the official policies of the

American Medical Association, it is rather curious to find that, among characters who are professional men, doctors, because of their scientific training, are usually most advanced in social attitudes. Teachers, to the contrary, are a sharply divided lot, and school administrators are uniformly depicted as the blackest of reactionaries. Perhaps because a number of the novelists were recent college graduates, schools and universities are often described as being, in Marx's phrase, mere extensions of the police power of the state. The most complete indictment is made in Edwin Seaver's *Between the Hammer and the Anvil*, which contains several high-flown episodes illustrating the violation of academic freedom and the difficulties experienced by radical student organizations in escaping administrative repression on the one hand while, on the other, attempting to arouse a lethargic student body. Finally, a special, personal wrath is reserved for those intellectuals who continue to support and be richly supported by "the system." The empty culture which they produce, it is charged — the escape movie, the escape poem, the escape novel — is no better than the cheap exhibitionism of the advertising men. Their bourgeois culture glistens like a dung heap, stinks like a corpse, with decay.

As one might expect, the central characters in these books have very little use for institutionalized religion. Except in *Studs Lonigan* and *Journal of a Young Man*, both strongly anticlerical, the Catholic Church receives relatively minor notice, being quickly dismissed as obscurantist and reactionary. The chief targets, perhaps because they had been more often part of a rejected home environment, are the Protestant sects. In the "bottom dogs" fiction a favorite object of criticism is the mission, where poor food and a hard bed are granted to homeless men only after they have sung at length about being washed in the Blood of the Lamb. Religion is obviously the opiate of the masses, but the astute Marxist recognizes the power of religion in the community as another of capitalism's protective institutions. In the novels about the industrial South, the reader is always informed either explicitly or implicitly that the evangelical ministers of the region helped to persuade the mountain people to come down into the mills and that they even now drain off incipient rebellion through revivalist ecstasies. In almost every instance where religion is mentioned in connection with strikes, ministers and priests are shown as taking the side of the owning class. Those few who still attempt to apply the social gospel are quickly ostracized by the solid citizens of the community.

Quite unlike the Socialist writers, moreover, the proletarian novelists have little use even for noninstitutionalized Christianity; a personal religion is the opiate of the individual. Although it is sometimes pointed out, as in *Beyond Desire*, that the founder of the faith would have been horrified to see what churches have made of it, Christ is much less often "the first worker-Socialist" to these later novelists than he is a swearword. With few exceptions, religion simply plays no part in the interior lives of the characters. Larry Marvin in *The Shadow Before* had once, to be sure, been a Baptist Sunday School teacher in a New Jersey mill town; but a worker had talked to him about One Big Union, whereupon Marvin broke off his fruitless attempt to apply the Sermon on the Mount within capitalist society and discovered the true brotherhood of man in a militant class consciousness. It is clear that the proletarian novelists and the protagonists in their fiction obtained certain quasireligious satisfactions from Marxism, but the fact is very rarely admitted consciously. Marxism is science, light, and progress; religion is superstition, darkness, and retreat.

Despite its opposition to religion as a form of antiintellectualism, despite its insistence that Marxism liberates the mind, this literature is primarily not one of ideas but of attitudes, a characteristic which, incidentally, it shares with most other American fiction of the thirties. It honors science, for example, but beyond the generalized word of praise and an occasional assurance that Communists favor technological advance it has little to say about the nature and momentous role of science in the twentieth century. Again, nothing in the proletarian novel resembles the earnest, rather clumsy discussions by the Socialist writers of how Darwinism might be reconciled with ethics; this fiction merely assumes without question that ethics are the product of environment and that all evil is contributable to the social relations within capitalism. Nor does any novel come to grips with the somewhat related problem, which is almost a theological paradox within Marxism — how necessity and freedom are actually related, how the future can simultaneously be predetermined and yet subject to human will, why men must —

how they even can — align themselves deliberately with history in order to try to hasten it when the historic process moves inexorably out of the relationships of production. No doubt these novels are often better as novels for not being more expository than they already are, certainly they are generally more competent in craftsmanship and more readable than the Socialist fiction; but the fact remains that, with the exception of the highly individualistic Waldo Frank, none of the authors cared to work out a dramatic scheme capable of carrying the philosophic weight of such works by European radicals as Koestler's *Darkness at Noon*, Silone's *Bread and Wine*, or, to pick an example more politically acceptable to them on its appearance, Malraux's *Man's Hope*.

Although little quarter is given to religion, to return to the subject at hand, the novelists show consistent tolerance in another direction. One of the most frequently recurring motifs is an attack on that vicious characteristic of American society, racial discrimination. Not only do all the novels about Gastonia emphasize that the Communist textile union's motto is, "Black and white, unite and fight," but a large majority of the others introduce episodes of varying length making similar appeals. Sometimes, as in *All Brides Are Beautiful*, the episode may consist simply of protest by an enlightened character when an unenlightened one uses the word "nigger." A more usual method is to introduce a Negro who is befriended or protected by a radical in the book. Although, in the highway-building sequence near the end of *The Disinherited*, a Negro has been used by the road boss as a pace-setter, Larry Donovan is not disturbed when he inadvertently drinks from the "nigger cup" in the water pail; and when the pace-setter collapses in the intense heat, Larry refuses to go back to work until a doctor has been called for the man. Occasionally the episode teaching racial tolerance appears to be dragged in like a homily with little concern for the structure of the story. In *The Green Corn Rebellion*, the Negro Bill Johnson appears briefly and unimportantly in the climactic section describing the actual uprising; but a preceding, almost unrelated chapter is in effect a short story, reminiscent of Erskine Caldwell's shockers, which tells how Bill is promised a load of wheat if he will eat a dead mouse and, when he does so sickeningly, is robbed of the wheat by its same Negro-hating owner. Finally, as in *A Sign for Cain*, a lynching may occur in spite of, or may be prevented by, the militant workers. In conversations among characters, lynchings are often referred to as evidence of native fascism.

At some point in most of the novels strong opposition is likewise registered against anti-Semitism and nationalistic hatreds; by contrast, of course, proletarian internationalism is praised. It is quite often a foreign-born character who brings the Marxist message to the potential American convert, and representatives of various nationalities may be brought together in a strike or demonstration as a kind of fictional prediction of a world-wide Union of Soviet Socialist Republics. Accompanying attacks on the nationalistic spirit, a very frequent motif is the condemnation of militarism, imperialism, or war. World War I is viewed as the bloody consequence of rival imperialisms, although the various characters may not analyze the causes of war in such abstract terms. The saying, "It was a rich man's war and a poor man's fight," is used by individuals in several different books; while a frequent device is the introduction of a minor character who goes or has gone through the war as a common soldier — officers are much less popular than in the fiction of World War II — and becomes disillusioned with the hypocritical slogans employed by capitalist countries to mask their ruthless drives for markets. Tom, in *Gathering Storm*, is beaten and jailed when he dares to talk against the war; the brother of Cass McKay, protagonist of *Somebody in Boots*, was gassed and spiritually wounded while a soldier in France; ex-private William Hicks of *In Time of Peace* discovers that the only war which the workers should fight in is that between the classes. Clearly the intent of these writers is not "pacifistic." It is, moreover, recognized in these novels that one of the "peacetime" functions of the Army and the National Guard, and of such militarist organizations as the American Legion, is the breaking of strikes and the containment of working-class discontent.

Because of their opposition to militarism and their support of internationalism, the authors of the earlier novels usually consider patriotism to be one of the last refuges of the bourgeois scoundrel; yet an oblique attack on false patriotism is occasionally made. When, for example, the striking mill workers march in *The Shadow*

Before, a mounted policeman gallops up to the boy carrying the American flag and roars: "*Pull that goddamned flag off the ground or I'll give you a kick in the goddamned . . .*" In the novels appearing after 1934, the attitude toward patriotism is given a new twist. In this later fiction, it is not infrequently argued, somewhat contradictorily, that international Communism is actually "true Americanism," since Communism is merely an extension of an American tradition of revolution.[43] When Granny, a declassed petty bourgeoise in *Marching! Marching!*, goes to a mass meeting, she hears one worker tell another:

"They talk about radical foreign stuff! Americanism! That's what! Americanism! Didnt we have a revolution to get founded? to get our American freedom of speech? to get ourselves a government for the people and by the people? And isnt the people the masses? By God, I'd like to know who we are if we aint the people! And now that the bosses and politicians is running the country like money kings, we got to take it away from 'em to run it for us people again. We've put kings under the earth before. We did it in 1776 and we'll damn well do it again!" [44]

Granny thereupon rises with the audience when it bursts into singing the *Internationale*.

It is the spirit of the *Internationale* which animates all of the class-conscious characters in these proletarian novels. Against what they conceive as capitalism's unjust laws, its vicious and vitiating institutions, its starvation and its wars, are set the sense of solidarity given by mass action and the light that the torch of Marxist knowledge brings to dark, suffering ignorance. In all of the strike and conversion novels, the central figure learns that he must lose his soul in order to find it, must submerge himself in the masses in order to discover true individuality. It is the fusing power of the mass which integrates and makes purposeful the drifting worker or the helpless, tortured member of the middle class; it is this fusing power which makes a strike possible, turns a congeries of individuals into one hard fist, hurls the working class again and again against its oppressors. Like the motif of solidarity, the motif of enlightenment informs these novels. So Mom, the paralytic in *Marching! Marching!*, remembers that before Matt, the Communist organizer, came, the world was not round. It was a flat road between shack and factory prison. Sometimes the looks of the shacks and workhouses changed, but the road was the same, with its surrounding wall of despair. There was an outlet — into the immense concentration camp of the unemployed. None escaped. No one who worked could save enough for the ladder to go clear over the wall. Now here they were, depressed, ground into the earth, stood against walls.[45]

Then into this world comes knowledge of the revolution. With knowledge comes power, the power whereby the prisoners of starvation may arise and bring a better world to birth.

IV

In the preceding discussion of its subject matter and "motifs" the proletarian novel has been largely considered as a distinct phenomenon in the American literature of its time. Such a procedure is of course arbitrary and has been followed for its convenience, much as certain physical factors may be isolated for analysis in a laboratory experiment. If, instead, this part is viewed as it relates to the whole of American fiction in the thirties, it will be seen that, beneath left-wing assertions that here literature was making an entirely new start, what actually happened was the adaptation of a radical ideology to what might be called the inherited literary consciousness. Despite a difference in ideologic viewpoint, the proletarians responded to that consciousness much as did other, nonradical writers; for the idol-smashing literature of the twenties had furnished a common nourishment.

It may be said at once flatly that the American proletarian writers were not appreciably influenced in their craft by the practice of Soviet novelists, and this for two obvious reasons: almost no American novelist or critic of any political persuasion could read the Russian language, and relatively few translations of the many current Soviet novels were available. These points were underscored at the time by the symposium "Where We Stand," published in *International Literature* for July, 1934, the contributors being Theodore Dreiser, Malcolm Cowley, Louis Adamic, Joseph Freeman, Isidor Schneider, Granville Hicks, Corliss Lamont, Joseph Kalar, and James Steele. Since each of these men regarded Russia

favorably and was intensely interested in Soviet affairs, their unani-
mous confession to substantial ignorance of Soviet literature, precisely because of language and translation difficulties, is particularly telling. The most pertinent explanation is Cowley's.

> Nobody here in the United States who doesn't read Russian knows
> very much about Soviet literature. A good many Soviet novels are
> translated, but they are always the novels read four or five years ago in
> Russia — thus, during the first five-year plan, we were getting the
> disillusioned books written during the NEP, and at present we are
> getting novels written in the first flush of the five-year plan — and we
> aren't getting enough of them.[46]

The contributors agreed that what Soviet fiction they had read
was "vigorous" and "optimistic"; but, most significantly, none felt
it to be helpful to American writers from the standpoint of technique — Adamic even considered it "technically inferior" to non-
Communist writing in capitalist countries — and Joseph Kalar, poet
and story writer, expressly declared that "for my Americans a
pessimistic literature is still to be desired, since it better reflects the
conditions of their own existence." If, finally, several contributors
praised *International Literature* for bringing them in translation at
least some selections from current Soviet writing, it is clear that
none considered selections a sufficient basis for literary imitation.

To repeat, then, certain matters of technique in the American
proletarian novel must be explained, not as borrowings from Soviet
novels, but rather as the result of efforts to combine Marxism and
the inherited literary consciousness. It has already been shown how
the widespread obsession with violence in the thirties relates to the
self-destructive endings of so many strike novels. Similarly a rough
quantitative parallel exists between the radical and the nonradical
novels of the decade in the extent to which the books in each group
rely on accepted fictional forms or instead search for new ones.
Since the writers of the twenties had firmly established realism as
the dominant tendency in American fiction, it is actually not surprising that a very large majority of proletarian novels use traditional realist forms and techniques. Likewise the attempt of a
minority to work out experimental forms corresponds to the proportionately smaller output of the unpolitical avant-garde. The
ratio of tradition to experiment in the proletarian novel is conveni-

ently represented by the six novels based on the Gastonia strike. Four of these — *Strike!*, *Call Home the Heart*, *To Make My Bread*, and *Gathering Storm* — are quite obviously realistic in literary method; while *The Shadow Before* is the classic example of proletarian experimentalism. If *Beyond Desire*, which combines realistic statement with a loosely handled stream-of-consciousness, is regarded as mainly realistic but with experimental trimmings, the proportion will be approximated: four realistic novels to one experimental, with a largely realistic hybrid to annoy those who like rigid categories.

As far as *technique* goes, the radical novels, like any other in the realist school, attempt to portray, or rather photograph, "things as they are." Most representative of traditional realism, perhaps, is such a book as Thomas Bell's quiet and surprisingly pleasant *All Brides Are Beautiful*, the record of the first two-and-a-half years of married life for a young working-class couple in Depression New York. Here the strikes and militant demonstrations impinge only on the periphery of the story, which is concerned rather with the harassments of a tight budget, Peter Cummings's unemployment — his wife, Susan, keeps them going with her small salary as a book-store clerk — and his reëmployment at the end of the book in a machine shop where he can help organize a militant labor union. More violent events than these make up the content of the greater part of the realistic novels, but violent events did occur plentifully in the Depression Decade, even though the slow cancer of unemployment was more the usual affliction than the fever of pitched battles with company thugs and the police.

Such familiar realist devices are used as the attempted reproduction of actual speech sounds or rhythms in the dialogue, careful analyses of the physical appearance of characters, and exactly detailed descriptions of settings or events. The influence of reportorial journalism is evident frequently in the desire to "get all the facts down" — and sometimes in the flatness with which they are got down. One characteristic device is the description, as Michael Gold had prophesied, of industrial or manual processes. Although similar passages of description occur in the Socialist novels, they are less common, less extensive, and less exact. The proletarian novels give more evidence that their authors might actually have worked with their hands. Jobs in a rubber factory, a steel mill, an auto plant are among those detailed in *The Disinherited*, which also includes a fine serio-comic scene in which Larry and Ed, though without experience, work very briefly as riveters on a high steel bridge project in order to get money for their journey back to Missouri. *Conveyor* gives the fullest picture of the nerve-racking task of keeping up with an assembly line; spinning mill operations are carefully described in *To Make My Bread*, *Strike!*, and *Beyond Desire*; the processes of lumbering and wood finishing form the background for *Lumber* and *The Land of Plenty*. Clara Weatherwax's *Marching! Marching!* becomes at times an occupational handbook for the Pacific Northwest, some of the processes detailed being lumbering, wood finishing, clam digging, stevedoring, the picking of fruit and vegetables by migrant workers, and even the cutting up of whales at a shore station.[47] Almost always these descriptions are presented in technical but still comprehensible language in order to increase the effect of verisimilitude. In a few instances, as with the turret lathe — a Warner-Swasey No. 4 — in Bell's *All Brides Are Beautiful*, the uninstructed reader feels as though his novel had been infiltrated by a trade school textbook.

The foreman snapped on the light over the machine. "She's all set up," he barked. "The day man set her up."
Peter could see as much; projecting from the turret, like so many diminutive cannon, were the necessary tools, front stop, spotting tool, drill, boring tool and a floating reamer, with chamfering, facing, and cut-off tools on the cross slide. He glanced at the blueprint; the legend in the corner, "FB 31, Stainless Steel," told him little, but the drawing was of an inch and a half collar, 7/8ths of an inch wide with a one-inch plug fit and a 1/16th, 45 degree chamfer. They were breaking him in on a comparatively simple job.[48]

The novels going beyond realism to naturalism add to this long list of processes such nonindustrial accomplishments as pimping, catching a fast freight, or preparing canned heat to make it drinkable; but true naturalistic novels are infrequent among the dominant realist trend. Because of naturalism's attempted inclusiveness and scientific objectivity, the few novels utilizing this technique tend to be those concerned with the "bottom dogs," where the intention is to show with cold completeness the debased, animalistic existence forced upon the refuse of an exploitative society. Nevertheless, the chief monument of naturalism in the 1930's, James Farrell's *Studs Lonigan*, is, somewhat paradoxically, one of the individual achievements of the proletarian novel.

As though to illustrate the complete triumph of realism since the days of Jack London, there is only one radical novel published in the thirties which was deliberately written as a romance. It is tempting to describe at length George Marlen's incredible *The Road: A Romance of the Proletarian Revolution* — the rescue of the wealthy, blue-eyed Vera from a runaway automobile by a young left-wing Socialist on a bicycle, remarkably like the rescue in Gene Stratton-Porter's *Freckles*, or the Socialist's golden dream of the future classless society where morning music has displaced the jangle of that capitalist product, the alarm clock — but fortunately the book, even to its stilted prose, is an unrepresentative anachronism.[49] Yet in a very limited sense even those of the novels which use the most realistic fictional techniques have about them something, if not of the literary romance, at least of literary romanticism. The realism of the proletarian novelists cannot ultimately be equated with a mere straightforward photographing of surfaces; rather, their method approximates *independently* that "socialist realism" which became the official technique in Soviet literature soon after April 23, 1932, when the Central Committee of the Communist Party, U.S.S.R., dissolved its chosen literary instrument, RAPP (Russian Association of Proletarian Writers), to make way for another, the all-inclusive Union of Soviet Writers. As defined by Edwin Seaver in *The New Masses*, socialist realism demands "that the author realize all the contradictions, the contrarities and the complexities of the world in crisis; which demands that the artists not only see things as they are — statically, but where they are going — dynamically; and which demands not only that the author see where things are going, but himself take a conscious part in leading the reader through the maze of history toward Socialism and the classless society." [50]

It is through the Marxist assumptions of "socialist realism," which has also been defined as the counterpart in art of dialectical materialism in philosophy, that the romantic element enters these novels. This is not to argue that dialectical materialism is itself "romantic" — and in such a discussion there would be needed more exact words than that one — nor is it to argue that nonsocialist realism is necessarily more "objective" — for by the very selection of his material any artist imposes some kind of arbitrary personal order on complex reality — but it is to argue a lesser and more relevant point. When the proletarian novelists insisted that their snapshots of strikes, demonstrations, conversions were exact portraits of the social developments implicit in that given point of history, they were not accurately photographing what a Marxist would call "the objective situation" existing in the United States during the 1930's. If anything is now clear concerning this country in the Depression Decade, it is that, despite the vast unrest, the larger social movements were not in the direction of revolution but of reform, not toward liberation under a new society but toward security under a modified form of the old. The dialectic may have been operating, to be sure, but the point is that if it was, it was not operating in the way these novelists said it was. If, then, they were photographically realistic in their literary techniques, the angle from which they set up their cameras and the type of lens they favored could distort the perspective of the finished picture, all the more so if the photographer himself were unfamiliar with his equipment. To this extent it might be said that the "literary consciousness" inherited by these writers from the twenties was in turn modified by radical ideology.[51]

American literary tradition was dominant, however, in the attitude of the proletarian writers toward formal experiment in the radical novel, and the contrast with the Russian situation in the thirties seems now particularly striking. In 1932 the Communist Party of the Soviet Union had decreed a single Union of Soviet Writers to insure that all literary production would be under centralized control. At the start the Party moved slowly and carefully in this new coercion of literary men, but beginning with the First Soviet Writers Congress of 1934 enforcement of the decree of socialist realism as the one acceptable technique seriously began. Thereafter any experimentation in form or technique was subject to virulent attack as "bourgeois formalism." Among the American proletarian novelists, to be sure, some scattered opposition to "formalism" was raised on the basis of supposed audience reaction

— Could a steel worker understand *The 42nd Parallel*? — but the Party in the United States had far less control over its fellow travelers, and in addition the habit patterns of the writers themselves were still powerfully operative. During the twenties, the word "experimental" had become too well established as synonymous, not with "bourgeois," but with "antibourgeois" to antagonize literary revolutionaries from the middle class. Furthermore, the term was less often associated in their minds with the elaborate verbal artifice of "decadent" James Joyce than with the presumably proletarian constructions of John Dos Passos, archetype for them until the late thirties of the social and literary rebel. The result was that a majority of the American writers and critics, even though more at home themselves with realistic methods, praised experimental novels as attempts to enlarge the boundaries of radical art.

It was certainly to Dos Passos's work that most of the technical experiments in the proletarian novel were indebted. To take the most famous example of its time, how much *The Shadow Before* owes to *The 42nd Parallel* and *1919* is immediately manifest. Particularly in the first half of William Rollins's novel, the descriptive passages, with their attention to imagistic color details and even the running together of words, is strongly reminiscent of Dos Passos's stylistic peculiarities. Like the Dos Passos method, too, is the introduction of Marjorie Thayer, the mill superintendent's daughter, in a rapid biographical manner; while two other figures, Ramon Vieira and Harry Baumann, are first presented in character-molding scenes from their respective childhoods, despite the fact that almost all of the book's action occurs when they are young men. Further, the novel is largely constructed of short sections, which are sometimes told through a single character, although, unlike Dos Passos's method, development of the action is primarily accomplished through scenes rather than the flow of narrative. Finally, newspaper headlines and stanzas of songs are used, but they are placed throughout the text and not gathered into separate "Newsreels."

A number of Rollins's devices seem less derivative. Occasionally thoughts and spoken words are telescoped into a single sentence without formal demarcation; at one point (pages 159–160) the author himself speaks as a strike leader; and there are semiexpressionistic attempts to reproduce the sight and feel of a spinning room:

Turning a corner, he pushed open the swinging door, three steps above the high dark room.
ARMS shoot out; ARMS shoot back.
Up and down the factory room of windows, windows, windows, ARMS shoot out; ARMS shoot back, in eightyfive machines. UP; down. UP; down. UP, the barren ceiling; down, the line of dwarf-like girls, who clamp the spools on spindles; twist the thread; then snap the empties off the spindles. UP; down. UP; down.[52]

The strikers' parade (pages 210–217) is shown partly by realistic description, partly in terms of how it is viewed by marchers or spectators, and partly through the devices of printing snatches of the song "Solidarity Forever," placing in large black type and in various languages the truncated slogan, "WORKERS OF THE WORLD UNITE! YOU HAVE NOTHING TO LOSE BUT YOUR," and reiterating a word formula — "tramp, tramp; tramp, tramp" — in isolation from the rest of the text. Another word formula,

thump   throb; *thump*   throb

which stands for the sound of the mill in operation, is introduced at the end of Book One as Marvin the organizer comes to the watchman's gate to ask for a job. The formula of course does not appear during the strike, which takes up the larger part of the book; but at the end, when the strike has been broken and the mill is running again, "*thump*   throb; *thump*   throb" reaserts itself as the machine rhythm governing the lives of the oppressed workers.[53]

The use or avoidance of experimental devices bears a close relationship to the kinds of novel structure adopted by proletarian writers. The realistic novels usually employ the traditional "biographical" or "dramatic" frameworks, or some combination of both;[54] technical experimentation, as a rule, is connected with efforts to write the "group" or "complex," heroless novel. Here was another reason why the experimental novel was accepted among most left-wing literary circles. By an analogy as forced as the one which asserts that modern poetry must have nervous rhythms to correspond to the nervous rhythms of modern society, a few critics in their fervor argued that only the heroless novel was possible in a collectivist culture. Even so, the one attempt at a true "collective" novel [55] is *Marching! Marching!*, acclaimed as a triumph by the Left in 1935, but now interesting, if at all, only as a period piece.

Marching! Marching! gives one the impression that its author had wished to collect into one place all the proletarian materials lying about like those of the *commedia dell'arte* — the courageous organizer, the converted college boy, the vicious representative of capitalism, the daily misery of the workers, the demonstration, the strike — and to combine them in a structure that would emphasize mass rather than individual. Mention has already been made of the book's full descriptions of manual processes and its compulsive conclusion. Furthermore, it manages to include all of the proletarian "motifs" previously listed, and introduces so complete a listing of the stands taken on political issues by the Communist Party that the contemporary "line" could be reconstructed almost from this source alone. The style seems to be Miss Weatherwax's own invention. It is a highly elliptical, impressionistic, unpunctuated style, which jumps without warning from character to character, from internal monologue to external action. For example, Pete Bayliss, the college boy, sees a lumbering accident from where he is sitting on a logged-over hill.

By God it's an accident really saying it loud without hearing himself without knowing he was already on his feet going downhill. Half sliding half stumbling his boots ripping through blackberry vines crushing salal monkey-ferns his thighs scattering blossoms of fireweed smashing tearing through stiff huckleberry jumping twist-rooted stumps scratching bruising flesh without the nerves' knowledge, the body's whole force bent on plunging downward and surviving the plunge.[56]

The novel describes the sufferings of the workers in a lumber town of the Pacific Northwest, the growth of class consciousness, a general strike, the brutal retaliations perpetrated by the owning class, and the final demonstration by the strikers in the face of the National Guard. Numerous characters, chiefly workers, are introduced, carried along briefly, dropped, picked up again in new combinations, their lack of individualization evidently being intentional so that they may be submerged in the great wave of the collective. When Mario, the Communist organizer, is beaten by thugs and left barely alive, his place is taken by Pete and by Joe, the class-conscious worker. When Pete and Joe — last names are usually reserved for the owning class and its tools — are brought to trial on a false charge of assault, the momentum is maintained by Mary, Joe's girl. And when the workers assembled in Mary's house are raided and clubbed by the police, yet another leader is cast up by the revolutionary ferment to rally the strikers into the mass demonstration which concludes the book. It is at this point that the author introduces her last "collective" device. As the final chapter opens, she shifts from using the grammatical third persons of her various characters, to the first person plural, and it is "we," those of us who have kept pace with her, who go marching staunchly up to the machine gun's mouth.

Such deliberate disregard for the individualization of characters is not frequent in the proletarian novel; the more usual lack, adequate characterization, springs from the inability of many of the novelists to breathe life into their creations. Just as in any kind of fiction, however, much depends on the general technical competence of the particular writer. For example, William Cunningham's episodic novel, *The Green Corn Rebellion*, is centered on the hard-working, impoverished farmer Jim Tetley, although several other characters, such as the Negro Bill Johnson, dominate whole chapters which are only loosely linked with the major action. Besides the looseness of structure, the chief defect of the novel is the casualness of motivation for Jim's acts. Understandably, Jim takes a holiday from his rather grim wife to have a quiet affair with her younger sister, Happy; and likewise understandably, the full-blooded Happy, bored by the drudgery on her father's farm, takes another lover in addition to Jim. The second lover, unfortunately, is a self-centered high-school athlete, who is careless enough to present Happy with both pregnancy and syphilis. When the girl learns of her double affliction, she shoots herself. Jim, though presumably much in love with Happy, receives the bad news from her father with what seems to be only a twinge of unhappiness, and at once sets off to take part in the rebellion. Again, after the uprising has collapsed, Jim, who hates war enough to rebel against the one going on, agrees to enlist, though reluctantly, almost as soon as his petty-bourgeois brother threatens to accuse him to Happy's father as the ultimate cause of the girl's suicide. Cunningham's primary concern is not to motivate Jim properly, but rather to get him and the reader through a certain sequence of events. On the other hand, careful and consistent characterization of workers and lower-middle-class individuals marks Bell's *All Brides Are Beautiful*, which is particularly successful in showing without sentimentality how an average young couple achieve a sense of healthy unity in their marriage despite the corrosive influences brought to bear on them by the Depression.

The tendency among many of these writers to subordinate character to purpose was emphasized by the Marxist principle, as stated by Granville Hicks, that "the most important thing about an individual is the social class to which he belongs," for "not only the individual's role in society but also his character are to a large extent determined by his economic function." [57] A mechanical application of this theoretical conclusion produced in the worst of the proletarian novels the situation complained of by nonradical critics, in which the workers have most or all of the virtues and the *bourgeoisie* all or most of the vices. Even so generally expert a novel as *The Land of Plenty* is partially weakened by this defect. Cantwell's semisyndicalist contention that workers themselves develop the ability to carry on the managerial functions within a factory can be supported by observation, but, not satisfied with demonstrating this point, the author depicts the managerial representatives of the owning class as utter incompetents. It is believable that Carl Belcher, the "efficiency expert," be self-centered and unpleasant; it is not believable that he should be ignorant of the existence of a sprinkler system in the factory and unacquainted with the rather simple mechanical principle on which it works. When Carl and MacMahon become lost in the bushes on the tideflat, the reader finally begins to suspect that if these are the best managers that the *bourgeoisie* can produce, capitalism should have collapsed some time ago out of sheer ineptitude.

But *The Land of Plenty* is likewise typical of the better proletarian novels, in fact of most of them, in that the workers or the class-conscious characters are by comparison more believably presented than are the representatives of the antagonistic owning class.

This phenomenon results from the fact that more space is given, as a rule, to the development of working-class characters and from the distinct tendency to villainize the capitalists or, as in Cantwell's novel, to make them appear at least incompetent and unpleasant. Only one of these books, Cuthbert's strike story, *Another Such Victory*, is primarily aimed, like such Socialist novels as *A Little Brother of the Rich*, at attacking the ways of the wealthy, but character contrasts are frequent between the owners and the disinherited. Basically the proletarian is a man of good will, the bourgeois one of ill. The proletarian resorts to violence only in retaliation for the bourgeois' compulsion toward it, and very few capitalists are depicted as trying to coöperate with their workers, most of them preferring to fight rebellion ruthlessly with all the many weapons at their command.

A further catalogue of the qualities assigned to the unreclaimably bourgeois or petty-bourgeois characters indicates that they tend to be physically unattractive or diseased, hypocritical, false and greedy, neurotic, antiintellectual, and spiritually dry, incapable of affection even for wife or family, and highly prone, in their filthy-mindedness, to sexual promiscuity. Although these books are no more, and no less, preoccupied with sex than is other fiction of the thirties, a chance is rarely lost to show that few bourgeois sex lives are normal. As compared with the Socialist novels, there is relatively little discussion of prostitution, though its economic basis in capitalism is occasionally referred to in passing; what is frequent is a charge missing from Socialist books, probably because it was "just not discussable" at the time, the charge that the bourgeois, in addition to indiscriminate sexualizing, have a penchant for the gaudier perversions. Particularly the incidence of homosexuality among the *bourgeoisie* by contrast with that among the proletariat is placed astoundingly high, so high, in fact, that it quite reverses the findings of Professor Kinsey's celebrated study of sexual behavior in the American male.[58] One suspects that for the proletarian novelist homosexuality came to stand arbitrarily as a convenient, all-inclusive symptom of capitalist decay. The most interesting point about the whole list of bourgeois characteristics, however, is that, with the possible exception of sexual perversion, they had been attributed to the *bourgeoisie* by writers long before the proletarian novel came into existence. The radicals were merely adding an economic basis to the old charges against Philistia.

Accusations to the contrary, only the poorest of these writers portray their worker characters as completely without faults. Frequently the workers are shown as physically and emotionally warped or unattractive because of the life which they have been forced to lead, and often their minds have been infected by the inanities of the capitalist press, movie, and radio. The rather self-consciously noble New Woman of Socialist fiction has disappeared, too, and her statuesque place is taken by an ordinary working girl with run-down heels, subject to much the same frailties as the laborer, who accepts her without question as an equal. Unlike the protagonists of the Socialist novels, moreover, these men and women are not generally depicted as being more chaste or monogamous than any other American male or female; but it is true that the number of successful proletarian marriages is extremely large in this fiction,[59] and the worker's sexuality is almost always considered in a matter-of-fact way as evidence of healthy vigor. That the explicit linking of political revolution and sexual freedom rarely appears, as it did in *Daughter of Earth*, is probably yet another reflection of the extent to which the social and literary mores achieved in the twenties had been taken for granted by the radicals of the thirties.

In most of these novels, then, a more or less successful attempt is made to limit the ever-present tendency toward idealization of the individual workers, although few pains are taken to present attractive bourgeois characters. William Rollins labored so hard not to idealize his workers in *The Shadow Before* that they appear to be as morally irresponsible and emotionally unstable as their antagonists. On the one hand, the mill manager's daughter manifests strong schizoid tendencies, several members of the owning class indulge in sexual promiscuity, and a judge is sexually stimulated when in open court he forces the father of an arrested girl picket to punish her with a spanking; on the other, as Rollins himself pointed out: "Of [the] four important strikers, the organizer was a neurotic (to a lesser degree), the girl betrayed a man to sleep with a scab, a third was a dipsomaniac, and the fourth a homosexual."[60] But no other proletarian novel, consciously or unconsciously, shows the working class so infected with symptoms of capitalist disintegration. A residue of idealization remains in most of them. Unlike the *bourgeoisie*, who are always associated with decay and death, the workers, whatever their faults as human beings, are always on the side of health and life.

The special concern of the proletarian novelists with the working class as protagonist led certain Marxist critics to proclaim that these writers had introduced not only new subject matter, new forms, new characters, but even a new "sensibility." James Farrell found, for example, that Edward Dahlberg, a product of city life, was developing a new fund of imagery to replace the outworn stock of Romantic figures of speech, which drew heavily from, among other sources, "the charms and attractions of nature."

[Dahlberg's] imagery in many cases is derived from words and associations taken from urban sights and sounds, and from comparisons between objects that are regularly seen by those whose experience is also urban. . . The attempt here is that of relying on a new set-up of associations, and on the fashioning of a language and an imagery that is more closely connected with his subject matter.[61]

Most of the proletarian writers, certainly, tended to draw their images from their immediate environment and, depending on their varying degrees of verbal awareness, to utilize the most exact ones while discarding the hackneyed; a reading of the proletarian novels indicates, however, that, with the possible exception of Dahlberg, the radical novelists drew these images from no other sources than those depended on by their nonradical contemporaries, who were just as likely to be urban in origin.

Actually the chief ingredient of the proletarian writers' sensibility was a predilection for irony, that age-old defense developed by man to meet the disparity between what is and what ought to be. A defense was indeed necessary to them in order to maintain psychological wholeness; for though they could live *for* the future, they must live *in* the present, and the immediate disparity was great. Yet irony, as always, was a method of attack too. Because of their acceptance of the Marxist dialectic, they conceived what ought to be as what would be. Unlike other participants in the tremendous drama of history, they knew its climax in its beginning and could reveal to these others the final scenes, how the blindness of an evil strength led inevitably to catastrophe, how the very ripeness of capitalism foreshadowed its decay. Combining anger and joy, irony pervades their novels, and the residual effect is somber only in those violent endings where the writer's faith in the future seems unconsciously to break down.

The most consistent use of irony is that made by John Herrmann in his novelette, "The Big Short Trip," which describes the last trip made before retiring by a jewelry salesman for a wholesale firm. By viewing the action almost entirely through the salesman's eyes, by showing his stock reactions to the growing effects of the Depression in the cities he visits, by registering the progress of the heart disease that finally kills him, Herrmann attempts to convey the sense of a whole social system running down. In contrast, the salesman's radical son, who appears in the story only through his father's thoughts and a letter, decides to go to the Soviet Union instead of on a long vacation with his father. The revolt of the younger generation is equated here, as occasionally in other proletarian novels, with social revolution. The father unwittingly points the "moral" when he bewails his son's decision.

"I don't mind giving up the trip with him although I've looked forward to it for years. It's his ideas. He's got radical ideas, regular Bolshevik ideas. If he believes in that, it makes everything I've worked for seem wrong. What I've worked for is nothing to him. He throws it all aside. It's only in his way. It doesn't help him. I'm no use to him, like I wanted to be. I'm a hindrance. He'll go his way. I'm just out of the picture, something to be cast aside." [62]

Less extended examples of the ironic treatment of material can be found in nearly every novel. Sometimes the irony may be contained in the title, as *The Land of Plenty* or "Season of Celebration," or in the choice of an epigraph. The most frequent method is the juxtaposition of contrasting scenes or characters. This juxtaposition may be on the fairly simple level so often employed by Upton Sinclair, the abrupt confrontation of the rich with the poor. In Boyd's *In Time of Peace*, for example, a street scene is described and a mood set in the following manner.

Bright autumn sunlight splashed over the concrete, the brick, the glittering store windows in City Hall Square, posed in prim smugness, and the soiled banner over the Republican Young Men's Club. It missed the dark, repulsive flow of seasonal workers, tramps, drunkards, and house prowlers from the basement entrance to the Black Maria waiting to take them to the county jail. Hicks muttered, his eyes jerking upward to the knurly crabapple face of Coolidge, "so this is Prosperity!" [63]

Often this ironic contrast of elements from conflicting classes stands at the edge of enlargement into symbolic statement. In *You Can't Sleep Here*, the unemployed hero helps to picket a New York hotel in a laundry strike for better conditions and union recognition. Since the hotel in the narrative is so situated that the wealthy sections of the city are on one side of it and the East Side slums on the other, the strike is obviously to be considered more than a battle in the class war; it is the class war itself. So also the conclusion to *The Executioner Waits* presents a symbolic situation wherein the declining middle class is ignored by the proletariat, the one class capable of overthrowing the power of the *grande bourgeoisie*.

Probably the most difficult problem for the proletarian novelist to solve satisfactorily was that of the conclusion to his book. For one thing, the widespread insistence that art was a weapon gave the ending of a story a disproportionate importance. Here obviously was the place where the reader could most emphatically be shown that what ought to be was in the process of becoming, and indeed radical critics and reviewers often adopted a kind of theory of literary ballistics: the most effective book like the most effective rifle was that with the highest velocity at the muzzle. Hence revolutionary optimism was considered a necessity; any hint of pessimism or defeatism might lower the explosive power of the charge. Another reason for the difficulty was of a different order. Since, as Michael Gold once pointed out, the United States had not yet undergone its October Revolution, the American, as opposed to the Soviet, novelists could not write of achieved fact — the White army cut to pieces, the cement factory restored, the steel quota surpassed, the dam flung across the Dnieper by sheer Socialist will. Instead the end of the strike, whether victory or defeat, had to be made to prefigure the coming revolution of the proletariat; the conversion of one individual to Communism had to point the way to the future liberation of all in the classless society. That which was coming must appear almost to be.

Given the stubborn facts of capitalist America, it is rather surprising that almost none of the novels, either good or bad, should have turned fully to symbolism as a solution to the problem of the ending; for the symbolic conclusion can be either a thrusting toward intensified vision or an easy retreat from it into verbal wish-fulfillment, a means of carrying out one's artistic duty more compellingly or of avoiding it altogether. The former is the case with Waldo Frank's *The Death and Birth of David Markand*, which, frenetic and self-consciously lush as it sometimes is, is also a complex study in depth and breadth of an individual and his age partly because of an elaborate symbol structure built up to the very end at numerous levels. The latter is the case with "Arnold B. Armstrong's" *Parched Earth*, the symbolic conclusion to which was originally hailed by Granville Hicks as a great technical advance, but which now seems only amusingly ingenious. The town of Caldwell, California, so this story goes, is named after the grasping industrialist who virtually owns it and its occupants. Opposed to his power are a few individualists and the rising resentment of the unemployed, led by the Communist organizer Dave Washburn. At the peak of the clash between these antagonists, Caldwell's illegitimate idiot son blows up the dam above the town, whereupon all the petty-bourgeois and bourgeois inhabitants of the town are swept to their death. Dave Washburn and his friends, however, find safety by climbing a windmill. Thus, capitalism has been destroyed by itself, while for the working class the receding flood waters presage a rich harvest out of the once-exploited land.

It is no doubt better that other radical writers confined themselves to at least approximately realistic methods. Yet the demand that the ending of the proletarian novel should affirm, a demand made both by the critic on the author and the author on himself produced in too many instances besides that of *Parched Earth* a failure of artistic nerve. The less skillful novelists, and those who were not really novelists at all but tractarians, simply "sloganized" their endings as they had sloganized their characters throughout, flatly asserting a doctrinal message in their own persons or through inadequately concealed mouthpieces. Others were less obvious in their methods, but nevertheless ended with the clenched fist of revolutionary hope whether it was consistent with the preceding action or not. Some, however, the best, simply did not consider the possibility of overt moralizing, refused any forced optimism and tried to show their revolutionary integrity by following out to the end what they saw as the logic of their design. If little David Schearl of *Call It Sleep* can at last begin to resolve the confusions and terrors of childhood, Studs Lonigan dies at the sordid end of his debaucheries, Cass McKay of *Somebody in Boots* wanders on blindly from flophouse to gin mill, and Johnny Hagen of *The Land of Plenty* weeps out his defeat in the rain.

But whatever the conclusion adopted, whether optimistic or not, it ultimately went back to the irony implicit in a view of world history which, though the opposite of tragic, was as fated as the tragedy of the Greeks. Capitalism, that which is, declines because of its own contradictions, because it must inevitably, yet unknowingly, produce its antithesis, the gigantic power of the masses which is to be. In this irony was resolved for the proletarian novelists both their hope for the future and their bitterness for their own day.

8.

LITERATURE AND POLITICS

ONE of the bits of news made in the thirties by *The New Masses*, never a magazine to avoid publicity, was the opportunity that it gave — once — for a group of writers to bite their critics. In the issue of July 3, 1934, appeared "Authors' Field Day: A Symposium on Marxist Criticism," containing replies from fourteen of the more than thirty authors who had been asked by the editors *"whether the criticism of their work in THE NEW MASSES had helped them and also what they expected from Marxist criticism."* [1] The replies showed that almost all of these writers, who were predominantly proletarian novelists, had been annoyed by the treatment accorded their own books, and that they found *New Masses* criticism in general to be seriously defective — vague, dogmatic, or "niggardly and patronizing." In an appended reply the editors admitted some faults, denied others in an aggrieved tone, and concluded that: "After all, revolutionary criticism, quite as much as revolutionary fiction, is a weapon in the class struggle." Granville Hicks, however, felt it necessary to append a supplementary rebuttal to Robert Cantwell and Josephine Herbst, his chief detractors. There were no more authors' field days, but the one of July, 1934, threw sudden light on a whole tangle of personal and ideological tensions which, pulling and hauling within the literary Left, soon was to reinforce the different and much more compelling cause for the swift decline of the proletarian novel.

What Eastman and Dell had been to the literary rebels of the middle 1910's, Granville Hicks was now trying to be to the revolutionary writers of the middle 1930's, and he did achieve wide reputation as an interpreter of the relation of literature to society by virtue of his enormous industry and fixed convictions, his authorship of the Marxist study *The Great Tradition,* and his strategic post of literary editor on *The New Masses* from its first appearance as a weekly at the opening of 1934 to the middle of the following year, when he began to give most of his time to writing a life of John Reed.[2] Prior to 1934, the critical policy of *The New Masses* had continued to be characterized, though decreasingly so, by the impassioned but unsystematic revolutionism represented by the emotional Michael Gold. Hicks, who had been born in Exeter, New Hampshire, had studied at Harvard, and had been a divinity student and college English teacher, was of more disciplined, perhaps overdisciplined, intellect. Although he had contributed to the 1932 symposium on "How I Came to Communism" and had written briefly on John Reed, his first considerable piece of work for *The New Masses* was an article in the issue for February, 1933, entitled "The Crisis in American Criticism," which illustrates the then rather dogmatic cast of his mind. Objecting to the "over-simplification" of Calverton's approach in *The Liberation of American Literature* because it "reduces aesthetic categories . . . to economic categories," he proposes in this article that the Marxist critics "refine" their procedure by requiring three qualities of any writer: (1) that he be concerned with the effects of the class struggle; (2) that he present experience with "intensity"; (3) that his viewpoint be "that of the vanguard of the proletariat." Evidently believing that insistence on these three essentials would represent an advance over Calverton's critical system, he concludes that this approach would give "not only a standard by which to recognize the perfect Marxian novel, but also a method for the evaluation of all literature." [3] Obviously, however, Hicks had not progressed beyond Calverton's position, which is indeed oversimplified; for the latter critic also demanded from the writer a Marxist viewpoint and likewise paid at least lip service to the requirement of technical excellence.

It is therefore not surprising to find that Hicks's Marxist history of post–Civil War American literature, *The Great Tradition,* which is still a pioneering book of some value, should be marred by almost as much oversimplification as was Calverton's volume. One of the more peculiar aspects of the book is that, although Hicks speaks of the tradition of social criticism as "the great tradition" of

American literature, both the first and, to a somewhat less extent, the second editions describe it as primarily a record of failure, compromise, or half-success;[4] yet the chief defect in the analysis and evaluation made of these writers is the "mechanical" manner with which Hicks applies his Marxism. He apparently assumes — incorrectly, from the standpoint of actual Marxist theory — that there is a direct and immediate connection between economics and literature,[5] and proceeds to discuss each literary figure in terms of that writer's comprehension of the contemporary socioeconomic situation, the extent to which he understood the nature of the class struggle, and the amount of devotion he displayed toward the "common man." Almost completely on the basis of this discussion, Hicks then evaluates the artistic achievement of the individual writer. For example, among current writers he dismisses William Faulkner as standing in "danger of becoming a Sax Rohmer for the sophisticated"; while he argues that Farrell's *Judgment Day* "is vibrant with a kind of awareness that Farrell had not shown before," not because he had increased his creative skill or was completing his grand design, but simply because "he moved to the left at the time he was completing the Studs Lonigan trilogy." In the face of such consistent question-begging, it is interesting to reflect that the original edition of *The Great Tradition* received more favorable notice among the academic reviewers than among the critics on the Left. E. A. Schachner in his long article for *The Windsor Quarterly*, "Revolutionary Literature in the United States Today," blasted Hicks as being a moralist rather than a Marxist; and the visiting Englishman John Strachey tempered praise with censure when, though describing the book as distinguished and its author as "the foremost Marxist literary critic of America," he remarked that Hicks "hardly seems to pay enough attention to the merits of writers as writers. . ."[6]

Starting from unlike beginnings, the revolutionary emotionalism of Gold and the almost puritanical dogmatism of Hicks reached, in effect, the same conclusion: that literature can almost automatically be evaluated according to the degree to which it consciously illuminates the class struggle and explicitly affirms allegiance to the proletariat. As a result, although many other Marxist critics and reviewers were by no means in complete agreement with them, the pressure of two leading shapers of *New Masses* literary policy was generally toward persuading the proletarian novelists, the less self-confident of whom would listen, that they should write in the manner described at the end of our preceding chapter — that they should deal with the more obvious aspects of the class struggle, melodramatize their characters into good workers versus evil *bourgeoisie*, and end on a carefully affirmative note whether the internal logic of the novel demanded such a conclusion or its opposite. Were it not for "Authors' Field Day," one might be tempted to assign both Gold and Hicks a larger share of the blame for the deficiencies of the proletarian novel.

The New Masses, however, could hardly be considered an organ for the literary theories of one man,[7] and Hicks, perhaps because of his exposed position, found himself under sharp fire in his own magazine and other left-wing periodicals, particularly in *Partisan Review*, where Philip Rahv, William Phillips, and others sniped scornfully at the Hicksian line. Plans for *Partisan Review* as the voice of the John Reed Club of New York had been begun in the fall of 1933, and the first issue of this "Bi-Monthly of Revolutionary Literature," financed by John Strachey's public lecture on Literature and Dialectical Materialism, was published in February, 1934. Like most little magazines, it opened with a manifesto, this one affirming loyalty to the current revolutionary line of the Party, but insisting that the main concern of the editors would be with literature. The magazine would attack the literature of the political Right, of course; at the same time — and here was the significant point — it would "resist every attempt to cripple our literature by narrow-minded, sectarian theories and practices." [8] That the manifesto was to be carried seriously into action was demonstrated in the same first issue by Rahv's review of Hemingway's *Winner Take Nothing*, when Rahv, while dismissing the author's subject matter as useless to the proletarian novelist, declared that the "cluster of formal creative means" which Hemingway, a "bourgeois" artist, had evolved might very well be used as a corrective to the sentimentality of much proletarian fiction.

From its first issue *Partisan Review* had become the base of operations for one side in a literary civil war which, now hidden, even sometimes from the contestants themselves, now open and

violent, had been going on among left-wing writers since the very
beginning of the thirties. Put simply, the cause of the war was a
basic division of attitude toward the creative process, a division
made public as early as 1930 by the announcement in the July
number of *The New Masses* of a debate to be held between Joshua
Kunitz and Michael Gold under the auspices of the (New York)
John Reed Club on the subject, "Can We Learn Anything from
the Bourgeois Writers?" The position each debater would take
was conveniently summarized in advance. Kunitz would assert:
"Are we forever doomed to relish the flat, grey stuff dished out
to us by so many of our writers? We must learn from the bourgeoisie just as the bourgeoisie had once learned from the aristocracy."
To this Gold would reply: "Nothing but academic banalism. There
is no 'style' — there is only clarity, force, truth in writing. If a
man has something new to say, as all proletarian writers have, he
will learn to say it clearly in time: if he writes long enough." [9]
Neatly objectified as debate, the split, then, was between those
who with Gold considered content more important than form and
those who with Kunitz considered form to be quite as important
as content, that split which has already been made familiar by the
closing section of the previous chapter in this book. Gold and Hicks
clearly favored content; those in control of *Partisan Review* — the
John Reed Club itself was deeply divided [10] — quite as clearly did
not.

By the time its third issue had appeared (June–July, 1934),
Partisan Review had further complicated the situation by conceiv-
ing of itself as speaking for what it called the "Centrist" element
among left-wing writers. In an article, "Problems and Perspectives
in Revolutionary Literature," Wallace Phelps and Philip Rahv
first mounted a major attack on the sectarian theories and practices
of the proletarian writers themselves, practices which they now
dubbed "Leftism" by literary analogy with Lenin's political polemic
against extremists within his own party, *"Left-Wing" Communism,
an Infantile Disorder*. "Leftism," they argued, consisted in arbitrarily imposing radical doctrine on awkward literary forms and
stemmed "from the understanding of Marxism as mechanical materialism." Since literature properly makes its appeal to the sensibility, "political content should not be isolated from the rest of ex-

perience but must be merged into the creation of complete personalities and the perception of human relations in their physical and
sensual immediacy. The class struggle must serve as a premise, not
as a discovery." [11] Then, shifting from primarily literary to primarily political categories, Phelps and Rahv concentrated a secon-
dary attack on a new, opposing right-wing tendency within the
Left itself, a tendency represented by writers who accepted the
revolutionary philosophy only halfheartedly. So *Partisan Review*
believed itself to hold a middle way which combined devotion to
revolution and devotion to literature.

That such a "Centrist" group did exist, and powerfully, was in
effect admitted by Joseph Freeman in *The New Masses* for September 11, 1934, though, like the public relations man he has become
since leaving the Party, he asserted that unity, not difference, characterized the Left. Noting with relief that fellow travelers were
being accepted far more readily into the Communist movement than
they had been even as recently as the previous year, he warned
against the danger that, not yet sufficiently educated in Marxism,
they might actually swing the movement too far to the Right.
Then he proceeded optimistically to pronounce nonexistent the
conflict between what *Partisan Review* now called "Leftist" and
"Centrist."

The writers and critics who today are in or near the revolutionary
movement may be divided roughly into two groups: those who have
spent the last ten years primarily in the movement, and those who,
during the same period have been engaged primarily in perfecting their
craft. The economic crisis has united these two groups politically; on
all burning questions of the day they fight side by side. It is no longer
necessary to convince able craftsmen like Isidor Schneider or John
Howard Lawson that it is not only permissible but obligatory for poets
and playwrights to raise their voices on behalf of the struggling working-class. . . On the other hand, it is no longer necessary to convince
writers who developed in the movement in isolation, during years when
loyalty was the primary test, that the revolutionary writer must perfect
his craft, that he must be not only revolutionary but a writer.
The merging of these two forces promises much for the development of a revolutionary literature in the United States.[12]

As Freeman must privately have been aware, however, the two
forces had merged only in the area of politics, not in that of craft.

Writer after writer appearing in *Partisan Review* attacked the "placard" or "slogan" method in fiction, insisted that a revolutionary viewpoint must grow out of rather than be imposed on a literary work, and demanded that the technical advances developed by bourgeois artists be adapted to the needs of proletarian writers.[13] Despite Freeman's attempt at reconciliation, the struggle went on through 1934, "Centrist" arrayed against "Leftist"; and gradually the former began to gather strength throughout all the John Reed Clubs. By the end of the year *Partisan Review* could publish a triumphant communiqué on the results of the Second John Reed Club Conference, announcing that the writers' commission had unanimously denounced "Leftism": "Together they showed that a living revolutionary literature could grow only out of genuine aesthetic recreation of the class struggle." Discussion at the meetings, the communiqué went on rather smugly, indicated that *"Partisan Review* was exerting a wide influence among the young writers." [14]

During the early months of 1935, in preparation for an event shortly to be described, the "Centrists" carried the fight into the strongest enemy position when a whole series of protests against "Leftism" began appearing in *The New Masses* itself. One of the first was Edwin Seaver's " 'Caesar or Nothing,' " which argued that: "Some of our middle-class critics have gone proletarian with such headlong momentum that today they are already several miles to the left of themselves."

From this infantile disorder of "Leftism," this romantic demand for Caesar or nothing, derives that schematicism whose alternate names are dogmatism and sterility and which would seek to eliminate objective realities by denying them. In the field of creative work — let us say, the novel — such schematicism takes the form of offering ideas or slogans without benefit of the creative act; without, that is, clothing such ideas and slogans in flesh and blood and giving them an emotional and human propulsion so that they come to life by their own right, and not by fiat of the author's. In the field of criticism, this schematicism takes the alternate form of wish-fulfillment or denial, the attempt to deduce certain political "truths" from the novel, which are not supported by the facts or, on the other hand, the tendency to kill a book because it does not bring out certain desired "truths" which fall outside the scope of the particular work.[15]

And Horace Gregory, although insisting that he looked for guidance to the Communist Party, went so far as to object that any revolutionary work of art was now expected to conform to the Party line of the moment.

I believe that all important works of art *do* change in meaning, but within Left cultural groups, aesthetic standards undergo daily revision. . . Here I would say that the instrument of dialectical materialism is being made to function as a political tool, not as a standard by which we measure works of art.[16]

The outstanding exploit of the whole campaign against the "Leftism" of Gold, Hicks, and their followers came, however, a whole year later when James Farrell published *A Note on Literary Criticism* (1936), the only extended discussion of Marxist aesthetics written from a Marxist standpoint in the United States during the thirties. Partly, perhaps, because several extremist reviewers had called for the display of more "class-consciousness" in the un-class-conscious characters of whom he wrote, Farrell had concluded that the critics of the Hicks school were perpetuating error and should be exposed before they could do further damage. Yet much more than personal pique and a taste for disputation went into *A Note on Literary Criticism;* for, although the author rejects any claim to being professional either as critic or Marxist, his book proves him to be honestly concerned with his subject and eager for truth. Considering the eminent position held by the object of his special displeasure, it also shows him to be a man of considerable intellectual courage.

The book constitutes a simultaneous attack and defense. The attack is directed against both "revolutionary sentimentalism," as represented by Gold, and "mechanical Marxism," as represented by Hicks. Since each of these two "Leftist" tendencies in literary criticism has, in its extreme emphasis on the functional ("use-value") aspect of literature, ignored the aesthetic aspect, they have together, Farrell argues, kept Marxist criticism weak, because they substitute measurement for judgment. Hence the critic's task, which is ultimately one of judgment, of evaluation, has been avoided. Nowhere is this more obvious than in the treatment accorded "bourgeois" literature. Farrell cites chapter and verse in order to demonstrate that Marx himself would accept an important primary conclusion: "Certain works of literature possess a human worth and a carry-over power which endow them with a relatively inherent persistence-value after they have been divorced from the material conditions and the society out of which they have been created." [17] In literature, unlike politics or economics, the categories of "bourgeois" and "proletarian" must be considered descriptive, rather than normative; for if all true works of art produced by any society have "persistence-value," the categories "are not the basis of value judgment *per se.*" One cannot, in other words, condemn a novel, as the "Leftists" do, merely on the ground that it is written from a non-Marxist point of view.

If the extremist critics have been obtuse about non-Marxist literature, the effect of their "mechanistic methods" on Marxist writing calls for even greater indictment.

First, writers have been led to create characters out of concepts — "the general" — instead of from life with the clarifying assistance that concepts provide. The result of this has been obviousness. The characters often illustrate concepts that have not been soundly applied. Second, such work has been unduly encouraged and praised, so that it has been tacitly set up as a literary model to be followed. In order to establish such unrewarding writing as a model, critics and reviewers have gone a step farther. They have utilized such models and the concepts they present, in order to diminish the reputation and the understanding of novels that do not conform to the standards governing this type. The novels thus regarded as models have generally restated ideas that have been repeatedly developed in books, articles, pamphlets, and editorials. In other words, they are a rehash, contributing no new understanding, giving no concrete sense of life and no help in the application of the concepts. Abstractions have merely been allowed to walk in at the wrong place.[18]

Nor have the extremists assisted their case by arguing that all literature is propaganda. Although any literary work must ultimately spring from an ideological point of view and can certainly influence a reader, nevertheless a novel, for example, is created by a far different process than is a strike bulletin, it must be worked out by its own inner logic, and it affects the reader, not in a simple, but in a very complex way. By, in effect, lumping the novel and the strike bulletin together as "weapons in the class struggle," the mechanistic critics have failed to distinguish properly among categories and among functions. It is this failure to distinguish and then to judge which is leading revolutionary literature into confusion and sterility rather than into clarity and new life.

If Farrell's own statement of the critic's function is not strikingly original,[19] if his dissection of the deficiencies of proletarian literature and criticism is, stylistically speaking, performed as much with a meat ax as with a scalpel, still the dissection itself was a thorough one. The extent to which he drew critical blood may, in fact, be gauged by the harshness of Isidor Schneider's review of the book in *The New Masses* and Hicks's "reply" to that review in an article entitled, with something less than accuracy, "In Defense of James Farrell." [20] But Farrell had his supporters as well as opponents, and one of those intramural battles typical of the literary Left burned for weeks in the columns of *The New Masses*, reaching a climax, but not an end, in the issue for August 15, which contained, under the heading "The Farrell Controversy": (1) a reply by Farrell to Schneider's review; (2) Schneider's rejoinder to Farrell's reply; (3) a letter from a subscriber defending Farrell; and (4) a communication from Morris U. Schappes attacking Farrell's "Mr. Hicks: Critical Vulgarian" in the April number of *The American Spectator*. The most important point which the controversy emphasized was that a sizable number of radical novelists and younger left-wing critics approved Farrell's attitude toward the creative process; but the most curious point about the controversy was that, like Andrew Jackson's Battle of New Orleans, a decisive fight occurred after the enemy had, for reasons of its own, capitulated. More importantly than in literature, as will soon be seen, "Leftism" had been for some time found wanting in the Party's own orientation.

II

A singular fact about the proletarian novels is that in the great majority of cases they, like their Socialist predecessors, were brought out by a variety of "bourgeois" publishing houses, since the Left established its own literary publishing apparatus only late in the thirties, when it took over Modern Age Books, perhaps the first really large-scale paperback book firm.[21] Yet even with the blandishments of capitalist advertising and the marketing facilities afforded by the Workers' Bookshop chain, the sales of proletarian novels were remarkably small. The only exact figures available on distribution are those given in the paper that Henry Hart read at the first American Writers' Congress in 1935.

Bernard Smith, the editor of Knopf's, recently gathered some figures on the sales of novels by revolutionary writers. These figures, from the publisher's point of view, that is, from the standpoint of profit, are very bad. Now it requires a sale of about 2,000 copies for a publisher to get back what he invested — before he makes anything. Cantwell's *Land of Plenty* had the largest sale — 3,000 copies. Jack Conroy's *The Disinherited* sold 2,700, but of these 1,000 were sold at a considerably reduced discount. William Rollins' fine novel *The Shadow Before* has not sold 1,200. Novels which all of you know, and have read, and admired, have sold less than 1,000 copies.

And he unhappily concluded:

Sales such as these mean that the bourgeois publishers are going to begin to refuse to publish our novels. And, of course, they are going to refuse to publish them as the present incipient fascism increases. At the moment, it is still possible for a publisher to say, as one of them said recently, "It's smart to be Communist." But, and I have heard it already said, proletarian and revolutionary novels don't sell.[22]

In order to stimulate the distribution of proletarian novels, as well as radical literature of all kinds, and thereby to insure that capitalist publishers would continue to bring out anticapitalist books, a left-wing book club, called the Book Union, was formed on the model of such established organizations as the Book-of-the-Month Club. Its first selection, the anthology *Proletarian Literature in the United States*, appeared in October, 1935. Other monthly offerings ranged from Henri Barbusse's *Stalin, A New World Seen Through One Man* to Hicks's *John Reed* and Freeman's *An American Testament;* and within a year from the initiation of the project, three proletarian novels were chosen for Book Union promotion: Fielding Burke's *A Stone Came Rolling*, Clara Weatherwax's *Marching! Marching!*, and Leane Zugsmith's *A Time to Remember*. Nevertheless, Malcolm Cowley partially confirmed Hart's doleful statement as being representative of the whole decade when, in summing up the literary activity of the 1930's, he wrote: "From the very beginning, the novels of social protest received a critical attention that was out of all proportion to their popularity, considering that very few had a sale of more than 2,500 copies. . . " [23]

Reasoning from Hart's statistics, Farrell, in *A Note on Literary Criticism*, was to make a neat practical point concerning the function of radical fiction: even if one accepted the premise that a proletarian novel, like all art, was merely propaganda, what was the value *as propaganda* of a piece of writing which had so slight a dissemination? This qestion had already been considered by Louis Adamic in an article for *The Saturday Review of Literature* entitled "What the Proletariat Reads: Conclusions Based on a Year's Study Among Hundreds of Workers Throughout the United States." Assuming the strongest justification for the proletarian novel to be that it was propaganda addressed to the working class, Adamic concluded from his conversations with workers throughout the year 1934 that 99.5 per cent of the American proletariat was not class-conscious and did not read proletarian novels at all, while a great majority of the .5 per cent of the class-conscious individuals could not afford to buy them.

> I met hundreds of workers, but among them only a few real proletarians (not recently radicalized middle-class would-be intellectuals) who had read or heard of one or more of the several recent proletarian novels, and these few told me that, so far as they know, they were the only persons in their towns who read anything at all apart from the local papers and the cheap magazines procurable at the corner newsstands.
>
> Worse yet, none of the workers outside of New York who had read one or more proletarian novels was entirely pleased with it or them.[24]

One worker preferred Upton Sinclair to Jack Conroy, factory girls in Flint, Michigan, thought Catherine Brody's *Nobody Starves*, a non-Marxist novel about the Flint proletariat, exaggerated and untrue, and all worker readers objected to "queer" writing, such as appeared in *The Shadow Before*.

Except for a possible objection to the reliability of Adamic's statistical methods, there was only one weak spot in his argument concerning the general reading habits of workers — his failure to mention the public libraries. In a carefully constructed refutation, Robert Cantwell showed how Adamic's "assumption that the working class cannot possibly provide the basis for a highly developed culture is emphatically challenged by a study of the users of the libraries and the quality of the books they read"; but Cantwell had to admit the immediate point: "It is impossible to dispute Mr. Adamic's charge that the working-class audience of proletarian novels is limited. . . " [25] Only one other person, quite unconnected with the radical movement, tried to get at some specific facts. As part of a doctoral dissertation submitted at Pennsylvania State College in 1939, a scholar named John Scott Bowman stated the results of a survey he had made of thirty-one public libraries in different parts of the country, one being the public library of Flint. Admitting that his data might be only indicative rather than conclusive, Bowman reported his survey as showing that "37.7 per cent of the borrowers of proletarian novels are from Labor, as against 50.9 per cent from White Collar"; and he felt three facts to be established: "that the borrowing record of proletarian novels compares favorably with that of best-sellers, considering that the latter are much better advertised and are more available; that the working-class readers of proletarian novels are at least not disproportionate to the percentage this class forms of library borrowers in general; and that labor forms a larger proportion of the readers of proletarian fiction than it does of the best-seller titles." [26] Here was evidence that with the assistance of Andrew Carnegie the proletarian novel might be somewhat more effective than Farrell and Adamic considered it to be, but clearly it was never effective enough to precipitate a revolution.

Whatever the extent of its distribution or effect or the class origin of its readers, there could be no doubt that the proletarian novel's glorious year was 1935 as far as the literary world was concerned. One of the lesser signs of success was the fact that in that year *The Year Book Review Digest*, in its Thirtieth Annual Cumulation, for the first time listed "Proletarian Literature" as a distinct classification for fiction. More important were Hicks's publication of the revised edition of *The Great Tradition*, with its entire new chapter on proletarian literature, and the appearance, late in the year, of *Proletarian Literature in the United States*, a collection containing examples of fiction, poetry, "reportage," drama, and literary criticism. With the publication of such an anthology, left-wing literature would seem to have reached the status of an institution, and the preface to the section on fiction was one cry of revolutionary triumph. "Five years ago the space given to fiction in this anthology would have been more than enough; today it is inadequate to give more than a few of the clearest *samples* of revolutionary fiction." [27]

Quite as exciting as the appearance of an anthology was the announcement of the results of a contest instituted by *The New Masses* and The John Day Company for manuscripts of novels written both from the viewpoint of and about the proletariat, the winning novelist to receive a prize of $750 in addition to the royalties deriving from the promised publication of the book. After running for a year, during which manuscripts poured in, the contest closed on June 1, 1935, and in September *Marching! Marching!* was announced the winner. In a *New Masses* article, Alan Calmer, one of the judges, subsequently gave some significant information concerning the novels that had been submitted. There were more than ninety of them, one third written by women; all but a dozen "dealt with working-class life or were proletarian in outlook"; over half were "explicitly Communist." The geographical distribution of the contestants, as given by Calmer, in fact corresponded closely to those areas of the country where radical political activity had been most evident and where the majority of the John Reed Clubs had been located: Midwest, twenty-eight; New England, four; South, ten; Rocky Mountain region, "three or four"; Eastern States — excepting New York City — "about half a dozen"; New York City, twenty; California — residence of the winning novelist — sixteen. The most interesting detail in the report is the statement that "all the contributors were unpublished authors"; no already-published proletarian novelist had submitted a manuscript in spite of the award offered. Speaking as a "Centrist" literary critic, Calmer attacked the "Leftist" tendencies to "sloganize" and to end with an unprepared-for conversion, tendencies that evidently marred the greater part of the manuscripts; and he objected to the lack of concern shown for literary technique. "These writers seem blissfully ignorant of all developments in modern fiction from Henry James on. All of them could stand a stiff dose of modern fiction — Hemingway and Faulkner, Joyce and Proust, as well as proletarian novelists." [28]

The outstanding left-wing literary event of 1935, however, was the first American Writers' Congress. Just as this year was both a peak and a pivot for the production of proletarian novels, so the Congress represented a culmination and, at the same time, a new direction. In *The New Masses* for January 22, 1935, was published a Call to the Congress, signed by numerous left-wing writers and opening with a militantly revolutionary paragraph, which declared capitalism to be crumbling so visibly that hundreds of literary men were now ready to assist in completing its destruction and establishing a workers' government. No less militant was the statement of the purpose of the Congress.

This Congress will be devoted to exposition of all phases of a writer's participation in the struggle against war, the preservation of civil liberties, and the destruction of fascist tendencies everywhere. It will develop the possibilities for wider distribution of revolutionary books and the improvement of the revolutionary press, as well as the relations between revolutionary writers and bourgeois publishers and editors. It will provide technical discussion of the literary applications of Marxist philosophy and of the relations between critic and creator. It will solidify our ranks.[29]

Unlike the practice of the John Reed Club conventions, the carefully selected writer-delegates were to represent only themselves; and the spontaneity of the proposed Congress's actions may be judged by the statement in the Call that: "We believe such a Congress should create the League of American Writers, affiliated with the International Union of Revolutionary Writers." By the time that the more than three hundred writers were assembling, on April 26 at Mecca Temple in New York, to create this continuing organization, *The New Masses* could already announce the apparent result of their efforts.

Out of this congress will emerge the League of American Writers, with the following program, which some 200 delegates have already pledged themselves, in their professional capacity, to support: "fight against imperialist war and fascism; defend the Soviet Union against capitalist aggression; for the development and strengthening of the revolutionary labor movement; against white chauvinism (against all forms of Negro discrimination or persecution) and against the persecution of minority groups and of the foreign-born; solidarity with colonial people in their struggles for freedom; against bourgeois distortions in American literature, and for the freedom of imprisoned writers and artists, and all other class-war prisoners throughout the world." [30]

The discussions of literature which took place at the Congress have already been examined to show how they illuminate the running quarrel as to a definition of the proletarian novel, and it is noteworthy that the dispute over literary "Leftism" was for the most part kept out of sight under the equally familiar wrangle concerning "subject matter" and "point of view." One of the Congress's surprises, actually, must have been Hicks's paper, "The Dialectics of the Development of Marxist Criticism," which was a flat admission, well before *A Note on Literary Criticism* was published, that the approach made by himself and "certain other critics" had indeed been extreme, that they had not sufficiently heeded the demands of proletarian writers for more attention to their technical problems, and that "a number of critics, notably some of those associated with *Partisan Review*" had quite properly been placing greater emphasis on "the complex relationship between experience and creation." [31]

The formal creation of the League, however, was even more significant than any of the literary debates which took place; for this organization replaced the John Reed Clubs, which had, in effect, committed suicide at their Chicago convention of September, 1934, and were now in New York officially dissolved. The structure of the League was less decentralized, and therefore more easy to manipulate, than that of the Clubs had been. There were to be no local branches, but rather the writers were to join as individuals a centralized organization headed by a chairman, with a powerful executive committee of seventeen members (all apparently either Party members or close fellow travelers) and a national council of about fifty.[32] Again unlike the John Reed Clubs, membership in the League would not be open to young writers learning their trade, but only to those whose published work had already placed them in a professional status. Obviously if, under this restriction, the League was to attain any size at all, a large percentage of the members could not be "proletarian" writers. This was indeed the case. Among the one hundred and twenty-five members who joined the League during its first few months were — along with

Josephine Herbst, Grace Lumpkin, Jack Conroy, James Farrell, and Granville Hicks — such less specifically committed figures as Vincent Sheean, Robert Morss Lovett, Lewis Mumford, Sidney Howard, and Van Wyck Brooks.

These organizational developments rather than the fiercely class-conscious addresses of the speakers, Hicks's conciliatory words on criticism rather than the militant definitions of the proletarian novel, indicated the new direction beginning to evolve at this congress which had had so revolutionary a Call. They were adumbrations of that official reversal in Communist policy known as the Popular Front. Left-wing literature was about to enter upon a new phase.

III

Although the tactic had been tried out earlier — notably in France in 1934 — it was not until the Seventh Congress of the Communist International met in July–August, 1935, that the United Front policy was formally affirmed and Georgi Dimitroff, the Comintern's General Secretary, could announce: "Ours has been a Congress of a *new tactical orientation for the Communist International.*" [33] The previous policy of revolutionary activity in defense of the Soviet Union had catastrophically failed in Germany, the key country of Europe, where the National Socialists utilized the split between Communists and Social Democrats as an avenue to power. When, contrary to Communist expectation, Hitler received widespread public support in Germany and was quickly successful in his efforts to suppress radical groups in both the Nazi Party and the State, the Soviet Union was furnished proof enough of the danger of a Fascist cordon of powers. While continuing the grand strategy of revolutionary extremism, the Comintern began to give greater emphasis, as a means of implementing it, to the already established tactics of the "United Front from Below," a device whereby the rank and file of "Social Democratic" parties and of "reformist" trade unions in capitalist countries were to be detached from their "social-Fascist" leaders and brought into the Communist orbit. Such tactics were remarkably unsuccessful throughout 1933. The Comintern next moved, in France, to include the party and union leaders as well; and on February 12, 1934, France's Popular

Front was born when the Communist and Socialist trade union organizations united in a one-day general strike. In the same year the Soviet Union itself joined the League of Nations and concluded treaties with France and Czechoslovakia. The final step in the reorientation of Comintern policy was that announced by Dimitroff. Though designed to operate differently in different countries according to the existing situation, fundamentally it proposed a common defense against Fascism by the Soviet Union and the same capitalist democracies which Russia had only recently been excoriating. Within the democracies themselves, the policy required coöperation between the Communists on the one hand and, on the other, the Socialists and liberal groups as well, all of whom shortly before had been under attack as "social-Fascist." The reversal had not come about overnight, but the extent of it, after August, 1935, was rather confusing.

In the United States the terms most frequently used by the Communist Party, U.S.A., to designate their new orientation were the "Popular Front," as in France, or the "People's Front," and some of its manifestations were startling. Earl Browder, after campaigning for the presidency in 1936 with the slogan, "Communism is Twentieth-Century Americanism," went so far as to "extend the hand of fellowship and cooperation to Republicans, Democrats and Socialists, as well as to those of no party at all" who would unite in a determination "to defend culture, to unite culture with the strivings of the people, to preserve and extend our democratic heritage, to assist our brothers in other lands who are suffering the bestial assaults of fascism." [34] The literary bedfellows were no less strange. For example, when reviewing Archibald MacLeish's *Poems, 1924–1933* in the issue of *The New Masses* for January 16, 1934, Margaret Wright Mather (frequently a pseudonym for Granville Hicks) had stated flatly: "Archibald is a Nazi, at least a kind of ur-Nazi." Yet two years later, in December of 1935, the poet, now miraculously denazified, was allowed to contribute to the magazine's Anti-Fascist Number; while in the issue for March 24, 1936, MacLeish's *Public Speech* was praised by Isidor Schneider as a "beautiful and moving collection of poems." [35] Under the revised dispensation, the Communist Party rapidly increased in size, claimed membership growing from 30,000 early in 1935 to 40,000 in

1936; 50,000 in 1937; and 75,000 in 1938. The Trade Union Unity League, which had been trying for six years to construct a framework of revolutionary unions, was dissolved in 1935 so that Communist organizers could help build the C.I.O.; the "25th Anniversary Number" of *The New Masses* had a press run in December, 1936, of 100,000 copies, the largest in its history; [36] and "People's Front" groups, either controlled by Communists directly or responsive to the current "line," flourished like gardens in the sun.

To the proletarian novel, for which a brilliant growth had been prophesied at the first American Writers' Congress, this weather was, however, like a killing frost. Instead of flourishing, it withered so quickly on the vine that by June, 1936, Joseph Freeman, in writing of the John Reed Club period, could casually refer to "those radical writers who in the 'sectarian' days were engaged in advancing what used to be called proletarian literature." [37] Such a complete reversal, the very timing of it, demands explanation, for Freeman's bland use of the past tense shows how ancient he considered this history to be. The "official" reason given for the sudden decline of the form in which "The Great Tradition" had presumably just culminated was, as Freeman suggested, that the revolutionary movement had matured away from the political sectarianism (that is, extremism) which, in some of its literary manifestations, Farrell was attacking.[38] The actual explanation significantly shifts the emphasis: the proletarian novel was not transformed by a dialetical process into a new synthesis; rather, it was almost destroyed by the political maneuver of the People's Front. From 1930 to 1935, the proletarian novel had been closely connected with the revolutionary policy of the Communist Party through the literary apparatus of the John Reed Clubs and *The New Masses*. It had developed, awkwardly yet quickly, because it offered the writer a sense of solidarity with one class in a common struggle against an antagonistic one. But the new Communist policy called for coöperation with many of the same social elements that had previously been attacked. It called politically for coöperation with President Roosevelt's New Deal; it called ideologically for an alliance with capitalist democracy; it called "culturally" for a joining of hands with those who wrote of social reform, even if that, rather than of social revolution. The consequence was inevitable. If the radically

orientated writer had, at least for the moment, to accept capitalist
democracy, obviously he could not emphasize the class divisions
implicit in a strike, he could not document the disintegration of the
middle class, he could not, as a convert to Communism, hurl defiance from a metaphorical barricade. Literature must no longer be
declared a class weapon, but simply a weapon; and the weapon must
be used, not against capitalism, the proletariat's oppressor, but
against Fascism, the oppressor of the "people." [39] In short, the
specific Marxist viewpoint must largely disappear. That many of
these writers did see the problem explicitly in terms of political
tactics may best be proved, in fact, by reference to the list of proletarian novels according to year in our Appendix. In one year
after its peak, the production of proletarian novels dropped off
60 per cent.

Set in this frame of reference, the deliberate destruction of the
John Reed Clubs to make way for the formation of the League of
American Writers takes on added meaning. The Clubs had rejoiced
in their revolutionary hatred of capitalism, and that "sectarian"
spirit as it was now termed, had indeed restricted the range of their
influence; but they had also been a means of bringing together
groups of young writers who were in the process of learning their
craft, such relatively unknown writers as had published the many
radical literary magazines or had contributed to the more than
ninety manuscripts in the *New Masses*–John Day proletarian novel
contest. The dissolution of the Clubs meant the destroying of part
of the subliterary soil out of which future radical talent could
have grown. Furthermore, the exclusion of unpublished writers
from the League, a device clearly intended to give the new organization greater prestige value and hence a wider and more powerful influence, must have made the excluded ones feel that they had
been sacrificed to expediency. Such a feeling would hardly increase
their desire to produce radical fiction.[40]

A majority of the John Reed Club writers had sided with the
opponents of "Leftism" in the conflict over a radical aesthetics, and
this conflict likewise was affected by the reversal in political policy.
As had been revealed by "Authors' Field Day" in *The New Masses*, by the attacks on "Leftism" published in that magazine just
before the American Writers' Congress, and by every issue of

Partisan Review, the proletarian writers with some sensitiveness for their craft had long questioned the extremist tendency to subordinate the creative process as a whole to the urgency of one part, the message, a subordination which, they saw, would immediately pose the problem later described by John Chamberlain.

The dilemma of the socially conscious writer is illustrated by a young novelist of my acquaintance who has been trying for years to finish a book about the San Francisco waterfront strike of 1934. He cannot finish the book because he is all at sea concerning the motivating philosophy behind it. From month to month and year to year his attitude toward the personal value of his protagonist keeps fluctuating with the movement of radical values, of radical morality, in a world of Moscow trials, undeclared wars, "Trojan-horse" tactics, and political "timing" that frequently works out into two-timing.[41]

Resisting the demands, as Alan Calmer was to put it, for a "pugnacious culture," these better writers — Algren, Cantwell, Farrell, Herbst, Roth — had concentrated on working out methods of expressing their own experience truthfully, yet in accordance with Marxism as they interpreted it. Seemingly they should have rejoiced in their victory when, even before the Farrell Controversy, Hicks had formally admitted their chief arguments; but with the introduction of the People's Front policy they found that the very premises of a revolutionary literature had been officially rejected. In its current zeal to be "democratic," the Party line had, if not repudiated Marxism, at least transformed it strangely. Any radical writer who was really concerned with aesthetic values was forced to face some unpleasant questions.

If, despite the best of intentions on the part of political leaders, the proletarian arts were chained to the exigencies of a political movement — which meant that esthetic ideals had to be sacrificed whenever they clashed with practical realities of the hour — how was literary sincerity possible? Of was there an insoluble contradiction between literature and momentary tactics? [42]

Those writers who accepted political expediency could easily abandon the proletarian novel for fiction of a generalized social-protest nature; those who felt that personal and artistic integrity would be compromised by writing according to each twist of Party policy fell to wondering whether "joining a political party irrevocably doomed intellectual freedom." [43] Such doubt and confusion paralyzed many writers — particularly those who were neither political hacks nor self-confidently creative artists — until that time when they could laboriously work out a personal solution. And at that, the People's Front reversal was far easier to accept than the other political shocks that history was reserving for them.

It has been argued that an explanation which makes the decline of the proletarian novel so closely dependent on political change is too "schematic"; yet the schematism is not of this writer's choosing, and other suggested reasons for the collapse of the proletarian boom are not ultimately convincing. The very "as-if"-ness of their conclusions show how weak their premises are. One alternative explanation goes as follows. After having once fictionalized his conversion to Communism or the facts of a strike with which he was familiar, the average writer who wished to be more than a reporter could put into a new novel the necessary sense of lived detail only by first experiencing some of that detail at first hand himself. If a worker-writer had once described the drift of migratory laborers or the life of the factory where he may have spent a number of years, it was useless to try to refashion the same material, a point which may indeed be verified by comparing Jack Conroy's *The Disinherited* with his feeble second novel, *A World to Win*.[44] Living through and understanding experience quite naturally takes time, and a marked feature of the proletarian novel, in fact, is the relatively small number of writers who produced more than one book. But even assuming what is not the case, that Communism had attracted no more writers after 1935, the time-lag in composition could hardly account for as much as a leveling off in the appearance of left-wing novels, let alone so sharp a drop as actually occurred. On the contrary, had the forces making for an intransigeantly radical fiction continued in the same direction, there would have been time for older writers to assimilate necessary experience, for new writers to contribute fresh vigor, for the excesses of "sectarianism" to be modified by even stronger opposition, and possibly for what was, after all, only a literary phenomenon to develop into a full-fledged movement.

Another argument assumes that the dire predictions of Henry

Hart came true, that capitalist publishers ceased to accept revolutionary novels because they were not a salable product. Such reasoning unconsciously makes the proletarian novel appear to be, far more than it actually was, a mere publishing fad; and the fact of the matter is that "bourgeois" firms published all except one of the examples of the form which, appeared in reduced number, like stragglers after a main column, in the last four years of the decade. Furthermore, it is hard to believe that, if the regular companies had refused to take any revolutionary books at all, an emergency publishing apparatus could not have been set up even before Modern Age Books — whose novels, by the way, were not specifically *proletarian* — and the problems of distribution solved through such agencies as the already functioning Book Union. The related assertion of changing taste on the part of the book-buying public is hardly operative here, as Hart's reports on the meagerness of sales should have demonstrated; yet as far as that goes, the opposition to "Leftism" was already making for greater creative flexibility on the part of radical authors, who could thereby have retained their revolutionary integrity while enlarging their audiences.

The explanation has also been offered by Howard Fast,[45] now the leading Marxist novelist in the United States, that left-wing writers of the later thirties were searching for new subject matter to replace the limited choices available in the "sectarian" days. Yet this is for several reasons an explanation which does not explain. Radical subject matter had already developed considerable variety in the first half of the thirties, as the preceding chapter of this book has demonstrated, and the climate of opinion at the first American Writers' Congress, while predominantly revolutionary, had favored the widest possible choice of theme. Most important of all, the majority of those speakers at the Congress who were concerned with defining the proletarian novel had insisted on the primacy of the Marxist viewpoint in clear distinction from subject matter. Subject matter was irrelevant. After all, Marxists claimed that their philosophy could be applied to every aspect of existence, and Marx himself had stated his favorite maxim to be, "I regard nothing human as alien to me." Surely that covered most of the subjects available for fiction.

Certain other explanations prove basically to be just as inadequate. If the gradual improvement of the country's economy and the intensification of the reformist spirit in the New Deal after 1935 helped to siphon off from the Left some of those whose commitment to Marxism had been slight, the Recession of 1937 and continued unemployment should have indicated that capitalism was still having difficulties, and actually Party membership and influence increased greatly in the second half of the thirties. The deliberate attempt by Communists to "infiltrate" the WPA writers' projects no doubt turned the immediate energies of some radical authors from their own creative work, but most of the proletarians never had been professional writers, always had had to try to support themselves at other jobs, and besides had been expected to combine writing and agitational chores from the beginning of their careers with the Left. Finally, beyond the ever-seductive lure of the capitalist literary world, there was Hollywood, the Klondike of the thirties, to which during the last years of the decade a large band of ex-proletarian prospectors did make their way in hopes both of finding gold and exerting the influence of the Left on a mass medium. This migration from New York to Hollywood, however, only serves to bring the reader himself back to the original proposition. The radical in Hollywood could, sometimes, insert in a movie a speech favoring the Spanish Loyalists or a suggestion that Russians might be human beings too or even a worker-part where the actor was not required to portray a clod or a clown; the radical would not, and for reasons other than the sheer impossibility of the thing under the Hays Code, try to suggest that the proletariat must rise up against those who held it in bondage. In short, he attempted to propagate, not Marxist doctrine, but the current nonrevolutionary Party line, which called for social reformism and the defense of democracy, any democracy, against Fascism.

Wherever one turns, then, for an explanation of the decline in the proletarian novel, one is ultimately brought back face to face with the political reversal contained in the People's Front. The maneuver, it should be emphasized, was an astute one from the standpoint of the Party. It brought Communism, if not Marxism, as closely into the mainstream of American development as Socialism had been brought in the years just before World War I; and liberals must acknowledge that the new Party line gave impetus to the movement for many much-needed reforms, even if at the same time the coöperation of the Left made that general movement more vulnerable to attack from the Right. In the course of that maneuver, however, the proletarian novel was dumped without ceremony by the roadside — though it refused quite to die in the ditch — and with it went very probably the last opportunity for a radical fiction of any size to grow in the United States out of Marxist doctrine.

Nothing makes the fact of the dumping more clear than the silence of *The New Masses* where before all had been clamor. After 1935, references to "the proletarian novel" or "proletarian literature" almost completely disappear from the critical articles of the magazine, being replaced by such adjectives as "anti-Fascist," "people's," "democratic," or, at most, "left-wing." The latter words too were applied in reviews of the now relatively few novels that were still proletarian by the accepted definition. So long had it been since the old term was used that when Henry Hart, reviewing *A Time to Remember* in the issue for September 22, 1936, stated that the book's second half equaled "anything that has yet been achieved in American proletarian writing," his words must have resounded like an unfortunate slip of the tongue in a public place. By December, 1936, William Phillips, in a review of *The New Caravan*, was facing the solemn conclusion.

[This collection omits] many of our more promising writers. . . But there is an even more distressing absence of our highly publicized proletarian literature, which cannot be traced simply to editorial judgment, for there are many other indications of a general recession. Have all our critical guarantees that proletarian literature would expand and mature to the point of dominating American literature been just so much professional optimism? If so, *The New Caravan* may be taken as a monument to the dispersal, if not the demise of proletarian literature — at any rate, as it has been defined all these years.[46]

The tone of tentative elegy in Phillips's remarks doubtless reflected the fact that only two months previously *Partisan Review* had ceased publication because two of its three surviving editors were becoming increasingly disillusioned with the Party.[47] To the end it had maintained its opposition to "Leftism" and its support for revolutionary literature. But almost no one was listening any more.

A whole year went by before Michael Gold suddenly made a reëxamination of "proletarian literature" in *The New Masses*, and the effort was illuminating. In "Notes on the Cultural Front," Gold first attacks the "Trotskyists" for their argument that Communist dictatorship had killed proletarian literature. Such an accusation, he maintains, is manifestly false, since there is no Communist dictatorship of literature. Their argument only succeeds in demonstrating that the Trotskyists are bourgeois intellectuals, who were useless even in the days when they were close to the Communist Party. Actually, American writers are facing a period of reconstruction, a difficult one because under the People's Front the "class struggle is more complex than it was five years ago." When Gold at last reaches a definition of the new proletarian literature, he makes it appear, except for working-class origin, little more than what Farrell had acidly called "literary populism," hardly distinguishable from that written by politically liberal authors.

Out of them [proletarianized white-collar workers and professionals], I believe, will come a new wave of proletarian literature, different and more complex than the last, more at home in the working-class world. For every white-collar renegade, there are thousands of these "new people." In the factories, mines, and mills are thousands of other lads whose whole outlook is being shaped by the C.I.O. The future of proletarian literature is in these hands. Labor is on the march. The farmers, professionals, small businessmen are stirring. Several thousand young American Communists and liberals are fighting in Spain. A labor party is being born. The American people are in motion.[48]

Gold's was, in fact, the first extended discussion of proletarian literature to appear in *The New Masses* for two years. It was another six months before Joshua Kunitz, like Gold one of the radicals of the twenties, simultaneously defended the use of the old name and admitted the need for "some such broad, inclusive term [as 'people's literature'], which would be the literary analogue of the political people's front or democratic front."[49] After this pronouncement, the silence indicated that old ways had ceased to function.

Even earlier, however, when the second American Writers' Congress was held in June, 1937, it was clear that the "literary front" of the Left was no longer dedicated to the overthrow of capitalist society, but solely to the task, certainly honorable enough in itself, of opposing Fascism. Quite unlike the Call to the first Congress, the Call to the second was anti-Fascist, but not in the least prorevolutionary; conflict now was not between class and class, but between, as Joseph Freeman was to put it, "the forces of progress and reaction." The crowded public meeting that opened the new Congress took place in Carnegie Hall rather than the Mecca Temple of the old, and new faces appeared among the speakers at the various sessions. Besides Browder, Cowley, and Hicks, who had spoken before the first Congress, the second was addressed by Hemingway, MacLeish, and Frances Winwar, all adherents to the People's Front. Spain, not Russia, was the country now most frequently named; politics, not literature, was the focus of attention; and the impossibility of true culture under Fascism, not the rich possibilities of culture under democratic societies, was the major theme. If some of the speakers did discuss literature, it was almost left to the political Earl Browder to formulate a statement of what literature should now attempt, and the formulation was even vaguer than the definitions of the proletarian novel had been: "The greatest literature of our day will deal with precisely this: the artistic recreation of the actual process of the development among the people of a broad, united, democratic front against, and its defeat of, fascism." [50] The League of American Writers was reorganized on a regional basis, though real control remained in the hands of an "active executive council" made up of those members of a national council who resided in the New York area; and the League was to be no longer the American Section of the International Union of Revolutionary Writers, but rather of the more politely named International Association of Writers for the Defense of Culture. Finally, a new president, Donald Ogden Stewart, was unanimously elected, no opposition candidate having been named. When one seeks to find an explanation for the unexplained disappearance of the first president, Waldo Frank, one finds it concealed behind Browder's statement that "I spoke in sharp terms against a proposal from Waldo Frank that I join him in rejecting the evidence and verdict of the Supreme Court of the Soviet Union in the trial of the Trotskyite wreckers and espionage-agents of fascism. . . " [51] Like the proletarian novel, though for quite different reasons, Waldo Frank had been found wanting and had been officially disposed of.

As his concluding words Donald Ogden Stewart announced that the Congress had been very successful, and indeed the whole Popular Front, while it lasted, proved to be the Left's most effective invention. At home the Left was able to swim with the tide toward greater political and social justice. It could support New Deal legislation and to a small extent exert influence on such results of it as the WPA writers' program with its potentialities for cultural self-consciousness; and it could give considerable aid in the massive organizing campaign of the C.I.O., which, with the strong advances made by the A.F. of L., drove up total trade-union membership from a low of just under three million in 1933 to nearly eight in 1939. Abroad the American Left could point to the successes of the Popular Front in France, to the "liberal" new Soviet Constitution of 1936, to Litvinov's work for collective security, to the last-minute offers of Russian assistance to a betrayed Czechoslavakia, to the front against Fascism everywhere. Above all it could point to Spain, that cross upon which for three years the conscience of the West was crucified.

If any proof was needed that Fascism must be opposed, Spain was the proof, and the greatest effort made by the Left during the whole thirties was to assist the Soviet Union in first aiding and then controlling the Loyalist resistance in the Spanish War. Every kind of gathering from the cocktail party to the mass meeting was used to promote Aid to Spain; and every bit of political influence available to American Communists was brought, unsuccessfully, to bear against the Neutrality Act of May, 1937, which by its professed impartiality in prohibiting the export of arms and munitions to either belligerent in effect prevented the same kind of support from the United States to the Loyalists that Germany and Italy were openly furnishing to the Insurgents. Meanwhile the writers of the Left, some of them, went to fight with the Abraham Lincoln Brigade; many more stayed home to suffer the self-torments of the imaginative man who feels he must somehow atone for remaining out of the immediate essential battle. Even some fifteen years later the then half-Marxist, now Zionist, Meyer Levin could write of his visit to the trenches of the Madrid front and his decision to go on to Palestine: "It seems to me that I am still apologizing a little for not having remained to fight in Spain." [52]

But history was moving too intricately for the Communists to exploit fully their position as defenders of the Spanish Republic. Shortly after the Franco revolt had broken out came the first of the several Moscow Trials, which, extending from August, 1936, to March, 1938, linked a number of prominent "Old Bolsheviks" with the hated name of Trotsky. In the United States the Trials brought doubt and division among Communist sympathizers and even within the Party itself, for the charge of treason against these men who had helped to create the Revolution posed a sickening alternative. If they were guilty of the crimes to which they so abjectly confessed, then how could they have been so corrupted and how many other corrupted leaders still existed unexposed? If they were innocent, then was not the Revolution itself betrayed? The first alternative was, to be sure, preferable, but had the judicial process itself been fair? Anyone disturbed by doubt would not be wholly relieved to find that John Dos Passos, and others, felt the trials to have been gigantic frame-ups. Dos Passos could be dismissed as a renegade — though Meyer Levin had not been entirely able so to dismiss him — for he had asserted that the Communists in Spain were chiefly interested in destroying the other groups in the Loyalist Popular Front and had already inaugurated the literature of anti-Communism in the final pages of *The Big Money;* but the doubt could remain and fester inwardly.[53]

And history was moving too rapidly as well as too intricately. The event which ended half a decade's triumph for the People's Front was of course the announcement on August 22, 1939, of the Nazi-Soviet Non-Aggression Pact. Writers and critics who, up to this point, had faithfully accepted both the changes in the Party line and the Purge Trials as necessary in the struggle against reaction and its appeasement, who had excoriated the hypocritical policy of the United States toward Spain, the betrayal of Czechoslovakia by England and France at Munich, now saw the country on which they had fixed their hopes match these obscene acts with one equally obscene. Like any other nation — the revelation was overwhelming — Soviet Russia could act for reasons of national expediency and could even join hands, no matter how temporarily, with its mortal enemy, with the mortal enemy of all decent men. Recantations of political belief, reaffirmations of faith in democratic liberties, which suddenly seemed really important, began to appear in press and periodical; and departures from the League of American Writers after it had officially supported the Communist interpretation of the Pact soon swelled to a flight.

The most celebrated case was that of Granville Hicks, who, despite his long identification with the affairs of the Literary Left, had the great courage to announce his doubts openly, to resign from the Communist Party — and what is more, to continue writing to this day both moderately and discerningly about the miscalled "Red Decade." It was Hicks, once the sternest of Marxist critics, who in 1940 repudiated years of effort with the statement that, although "the best of leftist writing will survive political catastrophes . . . I think a great deal, though by no means all, of left criticism has been invalidated by the events of the past year." And it was Hicks who pronounced, as though it were an epitaph for the decade, one of the soundest lessons to be learned by a literary man in the thirties: "Politics is no game for a person whose attention is mostly directed elsewhere." [54]

9.

THE LONG RETREAT

The rest of the journey in this book is mostly downhill, though it affords, as guidebooks say, several worthwhile views. During the war forties, the effect of American Communist policy on the radical novel was only a little less decisive than it had been during the depression thirties, but the history of the Party itself for the ten years after the Nazi-Soviet Pact presents a double paradox: in the first half of that decade its enemies, quite as much as its friends, caused it to survive and thrive; in the second half its friends, quite as much as its enemies, drove it headlong toward disaster. The Pact had been a grievous wound, and for nearly two years the American Party held on grimly to existence while the disillusioned membership bled away in streams. Forced to oppose the European struggle, though not the Russian attack on Finland, as "an imperialist conflict," the Communists would have repeated the fate of the Socialists, who had smashed up twenty-five years earlier against the herd-anger of a nation at war, except that six months before the Pearl Harbor disaster Hitler sent his planes and armored divisions across the Russian frontier. With relief the American Communists at once threw themselves into, not against, the effort to defeat the Axis powers, urging participation with even greater intensity than they had just been urging neutrality. Winston Churchill, wisely putting aside for the moment his lifetime anti-Communism, offered a military alliance between embattled England and embattled Russia. Americans of all political persuasions responded to the extraordinary resistance with which the Russian people met the German offensive, and when the United States finally declared war, the major capitalist democracies and the Soviet Union were comrades in arms.

A brief era of good feeling followed. The terminology of class struggle, put in storage during the Popular Front and brought out again after the Pact, was packed away yet once more. As loudly as anyone else the American Communists called on workers to refrain from strikes and to turn America into the arsenal of democracy. Aligned now with the "in-group," they could demonstrate allegiance to the United States as well as to the Soviet Fatherland, could advocate the suppression of dissent by any "out-group" remnants. Disregarding the implications of the newly passed Smith Act, which made it a crime to conspire to teach or advocate the overthrow of the government, they rejoiced when, during the second half of 1941, its provisions were invoked against the leaders of the Socialist Workers Party, a tiny Trotskyist group involved in a Minneapolis teamsters strike. They hailed the dissolution of the Communist International on May 22, 1943, as evidence that Soviet Russia and the United States could coexist peacefully, while exactly one year later Earl Browder announced the disbanding of the American Communist Party and its reorganization as a Political Association. Meanwhile Communist membership rose in 1944 to an all-time peak of 80,000, a record made partly possible, no doubt, by the praises that American generals, politicians, and newspaper editors showered on the unexpected valor of Russian arms. Under the stress of war emotions the Communists became for a short while almost respectable.

Within that initial paradox, however — that American Communism prospered in the early forties as much from its foes as its friends — lay a lesser one. While a policy of fraternization may outwardly have helped the Party toward greater popularity with the general public, inwardly it was as disruptive as the Pact of 1939. The metamorphosis from Party to Association and Browder's argument, on the basis of the Teheran meeting of Churchill, Roosevelt, and Stalin, that the three great powers could not only coexist peacefully but would actually coöperate after the war to create a new society — these developments were viewed by many of the tougher-minded Marxists as outright capitulation to capitalism.[1] Stalin, they felt, had not gone to Teheran as Chamberlain had to Munich; he had gone as serpent rather than dove. Their resultant bitterness turned to the advantage of William Foster, Browder's old rival, and Foster began to accumulate to himself the power of discontent. When, therefore, Jacques Duclos, secretary of the French Communist Party, gave one of the first signs of a hardening Soviet policy by publishing in the April, 1945, issue of the official *Cahiers du Communisme* a full-scale attack on Browder's position, the patient Foster was ready, after fifteen years, to resume leadership of the American movement. In June of that year Browder was expelled, the Association was changed back into a Party, and the Communists prepared to put into effect their share in the postwar program of the Soviet Union.

So began the second major paradox of the decade for the American Communists. While the Cominform was being established in September, 1947, as a successor to the Comintern, they themselves were calling for the formation of a Progressive Party, a party which was doomed to its fiasco in the elections of 1948 because the Communists, though not in complete control, held sufficient power within it to shape its candidate's campaign and to force into its platform an unqualifiedly pro-Russian foreign policy. Such a tactic was designed to meet Soviet needs in the postwar struggle against the United States; unfortunately for the Communists in this country it did not meet American needs. As the power struggle intensified, the position of the American Communists became a more and more exposed one, and it became increasingly clear that their Soviet friends had considered them in a precise military sense expendable.

They were, indeed, expended. Even before the election returns in 1948 had confirmed the failure of their tactics within the Progressive Party,[2] the Federal Government had indicted the twelve top Communist leaders under the same Smith Act to whose untender mercies those leaders had gleefully consigned the Trotskyists just before Pearl Harbor. By the end of the decade the enemies of the American Party were assuming complete responsibility for its destruction. Yet here again a lesser paradox resided, and still resides, within the greater one. The prosecution and conviction of the top Party leaders, while no doubt highly acceptable to a great majority of Americans, was being carried out under a law that made words punishable rather than deeds. Despite the fact that a Supreme Court majority affirmed the conspiracy conviction, many non-Communists concerned with the preservation of civil liberties agreed with the dissenting opinions of Justices Black and Douglas which held the Smith Act to be a clear and present violation of the rights of free speech and assembly set forth in the First Amendment. In the short view the Government's attacks were stamping out the Party; yet in the long view they were accomplishing for American Communism two ends that it could not accomplish by itself: they were bringing to an unwilling defense of the Party's political rights a number of citizens opposed to Communism precisely out of hatred for injustice of any sort, and they were creating the martyrs so essential to a militant faith. The American government, in short, was guaranteeing the survival of what it wished to destroy.

At the beginning of the new half-century, however, the most significant fact about the Party was its insignificance. In 1950 the number of actual Communists known to the well-informed Federal Bureau of Investigation had dropped to some 52,000. In 1951, as the attacks on the Party systematically continued, the number fell to 37,000; while in 1952, according to J. Edgar Hoover, there were just under 25,000 members. Caught between the anti-Communist hysteria at home and the genuine menace of Communism abroad, the wartime fellow travelers and sympathizers, who had briefly replaced the disillusioned intellectuals of the thirties, likewise fell away until the Party's influence was reduced almost to the little it had had in the twenties. Harried, hunted, and despised, pinned in a legislative trap which made it legal to become a Party member but illegal to be one, the American Communists had entered on a long winter. The remaining remnant no doubt awaited expectantly the collapse of the United States from economic contradiction or from military defeat at the hands of the Soviet Fatherland and a Soviet Asia; yet should another prolonged depression strike, the presence of powerful Communist adversaries in the world would more likely send the United States toward any solution but the Communist one, while the event of a third World War might well end human history even before, as Marx had argued, it could properly be said to have begun. Because of its growing roll of martyrs the Party could hope to exist. In the forseeable future it could hope for very little else.

II

Considering the fortunes of the Left through the forties and down to the present day, the true wonder is not that so little radical fiction has been written in this time, but rather that any has been written at all. The years of World War II were years of blight everywhere in American literature — perhaps too many writers were engaged too directly in the raw experience of future books — and the literary radicals, such few as remained, had the additional impediment of not wishing to disturb the sudden friendliness between the United States and the Soviet Union by inconvenient references to revolution. When the peacetime struggle for power supplanted wartime coöperation and when, as one result, the persecution of American radicals became fiercer, still no more than a few sparks of literary revolutionism flared, for Post-War was not the Hungry Thirties. Nevertheless a tradition of radical fiction has persisted, and despite the present isolation of the Communist Party, just enough novels in that tradition continue to be published so that the genre cannot be consigned to the dustbin of literary history.

Statistics describe the situation most quickly. In the fifteen years from 1940 through 1954, some forty radical novels were published, or an average of about three a year, a production level even below that of the last years of the Popular Front. The record, however, is uneven. No such works appeared at all in 1945, while 1947 and 1948 brought each the publication of four and 1943, 1951, and 1954 of five, the largest number published in a single year. Two more points should be noted at once about these figures, for in their quite different ways they bear on the present situation in the radical novel: one fourth of the entire total is the work of a single man, and at least another quarter was written, not by authors within the Communist orbit, but by independent leftists.

If the actual flow of radical novels has diminished from a small noisy torrent to a small quiet trickle, the subject matters have become a little more varied; somewhat less than a half of these books fall into the main categories established by the proletarian novel. Young people, a few at least, are still converted to the Marxist vision, as in the last two volumes of James Farrell's "Danny O'Neill" tetralogy,[3] books which so far mark his peak in the creation of characters; or in V. J. Jerome's antiquated tale of a Polish boyhood at the beginning of the century, *A Lantern for Jeremy*; or in Philip Bonovsky's *Burning Valley*. a passionate account of the conflict between Catholicism and Marxism in the mind and heart of a boy in a coal-mining town. Likewise the strike novel continues to appear, though infrequently. Howard Fast's *Clarkton*, Myra Page's *With Sun in Our Blood*, and Stefan Heym's *Goldsborough* make up the list except for Chester Himes's left-wing but strongly anti-Communist *Lonely Crusade*. The theme of the decaying middle class, with its corollary motifs of individual conversion and the rising power of the workers, is continued by Barbara Giles's *The Gentle Bush*, a long, densely-populated chronicle presenting the varied fortunes of a landed Louisiana family and a Cajun agrarian "proletariat." Finally, books dealing with the "bottom dogs" appear from time to time. To this last category, indeed, belong two of the most powerful novels of the forties, both by Negro novelists, one of whom was for a while a Communist Party member.

To Richard Wright literature and then, briefly, Communism had come as keys to the prison of his color. His bitter experience as a "free-born" American citizen in the Deep South, later re-created in the controlled terror of *Black Boy*, had burned into him a hatred of all oppression and a desire to set that hatred down in words. His name had become familiar to literary radicals by the middle thirties when his violently imaged free verse began to appear in *The New Masses* and Chicago's *Left Front*, of which he was an editor; but it was through his fiction that he moved into wider prominence. *Uncle Tom's Children* of 1938 is a late example of proletarianism. In actuality a collection of four novellas, it is so arranged as to give the effect of a novel's development because of the increasing order of militancy in the successive episodes. The first two novellas, "Big Boy Leaves Home," and "Down by the Riverside," show Negroes either fleeing the South or helplessly being killed. But in "Long Black Song," the Negro husband, whose wife has been seduced by a white man, shoots the man and then remains in his home, defending himself against a white mob, not crying out even when the house burns about him; and with "Fire and Cloud" the rising curve of resistance reaches its peak when hungry black and white citizens of a Southern town march together in a successful demonstration for food relief. As the demonstration triumphs, the Negro leader, a previously unmilitant minister, exultantly speaks the book's moral: *"Freedom belongs to the strong!"*

That the hard years of the Depression had shaped the whole American consciousness toward increased social awareness would be proved, if not in a hundred other ways, by the wide popularity of Wright's second book, *Native Son*, which sold a quarter of a million copies within a month after its publication in 1940. Defective though it may be in dramatic structure — Max is too obviously Wright's *raisonneur* as well as Bigger's defense attorney — the imaginative expansion of the book, the quality which survives both melodrama and didacticism, comes from the relating of the truncated lives of Negroes in the United States to those of all the other "have-not's," the humiliated and despised, who are goaded on by the American dream and whose American tragedy it is to be blocked from the dream's fulfillment. Whether or not Wright was correct in asserting shortly afterwards that the black and white Biggers of the world were potential of and would inevitably move toward either Fascism or Communism, there could be no doubting the other part of his analysis of social frustration: the Biggers would not accept the status quo. So Bigger Thomas, denied the alternative of organized, constructive action, goes to his death feeling that the murders he committed were good because he had at least been killing *for* something. The end of the book comes close to being a tract, but it is saved by the emotional force of its terrible warning.

An explicitly anti-Communist book, *The Outsider*, Wright's most recent work, lies beyond the province of the present volume; but it is worth noting that this melodrama of ideas, with its analysis of the Communist "systematization of the sensuality of power," quite reverses the environmentalism of *Native Son*. Unlike Bigger Thomas, Cross Damon is an Existentialist hero, the willed creator of his own past, present, and future within a chaotic and antagonistic world. On the other hand, in the short, lurid career of Nick Romano in Willard Motley's first novel, *Knock on Any Door*, the more traditional indictment of society is made, and with a thoroughness of detail which recalls Dreiser's defense of Clyde Griffiths. Nick's progress from altar boy to condemned criminal — by way of reform school, gang life and the pimps, bums, whores, jack rollers, stick-up men, thieves, and homosexuals of Chicago's West Madison Street — this progress is the result of his successive victimizations by an environment which first produces him, next impels him to act, and then punishes him for his action, the killing of an arrogantly vicious cop. Like the story of Clyde Griffiths, that of Nick builds toward a court trial where the real defendant, as the prisoner's attorney argues to the jury, is "you and me"; and again as with Clyde's case, that of Nick is used by the author to reveal all manner of corruption in the body politic. Here, to be sure, the judge presides fairly; but the police and the prosecuting attorney act illegally, the jurors' decision is a reflex of their more comfortable environments, and the newspapers slant the case without cease and without shame. The hands of the jurors, reflects one of the more sensitive of their number, shadow the hand of the executioner, and Nick's death in the chair, like Clyde's, only makes room for yet another Nick or Clyde to take his place.

The Chicago locale of *Knock on Any Door* reminds one of other American tragedies besides those described by Dreiser and Wright. Most of all it brings to mind the less spectacular but equally inexorable descent from innocence to corruption of Studs Lonigan, and just as Farrell introduces into that trilogy such contrast devices as the character Danny O'Neill and the Communist parade which Paddy Lonigan uncomprehendingly witnesses, so Motley introduces the figure of Tommy as both contrast and parallel to Nick. It is eleven-year-old Tommy who, in the reformatory, defies the Jim Crow code of the inmates by befriending a Negro boy, maintains his small dignity before the varied cruelties of the guards, manages to break out of the reform school briefly, takes his public lashing by the vicious superintendent, and binds Nick's loyalty to "Tommy's side" forever against the law. Tommy's career, moreever, in the few brief glimpses given of it in the remainder of the book, parallels that of Nick as opponent to established society. Tommy's way is constructive where Nick's is destructive, for his labor organizing activity at the rank-and-file level points toward the possibility of a more successful rebellion than does Nick's foredoomed singlehanded revolt; yet in the book's last agonizing sequence, shots of Nick awaiting execution for the crime which society committed are alternated by, among others, two glimpses of Tommy being slugged by bruisers while distributing strike leaflets in Denver and then wandering about the streets weeping after he sees a newspaper headline announcing that "Pretty Boy" Romano is about to die in Chicago. Then in the last two pages, Nick, in the chair, the black death mask pulled tight over his face, simultaneously relives the scene where Tommy receives his beating on the stage of the reform school assembly hall. The superintendent's arm rises with the coiled strap, the hands of the executioners lift to the four control buttons, the lash falls, the hands push home — and Tommy and Nick reach symbolic identity in their accusation of society's guilt.

In *Knock on Any Door*, Motley's concern for the hero as victim, though intense, is kept under artistic control; in his second and most recent novel *We Fished All Night* (1951), the control has slipped, or rather his material lies almost beyond control. Here what he attempts is to tell, not the story of one main victim, but that of three. Furthermore, where Nick's fate illustrates a unified, if limited, philosophic conception, the fates of Aaron Levin, Don Lockwood, and Jim Norris are intended to encompass all the myriad frustrations, dislocations, alienations, and defeats which Motley sees young Americans subjected to in a particular complex moment in history, the aftermath of World War II. Aaron Levin, alienated from his fellow men by his sense of Jewishness, achieves the complete self-separation of mental derangement and suicide. Chet Kosinski, attempting to erase the effects of his squalid home environment, constructs an image of himself as "Don Lockwood," becomes the "liberal" cat's-paw of a political boss, builds a boss-machine of his own, marries a wealthy girl, and learns to live with his corruption. If Don's career is reminiscent of Dan Minturn's, Jim Norris's recalls in part that of the labor organizer in the proletarian strike novel, with one important difference. Jim too has been so emotionally warped by a war experience that he is incapable of adequate sex relations with his wife and must fight an almost uncontrollable perverse desire for young girls. Here the working-class protagonist has become almost as twisted by the horrors of total war as the capitalist Emerson Bradley has become through his power over the lives of others; yet Jim finds himself at last in the strike against the Bradley plant, only to meet the traditional death at the hands of the police in a strike riot.

Politically Motley's novel is oriented toward the Progressive Party. (By working for this cause in the 1948 elections, one of Don's rejected girl friends, the woman who knows him best, finds personal integration.) Such an orientation no doubt helped to offset his caustic portrait of a Communist novelist who writes "novels approved by the party," whose second novel is admittedly damaged by doctrinaire Marxism, and who himself states that he robs his characters of humanity by turning them into symbols. At any rate a left-wing reviewer, writing of *We Fished All Night* early in 1952, praised the book highly, but found his chief objection in the characterization of Jim.[4] A "conscious idealist" like Norris, he argues, would have been more aware of war's brutalities and their tendency to produce psychic damage; hence, he would have been able to cope with his traumatic experience *before* it produced such devastating, if impermanent, results. Whether he knew it or not, this reviewer was demanding from Motley an idealized picture of the Communist hero, who became the most popular single subject for radical novelists from 1940 onward as though to compensate for the almost complete failure of the proletarian novel of the thirties to treat such a figure fully. Here also may be operating for the first time in the American radical novel an influence from Soviet fiction, which had been concerned throughout the thirties, and indeed still is, with the portrayal of "the new Soviet man"; but at least one sharp difference divides the American heroes from the Russian: unlike the latter, the former still dwell in a prerevolutionary society and must fight a preëminently hostile environment, rather than respond to a preëminently friendly one.

After the feeble *This Is Your Day* of 1937, the first radical novel to concern itself primarily with the life of a Communist Party member and the basis of his faith was Albert Maltz's *The Underground Stream* (1940), the action of which, given as it is in semi-dramatic form by a playwright turned novelist, is worth examining as an illustration of one of the difficulties involved in making a successful characterization of such a figure. This action resolves itself into a struggle between Princey, a hard-working but impulsive Communist organizer at "Jefferson Motors" in Detroit, and Jeffry Grebb, the company's personnel director, who has become a member of the "Iron Guard," a native Fascist organization — modeled by Maltz on Detroit's notorious Black Legion — as one step in a projected climb to political power. When Princey carelessly gets rid of his bodyguard, he is betrayed into the hands of the Iron Guard and imprisoned in an isolated house on the outskirts of the city. While his wife and comrades unsuccessfully search for him, Princey is given the choice of joining Grebb in the latter's plan to bring Fascism to the United States or of being killed. Refusing Grebb's offer to ride the whirlwind, he dies for Communism at the hands of the fanatic Iron Guard.

One of the defects of the book is the lack of realistic motivation for Grebb's acts, the central question being why he should have had any expectation whatever of winning over Princey to his own peculiar perversion of Marxism; yet the chief weakness is the ideological poverty revealed in the conversations between the two men when they finally and melodramatically confront each other. Princey "wins" the argument, not by means of dialectics, but simply through dogged self-discipline.

"Sure [he replies to Grebb], I'd like to see a Socialist world. But that ain't what makes me say Yes or No. The important thing is *I believe something*, and you want me to kick it out of the window! If I do that, I'll become something nobody would spit on, not even me. So I ain't going to do it."

He consoles himself merely with the holding of his purpose, rather than with any rightness of it. "*Beneath all else is this: A man must hold to his purpose. This — nothing less — is the underground stream of his life. Without it he is nothing. I cannot yield! A man is nothing who yields his purpose!*" The inadequacy of Princey's position is emphasized when the reader recalls the much earlier thoughts of Harvey Kellog, one of the hardened leaders of the Iron Guard.

His life, his entire fate, had become part of a secret current in American life . . . a current so deep-flowing, so powerful, that it would one day cast him upon a peak to which even the gentry of the Country Club would pay homage.

Kellog, too, has his "underground stream," or believes that he has; and if blind faith is alone the supreme good, Maltz would seem to have succeeded only in cancelling out Communism and Fascism against each other.

Despite its confusion between ideology and belief, however, *The Underground Stream* is historically important because it initiated the whole series of books chiefly concerned with an examination of the Communist's personality and faith or with a depiction of his life as the only fully admirable mode of existence available in the United States today. In this group, which includes at least seven out of the forty radical novels, clearly the chief problem faced by the writer was how to create a realistically believable leading figure while at the same time making him have meaning beyond himself. The urge to endow with meaning is always revealed in these books. Invariably the novelist attempts to establish implicitly or even explicitly that his Communist protagonist, usually the native-born son of proletarian immigrant parents, is more American than the Americans. Always his career is intended to demonstrate in microcosm the development of recent American history or the pressure of contemporary social and economic forces. Always his individual life and fate are in some way symbolic that the future belongs to the People of America and of the World, among whom he is a distinct but not separate unit, one cell in the great human body.

Such are, in fact, the emphases in Ruth McKenney's *Jake Home* (1943), which details the life of a brawny, redheaded Irish giant of the Left, whose nearly fabulous career carries him away from a white-collar railroad job to organizing activity for the Trade Union Educational League, work in the defense of Sacco and Vanzetti, near-catastrophe in his marriage to a wealthy neurotic, and finally back again to solidarity with "The Movement," where he is last seen as the "Big Red" who is happily leading a May Day parade in New York. Yet Ruth McKenney's grandiose conception of her hero produces a Jake suspiciously like a wish-fulfillment projection, a constructed myth rather than a created human being. All too frequently he suggests the cartoonlike drawings, striking within their own medium, which William Gropper often contributed to *The New Masses*, drawings in which a Paul-Bunyansized worker leads the masses pell-mell against their bloated oppressors.

In seeking to show the Hero of Our Times, Ruth McKenney succeeded in producing something close to unconscious caricature. Quite an opposite approach, that of deliberate caricature, was adopted by Isidor Schneider in *The Judas Time* (1946), which stands almost alone in radical fiction as a full-length satirical piece. Written primarily to define what a Communist is by describing what he is not, *The Judas Time* is the story of the repulsive Calvin Cain, a biologist at a New York university, who, by nature an egotist and an inquisitor, breaks with the Communist Party at about the time of the Spanish War, becomes a Trotskyist, travels to the Soviet Union on an espionage mission for the "Old Man" (Trotsky under one of the Devil's names), is unable, because of a psychosomatic illness, to carry out his plans, and brings back instead the "welcome" tidings that a Nazi invasion must drown Russia in blood before the Trotskyists can successfully return to power. Although occasional events are bitterly hilarious, the book is hardly convincing to the nonbeliever, who is apt to wonder why the Communist Party should have accepted the neurotic Cain and his fellow renegades in the first place. The satirical figure of Cain holds the center of attention, and the faithful Party members who are balanced against him are so faint as characters and as characterizations that one radical critic publicly grumbled: "[These] portrayals of ineptitude in individual Communists and Party activity serve only to reinforce prejudices created and spread by its enemies." [5]

In order to attain for the portrayal of the Communist man a more literal realism than caricature affords, two other novels — *Home Is the Sailor* (1948) by Beth McHenry and Frederick N. Myers, and *Swing Shift* (1951) by "Margaret Graham" (Grace Lois MacDonald) — admittedly are fictionalized biographies of actual worker radicals. Both are written as vigorously as their central characters lived, but in almost all other ways they are quite lacking in the art of the novel. *Swing Shift* is particularly marred by great lumps of straight exposition in which American socioeconomic history from the mid-1880's to the late 1930's is analyzed from a left-wing viewpoint before it is related to the fortunes of

"Mac," a tough and devoted railroad man. Thus only two final novels in this group actually succeed in favorably describing, in literary terms, the faith and works of presumably average, rank-and-file Communists.

The more recent of these books, Lloyd Brown's *Iron City* (1951), deals with the efforts of three Negro Communists, imprisoned as "politicals" just before Pearl Harbor, to organize a protest movement on the outside in defense of another Negro awaiting execution for a crime which he did not commit. Although the author, depite his subject, is unable to build such scenes of explosive violence as the far more gifted Wright and Motley excel in, he does carefully differentiate his three Communists as to personality and to motivation toward radicalism, he imbeds their lives in the observed minutiae of prison routine, and he establishes the "iron city" of the prison as a metaphor, not only for the Iron City (Pittsburgh, presumably) where the prison is located, but for the Iron City of capitalism itself, which is here conceived as encaging worker and prisoner alike. Unfortunately the book, for all its sincerity, seems overcome by the drabness of the routine which it describes; only at a few moments is the metaphor communicated with any sense of emotional intensity.

Equally informed in the daily lives of its proletarian characters, Alexander Saxton's *The Great Midland* (1948), has as its background the city of Chicago and the yards of one of the midcontinent railroads from the year 1912 to the outbreak of World War II. The rather complex web of lives and events, spun out within an arbitrarily shifting time sequence, is primarily centered on the relationship between the Communist railroad worker, Dave Spaas, and his wife Stephanie, although considerable attention in the first half of the book is also given to Dave's Negro comrade, Pledger McAdams, whose gradual acceptance of white men and of Communism is effectively handled. Dave, who had early been educated to radicalism by an I.W.W. uncle, is portrayed as a hard-working, single-minded man, willing to endure the slow, fatiguing work of organizing at the rank-and-file level. Stephanie, infected with a desire for the relative ease and security of the life in the university where she is studying biology, is torn between love for Dave and hatred of his capacity for subordinating their personal life to the demands of the Party. The instability of the relationship is understandable. At one point they separate, although, curiously, the actual scene of separation is never described but only hinted at; and when they are reunited, Stephanie's sense of insecurity begins almost immediately to drive them apart again. They can never expect more time together than the Party activity of each allows them; and their final reconciliation, after the outbreak of World War II and just before Dave takes a berth on a Liberty ship, actually leaves their basic conflict unresolved. Apparently because he consciously desires an "affirmative" ending, however, the author at this point violates the logic of the impasse relationship which he has so relentlessly been constructing. Without being informed of any new element in the situation which might produce a change of heart, the reader is simply told that, although Stephanie knows she will never feel completely secure, she has come to understand the nature of the ideal that could attract such men as Pledger McAdams and her husband. The portraits of Communists in this book, then, are more lifelike than the crude sketches in the proletarian novels of the thirties, but the conclusion is hardly more convincing.

Whatever the artistic limitations of these books about Communists, they do demonstrate an attempt to give what their authors consider truthful accounts of radical life. The most successful characterizations are of rank-and-file Party members or of lower-echelon "functionaries," men and women devoted to a cause, chronically overworked in Party activity, and harassed by the protective agencies of the established social order. They worry about bills, brush their teeth, fall in love, even marry before begetting children, have a beer or two with the boys of a Saturday night, like baseball or picnics or classical music, take a workman's pride in clean tools and a job well done — are fed with the same food, hurt with the same weapons, subject to the same diseases, healed by the same means, warmed and cooled by the same winter and summer, as non-Communists are. Quite obviously the accounts are in the main favorable; yet they are by no means lacking in what Party pronouncements delight to call "Communist self-criticism." If the Party itself is always considered incorruptible and infallible, still individual members may err in things both great and small.

They make take a beer too many or see a movie instead of reading
the back pages of *The Daily Worker*; some may be corrupted by
power or wearied into passivity; a few may let the blandishments
of capitalism cloud the eye of faith. If these books are no answer,
either in doctrine or in art, to the best of the anti-Communist novels
here and abroad, to Dos Passos's *The Big Money* or Silone's *Bread
and Wine*, still they suggest that the average Party member is
hardly the monster conjured up by the usual "anti-Red" thriller.
Although the radical writers may conceal some facts and sentimen-
talize others, they help to counterbalance the wild charges and melo-
dramatics on the opposing side. Probably truth lies somewhere
between.

Since 1940 a sizable part of the energies of the radical novelists
has gone into these portraits of the orthodox Communist by
writers who in general accept the orthodoxy. Quite another phenomenon is the appearance among the authors themselves of the
independent radical, affected by radical ideology but not committed to the Party as the sole repository of the faith. In this category, of course, stand at least James Farrell, Chester Himes, and
Willard Motley, probably Nelson Algren, and certainly the Joseph
Freeman of *Never Call Retreat*; to these must be added the
names of two other men — Norman Mailer, whose *The Naked and
the Dead* was one of the earliest and best of the novels to come
directly out of World War II, and Ira Wolfert, whose *Tucker's
People* remains one of the most distinguished American novels of
the whole forties.

Mailer's radicalism is of an indeterminate sort, the kind that
expresses itself preëminently, perhaps, in images and fictional constructs rather than in abstract schema. Never affiliated with the
Communist Party, he did affirm his stand with the Progressive
Party, for whose presidential candidate he campaigned in the
autumn of 1948. But *The Naked and the Dead* had already been
written before that time, from the summer of 1946 to the fall of
1947, and Mailer has stated that it was only after a European trip
taken subsequent to turning in the manuscript of the novel that he
overcame his dislike for any kind of collective action. This dislike
lies at the heart of his first novel and has often been interpreted as
making his critique of capitalist society an entirely negative one;

nevertheless *The Naked and the Dead* is a radical novel which affirms and does so within its own logic as a literary work.

Mailer's novel has a number of faults, not the least being that it sounds at times like a pastiche of the novels about World War I. The echoes of Dos Passos, another individualist rebel, are especially insistent: the interchapter biographies in *The Naked and the Dead* combine the techniques of the biographies and the narrative sections in *U.S.A.*, and the fact that all of these individual soldier lives are thwarted and stunted by a sick society seems clearly reminiscent of the social vision at the base of the trilogy. It is indeed a sick society that is being exposed to view in the microcosm of an army division which has been assigned the task, under Major-General Cummings, of seizing a Pacific island from the Japanese. If, as Mailer himself has stated, the book "finds man corrupted, confused to the point of helplessness," [6] these qualities particularly express the personality of that key figure, Lieutenant Robert Hearn, a confused liberal intellectual who, like the middle class in Marxist theory, is caught between the hammer and the anvil of great antagonistic forces. In him Mailer skillfully fuses form and content, for Hearn partakes in and thus links both of the power struggles which operate simultaneously in the book, in each holds a kind of ideological middle ground, and in each is defeated. In order to understand Mailer's radical purpose, however, it is necessary to see that the same alternative to defeat exists in both struggles.

At the top level Hearn comes into personal conflict with General Cummings, who, quite explicitly a proto-Fascist, seeks to convince his liberal aid that a successful army is structured as a "fear ladder," a tight hierarchy in which "you're frightened of the man above you, and contemptuous of your subordinates." Such a system of power morality as the Army, Cummings tells him, is "a preview of the future." When Hearn deliberately grinds a cigarette butt into the immaculate floor of the General's tent as a gesture of revolt, Cummings quite as deliberately shows how power, which he defines as always flowing from the top down, can burn out any "little surges of resistance at the middle levels." He humiliates Hearn, the one individual, successfully if temporarily, but even in his triumph he is forced to recognize within himself that he has not yet found the way to crush all six thousand men in his division.

When Hearn, as part of the punishment, is assigned to the reconnaissance platoon which Cummings sends out to reconnoiter the Japanese rear from the other side of the island, he finds himself in another struggle, that between Sergeant Croft, like the General a power moralist, and the men themselves. Croft ruthlessly takes care of Hearn by withholding from him the knowledge of a Japanese outpost and allowing the lieutenant to be cut down by an enemy machine-gun burst. Then he takes over full command of the men, beats down a nearly successful rebellion and, in order to cross the island, forces them up the heights of Mt. Anaka, which stands as a challenge to this perverted idealist. Although Hearn the liberal had been no match for Croft, the men are. Having dragged the exhausted soldiers almost to the summit, Croft blunders by pure chance into a nest of hornets, whose stings send the platoon into a wild tumble down the jungle-covered wall they have just painfully scaled. But it is not chance that the men, as they run, throw away weapons and equipments, for they sense that "if they threw away enough possessions they would not be able to continue the patrol"; and one crafty soldier sends his fellows into further panicky retreat by shouting what is not the case, that the hornets are still coming after them. In three more short paragraphs Mailer flatly describes Croft's weary acceptance of defeat, the platoon's return to the beach where they had landed, and Croft's half-conscious relief "that he had found a limit to his hunger."

Thus the point first stated in the Cummings–Hearn–army division struggle is here worked out once more: there are limits beyond which man in the mass cannot be pushed. And when, at the end of the book, Japanese resistance collapses before Cummings can put his master plan in operation, it becomes clear that Mailer seeks to demonstrate the inability of power moralists to manipulate history in opposition to mass will. If *The Naked and the Dead* is taken as the accurate sum of all its parts, it must be considered, as Mailer himself has declared,[7] a positive and hopeful book rather than a negative and pessimistic one. Though they are "a bunch of dispossessed . . . from the raucous stricken bosom of America," these foul-mouthed, insecure, embittered G.I.'s contain unknowingly in themselves the seeds of a less corrupt and sick society. More skillfully than most radical novelists Mailer has solved the problem of the ending which with artistic inevitability affirms the author's belief. Incident flowers organically into idea.

Like *The Naked and the Dead*, Ira Wolfert's *Tucker's People* has deficiencies that are minimized by a largeness of conception and a powerful presentation. Where Mailer's novel at times seems derivative, Wolfert's derives, if at all, only at its simplest level with a possible debt to the hard-boiled school of Dashiell Hammett and James M. Cain. The defects of *Tucker's People* are rather an occasional lapse into flat prose and a tendency to overanalyze the motivations of its characters. But even this latter emphasis indicates how Wolfert has increased the dimensions of the social novel. A knowledge of neurotic psychology has added depth, and cogency, to his broad social critique. Both *The Naked and the Dead* and *Tucker's People*, furthermore, develop a subject matter in such a way that a constantly suggested analogy always generalizes their major themes. If the Army is a preview of a future Fascist state with its power morality and its hierarchic organization, "policy" (the numbers racket) is pictured in Wolfert's novel as the mirror image of "legitimate business." In fact, since "policy" is always described in terms of "legitimate business" and "legitimate business" always in terms of "policy," eventually Wolfert achieves his purpose: both are merely forms of institutionalized economic activity, each devoted to satisfying to some extent the real wants of customers, and each equally unconcerned ultimately with the fate of individual human beings. Thus Leo Minch, forced out of a "legitimate" garage business with its own set of petty grafts, builds up a respectable small enterprise in policy, only to have it taken over by the ruthless Ben Tucker as one of the latter's first steps in effecting a projected monopoly. The methods of Tucker, it is suggested, are those of the usual business monopolist, and his excuses are the same: operating costs can be cut, policy can be run on an efficient basis, and Tucker himself, of course, will receive the enormous profits of a controlled market. Tucker is merely attempting to be a latter-day Robber Baron.

When Leo and the other small "bankers" are forced into Tucker's combination, Leo's employees must work for him on a new basis. Where formerly he was the paternalistic employer who derived ego-satisfaction from his small favors to them, he now must act as the corporation executive to whom individual lives are less important than the demands of the corporation itself. Thus in little becomes illustrated another of Wolfert's major theses: the universal product of a big-business society is a profound and permanent emotional insecurity in all its members. The brilliant Henry Wheelock, attorney of Tucker's corporation, has suffered and suffers from a lack of psychological wholeness, as does Joe Minch, Leo's brother, who handles business details for Tucker; even Tucker himself reflects the insecurity which he helps other businessmen to produce. But the supreme example in the book is that of Frederick Bauer, Leo's fear-ridden head bookkeeper, who is terrified into hysteria by two police raids on the "bank," irrationally accepts the help of a rival gangster's henchman as quite unnecessary protection against the people of Tucker's organization, betrays Leo into the hands of the rival, and has his head shot off by the henchman as reward. In the portrayal of Bauer, Wolfert moves most explicitly from the psychology of the neurotic individual to the psychology of the neurotic mass; Bauer's demoralized life, though not necessarily his violent death, is intended to stand for that of other "little men" in Depression America.

Bauer's relevance as twentieth-century victim extends, however, beyond his own country and culture. His desperate avowal of allegiance to one who promises protection is directly likened by Wolfert to the German people's fanatical acceptance of Hitler. Both Bauer and the Germans are "a climax to the modern world and its business game." Like theirs his act is an expression of a death-wish; like them he swims "drowning in the stream of history" toward destruction. The importance of Bauer in the book clarifies, indeed, Wolfert's subsequent declaration that his novel was a history of American business from Rockefeller to Hitler. Such is certainly the final purpose of a book which exists simultaneously on a rich variety of levels. *Tucker's People* is not only an exciting gangster story, journalist's report on a racket, account of the Depression, and analysis of the neurotic personality of our time; it is also a compressed image of modern capitalism as Wolfert sees it — or saw it — its quick ripeness, its sudden and terrible decay. However simplistic one may consider the view that Fascism is capitalism's final stage, this view nevertheless successfully unifies the varied aspects of the book. Because it is so many things and yet remains one, *Tucker's People* is a major achievement in contemporary American fiction.

III

Aside from the independent radicals, only one other left-wing writer since 1940 has produced any novels of better than average quality, and this man's work is perhaps most remarkable for its sheer quantity. In the lean years after World War I, the tradition of radical fiction had been kept alive largely by the efforts of Upton Sinclair. Now in as nearly lean years the same office is being performed by Howard Fast. Even more, in fact, than at first appears likely, Fast's position as writer resembles that of the older man. Besides being prolific in production, both have composed boys' stories as hackwork in professional writing careers, both have a flair for the tale of rousing adventure, both are pamphleteers of considerable skill, and both, though Fast is much the superior craftsman, regard their novels primarily as vehicles for their respective messages. Both have courageously refused to separate their writings from their lives, have been vigorous in direct agitation for their political beliefs, and have seen the insides of jails as a result of their determination to defend those beliefs openly. Finally, both Fast and Sinclair have at various times achieved wide popularity at home and abroad for their work, especially in the Soviet Union; and Fast's recent writing, like almost all of Sinclair's, has begun to suffer from some of the qualities which have helped to produce that popularity.

If Sinclair's chief contribution to modern American fiction was to help establish the novel of contemporary history, Fast's has been to show how an already established form, the traditional historical novel, may be used for radical ends. The conception basic to most of his work is a dialectic of revolutionary development whereby certain past events are viewed as acts in the extended drama of mankind's struggle toward a classless society. Fast's type-story is that of a revolt of the oppressed against their oppressors — Washington and his starving troops against the power of England, Spartacus and the gladiators or the Maccabees and their people against the power of Rome. Each of these struggles, Fast implicitly or explicitly argues, helped bring mankind closer to its inevitable future, and he hopes to persuade the reader of the magnitude of what might be called the tradition of revolt. But the usability of this past has a second element, particularly apparent in the latest books. If the past is seedbed of the future, it also affords parallel upon parallel with our own time, and Fast has always deliberately attempted "to link the trends" of a past revolutionary time "with the trends today." [8] The reader is not only to admire the past; he is to profit from it in his own time.

Although Fast has written of the ancient and foreign times of Palestine under the Maccabees (*My Glorious Brothers*) and Rome of the late Republic (*Spartacus*), his main efforts have so far gone into reëxamining American history, the current of which, he believes, "as expressed by the mass of American people is revolutionary." [9] Not including the three "straight" historical novels written prior to *The Last Frontier* (1941) — according to Fast this book was his first conscious attempt at radical fiction [10] — the books dealing with American history cluster around three different periods: the American Revolution, the second half of the nineteenth century, and the contemporary.

The contemporary novels — *Clarkton* (1947), *The Passion of Sacco and Vanzetti* (1953), and *Silas Timberman* (1954) — are significantly enough the thinnest of his work. *Silas Timberman*, the most recent, is an angry attempt to expose the forces behind the current suppressions of academic freedom, but Fast concentrates so hard on demonstrating all parts of the Communist analysis of these forces that he skimps the details needed to make his characters seem alive and engaged in human relationships. *The Passion of Sacco and Vanzetti* is the best of the three, for it at least gains a different and more successful kind of concentration by restricting itself in time to the twenty-four hours leading up to the execution of the Anarchists and by maintaining a consistent elegiac note, which even subdues the occasional bitterness of Fast's invective within an all-enveloping sorrow. Like any sensitive person Fast has responded to the final agony of these two men. In *Clarkton*, however, concentration is precisely what is lacking. Although only a little longer than the brief *Passion of Sacco and Vanzetti*, it attempts, by describing a postwar strike in a one-industry town of western Massachusetts, to present a group of Communists as human beings with quite human virtues and shortcomings. One is most struck by the shortcomings of all the characters. The owning class is represented by a cultivated "liberal," George Clark Lowell, who, finding himself less and less able to handle the developing strike situation, employs a professional strikebreaker and tries to benumb his conscience with drink and sexual promiscuity. Opposed to the disintegrating liberal are a group of Communists and their sympathizers, among them being a feckless strike organizer, a tired old lawyer, and, most important of all, a neurasthenic doctor named Elliott Abbott — the insistently New England names produce unconscious caricature — who is surprisingly friendly to Lowell but who maintains, with something less than scientific objectivity, that the Communist Party is "the only thing decent and good and real in this land." Unlike the strikes of so many proletarian novels, this one still holds as the book ends; yet even the class-conscious individuals on the workers' side are singularly cheerless in their conviction that the system they are fighting is a dying one. Like the other two novels, *Clarkton* is an *ad hoc* piece of work, and the weaknesses of all three suggest that, in order to speak out at once on contemporary issues, their overworked author is writing too fast and too abstractly.

Always Fast seems more at his ease with the novel about earlier times. The three dealing with the second half of the nineteenth century — *The Last Frontier* (1941), *Freedom Road* (1944), and *The American* (1946) — exhibit his technical versatility and as a group imply a conscious plan to cover as much of American society as possible. Geographically, for example, the first is concerned with the West, the second with the Reconstruction South, the third with the Midwest. (*Clarkton* and *The Passion of Sacco and Vanzetti* were subsequently to bring in New England, while the novels of the American Revolution concentrated on the Middle Atlantic states.) Again, in each of these three novels the fate of a different American minority group is emphasized: Indians in *The Last Frontier*, Negroes in *Freedom Road*, the foreign-born in *The American*. If it were not for the insistence on the inevitable revolutionary triumph toward which all this history tends, one might describe

Fast's work as an attempt to write a vast, many-faceted American tragedy, so brutally overwhelming are the forces arrayed in each case against the minority; yet any defeat that the oppressor inflicts is only appearance. Ultimate victory for the oppressed, these novels argue, is the reality.

Of the three books, *Freedom Road* and *The American* now seem for differing reasons markedly weaker than *The Last Frontier*. As history *Freedom Road*, though not unquestionable, appears mainly accurate in its account of the temporarily successful attempt by the newly freed Negroes and the poor whites of Reconstruction South Carolina to join political forces against the planters. But in a novel historical accuracy is not enough; all the characters except the dead ones, as Mark Twain said so scathingly of Fenimore Cooper's people, must appear to be alive. Gideon Jackson, Fast's Negro hero, is impossibly virtuous, as to a lesser degree are most of the other representatives of the two oppressed groups, and the white planters are almost unmitigatedly evil. Furthermore, the form of the novel, a spurious kind of folk epic, requires that Jackson be kept rather vague as an individual; while the language of the novel, a pseudo-Biblical, pseudo-"folksy" diction, ends by blurring all the characters rather than illuminating any of them sharply. On the other hand, *The American* succeeds in its portrait of the tough-minded, iron-fibred, yet compassionate John Peter Altgeld, Governor of Illinois and "Eagle Forgotten," who opposed President Cleveland's probably unconstitutional act of sending Federal troops into Illinois in 1894 to break the strike of Debs's Railway Union against the Pullman Company and who bravely put his career in jeopardy by pardoning as innocent men the three remaining Anarchists from the Haymarket Affair. The success of his characterization of Altgeld results in part from the many-angled view of the man made possible by what is perhaps Fast's favorite technique for the novel: successive clusters of related scenes, the scenes presented to the reader through the subjective viewpoint of one or more different characters and linked, like the clusters themselves, either by ironic juxtaposition or by swiftly moving bridge passages of author's narrative. Unfortunately Fast is less successful in his ultimate purpose, to reveal through the career of Altgeld the major forces in American socioeconomic history from the Civil War to the opening years of the present century; for his reading of that history is a decidedly simplified one in which the great liberal protest movements are discounted as utterly useless and unproductive of political progress, while the tradition of extreme revolt is held up as the one true source of strength against an imperialist oligarchy. How he overlooks distinctions in order to shape history to his own purpose is most obvious in his explicit attempt to present the Anarchists as forerunners of the modern Communists. History, even for the writer of historical fiction, simply is not that ductile.

If *Freedom Road* fails mainly for literary reasons and *The American* mainly for historical ones, *The Last Frontier* succeeds in all ways. Here at the outset of his career as a radical novelist Fast found the perfect "objective correlative" for both his beliefs and his powers. The subject of this fine novel, to date his best, is an extraordinary actual event out of America's frontier past. Among the Indians who were exiled to Oklahoma Indian Territory in the 1870's because the white Americans coveted their lands was a small band of Cheyennes from the fertile Powder River country of Wyoming and Montana. In 1878 this band, numbering less than three hundred men, women, and children, began a break for freedom which ended months and hundreds of miles later with half the band killed and half back in their old homeland despite the bitter opposition of over ten thousand veteran U. S. Army troops. At the end of the 1930's Fast came across an account of this event in Struthers Burt's *Powder River*. Now committed intellectually to Marxism and desirous of an adequate subject for its literary expression, he saw the story as "an epic in man's desire for personal freedom," knew he had his subject, and set off for Oklahoma in 1939 to gather the facts, which had long since become obscured and falsified. The details, when he discovered them, gave so complete a pattern that he needed to add only one fully fictitious character, a cavalry captain in whom pursuit of the Cheyennes becomes an obsession because of his admiration for their courage and indomitable purpose.

The novel is not simply admirable as history, however; it is admirable as literature and as radical literature. This rather short book takes on the quality of its incident, and in its spare, usually understated prose achieves indeed the stripped grandeur of an epic. Quite wisely Fast reveals the action only through the eyes of a variety of white characters so that the heart of the mystery, the almost instinctive drive of the Indians for freedom, is never explained but only manifests itself, calmly and irresistibly, like a force of nature. Quite wisely also Fast avoids suggesting his real theme directly except for a few brief passages. Thus, when Carl Schurz, erstwhile fighter on the barricades for German freedom and now a colder-blooded American Secretary of the Interior, signs the order returning a captured group of the Cheyennes to Oklahoma, he is portrayed as possibly thinking that such rebellions by minorities must not recur and then as "sensing something of a future where it would occur again and again and again, where the trail would not be the trail of three hundred primitive horsemen over a thousand miles of green prairie, but of thousands and millions across the blackened and tear-wetted face of the earth." Here the voice of the author sounds through that of his character, but almost everywhere else the radical theme resides in the incident itself, which produces its symbolic quality unaided. A struggle for freedom in the past implies a greater struggle for freedom in the future. Image and idea coexist, and a moment in history becomes, for literary purposes at least, a prophecy.

It was when he began work on *The Unvanquished* (1942) that Fast resolved to prove that the major current of American history has been revolutionary and to attempt, as he said, "a one-man reformation of the historical novel in America." Such being his resolve, it is not surprising that three of his many books are concerned directly with the American Revolution itself. *The Unvanquished* scrupulously details Washington's New York campaign in the fall of 1776 from the disaster of Brooklyn Heights to the crucial Battle of Trenton and shows the development of Washington from the fox-hunting landed gentleman to the man of steadfast devotion to the revolutionary cause; while *Citizen Tom Paine* (1943) Fast's most popular book despite the inevitable falling off of its second half, pictures the Revolution through the eyes of America's first professional revolutionary. These first two books were attempts to rescue two famous but quite different men from historical falsification, from the hagiologists in one case and from the demonologists in the other. Both were consistent portraits, that of Washington being the more convincing, but the critical and popular success both achieved resulted in part, no doubt, from the intensified patriotism of wartime, which was also willing to accept a revolutionary past in order to prove present idealism in a world fight.

When *The Proud and the Free* appeared in 1950, World War II was over, and the sudden, tentative friendliness between the Soviet Union and the United States had passed into hatred and suspicion. This third volume concerned with the American Revolution did not deal with already famous figures but with men so obscure that the names of most have been lost; it was far more explicit even than *Citizen Tom Paine* in revealing the revolutionary commitment of its author; and it was received with marked reservations or with rage. One reviewer attacked it so severely for supposed historical inaccuracies that Fast felt required to reply at length in the Marxist-oriented *Masses & Mainstream*. In his "Reply to Critics" he demonstrates that, contrary to the charge, he had done much careful research to assemble his facts concerning the mutiny of the veteran troops of the Pennsylvania Line's foreign brigades on January 1, 1781; nevertheless, the book and the reply suggest that as opposition to his political views becomes more bitter, as his popularity decreases precisely because of those views, he may be forcing the ideological arguments of his books to greater and greater extremes. The point is worth illustrating.

One may overlook the unimportant matter that Fast uses as his horrifying climactic episode a contemporary but second-hand account of the punishment of the leading mutineers even when that account is rejected as "fantastic" by Carl Van Doren in his *Mutiny in January*, a full-scale history of the little-known affair, one to which Fast himself quite properly assigns the major credit for establishing the facts.[11] What is really important is his interpretation of the mutineers' motives. As long as he keeps within the bounds set by established facts, of course, any historical novelist, whether Fast or, say, Kenneth Roberts, has the right to interpret the facts according to his own beliefs; yet just as Roberts's attempts to reëvaluate the character of Benedict Arnold ultimately smash up against the hard fact of his hero's subsequent treason, so Fast's attempts to make the mutineers a group of half-conscious Marxists smash up against other hard facts. The rebellious sergeants of the Pennsylvania Line's foreign brigades did throw off their officers, they did lead their troops in good order to Princeton, they did set up a well-conducted self-government and refused to be bribed over to the British — and then they resubmitted themselves to their officers. Fast's explanation for this significant conclusion of the revolt is that the sergeants knew they were caught in their own objective situation. Although they knew themselves to be the concentrated spirit of the Revolution, the conditions that would have enabled them to step upward to a new historical level lay in the future and did not then exist. "Thus, in surrendering, the Committee of Sergeants acted less from choice than from the strong pressures of necessity." [12]

What are the facts? The Pennsylvania Line mutinied for very excellent, but very specific reasons — mistreatment by officers, lack of pay, a disagreement over the term of enlistment. When their officers promised rectification of these abuses, the Committee of Sergeants voluntarily ended their rebellion. Since the order of events seems to show true cause and effect here, to argue that necessity rather than choice motivated their final decision is both gratuitous and questionable. Of course Fast may only be "interpreting," but his interpretation fails to supply motivation for a subsequent event. If the men of the foreign brigades were so far along on the unaccustomed way to becoming professional revolutionaries, why did a majority of them take the proffered chance to leave military service entirely instead of remaining in the essential fight? Finally, the mutiny in the Pennsylvania Line must be considered in relation to other mutinies that took place in the Continental Army at or near the same time, particularly that of the Connecticut Line. Not only did the latter occur six months previous to that of the foreign brigades and among a predominantly native-born body of troops, but it resulted from exactly the same kind of specific grievances. Nor was this mutiny ended by pacific agreement; rather it was put down by the threat of the guns of the Pennsylvania Line itself. If, according to Fast, the foreign brigades were the spearhead of the Revolution in January, 1781, then the Connecticut Line must have been the spearhead in the previous summer — and the Pennsylvania Line, "objectively" speaking, must of necessity have been acting at that time as a *counterrevolutionary* force. Such a conclusion would hardly suit Fast's interests, but it is the conclusion to which his premises lead.

That Fast's interpretations are becoming more and more extreme, and less and less convincing, is shown by his tendency, steadily on the increase since the end of World War II, to point up his parallels between past and contemporary history, a tendency perhaps motivated by a psychological need to meet present attacks against the Left with ever greater defiance. In *The American* he had pictured the Anarchists quite incorrectly as proto-Communists. In *The Proud and the Free* he apparently was trying to make the foreign brigades of the Continental Army stand for the foreign brigades on the Loyalist side in the Spanish War. In *Spartacus* (1951), his insistence on parallels sometimes turns the book into an ideological anachronism.

The revolt of Spartacus and the gladiators against Rome, a revolt which became the Gladiatorial War of 73–71 B.C., was of course a subject that was a "natural" for Fast; for it gave wide scope to his real gifts — a command of swift narrative, the ability to suggest through concrete details the felt sensuous everyday life of the past, a particular skill (one wonders at its source) with scenes of physical torment or other forms of violence. Even more suitable was the nature of the revolt itself, a spontaneous outbreak by slaves against masters, which in Fast's treatment becomes an explicit prophecy of a future, successful revolution by the proletariat against capitalist domination. The slaves of Rome, it is pointed out several times, are the producers, those who built "the cities, the towers, the walls, the roads and the ships," and who are forced into the "comradeship of the oppressed" by the unthinking, unfeeling cruelty of their owners. Under the leadership of Spartacus the gladiators of Capua, trained by their deadly profession not to make friends with each other, fight off in good order successively larger detachments of Roman soldiery and learn in these acts a sense of community which enables them to band together in a primitive communism where all men are equal and share with one another. That their effort ends in the thousands of crucified gladiators along the Appian Way only indicates that history is not yet ready, as it will be, for so much freedom.

On the improbable chance that the constant parallelizing of revolts might be missed, Fast at one point produces a scene out of a proletarian novel. A group of aristocrats is conducted through a perfume factory where rich materials are processed in filthy surroundings by nearly naked "free" workers, not slaves. The Roman capitalist who operates the factory points out that the factory owners of the country have smashed the laborers' guilds (read "unions"), and he scoffs at the notion that the workers might rebel like Spartacus; yet one of the aristocrats is filled with an inexplicable uneasiness as he sees the men go silently and efficiently about their tasks. Clearly, between *The Last Frontier* and this book Fast has not developed in the direction of greater subtlety and restraint.

The temper of the book is revolutionary throughout, and it comes as no surprise that there are many echoes of the motifs made familiar by the proletarian novel of the Angry Thirties. Roman justice is merely a means of protecting wealth and power; the politician is a "magician" who makes the common people believe in the illusion that "the greatest fulfillment in life is to die for the rich"; the wealthy Romans themselves are decadent and sexually perverse, while the slaves are normal, moral, and of course dedicated to Life. The victorious gladiators insist on equal rights for women, as well as conjugal fidelity for the men, and they reject national differences with an easy internationalism. Nor are race and religion barriers among them; with the gladiators, black and white unite and fight. In this context appears once more a pattern of characters which has become a formula with Fast beginning at least as early as *Clarkton* (1947) and recurring as well in *The Proud and the Free* and *The Passion of Sacco and Vanzetti*: always among the important figures are a Negro, a Jew, and a white Gentile. Though Fast's motive is certainly honorable, the repetition of the pattern becomes too glib and suggests that Fast's imagination is overly subjected to ideological habit.

Ideology certainly controls the characterization of Spartacus himself. Even through the hostile accounts of the Roman historians, one glimpses the man's genius and his humanity, but when Fast has filled in the gaps in his personality left by men who thought the deeds of slaves to be unimportant, what emerges is a kind of Soviet hero extrapolated into the first century B.C. The leader of the

gladiators is brave, calm, upright, and dignified, possessed of a remarkable "wholeness" of personality, devoted to his followers and
wife, who worship him, and to humanity as well. Such he might
have been, though Fast has come a long way from his portrait of the
admirable yet humanly limited George Washington in *The Unvanquished*. But real glibness appears when Spartacus is endowed
with a preternatural consciousness of history. Not only does he
agree with Marx that wealth is created solely by the workers, but
he almost repeats, or creates, Marx's most famous appeal when he
asserts to a Roman captive that the gladiators will build a new world
of equality, justice, and peace after smashing down the brutal
power of the owners: "The whole world will hear the voice of the
[slave] — and to the slaves of the world, we will cry out, Rise up
and cast off your chains!" [13] When Spartacus speaks with both the
accents and the vocabulary of *The Communist Manifesto*, the reader no longer needs to believe in him as a character of his time,

In a note at the end of *Spartacus*, Fast explains that the novel
was of necessity published by himself after he had learned that "no
commercial publisher, due to the political temper of the times, would
undertake the publication and distribution of the book." If such
be indeed the reason for the refusal of the novel, it is not one that
American publishing can be proud of; but even more serious for
Fast the writer than having to print his own books is the probability
that his defiant sense of crisis will impel him even farther along the
way of *Spartacus*, the way to a skillfully done but essentially sterile
melodrama of history. Then his best work will lie irrevocably behind him at the beginning of the forties, and a distinct, if limited,
talent will be quite lost to American letters.

IV

In a pamphlet published at the end of the 1940's, Howard Fast
spoke out with his customary emphasis against what he considered
to be one of the most evil symptoms of his desolate times, the treason of the intellectuals in the "fight for peace," their surrender to
the forces making for Fascism and war. This was not the way of it
in the thirties, he insisted, and mingling the tone of Ecclesiastes with
that of Jeremiah, he asked:

Where are the great ones of the 'thirties, the whole school of talented progressive writers who arose out of the unemployed struggles led by the Communist Party — and the great drive to build the C.I.O.? Where are the exciting regional spokesmen who made a new American literature in those years? To read off their names is like reading a roll-call of the dead, but none of them is dead; only the spark of compassion is gone from them.[14]

Like lamentations have continued to appear regularly during the 1950's in the pages of *Masses & Mainstream*, diminished monthly successor to the weekly *New Masses* and last stronghold of the once-proud literary Left.[15] Since they are unhappy admissions on the part of the Left itself that the Great Revolt is at least temporarily over, that the roaring offensive of the radical novel has shrunk to a kind of desperate holding action, it is possible at last to look back, particularly on the thirties, to assess the gains and losses.

The Socialist novel of the century's first two decades belongs as completely to the past as the day of the Socialist Party itself. If the very few novels noted at the end of Chapter Three, none of them of the first rank, can still speak to us across two wars, the influence of this whole body of fiction, its fight for realism, for example, has long since diffused out beyond trace into the great sea of our literary culture. The proletarian novel of the thirties, however, is still within the living memory of all but the youngest generation of writers and critics, and is still capable of provoking in them from time to time direct conscious reactions, mostly of a negative sort.

The deficiencies of the proletarian novel as a whole are obvious and have already been noted — the infatuation with violence for its own sake, the melodramatic confrontations, the oversimplification, and therefore falsification, of characters, the recurrence of stereotyped motifs, the "wish-fulfillment" endings, the tendency generally to tamper with the logic of the novel's own structure of relationships. Defects like these make most of the books, when read now, weigh heavy on the hand and light on the mind, or, in certain instances, cause the reader to feel, in the words of the *New Masses* review of the "poetic" strike novel *Jordanstown*, "as though he were reading an entire genre rather than a novel." [16] Yet the critic of the fifties who dismisses the proletarian novels as having been all of a bad piece overlooks a number of individual works which avoid quite successfully the defects of the school as an entirety. In Algren's *Somebody in Boots*, Bell's *All Brides Are Beautiful*, Cantwell's *The Land of Plenty*, the three books of Farrell's *Studs Lonigan*, Josephine Herbst's trilogy, and Roth's *Call It Sleep*, the framework of Marxist doctrine is imbedded almost out of sight but serves to bind the material of fiction firm; and these ten, if of unequal excellence among themselves, are probably the most durable achievements of the radical novel of the thirties. If the same indiscriminate critic objects that ten novels in ten years are little enough to show for the effort, he may recall that these are ten out of seventy novels and may then reflect whether all the examples of any other genre taken over a similar period would show any higher ratio of considerable excellence to mediocrity or worse.

The contributions of the proletarian novel considered as a whole, however, outweigh even those of individual books. Negatively, this literary phenomenon illustrated for later authors what pitfalls to avoid in writing the social novel, and it showed, to those who would see, the dangers involved when schematized thinking of any kind is inorganically imposed on the creative process. The positive contributions of the genre, despite the many individual faults and excesses, can perhaps be most quickly appreciated if they are simply enumerated. First, the proletarian novel introduced new experience and new characters into the range of American fiction. Second, it emphasized the relation of the individual character to his social environment, thus ultimately enriching our perceptions of both. Third, by its concern with the underprivileged third of the nation, it broadened the understanding in the writer and reader of the United States as a whole. Fourth, it led the writer toward a respect for important common experience and toward the realization that he was a man speaking to men. Finally, the "proletarian movement" itself helped to confirm the fact that one of the functions of the novelist was to be a citizen; and the collapse of the "movement" proved that he must, in addition, be an intelligent one.

Such contributions are unmeasurable, for they tend to operate indirectly; but that they did operate on writers and readers is demonstrated when one merely names two enormously successful novels published roughly a decade apart: Thornton Wilder's *The Bridge of San Luis Rey* in 1927 and John Steinbeck's *The Grapes of Wrath* in 1939. Obviously the whole experience of the Depression lay between these books, but the proletarian novel and even more the excited disputes that it roused had their part in formulating conscious responses to that great disaster. Not only is it unthinkable that *The Grapes of Wrath* would have been enthusiastically received at the beginning of the thirties, but it is even unlikely that Steinbeck, who was not a "proletarian novelist," [17] could have written the book without being aware of the efforts, crude or otherwise, made by the actual proletarians to solve the problems of ideological literature. And Steinbeck's novel is only one example — Meyer Levin's fine *Citizens* is another selected at random — of how the laboratory experiments, so to speak, of the radical novelists helped other writers to create literature that was sociological but was not just sociology.

This laboratory work of the thirties, its negative as well as its several positive findings, helps to explain also the achievements of the radical writers, mostly those of the independent Left, in the forties. It cannot be lost even on conservative critics that some of the best fiction of a not too brilliant literary decade has sprung from the radical tradition, for to the ten left-wing novels of the thirties that are still of some consequence may be added ten more from the subsequent decade: Algren's *Never Come Morning* and *The Man with the Golden Arm*, Fast's *The Last Frontier* and *The Unvanquished*, Farrell's last two Marxist-oriented novels, *Father and Son* and *My Days of Anger*, Mailer's *The Naked and the Dead*, Motley's *Knock on Any Door*, Wolfert's *Tucker's People*, and Wright's *Native Son*. The general level of excellence in the radical novel appears to have risen in the forties; though the number of examples of the genre dropped about one-half, the same number of volumes as in the thirties may be considered as having some permanent literary value.

Taken in its entirety, then, a half-century of the radical novel has had its effect on and made a contribution to American literature. It has also affected and contributed to American life, not just uniquely, however, but as part of the whole larger course of the novel of social protest, that tradition which has proliferated so variously in the troubled twentieth century and which extends back into the nineteenth through the early Hamlin Garland and the Utopians, through Mark Twain, in some of his moods, back to, and well before, Harriet Beecher Stowe, whose *Uncle Tom's Cabin* did as much to change the face of the nation as, perhaps, all the proletarian novels put together. This tradition, which is certainly a great, though not the only great one, the radical novel of the present century has helped to continue. Despite their orientation toward Marxism, the Socialist, the proletarian, the independently radical novelists have not been able to obscure the fact that in essential ways they represented yet another manifestation of the American middle-class conscience, which has been the major force behind the literature of social criticism from Harriet Stowe down even to the present day. Viewed as part of a developing process, the radical novel shares in the value of the whole, the value of protest against the still limited American democracy that is and of affirmation of the democracy that can be. For protest is valuable, quite as valuable as that acceptance without which no continuing social organization is possible. Whether wrong-headed or right, protest will always be essential in order to stir our civilization into self-awareness and thus prevent it from stiffening into an inhuman immobility. In the frequently unwise thirties this rather elementary final statement would have been assumed. That it must now be asserted indicates that the fifties have their own particular lack of wisdom.

Nor is the critic or the Congressman wise to insist that the Marxist novel be proscribed simply because it is Marxist and therefore presumably gives aid and comfort to the enemy. This argument is advanced from time to time, mostly by the politician, but actually it is only an unconscious assumption of the doctrinaire Communist's position, as so many attacks on freedom turn out to be. Both the doctrinaire Communist and the doctrinaire conservative assume that the expressed ideology of a book is its most important aspect; each denies the value of the book as literature. A novel, good or bad, may be about a conversion, but by itself it does not necessarily convert; the effect may indeed be quite the opposite. Instead the function of the novel, as with all literature, is to make the reader aware, and the better the book the greater the degree of possible awareness. A novel does not send its reader to the barricades or the altar, but rather enlarges his experience, makes him realize more fully the possibilities of the human being. The novel, whatever its formal ideology, is essentially a humanizing force.

The future of the radical novel — and it is a precarious one — probably lies almost wholly with the independent radical. On the one hand, it is still a question how much the Communist-oriented writer can produce or publish in so antagonistic a political climate; on the other, as the Communists have felt the danger threaten from without, they have insisted on greater and greater evidences of doctrinal purity within their decimated group. The resultant effect on the writer's imaginative freedom is vividly suggested by the issues drawn in the "Maltz Affair" of some years ago, which may stand as a final warning.

Early in 1946, as part of a postwar orientation discussion of Marxism and literature in the columns of the not yet defunct *New Masses*, Albert Maltz published an article entitled "What Shall We Ask of Writers," which argued that the errors of most writers on the Left largely flow from one source, "the vulgarization of the theory of art which lies behind left-wing thinking: namely, 'art is a weapon.' " To such an attitude Maltz attributed several harmful results, of which two, he thought, were most important:

First of all, under the domination of this vulgarized approach, creative works are judged *primarily* by their formal ideology.

There is an opposite error, corollary to this: NEW MASSES' critics have again and again praised works *as art* that no one (themselves included) would bother to read now, ten years later.[18]

After he had rejected these errors, he drew what seems a sound enough principle: "Literary taste can only operate in a crippled manner when canons of immediate political utility are the primary values of judgment to be applied indiscriminately to all books." Citing Engels's respect for the novels of the royalist Balzac, Maltz asserted that Steinbeck, Farrell, and Wright were good writers even though their political ideas were incorrect, and that a writer who repudiated a progressive political position did not *necessarily* show a decline in creative powers. The author, he concluded, must be judged in terms of art when writing, in terms of "citizenship" when acting.

If Maltz believed that his commonsense remarks would prove acceptable, he soon learned his mistake. Swiftly in succeeding numbers of *The New Masses* his position was bombarded by the big guns of the literary Left. Howard Fast warned that " . . . the end product of Maltz's direction is liquidation, not only of Marxist creative writing — but of all creative writing which bases itself on progressive currents in America"; Joseph North maintained that "Maltz's position . . . leads not to a mastery of Marxism, but to its abandonment"; while John Howard Lawson insisted that Maltz's argument meant taking "sides with reaction." [19] After a few weeks of siege, the writer surrendered unconditionally and, as one of the humiliating peace conditions, recanted his heresy in an article entitled, pitiably, "Moving Forward." So complete was the recantation that Maltz even reprimanded those who had protested the tone of abuse in the communications which had attacked him.

In such an atmosphere of intellectual terrorism a work of art can be created only by exception. In any atmosphere it can be created only to the extent that it holds unalterably to its own vision; for what shall it profit the writer to cease being a wage laborer if the alternative is to be a political tool? To conceive of literature as an absolute and independent category is to falsify its function as a record of — and, it should be remembered, as a part of — human experience. Such a conception is merely a critical fiction. But if literature is not an independent category within human experience, it is none the less a distinct one. It relates to all other forms of human activity, yet is not identical with any. To demand that literature identify itself with, let us say, religion or with politics is ultimately to rob it of its special function, a function that has long been a high one — to inquire relentlessly and unceasingly and on its own terms into the human condition.

APPENDIX: AMERICAN RADICAL NOVELS

1. THE SOCIALIST NOVEL, 1900–1919

1901

Friedman, I. K., *By Bread Alone: A Novel*, New York, McClure, Phillips & Co.

McGrady, The Rev. Father T[homas], *Beyond the Black Ocean: A Socialist Story*, Chicago, Charles H. Kerr.

Pemberton, Caroline H., "The Charity Girl," serialized in *The International Socialist Review*, March, 1901–February, 1902.

1903

Scudder, Vida D., *A Listener in Babel: Being a Series of Imaginary Conversations Held at the Close of the Last Century and Reported*, Boston, Houghton, Mifflin and Company.

Swift, Morrison I., *The Monarch Billionaire*, New York, J. S. Ogilvie Publishing Company.

1904

Raymond, Walter Marion, *Rebels of the New South*, Chicago, C. H. Kerr & Co.

1905

Brenholtz, Edwin Arnold, *The Recording Angel: A Novel*, Chicago, Charles H. Kerr & Company.

Scott, Leroy, *The Walking Delegate*, New York, Doubleday Page.

1906

Berman, Henry, *Worshippers: A Novel*, New York, The Grafton Press.

Sinclair, Upton, *The Jungle*, New York, Doubleday, Page & Company.

1907

Friedman, I. K., *The Radical*, New York, D. Appleton and Company.

Hurt, Walter, *The Scarlet Shadow: A Story of the Great Colorado Conspiracy*, Girard, Kansas, *The Appeal to Reason*.

McMahon, John R., *Toilers and Idlers: A Novel*, New York, Wilshire Book Company.

Steere, C. A., *When Things Were Doing*, Chicago, Charles H. Kerr & Co.

Teller, Charlotte, *The Cage*, New York, D. Appleton and Company.

1908

London, Jack, *The Iron Heel*, New York, The Macmillan Company.

Patterson, Joseph Medill, *A Little Brother of the Rich*, Chicago, The Reilly & Britton Company.

Sinclair, Upton, *The Metropolis*, New York, Moffat, Yard & Company.

—— *The Moneychangers*, New York, B. W. Dodge & Company.

1909

Brower, James Hattan, *The Mills of Mammon*, Joliet, Ill., P. H. Murray & Company.

Kaneko, Josephine Conger, *A Little Sister of the Poor*, Girard, Kansas, Progressive Woman Publishing Co.

Marcy, Mary E., *Out of the Dump: A Story of Organized Charity*, [Chicago, Charles H. Kerr & Co.].

1910

Jackson, Charles Tenney, *My Brother's Keeper*, New York, A. L. Burt Company.

Kauffman, Reginald Wright, *The House of Bondage*, New York, Moffat, Yard and Company.

Sinclair, Upton, *Samuel the Seeker*, New York, B. W. Dodge & Company.

1911

Cook, George Cram, *The Chasm*, New York, Frederick A. Stokes Company.

Glaspell, Susan, *The Visioning*, New York, Frederick A. Stokes Company Publishers.

Loux, Rev. Dubois H., *Maitland Varne: Or The Bells of De Thaumaturge*, New York, De Thaumaturge Co.

Oppenheim, James, *The Nine-Tenths: A Novel*, New York, Harper & Brothers Publishers.

Sinclair, Upton, *Love's Pilgrimage: a Novel*, New York, Mitchell Kennerley.

1912

Baker, Estelle, *The Rose Door*, Chicago, Charles H. Kerr & Company.

Converse, Florence, *The Children of Light*, Boston, Houghton Mifflin Company.

"Edwards, Albert" [Bullard, Arthur], *A Man's World*, New York, The Macmillan Company.

Kauffman, Reginald Wright, *The Sentence of Silence*, New York, Moffat, Yard and Company.

1913

"Edwards, Albert" [Bullard, Arthur], *Comrade Yetta*, New York, The Macmillan Company.

Kauffman, Reginald Wright, *Running Sands*, New York, Dodd, Mead and Company.

—— *The Spider's Web*, New York, Moffat, Yard and Co.

1914

England, George Allan, *Darkness and Dawn*, Boston, Small, Maynard and Company (Trilogy: *The Vacant World, Beyond the Great Oblivion, The After Glow*).

1915

England, George Allan, *The Air Trust*, St. Louis, Mo., Phil Wagner.

Poole, Ernest, *The Harbor*, New York, The Macmillan Company.

1916

England, George Allan, *The Golden Blight*, New York, The H. K. Fly Company.

Tobenkin, Elias, *Witte Arrives*, New York, Frederick A. Stokes Company.

1917

Cahan, Abraham, *The Rise of David Levinsky: A Novel*, New York, Harper & Brothers Publishers.

Sinclair, Upton, *King Coal: a Novel*, New York, The Macmillan Company.

1918

Beckley, Zoe, *A Chance to Live*, New York, The Macmillan Company.

1919

Sinclair, Upton, *Jimmie Higgins: A Story*, New York, Albert & Charles Boni.

Varney, Harold Lord, *Revolt*, New York, Irving Kaye Davis & Co.

II. NOVELS OF THE TWENTIES

1920

Sinclair, Upton, *100%: The Story of a Patriot*, Pasadena, Calif., published by the author.

1922

Sinclair, Upton, *They Call Me Carpenter*, New York, Boni and Liveright.

Tobenkin, Elias, *The Road*, New York, Harcourt, Brace and Company.

1923

[Ornitz, Samuel Badisch], *Haunch Paunch and Jowl: An Anonymous Autobiography*, New York, Boni and Liveright, Publishers.

1924

Sinclair, Upton, *The Millennium*, Girard, Kansas, Haldeman-Julius Company.

1927

Eastman, Max, *Venture*, New York, Albert & Charles Boni.

Hedges, M[arion] H[awthorne], *Dan Minturn*, New York, The Vanguard Press.

Sinclair, Upton, *Oil!* Long Beach, Calif., published by the author.

1928

Sinclair, Upton, *Boston: a Novel*, two volumes, New York, Albert & Charles Boni.

1929

Smedley, Agnes, *Daughter of Earth*, New York, Coward-McCann, Inc.

III. THE PROLETARIAN NOVEL, 1930–1939

1930

Dahlberg, Edward, *Bottom Dogs*, New York, Simon and Schuster.

Gold, Michael, *Jews Without Money*, New York, Liveright Publishing Corporation.

Harrison, Charles Yale, *Generals Die in Bed*, New York, William Morrow & Co.

Seaver, Edwin, *The Company*, New York, The Macmillan Company.

Vorse, Mary Heaton, *Strike!* New York, Horace Liveright.

1931

Colman, Louis, *Lumber*, Boston, Little, Brown, and Company.

Harrison, Charles Yale, *A Child Is Born*, New York, Jonathan Cape & Harrison Smith.

1932

Anderson, Sherwood, *Beyond Desire*, New York, Liveright Inc.

Bodenheim, Maxwell, *Run, Sheep, Run: A Novel*, New York, Liveright, Inc., Publishers.

"Burke, Fielding" [Dargan, Olive Tilford], *Call Home the Heart*, New York, Longmans, Green and Co.

Dahlberg, Edward, *From Flushing to Calvary*, New York, Harcourt, Brace and Company.

Farrell, James T., *Young Lonigan: A Boyhood in Chicago Streets*, New York, The Vanguard Press.

Herrman, John, "The Big Short Trip," *Scribner's Magazine*, XCII (August, 1932), 65–69, 13–128.

Lumpkin, Grace, *To Make My Bread*, New York, The Macaulay Company.

"Marlen, George" [Spiro, George], *The Road: A Romance of the Proletarian Revolution*, New York, Red Star Press.

Nearing, Scott, *Free Born: An Unpublishable Novel*, New York, Urquhart Press.

Page, Dorothy Myra, *Gathering Storm: a Story of the Black Belt*, New York, International Publishers.

Spivak, John L., *Georgia Nigger*, New York, Brewer, Warren and Putnam.

1933

Conroy, Jack, *The Disinherited*, [New York], Covici, Friede Publishers.

Herbst, Josephine, *Pity Is Not Enough*, New York, Harcourt, Brace and Company.

Levin, Meyer, *The New Bridge*, New York, Covici-Friede.

Pell, Mike, *S.S. Utah*, New York, International Publishers.

1934

"Armstrong, Arnold B.," *Parched Earth*, New York, The Macmillan Company.

Bodenheim, Maxwell, *Slow Vision*, New York, The Macaulay Company.

Cantwell, Robert, *The Land of Plenty*, New York, Farrar & Rinehart Incorporated.

Curran, Dale, *A House on a Street*, New York, Covici-Friede.

Dahlberg, Edward, *Those Who Perish*, New York, The John Day Company.

Endore, Guy, *Babouk*, New York, The Vanguard Press.

Farrell, James T., *The Young Manhood of Studs Lonigan*, New York, The Vanguard Press.

Frank, Waldo, *The Death and Birth of David Markand: An American Story*, New York, Charles Scribner's Sons.

Halper, Albert, *The Foundry*, New York, The Viking Press.

Herbst, Josephine, *The Executioner Waits*, New York, Harcourt, Brace and Company.

Levy, Melvin, *The Last Pioneers*, New York, Alfred H. King.

Newhouse, Edward, *You Can't Sleep Here*, New York, The Macaulay Company.

Rollins, William, Jr., *The Shadow Before*, New York, Robert M. McBride & Company.

1935

Algren, Nelson, *Somebody in Boots*, New York, The Vanguard Press.

Boyd, Thomas, *In Time of Peace*, New York, Minton, Balch & Company.

"Burke, Fielding" [Dargan, Olive Tilford], *A Stone Came Rolling*, New York, Longmans, Green and Co.

Conroy, Jack, *A World to Win*, New York, Covici, Friede Publishers.

Cunningham, William, *The Green Corn Rebellion*, New York, The Vanguard Press.

Farrell, James T., *Judgment Day*, New York, The Vanguard Press.

Irwin, Theodore, *Strange Passage*, New York, Harrison Smith and Robert Haas.

Kromer, Tom, *Waiting for Nothing*, New York, Alfred A. Knopf.

Lumpkin, Grace, *A Sign for Cain*, New York, Lee Furman, Inc.

Page, Myra, *Moscow Yankee*, New York, G. P. Putnam's Sons.

Roth, Henry, *Call It Sleep*, New York, Robert O. Ballou.

Schneider, Isidor, *From the Kingdom of Necessity*, New York, G. P. Putnam's Sons.

"Steele, James" [Cruden, Robert], *Conveyor*, New York, International Publishers.

Vogel, Joseph, *At Madame Bonnard's*, New York, Alfred A. Knopf.

Weatherwax, Clara, *Marching! Marching!* New York, The John Day Company.

1936

Bell, Thomas, *All Brides Are Beautiful*, Boston, Little, Brown, and Company.

Coleman, McAlister, and Raushenbush, Stephen, *Red Neck*, New York, Harrison Smith & Robert Haas.

Cunningham, William, *Pretty Boy*, New York, The Vanguard Press.

Delaney, Martin, *Journal of a Young Man*, New York, The Vanguard Press.

Farrell, James T., *A World I Never Made*, New York, The Vanguard Press.

Zugsmith, Leane, *A Time to Remember*, New York, Random House.

1937

Cuthbert, Clifton, *Another Such Victory*, New York, Hillman-Curl, Inc.

Halper, Albert, *The Chute*, New York, The Viking Press.

Johnson, Josephine, *Jordanstown*, New York, Simon and Schuster.

Newhouse, Edward, *This Is Your Day*, New York, Lee Furman, Inc.

Seaver, Edwin, *Between the Hammer and the Anvil*, New York, Julian Messner, Inc.

1938

Farrell, James T., *No Star Is Lost*, New York, The Vanguard Press.

Maltz, Albert, "Season of Celebration," novelette in *The Way Things Are and Other Stories*, New York, International Publishers.

Preston, John Hyde, *The Liberals: A Novel*, New York, The John Day Company.

Vogel, Joseph, *Man's Courage*, New York, Alfred A. Knopf.

Wright, Richard, *Uncle Tom's Children: Four Novellas*, New York, Harper & Brothers Publishers.

Zugsmith, Leane, *The Summer Soldier*, New York, Random House.

1939

Herbst, Josephine, *Rope of Gold*, New York, Harcourt, Brace and Company.

Lanham, Edwin, *The Stricklands*, Boston, Little, Brown and Company.

Trumbo, Dalton, *Johnny Got His Gun*, Philadelphia, J. B. Lippincott Company.

IV. NOVELS OF THE FORTIES AND FIFTIES

1940

Farrell, James T., *Father and Son*, New York, The Vanguard Press.

Maltz, Albert, *The Underground Stream*, Boston, Little, Brown and Company.

Wright, Richard, *Native Son*, New York, Harper & Brothers Publishers.

1941

Fast, Howard, *The Last Frontier*, New York, Duell, Sloan and Pearce.

Trumbo, Dalton, *The Remarkable Andrew: Being the Chronicle of a Literal Man*, Philadelphia, J. B. Lippincott Company.

1942

Algren, Nelson, *Never Come Morning*, New York, Harper & Brothers Publishers.

Fast, Howard, *The Unvanquished*, New York, Duell, Sloan and Pearce.

1943

Farrell, James T., *My Days of Anger*, New York, The Vanguard Press.

Fast, Howard, *Citizen Tom Paine*, New York, Duell, Sloan and Pearce.

Freeman, Joseph, *Never Call Retreat*, New York, Farrar & Rinehart.

McKenney, Ruth, *Jake Home*, New York, Harcourt, Brace and Company.

Wolfert, Ira, *Tucker's People*, New York, L. B. Fischer.

1944

Fast, Howard, *Freedom Road*, New York, Duell, Sloan and Pearce.

1946

Fast, Howard, *The American: A Middle Western Legend*, New York, Duell, Sloan and Pearce.

Schneider, Isidor, *The Judas Time*, New York, The Dial Press.

1947

Fast, Howard, *Clarkton*, New York, Duell, Sloan and Pearce.

Giles, Barbara, *The Gentle Bush*, New York, Harcourt, Brace and Company.

Himes, Chester, *Lonely Crusade*, New York, Alfred A. Knopf.

Motley, Willard, *Knock on Any Door*, New York, D. Appleton-Century Company, Inc.

1948

Fast, Howard, *My Glorious Brothers*, Boston, Little, Brown & Co.

McHenry, Beth, and Myers, Frederick N., *Home Is the Sailor*, New York, International Publishers.

Mailer, Norman, *The Naked and the Dead*, New York, Rinehart & Co., Inc.

Saxton, Alexander, *The Great Midland*, New York, Appleton-Century-Crofts, Inc.

1949

Algren, Nelson, *The Man with the Golden Arm*, Garden City, New York, Doubleday and Company.

Lampell, Millard, *The Hero*, New York, Julian Messner, Inc.

1950

Fast, Howard, *The Proud and the Free*, Boston, Little, Brown and Company.

Page, Myra, *With Sun in Our Blood*, New York, The Citadel Press.

1951

Brown, Lloyd L., *Iron City*, New York, Masses & Mainstream.

Fast, Howard, *Spartacus*, New York, published by the author.
"Graham, Margaret" [MacDonald, Grace Lois], *Swing Shift*, New York, The Citadel Press.
Mailer, Norman, *Barbary Shore*, New York, Rinehart & Co., Inc.
Motley, Willard, *We Fished All Night*, New York, Appleton-Century-Crofts.

1952
Jerome, V. J., *A Lantern for Jeremy*, New York, Masses & Mainstream.

1953
Bonosky, Philip, *Burning Valley*, New York, Masses & Mainstream.
Fast, Howard, *The Passion of Sacco and Vanzetti: A New England Legend*, New York, The Blue Heron Press, Inc.

1954
Fast, Howard, *Silas Timberman*, New York, The Blue Heron Press, Inc.
Heym, Stefan, *Goldsborough*, New York, The Blue Heron Press, Inc.
Kahn, Arthur, *Brownstone*, New York, Independence Publishers.
Lardner, Ring, Jr., *The Ecstasy of Owen Muir*, London, Jonathan Cape.
Lawrence, Lars, *Morning, Noon and Night*, New York, G. P. Putnam's Sons.

NOTES

1. Quoted from John D. Hicks, *The Populist Revolt: A History of the Farmers' Alliance and the People's Party*, Minneapolis, The University of Minnesota Press, 1931, p. 440.

2. The English edition of 1887, itself in two volumes, was distributed in the same year in the United States by Scribner and Welford, though the cost of the two volumes, twelve dollars, could not have been conducive to a wide sale among radical circles. The first actual American edition of *Capital* (Volume One) was published in 1889 by D. Appleton and Company.

3. "A Review of the World," *Current Literature*, XLI (August, 1906), 121–152, p. 146.

4. Edward and Eleanor Marx Aveling, *The Working-Class Movement in America*, second edition, London, Swan Sonnenschein & Co., 1891, pp. 17–18.

5. "Edmund Boisgilbert, M. D." [Ignatius Donnelly], *Caesar's Column: A Story of the Twentieth Century*, Chicago, F. J. Schulte & Company, 1891, p. 203.

6. That *Caesar's Column* could nevertheless have a radical *effect* is illustrated by a comment in *Fighting for Freedom* (Kansas City, Missouri, Simplified Economics, [1953]), the recollections of George H. Shoaf, a highly militant Socialist reporter. Meeting that famous radical "Big Bill" Haywood for the first time, Shoaf concluded at once that here was the perfect antagonist of capitalism. "In all these respects he immediately became the god of my idolatry. I had reveled in 'Caesar's Column,' by Ignatius Donnelly, the book which depicted the destruction of modern capitalism by working people outraged beyond endurance, and in Haywood I envisaged the leader who would make real what Donnelly wrote." (P. 62.)

7. Such books have been excluded from the following chapters on the Socialist novel for two reasons: first, the "socialism" for which many of them call often turns out to be only some kind of modified capitalism; second, since Nationalism had completely died out as an organized movement, these books were not written under the same conditions as those by authors associated, like the Socialists, with an active political party. The fullest discussion of these Utopias is in Vernon Louis Parrington, Jr., *American Dreams: A Study of American Utopias*, Providence, Rhode Island, Brown University, 1947.

8. I. K. Friedman, *By Bread Alone: A Novel*, New York, McClure, Phillips & Co., 1901, pp. 479–480.

CHAPTER TWO: REALISM AND REVOLUTION

1. Charles Edward Russell, *Bare Hands and Stone Walls: Some Recollections of a Side-Line Reformer*, New York, Charles Scribner's Sons, 1933, p. 193.

2. Quoted from "Socialism" in Finley Peter Dunne, *Mr. Dooley: Now and Forever*, selected by Louis Filler, Stanford, California, Academic Reprints, 1954, p. 253. *Dissertations by Mr. Dooley*, in which "Socialism" was collected, was published in 1906.

3. "Greeting," *The Comrade*, I (October, 1901), 12. The editorial board consisted of Leonard D. Abbott, George D. Herron, John Spargo, William Mailly, Morris Winchevsky, Algernon Lee, and Peter E. Burrowes.

4. A. M. Simons, "Editorial," *International Socialist Review*, I (November, 1900), 316–320, p. 318.

5. The installments of "The Charity Girl" ran from March, 1901, to February, 1902. It was never published in book form.

6. Caroline H. Pemberton, "The Charity Girl," *International Socialist Review*, II (February, 1902), 609–621, p. 620.

7. Edwin Arnold Brenholtz, *The Recording Angel: A Novel*, Chicago, Charles H. Kerr & Company, 1905, p. 245.

8. Clarence Darrow, *Realism in Literature and Art*, Chicago, Charles H. Kerr & Company, 1899, p. 25.

9. Lincoln Steffens, *The Autobiography of Lincoln Steffens*, one-volume edition, New York, Harcourt, Brace and Company, 1931, p. 434.

10. Letter to *The Appeal to Reason*, November 18, 1905.

11. Upton Sinclair, *American Outpost: A Book of Reminiscences*, New York, Farrar & Rinehart, 1932, pp. 12–13.

12. *Ibid.*, p. 143.

13. For an example out of the late twenties, see Edward Newhouse, "Transition — 1929," *New Masses*, V (July, 1929), 8: "Then the revelation . . . Upton Sinclair. Here was somebody who could offer an explanation to the perplexing chaos." Newhouse was subsequently to publish two "proletarian novels."

It is worth noting that the influence of *The Jungle* on a number of our contemporary non-Communist labor leaders has been considerable. Walter Reuther includes it in a list of books "which most influenced me in my youth," as does Jacob S. Potofsky, president of the Amalgamated Clothing Workers, and "many of his colleagues." See Mark Starr, "American Labor and the Book," *The Saturday Review*, XXXVII (September 4, 1954), 10–11, 32–34.

14. Jack London, *Revolution and Other Essays*, New York, The Macmillan Company, 1912, p. 38. "Revolution," the title essay, was delivered as the address at New Haven on January 26, 1906.

15. T. K. Whipple, "Jack London — Wonder Boy," *Study Out the Land*, Berkeley, University of Calfornia Press, 1943.

16. Jack London, "How I Became a Socialist," *War of the Classes*, New York, The Macmillan Company, 1905, p. 278.

17 Jack London, *The Iron Heel*, Sonoma Edition, New York, The Macmillan Company, 1925, p. 97.

18. *Ibid.*, pp. 326–327.

CHAPTER THREE: VIEW OF AN ERA

1. (Mrs.) L. H. Harris, "The Walking Delegate Novelist," *The Independent*, LX (May 24, 1906), 1213–1216, p. 1215.

2. Robert F. Hoxie, "'The Rising Tide of Socialism': A Study," *Journal of Political Economy*, XIX (October, 1911), 609–631, p. 615.

3. Madeleine Z. Doty, "The Socialist in Recent Fiction," *Charities and the Commons*, XVII (December 15, 1906), 485–488, p. 485.

4. William Balfour Ker's illustration, "The Hand of Fate," which was described at the end of Section II in our Chapter One, faces page 200 in this novel. It was later reproduced in Upton Sinclair's anthology of protest literature, *The Cry for Justice*.

5. "Chronicle and Comment," *The Bookman*, XXVII (April, 1908), 119–124, p. 120.

6. "Albert Edwards" [Arthur Bullard], *Comrade Yetta*, New York, The Macmillan Company, 1913, p. 250.

7. Ernest Poole, *The Harbor*, New York, The Macmillan Company, 1915, p. 351.

8. Ernest Poole, *The Bridge: My Own Story*, New York, The Macmillan Company, 1940, p. 195.

9. Poole, *The Harbor*, p. 386.

10. *Ibid.*, p. 387.

11. George Allan England, *The Air Trust*, St. Louis, Missouri, Phil Wagner, 1915, p. 138. This book, incidentally, contains six illustrations by John Sloan, the American artist.

12. Charlotte Teller, *The Cage*, New York, D. Appleton and Company, 1907, p. 333.

13. From the "Publisher's Note," in Walter Hurt, *The Scarlet Shadow: A Story of the Great Colorado Conspiracy*, Girard, Kansas, *The Appeal to Reason*, 1907, p. 9.

14. George Shoaf, the Socialist reporter for *The Appeal to Reason* on whom Shoforth is based, had formerly been less opposed to violence than was his fictional representative. See the following note. "Daniel Melnotte" is clearly intended as a portrait of David H. Moffat, banker, railroad builder, and mine owner, who was popularly known at the time as the richest man in Colorado.

15. To take only one example, the character Hoostman appears to have as his prototype Walter Vrooman, eccentric son of a Populist leader in Missouri, who, after marching with Coxey, started a movement ostensibly directed toward expelling all Chinese from American soil, but actually designed for recruiting a secret army to capture the national government. George Shoaf states in *Fighting for Freedom* (see pp. 34–42) that, as Vrooman's secretary in Chicago during 1900–1901, he assisted him in draw-

ing up plans for attracting telegraph operators and coal miners into the movement and for dynamiting rail bridges to disrupt transportation. According to Shoaf, however, Vrooman was frightened away from his scheme by the assassination of President McKinley in September, 1901, and, instead of being blown up by his own dynamite, later lost his mind and died in a mental institution.

16. Hurt, *The Scarlet Shadow*, pp. 304–305.

17. Joseph Medill Patterson, *A Little Brother of the Rich*, Chicago, The Reilly & Britton Company, 1908, pp. 290–291.

18. *Ibid.*, pp. 167–168.

19. Reginald Wright Kauffman, *The House of Bondage*, New York, Moffat, Yard and Company, 1910, p. 260.

20. *Ibid.*, p. 466.

21. Florence Converse, *The Children of Light*, Boston, Houghton Mifflin Company, 1912, pp. 133–134.

22. James Oppenheim, *The Nine-Tenths: A Novel*, New York, Harper & Brothers, 1911, p. 168.

23. George Cram Cook, *The Chasm*, New York, Frederick A. Stokes Company, 1911, p. 191.

24. Vida D. Scudder, *A Listener in Babel: Being a Series of Imaginary Conversations Held at the Close of the Last Century and Reported*, Boston, Houghton, Mifflin and Company, 1903, p. 156.

25. Hurt, *The Scarlet Shadow*, p. 262.

26. James Hattan Brower, *The Mills of Mammon*, Joliet, Ill., P. H. Murray & Company, 1909, p. 298.

27. Teller, *The Cage*, pp. 163–164.

28. Kauffman, *The House of Bondage*, pp. 221–222.

29. Quoted from Melech Epstein, *Jewish Labor in U.S.A.: An Industrial, Political and Cultural History of the Jewish Labor Movement, 1882–1914*, New York, Trade Union Sponsoring Committee, 1950, p. 392. See chapter 22 of this book for a history of "The Great Revolt" in the garment industries.

30. Zoe Beckley, *A Chance to Live*, New York, The Macmillan Company, 1918, p. 106.

CHAPTER FOUR: FROM MOTHER EARTH TO THE MASSES

1. From the "Call to Organization," quoted by Paul Frederick Brissenden, *The I. W. W.: A Study of American Syndicalism*, New York, Columbia University, 1919, p. 59.

2. See, for example, Wallace Stegner, "Joe Hill: The Wobblies' Troubadour," *New Republic*, CXVIII (January 5, 1948), 20–24, 38; and the reply by Friends of Joe Hill Committee, "Joe Hill: IWW Martyr," *New Republic*, CXIX (November 15, 1948), 18–20.

3. How one leading Wobbly regarded art in general is reported by Mabel Dodge Luhan in *Movers and Shakers: Volume Three of Intimate Memories*, New York, Harcourt, Brace and Company, 1936, p. 90. (In the early 1910's, Mabel Dodge's "Evenings" were a meeting place for all groups of the New York intelligentsia, including writers and radicals.)

"One night the artists were there listening to 'Big Bill' Haywood tell them that he thought artists thought themselves too special and separate, and that some day there would be a Proletarian Art, and the State would see to it that everybody was an artist and that everybody would have time to be an artist."

4. Floyd Dell, "Three Leaders of Revolt," *Liberator*, II (July, 1919), 45–46, 48–49, p. 48.

5. "Publishers' Department," *International Socialist Review*, IX (July, 1908), 79–80, p. 79.

6. These figures are taken from Nathan Fine, *Labor and Farmer Parties in the United States: 1828–1928*, New York, Rand School of Social Science, 1928, p. 232.

7. Thomas Seltzer, untitled editorial, *Masses*, I (January, 1911), 1.

8. Thomas Seltzer, "Socialism and Fiction," *Masses*, I (February, 1911), 3.

9. Unsigned and untitled editorial, *Masses*, IV (December, 1912), 3.

10. Max Eastman, *Enjoyment of Living*, New York, Harper & Brothers, 1948, p. 409, footnote. This book is the first volume of Eastman's projected autobiography.

CHAPTER FIVE: THE YEARS BETWEEN

1. These figures are taken from Harvey Wish, *Contemporary America: The National Scene Since 1900*, New York, Harper & Brothers Publishers, 1945, pp. 99–100, 404.

2. Randolph Bourne, *Untimely Papers*, edited by James Oppenheim, New York, B. W. Huebsch, 1919, pp. 171–172.

3. These figures are taken from C. Wright Mills, *The New Men of Power: America's Labor Leaders*, New York, Harcourt, Brace and Company, 1948, p. 53. By comparison, unionized workers in 1950 represented approximately 25 per cent of the total labor force.

4. In 1925, the Workers' Party of America changed its name to the Workers (Communist) Party of America, and in 1929 the present name was assumed: Communist Party of the United States of America (CPUSA).

5. Membership totals of the Communist Party in the 1920's are notoriously difficult to estimate. The numbers given for 1919, 1925, and 1929 come respectively from James Oneal and G. A. Werner, *American Communism: A Critical Analysis of Its Origins, Developments and Programs*, New York, E. P. Dutton & Co., 1947, p. 89; Nathan Fine, *Labor and Farmer Parties in the United States: 1828–1928*, New York, Rand School of Social Science, 1928, p. 329; Earl Browder, *The Communist Party of the U. S. A.: Its History, Role and Organization*, New York, Workers Library Publishers, Inc., 1941, p. 13.

6. It is worth noting that Lewis, at least by 1920, was considering a novel about the American labor movement to be based on the career of Eugene Debs and to be entitled *Neighbor*, but he never succeeded in actually writing it. See Harrison Smith (editor), *From Main Street to Stockholm: Letters of Sinclair Lewis, 1919–1930*, New York, Harcourt, Brace and Company, 1952, pp. 60, 138.

7. "Ernita," one of the long story-sketches in Dreiser's *A Gallery of*

Women (1929) describes objectively a woman who becomes an I.W.W., goes to the Soviet Union, and eventually decides to devote herself to Communism. Theodore Dreiser, *A Gallery of Women*, New York, Horace Liveright, 1929, I, 299–358.

8. Opening statement by "The Editor," *Liberator*, I (March, 1918), 3. The March issue was actually published in February.

9. Irwin Granich ["Michael Gold"], "Towards Proletarian Art," *Liberator*, IV (February, 1921), 20–24, p. 23.

10. Floyd Dell, *Homecoming: An Autobiography*, New York, Farrar and Rinehart Incorporated, 1933, p. 337. The parts of "Literature and the Machine Age" appeared from October, 1923, to October, 1924, the latter date being that of the last issue of *The Liberator*.

11. Floyd Dell, "Literature and the Machine Age," *Liberator*, VII (July, 1924), 27–29, p. 27. (*Intellectual Vagabondage: An Apology for the Intelligentsia*, New York, George H. Doran Company, 1926, p. 176.)

12. Freeman gives in his autobiography, *An American Testament: A Narrative of Rebels and Romantics* (1936), an extremely interesting and informative survey of the radical political and literary world in New York from the end of World War I to 1927. As a convert to the Communist Party, Freeman tells "the story of that no-man's land which lay, during the postwar period, between the myths of an old culture and the realities of the new, and how one man, typical of thousands, made the crossing." Joseph Freeman, *An American Testament: A Narrative of Rebels and Romantics*, New York, Farrar & Rinehart, 1936.

13. Except for its suspension during 1930–31, this magazine continued publication until fall, 1940, the year of Calverton's death. From February, 1933, to June, 1938, it came out twelve times a year as *The Modern Monthly*.

14. Although the purpose of *The Newer Spirit* lies for the most part outside the scope of this book, it should be noted as being, far more than Dell's *Intellectual Vagabondage*, an early attempt to formulate a Marxist theory of literary criticism. According to Calverton, only a Marxian analysis of the social forces which have produced a work of art can give a full understanding of the work. The incompleteness of his methodology is demonstrated by his tendency to assume *in practice* that sociological description is a sufficient substitute for critical evaluation.

15. Cf. Freeman, *American Testament*, p. 379: "Among the fifty-six writers and artists grouped around the *New Masses* only two were members of the Communist party, less than a dozen were sympathetic to it."

Unfortunately, an extended footnote concerning the relationship of *The New Masses* to *The Masses-Liberator* is necessary at this point. In a lengthy footnote of his own in his autobiography, *Enjoyment of Living*, p. 415, Max Eastman attempts with some success to discredit the notion that the former magazine was a continuation of the latter. "*The Masses*," he states, "was nine years dead, and even its successor, *The Liberator*, three years in its grave [Eastman must here be reckoning from his resignation as editor in April, 1923, instead of from the last issue of this magazine dated October, 1924], when *The New Masses* was founded by an entirely different group of artists and writers. The old editor-owners were not consulted; nothing but the name was borrowed, and that after some dispute." In the absence of any evidence to the contrary, the final statement must be accepted as correct; but that "an entirely different group of artists and writers" founded *The New Masses* is not quite true. Eastman accurately points out that of the six editors and sixteen members of the executive board (twenty-two individuals in all) named in the first issue of the magazine, only two had ever been contributing editors of *The Masses*. He is not, however, accurate in saying that "only two of the twenty-two had ever been contributing editors of *The Liberator*," for there were actually five such: Becker, Freeman, Gellert, Gold, and Gropper. All five, it should be noted, had been editors of *The Liberator* prior to Eastman's resignation, while Freeman, Gellert, and Gold constituted one half of the six editors of *The New Masses*. Further, if one compares the list of *contributing editors* of *The New Masses* with the editorial lists for *The Masses* and *The Liberator*, one will find a sizable proportion of names common to all three.

Eastman concludes: "During the year or two in which *The New Masses* tried sincerely to be a 'free magazine', it had some similarity, though no historic identity, with the magazine whose name it borrowed." Technically, Eastman is correct in objecting to the celebration in December, 1936, of a "twenty-fifth anniversary" of *The New Masses*, "which was then in its tenth year"; but on his own side he minimizes the considerable identity in personnel between even *The Masses* and *The New Masses*, and the continuing desire of a group of artists and writers to maintain a meeting place for art and radical ideas. Having certainly suffered for the past twenty years at the hands of the "historical rewrite men associated with the Communist Party," Eastman evidently could not resist the temptation to make out too good a case against them.

It is interesting to compare his present position on this matter with a note in "In This Issue," *New Masses*, III (June, 1927), 3: " 'What the NEW MASSES needs is a *Max Eastman!*' say hosts of of critics, who will be elated to know that Max Eastman has returned from abroad, that he is a member of the NEW MASSES executive board, and that he promises to be a frequent contributor to our pages."

16. Robert Wolf, "What There Isn't and Why Not," *New Masses*, III (February, 1928), 18–21, p. 18. The failure to consider Socialist literature may be partly due to the fact that Wolf, a contributing editor of *The New Masses*, had first given this paper as a lecture at the Communist Academy in Moscow on December 15, 1927, during a tour of the Soviet Union.

17. G. Louis Joughin and Edmund M. Morgan, *The Legacy of Sacco and Vanzetti*, New York, Harcourt, Brace and Company, 1948, p. 233. Cf. p. 234: "It is significant that three years later in December, 1924, in a roundup of world opinion, the Defense Committee quotes from only one well-known American writer, H. L. Mencken."

18. An illuminating example of the effect of the case on a writer who did not participate openly in the defense is furnished by Sinclair Lewis's reaction as reported by Ramon Guthrie: "Although he felt no militant interest in the case, Red [Lewis] talked about it frequently and saw analogies between Sacco and Vanzetti, as martyrs to a reactionary society, and Debs persecuted and imprisoned by similar interests." [Ramon Guthrie,

"The 'Labor Novel' That Sinclair Lewis Never Wrote," *New York Herald Tribune Book Review*, XXVIII (February 10, 1952), 1, 6, p. 1.]

19. "Artists and Writers Appeal for Sacco," New York *Times*, August 11, 1927, p. 3. Most of the signatures are of minor people in the arts, but the names of Paul Robeson, Susan Glaspell, and Carl Van Doren appear.

20. "Blocked in Federal Plea, Sacco Counsel Ask Fuller for Stay as Last Hope," New York *Times*, August 21, 1927, I, pp. 1, 19.

See also "Intellectuals Ask New Sacco Respite," New York *Times*, August 22, 1927, p. 3. This appeal to Governor Fuller was signed by "Hundreds of Professional Men and Women" representing twenty-two states. It "includes signatures of Judges, lawyers, physicians, social workers, ministers, engineers, business men, artists, editors, authors and professors. . ." Among a selected list of "Writers and Editors" are given the names of Mary Austin, Howard Brubaker, Florence Converse, Lewis Gannett, Hugh Lofting, Hendrik Van Loon, W. E. Woodward.

21. Robert Morss Lovett, "Liberalism and the Class War," *Modern Quarterly*, IV (November, 1927–February, 1928), 191–194, pp. 192, 194.

22. Malcolm Cowley, "Echoes of a Crime," *New Republic*, LXXXIV (August 28, 1935), 79. Joughin, incidentally, speaks highly of Cowley's social analysis in this one-page article.

23. John Dos Passos, *U. S. A.*, New York, The Modern Library, 1937, *The Big Money*, p. 462.

CHAPTER SIX: CLASS WAR

1. [V. F. Calverton], "The Pulse of Modernity: The American Scene," *Modern Quarterly*, V (November, 1928–February, 1929), 1–4, p. 1.

2. Dixon Wecter, *The Age of the Great Depression: 1929–1941*, New York, The Macmillan Company, 1948, p. 17.

3. *Ibid.*, p. 250. See also the source of much of Wecter's information on the decade's publishing activities: Douglas Waples, *People and Print: Social Aspects of Reading in the Depression*, Chicago, The University of Chicago Press, [1938], chapter III.

4. "Library Can Buy Only 50,000 Books," New York *Times*, February 10, 1933, p. 15. This report goes on to state that: "Circulation figures, meanwhile, are shootin[g] upward. In 1932, 13,408,909 books were borrowed, a gain of 1,053,807 over 1931."

5. Production in the U.S.S.R. rose from an index base of 100 in 1929 to 130.9 in 1930, 161.3 in 1931, and 183.4 in 1932. (See *Statistical Year-book of the League of Nations, 1938–39*, Geneva, published by the Economic Intelligence Service, 1939, p. 181.) Similar figures were available in the early thirties and were made much of in, for example, *The New Masses* and *The New Republic*.

6. "Editorial Comment," *New Masses*, X[IV] (February 26, 1935), 5. Cf. "Book Notes," *New Masses*, XIII (October 16, 1934, 26–27, p. 27:

"Last year the business of the chain of workers' bookshops in New York City increased in two and a half years from $300 a month to over $11,000. This included pamphlets, books and periodicals, and the items handled numbered 150,000 a month. A few capitalist publishers began to see a possibility in pamphlet publishing and a few capitalist bookshops now are putting in a stock of Marxist literature."

In October, 1935, Random House and International Publishers began to distribute Emile Burns's *A Handbook of Marxism*, originally published by Gollancz in England. This rapidly became the standard introductory work for the prospective Marxist.

7. Max Bedacht, "The Major Problem Before the Seventh Convention of the C.P.U.S.A.," *The Communist*, IX (June, 1930), 494–499, p. 498. Bedacht was then the editor of this Party publication.

8. See E. A. Schachner, "Revolutionary Literature in the United States Today," *Windsor Quarterly*, II (Spring, 1934), 27–64, p. 27.

9. In corroboration of this point, see, for example, James A. Wechsler, *The Age of Suspicion*, New York, Random House, 1953. Wechsler, who was a member of the Young Communist League in the middle thirties, has since that time been consistently an anti-Communist without becoming a reactionary.

10. League of Professional Groups for Foster and Ford, *Culture and the Crisis*, New York, Workers Library Publishers, 1932, p. 3. Fifty-two signatures are attached to this document.

It is easy, in varying situations, either to underestimate or overestimate the influence of radicalized intellectuals. In the 1932 election, Foster and Ford received the highest total of votes ever cast for Communist presidential candidates in the United States; this total, however, was only 102,991. By comparison, in the same election Norman Thomas, the Socialist candidate, received 884,781 votes, though it has been estimated that as many as two thirds of these were of the "protest" variety.

11. Joseph Freeman, "John Reed," *New Masses*, XIX (June 16, 1936), 23–24, p. 23.

12. The American delegates were Fred Ellis, Michael Gold, William Gropper, Joshua Kunitz, A. B. Magil, and Harry Alan Potamkin. Two "guest delegates . . . representing the sympathetic writers" were John Herrmann and Josephine Herbst. See Fred Ellis and others, "The Charkov Conference of Revolutionary Writers," *New Masses*, VI (February, 1931), 6–8, for a detailed report of the Conference and of the Union.

The International Union of Revolutionary Writers had been organized rather casually in Moscow in 1927 by a group of individual authors who were there to attend the Tenth Anniversary of the October Revolution. A minimal political program had been adopted at that time. Since then world Communism had entered its militant "Third Period," and at the Second Conference the emphasis was carefully placed on a "political platform of a broader and more concrete character," and on the organizing of writers to carry it out. For further information see also Rufus W. Mathewson, Jr., "Soviet-American Literary Relations: 1929-1935," unpublished dissertation for Master of Arts degree, Columbia University, 1948.

13. Ellis and others, "The Charkov Conference," p. 7.

14. Secretariat of the IURW, "To All American Revolutionary Writers," *New Masses*, VI (April, 1931), 21.

15. "The officers elected were Oakley Johnson, of New York, National Executive Secretary, and Louis Lozowick, of New York, International Sec-

retary. The nine other members of the Board are Joseph Freeman, William Gropper, and Whittaker Chambers, of New York; Eugene Gordon, Boston; Conrad Komorowski, Philadelphia; Duva Mendelsohn, Detroit; Jan Wittenber, Chicago; Charles Natterstad, Seattle; and Harry Carlisle, Hollywood." Oakley Johnson, "The John Reed Club Convention," *New Masses*, VIII (July, 1932), 14–15, p. 15.

16. See Alan Calmer, "Portrait of the Artist as Proletarian," *Saturday Review of Literature*, XVI (July 31, 1937), 3–4, 14. For a more detailed description of the activities of one of the Clubs, that in Chicago, see Richard Wright, "I Tried to Be a Communist," *Atlantic Monthly*, CLXXIV (August, 1944), 60–70, and (September, 1944), 48–56. Wright states that after he was elected secretary of the Chicago Club, he was required by the Communist Party to become a Party member if he wished to continue in that position. He did so, but later broke with the Communists.

17. Orrick Johns, "The John Reed Clubs Meet," *New Masses*, XIII (October 30, 1934), 25–26, p. 25. See this report for an account of the Conference.

18. *Ibid*, p. 26.

19. "Resolution on the Work of *New Masses* for 1931," *New Masses*, VIII (September, 1932), 20–21.

20. Joseph Freeman, "Ivory Towers — White and Red," *New Masses*, XII (September 11, 1934), 20–24, p. 22. The section of the article from which this quotation is taken is part of a report submitted by Freeman to the New York John Reed Club, November 4, 1932; the rest of the article illustrates how within two years the "unprecedented problem" had been met.

21. See the autobiographical comments in Michael Gold, "The *Masses* Tradition," *Masses & Mainstream*, IV (August, 1951), 45–55, pp. 45–46. Out of work in the unemployment crisis of 1914, at the age of nineteen, and with "no politics then, except hunger," he went to a demonstration in Union Square, where he bought a copy of *The Masses*, listened to the speakers, helped fight a police charge on the crowd, and was knocked down by a cop.

"That's how I got one of my first lessons in applied capitalism. *The Masses* continued the education, gave it intellectual form and significance, for I was soon its passionate reader. . . Oh, that holy hour when a worker first learns that poverty is not divinely ordained, that his chains are manmade and can be removed by man's effort!"

22. Michael Gold, "Notes of the Month," *New Masses*, VI (September, 1930), 3–5, p. 4.

23. Michael Gold, "Wilder: Prophet of the Genteel Christ," *New Republic*, LXIV (October 22, 1930), 266–267, p. 266.

24. Edmund Wilson, "The Literary Class War: I," *New Republic*, LXX (May 4, 1932), 319–323, p. 320.

25. Quoted from a letter dated March 26, 1938, written by Dos Passos in reply to an inquiry by William H. Bond concerning the ideological basis of *U. S. A.*

26. In conversation with the present writer, June 11, 1951.

27. John Dos Passos, *Facing the Chair: Story of the Americanization of Two Foreignborn Workmen*, Boston, Sacco-Vanzetti Defense Committee, 1927, p. 126.

28. In his violently anti-Communist novel, *Most Likely to Succeed* (1954), which is not one of his better productions, Dos Passos gives a scabrous picture of the activities of this group and of the subsequent careers of several members as Hollywood Communists and fellow travelers.

29. See John Dos Passos, "Back to Red Hysteria!" *New Republic*, LXIII (July 2, 1930), 168–169, p. 169.

30. For Dos Passos's complete answers see "Whither the American Writer: (A Questionnaire)," *Modern Quarterly*, VI (Summer, 1932), 11–12.

31. John Dos Passos, *The Big Money*, New York, Harcourt, Brace and Company, 1936, pp. 101–102. It should be noted that this biography, which runs to thirteen pages, is the longest in the trilogy.

32. That the over-all conception of *U. S. A.* did not change from volume to volume may be seen by an examination of the preliminary working of the materials in *The Big Money* contained in Dos Passos's play *Airways, Inc.* (published 1928, produced 1929). Here, among other motifs, are the stories of an aviator-inventor who fails in the "big money" and of a labor organizer who, framed on a murder charge, is executed in a Sacco-Vanzetti-esque atmosphere.

33. Dos Passos, *The Big Money*, p. 150.

34. *Ibid.*, p. 437.

CHAPTER SEVEN: "ART IS A CLASS WEAPON"

1. Since most of these novelists were fellow travelers rather than Party members, they were not directly subject to discipline, though doubtless they were themselves anxious to be doctrinally correct in order to prove their revolutionary loyalty. The present writer has been able to find assertions by only two individuals that anyone in an official position on the Left attempted directly to compel an author to change the shape of a creative work.

The first instance is that of Grace Lumpkin, who on April 2, 1953, testified before the Senate Permanent Investigating Sub-Committee "that she had written Communist propaganda into a 1934 novel [*A Sign for Cain*, published 1935] after being told that Communist book reviewers would 'break' her literary career if she did not." (" 'Red Line' in Book, Novelist Admits," New York *Times*, April 3, 1953, p. 10.) Althought asserting that she was never a Party member, she "said that she was under Communist discipline for several years." One would find her charge of coercion more compelling if she had not already, apparently on her own initiative, "written Communist propaganda" into *To Make My Bread*, published in 1932.

The second instance is that of Budd Schulberg. See his "Collision with the Party Line," *Saturday Review*, XXXV (August 30, 1952), 6–8, 31–37, for a description of his experience with a humorless Communist youth group and a cultural commissar in Hollywood. When they attempted to make him change *What Makes Sammy Run?* so that it would conform to the current Party line, Schulberg, unlike Miss Lumpkin, parted with the Communists at once and continued to write his novel in his own "un-Marxist" way.

2. An admirably thorough account of RAPP, correcting the inaccurate

legend that has grown up around it, is Edward J. Brown, *The Proletarian Episode in Russian Literature, 1928–1932*, New York, Columbia University Press, 1953. See this book for a full discussion of what "proletarian literature" meant to *Soviet* writers.

3. The term "bourgeois" was employed frequently, and often loosely, by the literary Left. In general it referred to the writing of anyone who basically accepted "capitalist" ideology and hence to most of the books published by most American book publishers. The term usually carried also the abusive connotations made famous by Flaubert — dullness, pettiness, and stolid resistance to creativeness of any kind.

4. V. F. Calverton, *The Liberation of American Literature*, New York, Charles Scribner's Sons, 1932, p. 461.

5. Schachner, "Revolutionary Literature in the United States Today," pp. 59–61, footnote. Before stating his own definition, Schachner admits that it is quite opposed to the current usage of the term.

6. Hart, Henry (editor), *American Writers' Congress*, New York, International Publishers, 1935.

7. *Ibid.*, p. 76.

8. *Ibid.*, pp. 100–101.

9. A. B. Magil, "Pity and Terror," *New Masses*, VIII (December, 1932), 16–19, p. 19.

10. Granville Hicks, "Revolutionary Literature of 1934," *New Masses*, XIV (January 1, 1935), 36–38, p. 36.

11. For a first-hand account of the events of the strike, see Fred E. Beal, *Proletarian Journey: New England, Gastonia, Moscow*, New York, Hillman-Curl, Inc., 1937. While their sentences were being appealed, Beal and the others jumped bail and went to the Soviet Union; but Beal returned to the United States, disillusioned and strongly anti-Communist. After several years as a fugitive, he was arrested in 1938, served four years of his sentence, was paroled, and in May, 1948, returned to Gastonia, where his United States citizenship was restored to him.

One example of the nation-wide repercussions of Gastonia is the statement by Elizabeth Bentley, erstwhile spy for the Soviet Government, that she had been much impressed as a college girl at Vassar when a group of strikers came to solicit funds and gave "a horrible description of conditions then prevalent in the textile industry." See *Out of Bondage: The Story of Elizabeth Bentley*, New York, The Devin-Adair Company, 1951, p. 4.

12. Seven of the strike novels are set in the South, three in the Northwest, one each in the states of California, Massachusetts, Missouri, and Oklahoma, and two in New York City, if one counts the "strike" (technically a mutiny) on board the *S.S. Utah*.

13. These are: *Strike!, Lumber, Beyond Desire, Call Home the Heart, To Make My Bread, Gathering Storm, S.S. Utah, Parched Earth, The Land of Plenty, The Shadow Before, A Stone Came Rolling, Marching! Marching!, A Time to Remember, Another Such Victory, Jordanstown*, and *The Stricklands*, this last dealing with the organization of a tenant farmers' union in preparation for future strikes.

14. This incident forms the background of Cantwell's story "Hills Around Centralia," published for the first time in Granville Hicks and others (edi-

tors), *Proletarian Literature in the United States: An Anthology*, New York, International Publishers, 1935.

15. Robert Cantwell, *The Land of Plenty*, New York, Farrar & Rinehart Incorporated, 1934, p. 298.

16. *Ibid.*, p. 369.

17. "Authors' Field Day: A Symposium on Marxist Criticism," *New Masses*, XII (July 3, 1934), 27–32, p. 27.

18. Robert Cantwell, "A Town and Its Novels," *New Republic*, LXXXVI (February 19, 1936), 51–52, p. 52.

19. These are: *Jews Without Money, Run, Sheep, Run, The Road, The Disinherited, The New Bridge, Slow Vision, A House on a Street, The Death and Birth of David Markand, The Foundry, You Can't Sleep Here, In Time of Peace, A World to Win, From the Kingdom of Necessity, Conveyor, All Brides Are Beautiful, A World I Never Made, No Star Is Lost,* and *The Liberals*. Sometimes "conversion" is actually intensification of belief; in *All Brides Are Beautiful*, for example, the hero accepts Communism from the beginning of the book, but at the end he is prepared to act on his beliefs rather than merely hold them.

20. Thomas Boyd, *In Time of Peace*, New York, Minton, Balch & Company, 1935, p. 309.

21. Jack Conroy, *The Disinherited*, [New York], Covici, Friede, Publishers, 1933, p. 286.

22. *Ibid.*, p. 310.

23. There are eight of these: *Bottom Dogs, A Child Is Born, From Flushing to Calvary, Somebody in Boots, Call It Sleep, Journal of a Young Man,* "Season of Celebration," and *Man's Courage*. In some respects *Jews Without Money* and *Lumber* could be classified with this group.

24. The epigraph for "Part Three: Chicago" is from Marx: "The 'dangerous class,' the social scum (lumpenproletariat), that passively rotting mass thrown off by the lowest layers of old society, may, here and there, be swept into the movement by a proletarian revolution; its conditions of life, however, prepare it far more for the part of a bribed tool of reactionary intrigue." Strictly speaking, *Somebody in Boots* is the only novel in this group which deals with the "lumpenproletariat," the true bottom of the Social Pit described by Jack London in *The Iron Heel*. The others deal with the lower layers of the working class.

25. See Henry Roth, *Call It Sleep*, New York, Robert O. Ballou, [1935], p. 401. The description of what David sees when he first comes out on the roof illustrates very well the combination in Roth's style of the realistic and the apocalyptic, and the extent to which symbolism penetrates the book. Another of Roth's stylistic devices is an effective phonetic rendering of the Yiddish-English language of the East Side children.

26. Roth, *Call It Sleep*, p. 566.

27. *Ibid.*, p. 569.

28. *Ibid.*, pp. 598–599.

29. "Brief Review," *New Masses*, XIV (February 12, 1935), 27.

30. David Greenhood, "Another View of 'Call It Sleep,'" *New Masses*, XIV (February 19, 1935), 20. (Letter.)

31. Edwin Seaver, " 'Caesar or Nothing,' " *New Masses*, X[IV] March 5, 1935), 21.

32. For a discussion of John Dos Passos and *U. S. A.*, see the end of Chapter Six, where it is argued that Dos Passos cannot be considered a "proletarian" author.

The novels of middle-class decay, which number a few more than those about the "bottom dogs," are: *The Company;* the three novels comprising *Studs Lonigan;* "The Big Short Trip"; the trilogy by Josephine Herbst (*Pity Is Not Enough, The Executioner Waits, Rope of Gold*); *The Chute; At Madame Bonnard's; Between the Hammer and the Anvil; The Summer Soldier.*

33. Quoted from Stanley J. Kunitz, and Howard Haycraft, *Twentieth Century Authors: A Biographical Dictionary of Modern Literature*, New York, The H. H. Wilson Company, 1942, p. 641.

34. Josephine Herbst, *The Executioner Waits*, New York, Harcourt, Brace and Company, 1934, p. 371.

35. *Georgia Nigger* is included among the radical novels with some reservation. It is the fictionalized version of a journalist's report, and Spivak at the time he was gathering his facts and writing the book had apparently only begun to move toward his pro-Communist position of the middle thirties; nevertheless, the book is listed several times in radical publications as a "proletarian novel" and was obviously accepted as such in its time.

36. Hugh M. Gloster, *Negro Voices in American Fiction*, Chapel Hill, The University of North Carolina Press, 1948, p. 197.

37. Claude McKay's *Home to Harlem* (1928) and Langston Hughes's *Not Without Laughter* (1930) deal with Negro working-class life, but neither shows much class-consciousness in addition to race-consciousness even though both men were associated with the radical movement.

For the unsuccessful attempts of the Communist Party to attract Negroes, see Wilson Record, *The Negro and the Communist Party*, Chapel Hill, University of North Carolina Press, 1951.

38. Under the title *Can You Hear Their Voices*, the story was published as a pamphlet and was turned into a play produced by the Vassar Experimental Theatre.

The radical critic Charles Humboldt writes that, in 1929, " . . . Theodore Dreiser published the first important study of an American Communist, the long story 'Ernita' in Volume I of *The Gallery of Women*." ["Communists in Novels," *Masses & Mainstream*, II (June, 1949), 13–31, p. 13.] Ernita's decision to break with the I.W.W. and become a Communist occurs, however, late in the story.

39. It is rather curious that in his two-part article, "Communists in Novels," Charles Humboldt does not mention this book. Newhouse has, indeed, broken with the Party, his novel *The Hollow of the Wave* (1949) being a statement of disillusion; yet Humboldt manages to derive considerable justified enjoyment from attacking the conception of the hero of *Jake Home* (1943) by Ruth McKenney, who was expelled from the Party in 1945 as a follower of Browder.

This Is Your Day was extravagantly hailed by the Left upon its appearance in 1937. Cf. Leane Zugsmith, "A New Novel by Contributor Newhouse . . . ," *New Masses*, XXII (February 16, 1937), 23: "Dating from the publication of this book, it will be appreciably easier to write imaginative, not imaginary, works about persons in the Communist movement; it will not be easy to write a better book about them than *This Is Your Day*."

40. Sinclair Lewis, "Onward Chicago!" *Newsweek*, X (October 4, 1937), 32.

41. Leane Zugsmith, *A Time to Remember*, New York, Random House, 1936, pp. 289–290.

42. Henry Hart's *The Great One: A Novel of American Life* (New York, The John Day Company, 1934) is a political novel, being an interpretation of the career of Boies Penrose. Hart subsequently argued in *The New Masses* that he had been trying to show the helplessness of the individual in a society which was making individualism impossible, but the reasons given in the book to explain the hero's turn from reform to reaction are hardly those a Marxist would assign.

43. Cf. Browder, *Communist Party of the U. S. A.*, p. 16: "Beginning with the Party's Eighth National Convention in 1934, was launched our systematic campaign to revive American revolutionary traditions, for rediscovery and re-evaluation of American history in general." Browder's presidential campaign slogan in 1936 was: "Communism is Twentieth-Century Americanism."

Cf. also Edward Newhouse, *This Is Your Day*, New York, Lee Furman, Inc., 1937, p. 151: "Mike had read plenty of mimeographed study courses prepared by the district agitprop committee, with instructions to 'utilize the revolutionary traditions of the American proletariat and of the toiling agrarian masses' . . . "

44. Clara Weatherwax, *Marching! Marching!* New York, The John Day Company, 1935, p. 208.

45. *Ibid.*, pp. 60–61.

46. "Where We Stand," *International Literature*, [no volume], No. 3 (July, 1934), 80–94, p. 82. Cf. Cowley's subsequent statement in "Letter to England," *New Republic*, LXXXII (February 13, 1935), 22–23, p. 23: "It can scarcely be said that the new foreign influence [on American writing] is Russian so far as technique is concerned. There is no doubt, however, that many of the younger novelists and poets are being inspired by the world revolutionary movement. . . "

47. One of the least successful of the author's dramatic devices is the interruption of a mass meeting of angry workers with a six-page description of the dangerous work in a lumber mill. Obviously she is attempting to show why the men are justified in striking, but this didactic interlude disperses whatever excitement may have been aroused in the reader by the previous events of the meeting and hence weakens the climax of the scene.

48. Thomas Bell, *All Brides Are Beautiful*, Boston, Little, Brown, and Company, 1936, p. 288.

49. In the introduction to his *Earl Browder: Communist or Tool of Wall Street* (1937), Marlen reveals that *The Road* was written between 1917 and, approximately, 1927. Hence from the standpoint of composition it is properly a late left-wing Socialist romance. George Marlen, *Earl Browder: Communist or Tool of Wall Street*, New York, [Red Star Press], 1937.

50. Edwin Seaver, "Socialist Realism," *New Masses*, XVII (October 23, 1935), 23–24. His article is a review of *Problems of Soviet Literature: Reports and Speeches at the First Soviet Writers' Congress*, by A. Zhdanov and others (New York, International Publishers, 1935). This Congress, which prompted the American Writers' Congress in the following year, was held in August, 1934.

Edward J. Brown states in *The Proletarian Episode in Russian Literature*, p. 283, footnote 46, that: " 'Socialist realism' as the proper style for Soviet literature was already well-established by October, 1932." Although the term "socialist realism" appeared in *International Literature* from 1932 on, it rarely occurred in *The New Masses* before Seaver's review. Because of this "cultural lag," the term played little part in discussions in the United States of the proletarian novel. Since World War II, it has come into great favor with American left-wing critics.

51. It is interesting to note that Seaver continues his definition by quoting from N. I. Bukharin's address at the Soviet Writers' Congress to prove that "socialist realism does away with the split between realism and romanticism":

"If socialist realism is distinguished by its active, operative character; if it does not give just a dry photograph of a process; [. . .] if it raises the heroic principle to the throne of history — then revolutionary romanticism is a component part of it. . . [s]ocialist realism does not merely register what exists, but, catching up the thread of development in the present, it leads it into the future, and leads it actively. Hence, an antithesis between romanticism and socialist realism is devoid of all meaning." For the original of the quotation see "Poetry, Poetics and the Problem of Poetry in the U.S.S.R.," *Problems of Soviet Literature*, pp. 253–254.

52. William Rollins, Jr., *The Shadow Before*, New York, Robert M. McBride & Company, 1934, pp. 91–92.

53. Myra Page's *Moscow Yankee* exemplifies realism with a few "experimental trimmings," touches which again seem to be borrowed from Dos Passos. In the midst of this narrative of socialist construction, the author places a poem, "Look Here, Stalingrad," which calls to the Stalingrad Tractor Plant to increase production; and the hero receives a letter from America into which the author ironically inserts headlines from American newspapers and comments on the Depression. Myra Page, *Moscow Yankee*, New York, G. P. Putnam's Sons, 1935.

54. See Granville Hicks, "Revolution and the Novel: 3. Drama and Biography as Models," *New Masses*, XI (April 17, 1934), 24–25, for an extended discussion of these structural types, which is admittedly based on Edwin Muir's *Structure of the Novel*, London, The Hogarth Press, 1928. Hicks points out that *Strike!* approximates the tightly constructed dramatic form made up of individual scenes, while *To Make My Bread* represents the more discursive biographical form.

55. In "Revolution and the Novel: 2. Complex and Collective Novels," *New Masses*, XI (April 10, 1934), 23–25, Hicks makes a valid distinction between the two types: "The collective novel not only has no individual hero; some group of persons occupies in it a position analogous to that of the hero in conventional fiction. . . The complex novel has no individual hero, no one central character; but at the same time the various characters

do not compose a collective entity. . ." In 1934, he finds no American examples of the first form, but of course cites *The 42nd Parallel* and *1919* as examples of the second.

56. Weatherwax, *Marching! Marching!* p. 14. See Alan Calmer, "Reader's Report," *New Masses*, XVI (September 10, 1935), 23–25, p. 25, for the opinion of one of the judges in the contest in which this book won first prize. Stating that the choice of *Marching! Marching!* should please everyone, he concludes: "The layman will find a short, swift story that holds his interest and is jammed with 'militant' episodes; the literary critic will, I believe, find its writing to be first-rate."

It suggests the climate of the thirties to note that the Left was not entirely alone in its praise. Reviewing the book in *The Saturday Review of Literature*, the unproletarian Henry Seidel Canby wished that the author "had been a little less radical in her punctuation," but declared nevertheless that *Marching! Marching!* "is the nearest approach in the current school of so-called proletarian fiction to those passionate works of the imagination which have accompanied every great attempt at reform." Henry Seidel Canby, " 'Workers, Unite!' " *Saturday Review of Literature*, XIII (January 4, 1936), 12.

57. Granville Hicks, "Revolution and the Novel: 4. Character and Classes," *New Masses*, XI (April 24, 1934), 23–25, p. 23; and "Revolution and the Novel: 5. Selection and Emphasis," *New Masses*, XI (May 8, 1934), 22–24, p. 22.

58. See Alfred C. Kinsey, Wardell B. Pomeroy, Clyde E. Martin, *Sexual Behavior in the Human Male*, Philadelphia, W. B. Saunders Company, 1948, pp. 357–362. Kinsey's figures indicate that the homosexual outlet varies both in frequency and incidence inversely according to educational level and occupational class from the daylabor to the professional group, as do also premarital intercourse and extramarital intercourse. Although from his scale of nine classes by occupation he omits numbers one (underworld), eight (business executive group), and nine (extremely wealthy group) on the grounds that they "are not represented by large enough series in the sample," he nowhere indicates that his available data on these groups suggest a significant departure from his above conclusion.

59. Only in one novel, Nearing's *Free Born*, does a major radical character expressly uphold the doctrine of "free love" as opposed to marriage.

60. William Rollins, Jr., "What Is a Proletarian Writer?" *New Masses*, XIV (January 29, 1935), 22–23, p. 22. In characterization as in technique, Rollins seems to reflect the influence of Dos Passos, whose characters are frequently neurotics and are never capable of maintaining a stable sexual relationship.

61. James T. Farrell, "In Search of the Image," *New Masses*, XIII (December 4, 1934), 21–22, p. 21. Another critic, Stanley Burnshaw, accepted Farrell's comments on Dahlberg, but took issue with the argument that inherited nature imagery creates "a dichotomy between the objects and sensations they [contemporary American writers in general] have sought to describe, and the language and symbolism they have inherited as that of a literary tradition." In the remainder of his reply, Burnshaw cited a number of nature images from Cantwell and other proletarian writers in order to

prove his point. See Stanley Burnshaw, "A New Direction for Criticism," *New Masses*, XIV (January 15, 1935), 23–24.

62. John Herrmann, "The Big Short Trip," *Scribner's Magazine*, XCII (August, 1932), 65–69, 113–128, p. 122. An indication of the rising interest in the proletarian novel in the early thirties was the announcement of this novelette as "One of the Two Winners in the *Scribner's Magazine* $5000 Prize Short Novel Contest." The other winner was Thomas Wolfe's "A Portrait of Bascom Hawk."

63. Boyd, *In Time of Peace*, p. 192.

CHAPTER EIGHT: LITERATURE AND POLITICS

1. "Authors' Field Day," p. 27.

2. Hicks remained on the editorial staff of the magazine, however, and contributed frequent articles and reviews until his resignation from the Communist Party on September 26, 1939.

3. Granville Hicks, "The Crisis in American Criticism," *New Masses*, VIII (February, 1933), 3–5, p. 5. Hicks's reference to "the perfect Marxian novel" is characteristic and revealing. Compare his recipe for the Great Proletarian Novel in "Revolution and the Novel: 7. The Future of Proletarian Literature," *New Masses*, XI (May 22, 1934), 23–25, p. 25: "But if we can imagine an author with Michael Gold's power of evoking scenes, with William Rollins's structural skill, with Jack Conroy's wide acquaintance with the proletariat, with Louis Colman's first-hand knowledge of the labor movement, with all the passion of these and a dozen other revolutionary novelists, with something of Dreiser's massive patience, we can see what shape a proletarian masterpiece might take."

4. *The Great Tradition* was first published in September, 1933. In the revised edition, published in November, 1935, an entirely new chapter was added in order that the book might include an extensive account of proletarian literature, in which development "the great tradition" is viewed as culminating.

5. Cf. Karl Marx and Friedrich Engels, *Correspondence, 1846–1895: A Selection with Commentary and Notes*, New York, International Publishers, [1935], p. 475: "According to the materialistic conception of history the determining element in history is *ultimately* the production and reproduction in real life. More than this neither Marx nor I have ever asserted. If therefore somebody twists this into the statement that the economic element is the *only* determining one, he transforms it into a meaningless, abstract and absurd phrase." Letter from Engels to J. Bloch, September 21, 1890.

6. John Strachey, *Literature and Dialectical Materialism*, New York, Covici, Friede, Publishers, 1934, p. 52.

7. The Communist Party, of course, continued to maintain a close check on the magazine. In a letter dated July 22, 1951, Granville Hicks stated to the present writer: "During the period when I was connected with the New Masses, there was always someone on the board who had close connections with party headquarters. Through this person the party exerted its influence when it so desired. Within the general framework of the party line, the magazine had a certain amount of leeway, but 'the ninth floor' [Party head-

quarters] always could crack the whip and frequently did." Cf. also Orrick Johns, *Time of Our Lives: The Story of My Father and Myself*, New York, Stackpole Sons, 1937, p. 340: "The Central Committee of the Communist Party had its say in questions of policy, and even of specific pieces. The C. C. was usually represented by Joe North, whose style of *reportage* in reporting strikes became popular with our readers." Johns had become one of the editors of *The New Masses* shortly after it had begun to appear as a weekly, on January 2, 1934, and remained on the staff for about a year and a half.

8. Editorial statement, *Partisan Review*, I (February–March, 1934), 3–4, p. 4. See "In Retrospect: Ten Years of *Partisan Review*," in William Phillips and Philip Rahv (editors), *The Partisan Reader: Ten Years of Partisan Review, 1934–1944: An Anthology*, New York, The Dial Press, 1946, pp. 679–688, for a survey of magazine policy.

9. "A Debate: Can We Learn Anything from the Bourgeois Writers?" advertisement in *New Masses*, VI (July, 1930), 21.

10. Some years later, in arguing against the charge that the Marxist literary criticism of the thirties had been regimented, Hicks indicated the lack of harmony within this organization: "Disagreement on literary issues was the rule, not the exception. Every meeting of the John Reed Club I ever attended was a battle, not a conspiracy." See Granville Hicks, "The Failure of Left Criticism," *New Republic*, CIII (September 9, 1940), 345–347, p. 346.

11. Wallace Phelps and Philip Rahv, "Problems and Perspectives in Revolutionary Literature," *Partisan Review*, I (June–July, 1934), 3–10, p. 8.

12. Freeman, "Ivory Towers — White and Red," p. 24.

13. See, for example, Wallace Phelps, "Three Generations," *Partisan Review*, I (September–October, 1934), 49–55, and Jerre Mangione, "Proletarian Magazines," *Partisan Review*, I (November–December, 1934), 57–59. In his article, Phelps quite typically praises T. S. Eliot, not for his religious views, but for his technical skill; by contrast Eliot was one of Gold's favorite whipping-boys.

14. "National John Reed Club Conference," *Partisan Review*, I (November–December, 1934), 60–61, p. 60.

15. Seaver, " 'Caesar or Nothing,' " p. 21. It should be noted that where Joseph Freeman, in "Ivory Towers — White and Red," attributed "Leftism" to the "Old Bolsheviks" of the literary Left, Seaver here attributes it to some of the recent middle-class converts. Actually both old and new personnel could be found on each side of the dispute.

16. Horace Gregory, "One Writer's Position," *New Masses*, XIV (February 12, 1935), 20–21, p. 21.

17. James T. Farrell, *A Note on Literary Criticism*, New York, The Vanguard Press, 1936, p. 46.

18. *Ibid.*, pp. 129–130.

19. For the summarized statement see *A Note on Literary Criticism*, pp. 216–217.

20. See Isidor Schneider, "Sectarianism on the Right," *New Masses*, XIX (June 23, 1936), 23–25, and Granville Hicks, "In Defense of James Farrell," *New Masses*, XX (July 14, 1936), 23. Hicks argues that, Schneider to the

contrary, *A Note on Literary Criticism* does have a Marxist foundation, but that Farrell has "built badly" on it.

21. International Publishers continued to confine itself almost entirely to nonliterary Marxist publications, although it did publish four proletarian novels. The leading publisher of these novels was The Vanguard Press, which, however, brought out only ten of the seventy titles, five of them being by one author, James Farrell.

22. Henry Hart, "Contemporary Publishing and the Revolutionary Writer," *American Writers' Congress*, p. 161.

23. Malcolm Cowley, "A Farewell to the 1930's," *New Republic*, CI (November 8, 1939), 42–44, p. 43. In a conversation with the present writer on August 18, 1950, Cowley later estimated the sale of an average proletarian novel to be from 1200 to 2700 copies, somewhat higher than the figures announced by Hart.

24. Louis Adamic, "What the Proletariat Reads: Conclusions Based on a Year's Study Among Hundreds of Workers Throughout the United States," *Saturday Review of Literature*, XI (December 1, 1934), 321–322.

25. Robert Cantwell, "What the Working Class Reads," *New Republic*, LXXXIII (July 17, 1935), 274–276, p. 276. Summarizing the results of several surveys, he concludes: ". . . most library students agree that the quality of the books taken out is relatively high, and that most of the borrowers are working people." Cf. Waples, *People and Print*, chapter V.

26. John Scott Bowman, "The Proletarian Novel in America," unpublished doctoral dissertation submitted at Pennsylvania State College, 1939, pp. 170 and 183–184.

27. Hicks and others (eds.), *Proletarian Literature in the United States*, p. 34.

28. Alan Calmer, "Reader's Report," *New Masses*, XVI (September 10, 1935), 23–25, p. 23. The board of judges had, incidentally, consisted of "Granville Hicks . . .; William F. Dunne, labor organizer and former editor of The Daily Worker; Alan Calmer. . . ; Richard J. Walsh, president of The John Day Company; and Critchell Rimington, vice-president of The John Day Company." ["NEW MASSES Novel Contest," *New Masses*, XVI (September 3, 1935), 7.]

29. "Call for an American Writers' Congress," *New Masses*, XIV (January 22, 1935), 20.

30. "Our First Congress of Writers," *New Masses*, XV (April 30, 1935), 9. Considering the remarkable reversal in policy soon to be announced by the Comintern as the Popular Front, it is highly interesting that, with the omission of one clause, the addition of another, and a very few changes of language, this "literary" program is identical in its elements and its wording with the political platform enjoined upon the American delegation by the I.U.R.W. at the Kharkov Conference in 1930, in the midst of the "Third Period" of revolutionary extremism.

31. See Granville Hicks, "The Dialectics of the Development of Marxist Criticism," *American Writers' Congress*, pp. 96–97. Hicks continues with a warning lest the overcorrection of "Leftist" errors lead to "formalism" and "the art-for-art's sake dogma."

Farrell mentions this paper in *A Note on Literary Criticism* (see p. 35), but argues that it is one thing to state formally how problems may be resolved and another to demonstrate the resolution in a concrete situation.

32. Waldo Frank was selected as the first chairman of the League. The executive committee consisted of Kenneth Burke, Harold Clurman, Malcolm Cowley, Waldo Frank, Joseph Freeman, Michael Gold, Henry Hart, Josephine Herbst, Granville Hicks, Matthew Josephson, Alfred Kreymborg, John Howard Lawson, Albert Maltz, Isidor Schneider, Edwin Seaver, Genevieve Taggard, and Alexander Trachtenberg. See *American Writers' Congress*, p. 188, where are also given the names of the thirty-nine original members of the National Council.

33. Georgi Dimitroff, *The United Front: The Struggle Against War and Fascism*, New York, International Publishers, 1938, p. 136. The selection is from Dimitroff's closing speech at the Congress on August 20, 1935. The italics are his.

For a description of the permutations of Comintern policy, see F. Borkenau, *World Communism: A History of the Communist International*, New York, W. W. Norton & Company, Inc., 1939.

34. Earl Browder, "Writers and the Communist Party," *The People's Front*, New York, International Publishers, 1938, p. 281. In this address, given at the second American Writers' Congress in June, 1937, Browder reiterated the official stand of the Communist Party which he stated at the first Congress, that the writer's work was merely to write.

It may be noted that in the 1936 presidential campaign Browder centered his attack largely on Roosevelt's opponents. In the following year the Communists plumped strongly for the President on the issue of enlarging the Supreme Court.

35. Isidor Schneider, "MacLeish and the Critics," *New Masses*, XVIII (March 24, 1936), 21–22, p. 21. Schneider insists that MacLeish's poetical career from "To the Social Muse" onward shows how salutary Left criticism was for him, but admits, rather revealingly, that Left criticism must "rid itself of its remnants of sectarianism, as antiquated equipment. . ."

36. Cf. "Between Ourselves," *New Masses*, XXI (December 22, 1936), 2: "At this writing (Monday, Dec. 14), with returns very incomplete, we can report 55,000 copies of the Dec. 15 issue already sold — a new high for this magazine."

37. Freeman, "John Reed," p. 23.

38. The explanation advanced ten years later was that the literary left-wing offensive met the same reactionary counteroffensive suffered by the New Deal after the 1936 presidential campaign. See, for example, Isidor Schneider, "Background to Error," *New Masses*, LVIII (February 12, 1946), 23–25. That this explanation is not in accord with the facts should become clear from the remainder of this chapter.

39. It is ironical to note that when, at the first American Writers' Congress, Kenneth Burke read a paper suggesting *"purely from the standpoint of propaganda"* that "the people" was a more effective symbol in America than "the worker," the subsequent discussion brought forth nothing but strong opposition. See Kenneth Burke, "Revolutionary Symbolism in America," *American Writers' Congress*, pp. 87–94, and "Discussion and Proceedings," pp. 167–171.

40. In support of these statements one among several pieces of evidence may be adduced. Five contributors to *Left Front*, the organ of the Chicago John Reed Club, are listed either in the four issues of this magazine (1933–34) or in *International Literature* as being at work on radical novels; but none of these books by John Alroy, Jack Balch, Joseph Kalar, Norman MacLeod, or Mark Marvin was subsequently published. Obviously the failure to publish may very well have resulted from other causes than the break-up of the Clubs; however, Alroy, Kalar, and Marvin never did publish books, while the first novels of Balch and MacLeod to appear express disillusionment with Communism.

41. John Chamberlain, "Literature," in Harold E. Stearns (editor), *America Now: An Inquiry into Civilization in the United States*, New York, Charles Scribner's Sons, 1938, p. 37. If Chamberlain's own fluctuating attitude toward the radical movement be felt to have put this statement under suspicion, compare Albert Maltz, "What Shall We Ask of Writers," *New Masses*, LVIII (February 12, 1946), 19–22, p. 22: "I know of at least a dozen plays and novels discarded in the process of writing because the political scene altered." Maltz later repudiated the latitudinarian arguments of this article under the most humiliating conditions, but he presumably did not also repudiate his memory.

42. Alan Calmer, "Portrait of the Artist as Proletarian," *Saturday Review of Literature*, XVI (July 31, 1937), 3–4, 14, p. 14. Calmer reiterates that the young proletarian was not retreating to the ivory tower; ". . . what he objected to was the way in which these *related* factors [literature and politics] were *identified*, as, for example, the way in which an act of literary evaluation was subsumed within an act of persuading a person to join up." Calmer's excellent article is the best analysis of the decline of the proletarian novel from the standpoint of the young proletarian writer's psychology. The best analysis in political terms is the embittered but essentially accurate "Proletarian Literature: A Political Autopsy," by Philip Rahv in *The Southern Review*, IV (Winter, 1939), 616–628.

43. Calmer, "Portrait of the Artist as Proletarian," p. 14.

44. In the latter novel, Conroy does try a new departure by adding to the story of a wandering worker that of the worker's half-brother, who goes to college and leads a Bohemian existence. When the book concludes, both brothers have been converted to Communism. Conroy's handling of the worker adds nothing to the picture given by the figure of Larry Donovan in *The Disinherited*, while his treatment of the Bohemian suggests a lack of experience with such individuals.

45. In conversation with the present writer, December 29, 1950. Cf. Howard Fast, *Literature and Reality*, New York, International Publishers, 1950, p. 63.

46. William Phillips, "Marking Time?" *New Masses*, XXI (December 22, 1936), 23–24.

47. After the dissolution of the John Reed Clubs, *Partisan Review* had been reorganized. Cf. "Partisan Review No. 8," *Partisan Review*, II (July–August, 1935, [2]: "Beginning with this issue PARTISAN REVIEW will not be published as the organ of the John Reed Club of New York but as a revolutionary literary magazine edited by a group of young Communist

writers, whose purpose will be to print the best revolutionary literature and Marxist criticism in this country and abroad." As before, however, the real shapers of policy were Phillips and Rahv. Becoming *Partisan Review & Anvil* with the issue for February, 1936, it ceased publication after its October, 1936, number on the decision of these two men. After an interval of slightly over a year, Phillips and Rahv started bringing out the magazine again, this time on its present independent, "anti-Stalinist" basis.

48. Michael Gold, "Notes on the Cultural Front," *New Masses*, XXV (December 7, 1937), literary supplement, 1–5, p. 5.
For another discussion of the new "literary populism" see Stanley Hyman, "*Bread and a Stone*," *New Republic*, CV (December 15, 1941), 834–835.

49. Joshua Kunitz, "In Defense of a Term," *New Masses*, XXVIII (July 12, 1938), section 2, 145–147, p. 147.

50. Earl Browder, "The Writer and Politics," *The Writer in a Changing World*, edited by Henry Hart, [New York], Equinox Cooperative Press, 1937, p. 54. See this volume for a record of the second Congress.

51. Hart (ed.), *The Writer in a Changing World*, p. 51.

52. Meyer Levin, *In Search: An Autobiography*, New York, Horizon Press, 1950, p. 113.

53. Turnover in Communist membership had always been high, but from 1936 to 1938 even official Party figures set it at 50 per cent in New York City, the center of radical activity.

54. Granville Hicks, "The Failure of Left Criticism," *New Republic*, CIII (September 9, 1940), 345–347, pp. 345–346.

CHAPTER NINE: THE LONG RETREAT

1. The old-line Party members must have writhed when Browder addressed the delegates to the newly created Communist Political Association on May 22, 1944, not as "Comrades," but as "Ladies and Gentlemen."

2. Henry Wallace, who repudiated the Progressive Party at the outbreak of the Korean War, received only 1,156,103 popular votes as the party's Presidential candidate, or a little over 2 per cent of the total vote. This number was some 13,000 less than that for the candidate of the Southern conservative States' Rights Democrats. The present political impotence of the other radical parties in the United States is strikingly illustrated in the number of votes cast for their candidates in these elections: Socialist Party — 139,009; Socialist Labor Party — 29,061; Socialist Workers Party — 13,613.

3. *Father and Son* and *My Days of Anger*, bringing the autobiographical Danny up to his acceptance of Marxism and his departure from Chicago for New York, were presumably written while Farrell still considered himself an independent Marxist. Since then he has repudiated this ideology as inadequate — this was confirmed in conversation with the present writer on December 29, 1950 — and has described his New York adventures on the literary Left in the Bernard Carr (Clare) trilogy: *Bernard Clare* (1946), *The Road Between* (1949), and *Yet Other Waters* (1952). The latter two make up a detailed and thinly disguised history of the "proletarian movement" of the thirties, and belong in outlook to the growing body of anti-Communist fiction.

4. David Alman, "After the War," *Masses & Mainstream*, V (February, 1952), 61–64.

5. Charles Humboldt, "Communists in Novels: II," *Masses & Mainstream*, II (July, 1949), 44–65, p. 48.

6. "Rugged Times," *The New Yorker*, XXIV (October 23, 1948), 25.

7. *Ibid*. In this record of an interview Mailer is quoted as rejecting the charge that his book is pessimistic: "'People say it is a novel without hope. . . Actually, it offers a good deal of hope. I intended it to be a parable about the movement of man through history. I tried to explore the outrageous propositions of cause and effect, of effort and recompense, in a sick society. The book finds man corrupted, confused to the point of helplessness, but it also finds that there are limits beyond which he cannot be pushed, and it finds that even in his corruption and sickness there are yearnings for a better world.'"

A case might also be made for an affirmative ending to Mailer's second, much less impressive, novel, *Barbary Shore*; however, this odd, perverse tale of alienation too much reflects the unhappiness that may come over the independent radical when he fully realizes that he must depend for emotional sustenance, not on a sense of community in an organization of like-minded comrades, but solely on a faith in the purity of his own individual beliefs.

8. Howard Fast, "Reply to Critics," *Masses & Mainstream*, III (December, 1950), 53–64, pp. 62–63.

9. Quoted in "Howard Fast," *Wilson Library Bulletin*, XVII (October, 1942), 82.

10. In conversation with the present writer, December 29, 1950.

11. Fast argues concerning this report that, "Too many of the accounts introduce the same note of horror for this to be entirely an invention." ("Reply to Critics," p. 63.) But for the purposes of his novel he accepts the account as entirely true, which is something else again. For Van Doren's rejection of the report, see *Mutiny in January: The Story of a Crisis in the Continental Army. . .* , New York, The Viking Press, 1943, appendix, pp. 250–251.

12. Fast, "Reply to Critics," p. 61.

13. Howard Fast, *Spartacus*, New York, published by the author, 1951, p. 215.

14. Howard Fast, *Intellectuals in the Fight for Peace*, New York, Masses & Mainstream, Inc., 1949, p. 14.

15. In January, 1948, because of its growing deficit, *The New Masses* suspended publication as a weekly, along with *Mainstream*, a Marxist literary quarterly that had been launched only the previous winter. Both were succeeded by *Masses & Mainstream*, a "cultural-ideological" magazine appearing monthly, its first issue being dated March, 1948. With an announced circulation in May of only 17,000, it almost immediately began a series of appeals for more subscriptions and other financial assistance.

Although chronically about to collapse, apparently, it has become a focal point of radical publishing. Under its own imprint it has brought out, through 1954, three novels (*Iron City*, *A Lantern for Jeremy*, and *Burning Valley*), a book of personal reminiscences by a participant in the Spanish

War (Steve Nelson's *The Volunteers*), and several miscellaneous volumes concerned with the arts.

16. William Phillips, "Small Town Idyll, Plus," *New Masses*, XXIII (April 20, 1937), 30–31, p. 30.

17. The present writer is indebted to Richard M. Ludwig of Princeton University for the opportunity to read Steinbeck's pamphlet, *Their Blood Is Strong*, San Francisco, published by the Simon J. Lubin Society of California, Inc., 1938. In this "Factual Story of the Migratory Agricultural Workers in California," Steinbeck offers specific suggestions for alleviating and finally eradicating the conditions which he describes. His proposals are aimed at integrating these families into society, not at the creation of further class antagonisms.

In Dubious Battle (1936), an excellent strike novel, is not proletarian in the sense of the term used in this book, although it was undoubtedly affected by the proletarian novels of labor conflict.

18. Maltz, "What Shall We Ask of Writers," pp. 19, 20.

19. Howard Fast, "Art and Politics," *New Masses*, LVIII (February 26, 1946), 6–8, p. 6; Joseph North, "No Retreat for the Writer," *New Masses*, LVIII (February 26, 1946), 8–10, p. 9; John Howard Lawson, "Art Is a Weapon," *New Masses*, LVIII (March 19, 1946), 18–20, p. 20.

INDEX

The following items have been indexed: names of persons, books, pamphlets, short stories, periodicals, newspapers, articles, and reviews.